Preface

The major goal of all teachers, regardless of the grade level or content area of specialization, is to help students to learn. The ability of students to comprehend information is related to their language, reading, and thinking abilities.

These processes have been examined in *Teaching Students to Read*. The major objective of this text is to assist every teacher in understanding the integral process of teaching students to read many different types of written material. In an attempt to accomplish this goal, we have divided *Teaching Students to Read* into four major sections: (1) The Teacher, (2) The Student, (3) The Reading Process, and (4) The Reading Curriculum.

Since the teaching profession requires an enormous commitment, we have introduced and discussed in Section 1, The Teacher, the professional responsibilities of teachers in general and teachers of reading in particular. This section provides assistance to the teacher who is asked to make many decisions about the role of a teacher, the students' needs, and the curriculum.

The second section of the book, The Student, provides information that will enable you to understand your students in light of current biological, psychological, and linguistic factors that affect and influence their development. This section includes detailed information about the development of children from infancy to preschool and on to the school years. Current trends in preschool reading programs, the importance of parental involvement in the education of the child, and the effects of television are discussed. Various activities for the preschool reading program as well as language arts activities for primary-, intermediate-, and middle-school-aged children are provided as well.

The third section of the text, The Reading Process, focuses on two distinct aspects of the reading process: decoding and comprehending. An understanding of "decoding" will help the teacher to instruct students in the beginning steps of reading: visual and auditory discrimination and recognition of letters, sounds, and words. Activities that will reinforce these early activities for beginning readers are included throughout this section of the text. As the focus shifts to "comprehending," we introduce the topics of implicit and explicit understanding of texts, reading study skills strategies, and content area learning. Many activities that will help to develop an effective reading program are included in this section of the book.

The fourth and final section of this book, The Reading Curriculum, provides information and methods to assist you, the teacher, in understanding and designing a diagnostic-prescriptive reading program. This section includes a chapter on special needs students, entitled Teaching Reading to Special Students, to help you to understand and meet the needs of special students who may be in your classroom. There is a thorough discussion of Public Law (P.L.) 94-142 and mainstreaming, along with important theoretical and practical applications for the classroom teacher.

The entire fourth section of the text focuses on the integration of theory and practice. In addition to the needs of mainstreamed students, this section includes chapters on the bilingual student, students' interests and attitudes, assessment, and ways in which to manage an effective reading program.

The teacher's tasks are difficult, complex, and exciting. As a teacher, one of your most significant tasks will be to provide instruction that will enable all your students to be good readers of *all* their texts. The accomplishment of this task is imperative since reading is essential to a student's success in school and in life. You, the teacher, are the key to each student's success. Remember, your students *will* learn to read, with your help.

We gratefully acknowledge the assistance of Jacqueline Collins and Dr. Linda Lungren, both of whom have contributed in numerous ways to the completion of this text.

Diane Lapp
James Flood

To Lloyd Chilton, our friend, advisor, and editor.
Thank you for your help throughout the years.

1986

W

Teaching Students to Read

DIANE LAPP / JAMES FLOOD
San Diego State University

MACMILLAN PUBLISHING COMPANY
New York

COLLIER MACMILLAN PUBLISHERS
London

Macmillan Publishing Company
866 Third Avenue, New York, New York 10022

Collier Macmillan Canada, Inc.

Library of Congress Cataloging in Publication Data

Lapp, Diane.
　Teaching students to read.

　Includes bibliographies and index.
　1. Reading.　　2. Child development.　　3. Reading compre-
hension.　　4. Reading—Curricula.　　5. Handicapped children—
Education—Reading.　　I. Flood, James.　　II. Title.
LB1050.L366　1985　　　　372.4'1　　　　84-27160
ISBN 0-02-367660-4

Printing: 1 2 3 4 5 6 7 8　　　　Year: 6 7 8 9 0 1 2 3 4 5

CHAPTER OPENING EPIGRAPHS/VERSE

Chapter 1　T. Johnson, ed., *Complete Poems of Emily Dickinson* (Boston: Little, Brown and Company, n.d.).

Chapter 2　P. Dale, *Language Development: Structure and Function,* 2nd ed. (New York: Holt, Rinehart and Winston, 1976), p. 18.

Chapter 3　Mario Pei, *The Story of Language* (Philadelphia: J. B. Lippincott Company, 1965), pp. 440–441.

Chapter 4　Abraham Lincoln, *Speeches and Letters,* in *The Oxford Dictionary of Quotations,* 2nd ed. (London: Oxford University Press, 1966), p. 314.

Chapter 5　Noah Webster, *The American Spelling Book,* 1831 (Reprinted, New York: Bureau of Publications, Teachers College Press, Columbia University, 1962), p. 19.

Chapter 6　D. Berlo, *The Process of Communication* (New York: Holt, Rinehart and Winston, 1960), p. 175.

Chapter 7　N. Lueers, "The Short Circuit of Reading: A Synthesis of Reading Theories," *Reading Psychology,* 4 (January–March 1983), 80.

Chapter 8　R. Tierney, "Learning from Text," in A. Berger and H. A. Robinson, eds., *Secondary School Reading: What Research Reveals for Classroom Practice* (Urbana, Ill.: ERIC Clearinghouse on Reading and Communication Skills and the National Conference on Research in English, 1982), p. 109.

Chapter 9　D. Moore and J. Readence, "Approaches to Content Area Reading Instruction," *Journal of Reading,* 26 (February 1983), 397.

Chapter 10　R. Farr and N. Roser, *Teaching a Child to Read* (New York: Harcourt Brace Jovanovich, Inc., 1979), p. 425.

Chapter 12　Patricia Anders, "Tests of Functional Literacy," *Journal of Reading* (April 1981), 618.

Chapter 13　G. Cook, "Breaking the Code," *Journal of Reading,* 25 (May 1982), 730.

Chapter 14　J. Gillet and C. Temple, *Understanding Assessment and Instruction* (Boston: Little, Brown and Company, 1982), p. 291.

Chapter 15　A. Archer, "Initial Assessment: Determining What to Teach," in J. Affleck, S. Lowenbraun, and A. Archer, eds., *Teaching the Mildly Handicapped in the Regular Classroom* (Columbus, Ohio: Charles E. Merrill Publishing Company, 1980), p. 61.

ISBN 0-02-367660-4

Contents

1 The Teacher

2 *The Student*

3 The Reading Process

5. Decoding: Word Analysis Through Phonics   77

6. Strategies for Vocabulary Development

7. Understanding Comprehension

4 *The Reading Curriculum*

10. *Approaches to Teaching Reading*   *231*

11. Encouraging Reading Attitudes and Interests

12. Assessing Students' Strengths and Needs   285

13. Reading for Bilingual and ESL Students   315

14. Teaching Reading to Special Students   355

15. Developing and Managing Your Reading Program   383

The Teacher

1 Teaching Reading to Every Student

He ate and drank the precious words,
His spirit grew robust;
He knew no more that he was poor,
Nor that his frame was dust.
He danced along the dingy days,
And this bequest of wings
Was but a book. What liberty
A loosened spirit brings!
[Emily Dickinson]

Goals

To help the student understand
1. The importance of formulating a personal definition of reading
2. The multifaceted role of the reading teacher
3. That readers are individuals
4. That a variety of possible reading curricula is needed

A teacher has the most important job society has to offer: the education of its young. Teaching requires years of preparation, long hours, patience, and enduring frustrations. A teacher experiences life in a way that no other professional person can. As a teacher, you will touch the lives of hundreds of people, some of whom you will cherish and always remember. The following is one teacher's reminiscence of such an experience:

I have taught school for ten years. During that time I have given assignments, among others, to a murderer, an evangelist, a pugilist, a thief, and an imbecile.

The murderer was a quiet little boy who sat on the front seat and regarded me with pale blue eyes; the evangelist, easily the most popular boy in school, had the lead in the junior play; the pugilist lounged by the window and let loose at intervals a raucous laugh that startled even the geraniums; the thief was a gay-hearted Lothario with a song on his lips; and the imbecile, a soft-eyed little animal seeking the shadows.

The murderer awaits death in the state penitentiary; the evangelist has lain a year now in the village churchyard; the pugilist lost an eye in a brawl in Hong Kong; the thief, by standing on tiptoe, can see the windows of my room from the county jail; and the once gentle-eyed little moron beats his head against a padded wall in the state asylum.

All of these pupils once sat in my room, sat and looked at me gravely across worn brown desks. I must have been a great help to these pupils—I taught them the rhyming scheme of the Elizabethan sonnet and how to diagram a complex sentence. (White, 1937, pp. 151, 192)

White's message is clear. We must attempt to make our curriculum relevant to the lives and needs of our students. We must focus on our

As a teacher, you will touch the lives of hundreds of people, some of whom you will cherish and always remember. (Photo by Linda Lungren.)

students' interests rather than relying on the familiar components of a "classical" education. During the course of your career, all of the students described by White will be seated before you.

Purpose of This Book

This book is designed to help you plan learning experiences that will make a difference in the lives of your students. If you are concerned about being a member of a reading methods class, take pride and remember that you must teach reading regardless of your content specialization. All content areas present students with facts to be learned and texts to be read. Students are required to read and reread in their attempts to learn. Your role is to provide students with the skills that will enable them to read for information and enjoyment. *All* teachers at *all* grade levels in *all* content areas need to help their students to learn from texts. To do so, all teachers need to understand the processes engaged in as one reads a text.

To prepare you for this task, each chapter of this text deals with important issues in the field of reading and presents current theoretical concerns and effective instructional applications. This book is designed to explore those processes and to provide instructional practices that will assist you in helping your students to learn from their textbooks.

Reading: What Is It?

If you were to ask a hundred people to define "reading," you would probably get a hundred different responses. Volumes of books have been written on the subject, frequently with contradictory definitions, each emphasizing a different aspect of the reading process. It would be counterproductive to present a long list of definitions here because each of you will have to develop your own definition of the process after you understand its components. It is this development that should be your *end goal* in reading this text. Your definition will continue to change and grow with new information. However, it is extremely important that you formulate a definition of reading because you will be forced to develop an instructional program as soon as you enter the classroom.

Some research studies suggest that classroom teachers are influenced by theoretical orientations toward reading. Mitchell (1980) states, "If teachers' reading instruction is being influenced by their knowledge base and/or belief system, then they need to become aware of what these influences are" (p. 259). If you have not given any thought to the question, *What is reading?* your program will probably suffer from a fragmented approach to the reading process.

In general, all definitions of reading fall into two categories. First, there are those who view reading primarily as a *decoding process*, in which the reader is taught how to "say" the word in print. In a second view, *reading* for *meaning* is emphasized from the very earliest stages of instruction; in this approach, reading for comprehension is stressed.

Although there are differences of opinion about a precise definition of reading, most educators agree that the reading process includes

1. Letter and word recognition
2. Comprehension of the concepts conveyed by the printed word(s)
3. Reaction to and assimilation of the new knowledge from the printed page with the reader's past experience

All instructors of reading must decide for themselves what reading is. Many educators have considered the problem, devised definitions, and established an approach on the basis of their definition. These approaches, along with other definitions of reading, will be presented in detail in Chapter 10.

We believe that reading is an interaction between the author and the reader. To understand the printed message, the reader must perceive, interpret, hypothesize, and evaluate. These processes occur in varying degrees depending on the readers' familiarity with the content of the text and with their purposes for reading.

The processes of perceiving, interpreting, hypothesizing, and evaluating occur quickly in the mind of a proficient reader, but the amount of time itself may not be the critical element; rather, *active participation* by the reader may be the critical element.

The following suggestions will help students to participate actively with the text:

1. Teach strategies that develop comprehension of concepts prior to reading.
2. Explain activities that foster concentration and observation as part of the reading process.
3. Give students clear goals.
4. Fill your classroom with materials that tap students' interests.

Given this general framework of what reading is and what the reading process entails, we now turn to the most important elements in the reading process: the teacher and the learner. The act of teaching reading is a play with two main characters, teacher and learner; each depends on the other to produce a masterpiece. Each character is important; each receives cues from the other before progress is made.

The Teacher

Many research studies have shown that the teacher is extremely important to the student in the process of acquiring reading proficiency. In fact, after reviewing the massive federally funded study, "The Cooperative Re-

As a teacher, you need to be certain that children who spend one year of their lives with you are helped in the development of knowledge that will help them become successful in life. (Photo by Linda Lungren.)

search Program in First-Grade Reading Instruction," Malmquist (1973) stated, "Studies indicate that the teacher is a more important variable in reading instruction than are the teaching methods and instructional materials" (pp. 142–155). Likewise, Goldbecker (1975) stressed the importance of the teacher in a reading program by stating, "The salient point remains that no reading program operates by itself. The teacher is still the single element who can determine success or failure of a reading program no matter where its emphasis lies" (p. 4). It is, therefore, important for you, as the teacher, to examine your values, assess your philosophy of teaching, and learn about your students. Furthermore, you must consider theories of learning as well as all of the information that is available about the ways in which students develop.

This book will provide you, the teacher, with a great deal of the background information essential for teaching reading. However, it cannot provide you with your philosophy of teaching; only you can do that.

Every individual has several roles in life, roles that overlap and are interrelated to varying degrees. Your role as a *teacher* is a reflection of your role in society, in the school, and in the classroom.

As a teacher, you need to be certain that students who spend one year of their lives with you are helped in the development of knowledge that

will help them become successful in life. You will occasionally encounter
students who are having difficulties with some task, and you will need to
know how to help them. One of the first steps is to identify your most
effective style of relating to students to encourage comfortable teacher-
student interaction and to promote maximum learning.

The Student

Now that you have explored some questions about yourself, you must come
to appreciate many facts about your students. It is essential that you begin with the idea that you are educating the *whole* student. For decades,
educators such as Dewey (1938), Drucker (1957), and Rousseau (1964) have
been espousing the development of the total child. Cleland (1980) succinctly stated, "Reading is a personal process deeply rooted within the
reader, and . . . any complete understanding of reading must necessarily
concern itself with the totality of the person engaged in the reading act."

To achieve the goal of educating the whole child, the teacher of reading must understand four different factors that affect the reading ability
of a child:

1. Language factors
2. Cognitive factors
3. Sensory and perceptual factors
4. Socioeconomic factors

Language Factors

The ways in which language is developed is a subject of constant research
and debate. Some theories, like Lenneberg's (1970), stress the innate aspects of language acquisition, whereas others, like Skinner's (1972), emphasize behavioral reinforcement as a prime factor in language development. Still others, like Piaget's (1962), focus on the child's interactions
within his environment as an essential factor in establishing concepts that
are communicated through language.

Klein (1981), in a discussion of generalizations about children's language, suggests that language is acquired in orderly stages. He states,

> Children do not learn language by simply imitating adults, nor do they ac-
> quire language accidentally. Instead, they develop language systematically
> with the system becoming more complex and language use more elegant
> throughout the years. Each of the various stages of development from be-
> ginning of speech through the beginning school years reflects attributes
> common to all children in the stage. (p. 445)

Although there is a need for continued research on language development, existing theories, like the one offered by Menyuk (1984) in which

she suggests that children need to possess certain oral language skills before reading, offer much of what is needed in understanding the language base of the reading process. A student may enter school with a "private" language (dialect) as well as a "formal" (public) language. If the private language is better developed than the formal public language, the student may find reading to be a difficult task since most reading materials are written in formal public language. Students from other cultural backgrounds may have difficulty with school experiences because their private language is often misunderstood or misinterpreted. All students must be encouraged to accept both their private and public languages while becoming aware of the phonological and grammatical variations that exist between these two languages.

We believe that language refinement and growth is highly dependent upon teacher understanding and acceptance. We encourage you, as reading teachers, to accept the language presented by the student and then provide further learning through interaction. For example, if your first-grader says, "I busted it!" you reply, "I see that you broke it. Delicate things break easily. Broken things are hard to repair, but let's try." In this way, you help the student to acquire public language skills while accepting private language. If you can offer students such nonthreatening interactions, they will grow in language skills.

Cognitive Factors

Cognitive factors related to reading achivement represent an array of mental processes. Gordon (1961), Piaget (1962), and many other psychologists and educators have dealt with developmental stages of mental growth. They assert that a large portion of cognitive growth takes place in the early years and is a biological function. Cannella (1980) however, cautions that "Results concerning cognition and reading have been tentative and nonconclusive." For this reason, a more detailed discussion on cognition and its relation to learning will be presented in Chapter 2.

INTELLIGENCE

> After an Old Home Week in the school system, when those we flunked return in Rolls-Royces to patronize us, we are positive of one thing:
> Either it takes no intelligence to make money, and education is of comparatively little value, or teachers don't know a smart child when they see one. (Preston, 1938, p. 176)

Many researchers and educators have conducted studies to examine the relationship between intelligence and reading. M. Tremans-Ziremba et al. (1980) found that "The relationship between intelligence and reading achievement found in previous studies was verified."

There are many definitions of intelligence in operation; we will define intelligence as a combination of biological factors and environmental experiences. Unfortunately, the most common computation of the IQ score, while considering MA (mental age) and CA (chronological age), gives little attention to the experiential background of the child. Generally, it focuses on a child's current level of intellectual functioning. Often, an IQ score is computed, a child is labeled "bright," "average," or "dull," and the case is closed. In so doing, the following questions remain unanswered:

1. Was the child ready to be tested?
2. Was the child motivated?
3. Were the child's life experiences similar to those of the "average" child?
4. If these experiences were different from the norm, which set of experiences should be tested?
5. Does the child need exposure to a specific set of experiences before being given a particular test?

Many students who score poorly on intelligence tests in the first grade are erroneously labeled "dull" or "retarded." Often, they are assigned to the lowest reading group, where they deteriorate for the remainder of their school lives. Given this fact, the findings of Cohen and Glass (1968) are frightening: they state that there is no significant relationship between first-grade reading ability and IQ scores but that there are significant relationships by grade 4.

The exact nature of the relationship between reading and intelligence is still unknown. Much of the research is contradictory and sheds little light on this topic because the larger question of the precision of IQ testing is still unanswered.

Sensory and Perceptual Factors

One of the initial concerns for the teacher of reading is a student's visual and auditory readiness for printed materials. It has been suggested that there is no one best age at which a student should begin a visual or auditory readiness program.

Neuman (1981) conducted a study that showed that first-grade students can be taught auditory perceptual skills; this training, however, did not have a significant effect on their reading skills. It should be noted that perceptual development as well as sensory development often is dependent on physical, emotional, linguistic, and environmental factors. The specifics of assessment of readiness factors will be discussed in detail in Chapter 2.

Socioeconomic Factors

There are more questions regarding the relationship between reading and socioeconomic status than there are answers. Many reading studies have shown high correlations between reading failure and low socioeconomic status. However, M. Tremans-Ziremba et al. (1980) suggest that "it is necessary to obtain a better description of the ongoing family environmental processes that influence reading, before a full understanding of the relationship between reading and socioeconomic status can be obtained." In Chapter 2, we will discuss several issues concerning the home and the preschool experiences of students who are beginning to learn to read.

Curriculum

What do I do to be an effective reading teacher? The role of the classroom teacher is extremely complex and will demand extensive treatment throughout the book. The "What do I do?" part of this question will be discussed in depth in Chapter 15.

Both your philosophical and methodological beliefs will determine the structures of your classroom. You must consider such questions as, "How will information be transmitted to my students?" and "What type of student-teacher interactions will I try to develop?" Such questions will help you continuously to reassess existing curricula, methods, and materials as the strengths and needs of your students change. As a teacher of reading, you will be called upon to make many similar curricular decisions.

When the close of summer signals the start of the school year, teachers begin to think about their curriculum and begin to plan their teaching strategies.

As you begin to do this, ask yourself the following questions:

Teacher

1. What is my view of the world? What part does education play in my view of the world?
2. What is my role as a teacher? Who am I to my students? Which term best describes my role: *facilitator, expert, resource person, co-equal, confronter?*
3. What societal values do I want to convey to my students?
4. What is my view of humanity? What am I specifically doing through day-to-day interactions to produce the ideal, mature, human being?
5. What are my basic values? Do I encourage students to accept my value structures, or do I teach them a process for developing and selecting their own value system?
6. With what type of student-teacher interactions am I most comfortable? Is the flow of communication one-way or two-way, open-ended, or planned and determined?
7. To what types of motivational sources do I ascribe? Does motivation

come from within the student, or does it come from an external re-
ward system, or both? Does my motivational source distort the learning process or insert noneducational values into the educational process?

8. What types of discipline will I use? How do I handle individual problems? Group problems? Total class problems? What are the emotional
and educational results of my discipline?

Students

1. What will be the role of the student in my class? What expectations
do I have for him?
2. Who are these young people? What do I know of their experiential
readiness for learning?
3. Which word or phrase best describes the relationship of the students
to me and to the learning process: *receivers of the word, creators, in-
dividualists, technicians, obedient children?*
4. How do children learn? How do they view my role as a teacher?
5. How are students evaluated? Do they have a clear understanding of
the evaluative process? How are these children emotionally, socially,
and cognitively affected by the evaluative processes of the classroom?

Curriculum

1. What will be the learning climate of my classroom? Will it be quiet,
active, friendly, individually oriented, teacher dominated, task oriented, almost unstructured, enthusiastic, altering in tempo, or even
paced? Will the atmosphere be friendly, fearful, respectful, "hard-at-
work," or personal growth oriented? What will be my role in determining the learning environment?
2. What will be the major purpose, or goal, of education in this classroom? What specific social, psychological, emotional, and cognitive
learning will occur within the classroom?

Although the process of answering these questions may seem burdensome, we encourage you to attempt to formulate answers that will help
you to integrate your philosophical, psychological, and curricular beliefs.
You may begin by describing the principles of your philosophy and the
effects of these principles on the psychological development of your students.

Once you have formulated and refined your educational beliefs, you can
begin to plan a curriculum that will provide your students with the experiences and information needed to become successful readers.

Our role in this process is to provide you with a comprehensive view
of reading and methods for implementing this theory. You will then be a
practitioner as well as a *theoretician*.

Suggested Readings Related to Goals   We encourage you at this time to review the goals at the beginning of this chapter. If you feel you would like to explore one or more of these areas in greater depth, please refer to the cross-indexed bibliography at the end of the book.

2 Factors Affecting the Reader's Early Development

Around eighteen or twenty months of age children begin to put words together. In the sense that language is essentially a systematic means for expressing and understanding an unlimited number of ideas, this point is the true beginning of language. Although child language at this stage is simple, it is particularly interesting because it reflects the child's initial organizing strategies.

[P. Dale]

Goals

To help the student understand
1. The early stages of cognitive development
2. How children acquire and develop language
3. How the home environment and family influence young children
4. How television influences the developing reader

It is important for the prospective teacher of reading to have an understanding of the cognitive and linguistic development of each student and to understand the influence of home and family on each student's growth because these influences will affect each student's success in school.

In a broad sense, we can categorize the factors that influence school success into two broad areas: internal growth stimulants (cognitive and language development) and external stimulants (family and environmental factors). Obviously, there is some overlap and interplay between external and internal stimulants. We will begin with a brief discussion of the internal stimulants to human growth.

Human Development: Internal Stimulants

We recognize that there is a wide array of internal factors that affect human development. The following four areas have been designated for discussion in this chapter because they are thought to be the factors most closely related to later reading success:

1. Cognitive development
2. Perceptual development
3. Language development
4. Human performance and information processing

Cognitive Development

Babbs and Moe (1983) state that cognition "refers to the intellectual functioning of the human mind and is characterized by remembering, comprehending, focusing, attention, and processing information" (p. 423). These mental, or thinking, processes can be categorized under two broad headings that indicate two somewhat different mental processes. The first of these, *logical thinking*, deals with the formal, well-structured thought processes used in the ordered solving of problems. The second, *creative thinking*, is an informal, divergent kind of thinking. In any curriculum designed to nurture the individual, the teacher must be concerned with both kinds of thought processes.

LOGICAL THINKING

To understand logical thinking and its growth in students, we will look at four processes that result in logical thought:

1. Concept formation
2. Concept realization
3. Generalizing
4. Hypothesis and prediction

Concept Formation.   From the outset, it is important to distinguish *concept* from *concept formation*. A concept is a word or phrase that identifies or classes a group of objects, events, or ideas. The designation of a concept in words is called a *term*. Concept formation is a mental process in which we construct an understanding of objects and experiences, particularly in relation to other objects and experiences.

We tend to observe similarities and differences in any group of objects and then classify the similarities under a concept label. A concept may be concrete (e.g., dog, car) or it may be abstract (e.g., patriotism, love). A concept may be more or less inclusive (e.g., *animal* is more inclusive than *mammal; mammal* is more inclusive than *cat; cat* is more inclusive than *Siamese*).

*It is important to have an understanding of the cognitive and linguistic devel-
opment of each child and to understand the influence of home and family on
each child's growth because these influences will affect each child's success in
school (Photo by Linda Lungren.)*

It is a complex transition from mere awareness (perception) to conception, and much remains to be learned about it. Dasch (1983) summarized
its importance when she noted that Piaget (1963) "holds that cognitive
abilities (thinking and comprehending skills) are dependent upon the development and organization of cognitive structures. These structures . . .
are based on sensorimotor experiences that have been transformed into
mental representations. . . . The more highly developed and organized
the structures are, the more useful they are . . ." (p. 429).

In another detailed study of the complex process of concept formation,
Vygotsky (1962) concluded that a student, in his or her early years, associates a number of objects with a word. Sometimes the association is based
only on a chance impression; for example, *doggie* may equal *horse, cow,*

cat, donkey, oddly shaped chair, and *teddy bear*. For this somewhat random collection of objects, the student improves the unorganized *congerie*, or "heap" (Vygotsky's term), in three ways: trial-and-error methods, organization of the visual field, and reorganization of the "heaps" by associating elements from different heaps with a new word. This tendency continues as the student matures; however, he or she begins to think about objects on the basis of more concrete or factual bonds. The student does not yet distinguish between the essential and the nonessential (relevant and irrelevant) attributes of objects. The student may associate objects on the basis of similarities, contrasts, or proximity in space or time or on the basis of his or her own practical experiences. In this phase of concept formation, which Vygotsky refers to as thinking in complexes, the subjective associations are supplemented by more objective bonds, but the student still groups objects in toto with all of their attributes, regardless of their importance.

Finally, the stage is reached in which the student isolates elements and is able to consider these elements apart from the concrete experience in which they were encountered. Applying a concept to new situations is even more difficult for a student. "When the process of concept formation is seen in all its complexity, it appears as a movement of thought within the pyramid of concepts, constantly alternating between two directions from the particular to the general and from the general to the particular" (Vygotsky, 1962, pp. 80–81).

Concept Realization.   Three major factors affect concept realization or attainment. They are

1. The kind of concept (concrete or abstract)
2. The developmental age of the student
3. The number and degree of intensity of experiences the student has

This suggests that there is a time and a kind of experience that is appropriate for a student. Piaget notes this phenomenon when he differentiates between accommodation and assimilation:

1. Accommodation: When the individual encounters something new which does not fit his existing mental structure, he accommodates the new by modifying or reorganizing his present structure of thought.
2. Assimilation: When the individual internalizes the change so that he can handle the new experience with ease, as a part of his own life space, he has assimilated the new information.

This accommodation/assimilation process can be called adaptation. A student adapts to the environment when the concepts of accommodation and assimilation are integrated.

Generalizing.   A generalization is formed when a person differentiates ideas and then synthesizes them. For a student to make sense of the innumerable facts in a life experience, the facts and ideas must be ordered and connected, that is, generalized. The learner must be the primary agent in generalizing meaning in his or her own collection of facts.

Hypothesis and Prediction. Once a student has begun to generalize about facts and ideas, predictions are possible. Humans must invoke the aid of analogy to predict. While we base our prediction on as large a number of facts as possible, we can never be sure that further investigation will support our hypothesis (Poincaré, 1952). Even so, it is far better to predict without complete certainty than not to hypothesize at all because prediction enables the learner to continue investigating knowledge. It is important that students learn to hypothesize and then carry out experimentation that will verify or negate their hypotheses.

CREATIVE THINKING

As Dasch (1983) succinctly pointed out, "If teachers actually are going to 'teach to the child' then they must teach to the whole child" (p. 434). We believe that one of the teacher's responsibilities is to provide ample opportunities for creative thinking.

Kagan (1971) maintained that "the mission of education is to persuade each child that he is a richer source of ideas than he suspects and to enable him to experience the exhilaration that is inherent in the creative use of mind" (p. 73). Perhaps the best way for a teacher to encourage creativity is by serving as a model, demonstrating interest in novel situations and curiosity about different and unique ideas. Having shown this interest and delight in learning to a student you must provide him or her with opportunities to develop and pursue such interests in learning. Some educators call this approach *discovery learning*. There are several advantages to discovery learning:

1. It enables the student to identify problems and possible solutions.
2. It develops the learner's self-confidence and attitudes toward trying alternative solutions.
3. It encourages the student to discover broad principles and larger connections between different bodies of knowledge.

Regarding the process of discovery learning, it must be noted that there can be something arbitrary about the ideas of knowledge gained. A sense of ownership emerges about the conclusions; that is, "Because I discovered it, it must be right." Continuous self-evaluation of one's ideas may be difficult; for this reason, there is a need for highly skilled teacher guidance in the discovery process.

Perceptual Development

A student's perceptual ability involves seeing (visual), hearing (auditory), touching (kinesthetic), smelling, and tasting. Perception and its relationship to the reading process has been a topic of research for decades, particularly with regard to visual and auditory perception. The question of when a student's perceptual abilities are mature enough to cope with the reading process is central to "reading readiness" research and will be discussed in greater detail in Chapter 3.

Even allowing for individual differences, Vernon (1959) maintains that there are four perceptual processes related to reading: (1) discriminating a visual stimulus from its background characteristics, or recognizing that sound patterns within words are separate entities; (2) recognizing essential similarities necessary for the general classification of sound patterns into a succession of word patterns; (3) classifying visual symbols within their broader class, which are reflected as sounds; and (4) identifying words, usually through naming.

Perception involves the process of associating meaning with a concept that previously has been isolated through experience. After successful identification and recognition, the student attempts to modify and relate the previous association with the present situation. Thus, the student refines the factors of *identification* and *recognition, categorization, generalization, analysis,* and *synthesis* to arrive at an understanding of the world at large.

Language Development

The National Council of Teachers of English (1983) described the importance of language as the core of the school curriculum when it stated, "Language is a primary way individuals communicate what they think and feel. They find self-identity through language, shape their knowledge and experience by means of it, and depend upon it as a lifelong resource for expressing their hopes and feelings" (p. 185).

It is almost axiomatic to say that teachers who are preparing to instruct students in reading need to know a great deal about language, language development, and language acquisition. The relationship between language development and reading has become a major issue in linguistic and educational research in recent years. In the next section, we will present a brief overview of the current research relating to language development and acquisition.

LANGUAGE ACQUISITION

Despite being born with an immature nervous system, human infants are capable of communicating their basic needs in a primitive linguistic manner (Flood and Salus, 1984). In time, infants learn to control their muscles, and with this maturation, they become more capable of discriminating between sets of sounds, shapes, and colors. Researchers have reported a time schedule for certain types of linguistic performance. For almost all children the schedule looks something like this:

Age	Vocalization
At birth	Crying
1–2 mo.	Cooing and crying
3–6 mo.	Babbling, cooing, and crying
9–14 mo.	First words
18–24 mo.	First sentences
3–4 yr.	Almost all basic syntactic structures
4–8 yr.	Almost all speech sounds correctly articulated
9–11 yr.	Semantic distinctions established

The stages shown in this table are sequential. Although each includes an age range, Lenneberg (1967) has stated that they occur in the same order for every child. Furthermore, newborns are not equipped either to perceive or produce speech. The sounds they make are not directly related to those that will eventually become part of their language.

Chomsky (1962) and other linguists have advanced the idea that humans possess an innate specific language acquisition device. They tell us that all infants acquire this language tool without overt teaching; that is, given a minimal amount of language input, all physiologically "normal" children learn to talk.

LANGUAGE COMPONENTS

In the following section, we will discuss the four basic components of language and the specifics of their acquisition in children. These components are

1. Phonology—the sound system
2. Morphology—inflections, tense markers
3. Syntax—the order of words
4. Semantics—the meaning of words

Phonology. The study of the specific speech sounds that make up language is called phonology. Many researchers believe that the reading process includes the deciphering of speech transferred to print; therefore, it is important that teachers of reading understand how the child acquires and uses the phonology of his language.

Jakobson (1968) asserts that the development of the phonemic system is the result of the child's attempts to establish a system of oppositions within a sound continuum. The first oppositions are maximal ones between a consonant and a vowel; usually they are the opposition between the most open, central, farthest back vowel, /a/, and the farthest front, stopped consonant, /p/. Thus, /a/ is the "optimal" vowel, and /p/ the "optimal" consonant. There is great frequency of /papa/ as a first-syllable sequence in young children. Sometimes there is less than optimal control over the larynx and over the velum, the flap of skin at the back of the roof of the mouth. In this case, the first-syllable sequences are /baba/ or /mama/. Jakobson points out that this is why "papa," "baba," and "mama" are often the child's first-remembered or quoted sequences; it also explains why they are used as parental names/substitutes in many cultures.

A child's ability to use a wider variety of consonant sounds continues as the child develops. Some linguists suggest rough age correlates for production of English consonants:

Age	Proficient Consonant Articulation
$3\frac{1}{2}$	b p m w h
$4\frac{1}{2}$	d t n g k ɔ y
$5\frac{1}{2}$	f
$6\frac{1}{2}$	v ð ž š l
$7\frac{1}{2}$	s z θ f

For a more detailed discussion of developmental distinctions between speech sounds and how and where they are formed in the mouth, see Flood and Salus (1984).

Morphology.   The smallest units of meaning in language are called morphemes. Inflectional endings and tense markers, as well as the root words to which they are attached, all represent types of morphemes. In the study of morphology, the teacher is interested in looking briefly at how the student demonstrates growth in understanding about the effect that inflectional endings and tense markers have on meaning in language.

In an important study on the acquisition of morphology, Jean Berko-Gleason (1958) showed students a picture of a cartoon figure, telling the students in the study, "This is a *wug*." She then told the students that there were two animals, showed them a picture, and said, "These are two _____," expecting the students to supply the plural "wugs" /wugz/. She used nonsense words that elicited all three of the English plural morphemes (/-s/ as in hats; /-z/ as in rugs; and /iz/ as in doses). Berko-Gleason found that youngsters in the age range of 4 years made 6 percent errors with the /-iz/ forms, and 25 percent errors with the /-z/ forms. She also found that they have /iz/ forms in their lexicons, for 91 percent had the correct plural for glass. She concluded that at a relatively early age children are able to account for morphological changes in language.

Syntax.   The arrangement of words in a meaningful order is what linguists call syntax. As children progress from single-word utterances, there is a need for consistency in ordering these utterances so that they will be understood. Since clarity of meaning in written language also depends on this consistent ordering, a child's ability to use proper syntax when speaking may facilitate understanding written sentences.

Telegraphic Speech and Pivots. Within six months of the time a child produces his first word, he acquires a vocabulary of approximately fifty words. At this time, his first attempts to combine words together result in what is called *telegraphic speech.* Some examples might be, "Milk gone," "Mommy home," or "Baby cookie." According to Brown and Fraser (1963), articles, prepositions, and auxiliaries are not used at this stage.

Shortly thereafter, children begin to use some of their words as "pivots"—that is, the pivot words are fixed, and other words are attached to them. The following examples illustrate this phenomenon:

Position Pivot 1	Position Pivot 2
allgone truck	shoe on
allgone cracker	hat on

Brown and Fraser (1963) also indicate that children divide their lexicon into "function" words and "object" words. These divisions may be the basis of functional divisions that later become formal word classes—for example, nouns, verbs, and adjectives. As such, this process may lay the groundwork for contextual word analysis when the child begins the task of reading.

Slobin (1979) presents examples of some of these pivot structures:

Function	English	Function	English
Modify, qualify	pretty____	Describe act	____away
	my____		____on
	allgone____		____off
	all____		____it
Locate, name	there____	Demand	more____
	here____		give____
	see____	Negate	no____
	it____		don't____

Complex Syntactic Forms. Children acquire the ability to use more complex syntactic forms gradually. For example, in the early stages, children pose questions simply by incorporating the rising intonation of typical English sentences into the same sentences they used for statements, for example, "Daddy home?" More complex questions using a verb or auxiliary in the initial position ("Does Ryann go to school?") and the wh-questions (who, what, why, where, when, how) begin to appear as the child progresses with language comprehension. *Relative clauses* are one of the last syntactic concepts to be understood by children. Chomsky (1969) has found that many 8-year-olds do not fully understand a sentence such as, "Tell Hugo what to buy at the store." She further suggests that most students between the ages of 5 and 10 regard the first noun phrase in a sentence as the subject and the second noun phrase as the object. In a sentence like, "The cupcake was baked by Bill Deacon," the cupcake is thought of as the subject perpetrating a horrible fate on the object, Bill Deacon.

A student's ability to produce more complex syntactic structures and to understand potential syntactic complications such as relative clauses is essential to reading comprehension. As students acquire competence with these language forms, their ability to proceed through a written text smoothly increases.

Semantics.   An often-quoted definition of semantics is that it is the study of word meaning. While this is true, semantics also includes phonology, syntax, and contextual usage. Single words often have multiple meanings for the child, and even "fixed" multiple meanings can be altered by syntactic and contextual constraints. A 4-year-old knows that a figurative meaning is being attached to the word puppy when his mother says, "Paul, you're acting like a puppy." Furthermore, the child knows if "puppy" is being used in a good or bad sense by his mother's tone and by contextual considerations (for example, is Paul chewing on the sofa?).

Taking this example one step farther, if the utterance is changed to "Paul, you're acting like a zumtoadbat," the child can use his knowledge of syntax, intonation, and context to arrive at an acceptable synonym for "zumtoadbat." Semantics, then, is the study of word meaning, along with phonology, syntax, and contextual usage.

While the importance of semantics in the acquisition of syntax has been both minimized (Chomsky, 1972) and emphasized (Clark, 1976), there is little argument that knowledge of word meaning including phonology, syntax, and contextual usage is essential to reading comprehension. Simply breaking the code phonetically does the reader little good without the semantic information necessary to give it meaning.

Students come to school with incomplete notions about language; it is your job to help them develop their language skills. In Table 2-1, modeled after the work of Menyuk (1984), we have listed both the elements of language that the children have acquired before school and the elements of language that they will acquire during their school years.

Human Performance and Information Processing

An area of study which has been of great interest in recent years to educators is that of human information processing. Such complex areas of human performance as the role of perception and memory in processing information, the speed and quantity of information processing and storage, and what type of information is most easily processed and stored by the

Table 2-1
Elements of Language Development Before and During School

	Phonology	Morphophono-logical	Syntax-Semantics	Lexicon	Pragmatics
Learned before 5 years of age	1. Discrimination of all phonological elements that are critical for word identification 2. Production of all phonological elements except strident clusters (e.g., *scr*eam)	1. Pluralization 2. Tense markers	1. Basic syntactic structures 2. Basic semantic structures	1. Sizable structured lexicon that include 2,000–3,000 words 2. Reliance on physical and linguistic cues for meaning	1. Conversational rules 2. Speech acts (e.g., assertion, commanding, and request-ing).
Learned in school by acquiring more knowledge *and* greater depth of knowledge	1. Segmentation 2. Rhyming 3. Recognition and production of initial, medial, and final pho-nemes	1. Rules of stress (e.g., minute-minute) 2. Rules of phono-logical change (e.g., sane-sanity)	1. Complex functions 2. Structural para-phrase (e.g., The dog was given to her by her brother. Her brother gave her the dog.) 3. Ambiguity clarification (e.g., The duck is ready to eat.)	1. Increased hierarchical organizational schemes, for example, I. Dog A. Shepherd 1. Irish 2. German 2. Multiple mean-ings (e.g., She wanted to be a *star* in the theater, i.e., a success in her acting career.)	1. Domains of discourse (e.g., narrative, exposition, poetry) 2. Speech acts requiring hypothetical physical conditions (e.g., If I were king, I would . . .)

Meaning 1: The duck is ready to eat the grain.
Meaning 2: The duck has been cooked and is ready to be eaten.

SOURCE: P. Menyuk, "Language Development in Children," in L. Carmichael, ed., *Manual of Child Psychology*, 2nd ed. (New York: John Wiley & Sons, Inc., 1984), pp. 492–639.

human brain are all being examined. An understanding of how we process perceptual and linguistic information will enhance our comprehension of the reading process. How does the human intellectual system function? How is the functioning related to the acquisition of knowledge? The information being gleaned crosses many disciplines and involves a great deal of technical and experimental research.

For example, *psychologists* have moved us from vague concepts of short-

and long-term memory to a greater understanding of the components necessary to *acquire, understand, synthesize, retain, retrieve,* and *evaluate information.* Their insights are important when planning instruction because, to retrieve information from long-term memory, it must be rehearsed and attached through example to prior knowledge.

From *sociologists* we have developed an appreciation for the strong contextual base of human cognitive development. How do differences in students' culturally organized experiences affect the way in which they process information?

Still another contribution comes from the intense study of *biological, neurological,* and *physiological* life systems. Scientists in these areas have begun to sketch a profile of the human brain. This profile, although still woefully scant, has provided greater understanding of genetic transcription and translation, metabolic processes, and synaptic connections. This matching of particular human functions with specific brain parts offers both an explanation for certain phenomena and a more clearly defined direction for further exploration.

An example of this information that is important to teachers in planning curriculum is the realization that the cerebral cortex (the outer surface of the forebrain) tells the limbic system (the inner emotional brain) the kind of response to make. The limbic system adjusts the response level from mild enjoyment to ecstasy or from vague displeasure to intense hatred. This information is the basis for our discussions of the significance of the *affective* domain, or one's attitudes and interests in planning learning experiences.

Although other information processing activities have not yet been coupled with specific areas of the brain, the exploration of such strategies has yielded important insights that have relevance for instructional development.

For instance, researchers in the area of complex analogical reasoning have defined structural components of problem-solving analogies that significantly increase a learner's ability to develop strategies to solve the new problem. The ability to recognize similar causal relationships within different problem situations or reading experiences facilitates our ability to transfer such problem-solving strategies effectively to a broad range of novel situations regardless of the degree of similarity in their actual content or text.

An understanding of the strategies used in processing information allows the teacher to develop and sequence instruction in a manner that promotes optimal learning and retention.

Human Development: External Stimulants

Along with the complex internal stimulants we have discussed, children are also shaped physically, emotionally, and psychologically by external stimulants, that is, factors within their environments. In the past, the significance of the environment as an influence on learning has been under-estimated. Recently, educators have found that external stimulants are equally as important as, and perhaps more important than, inherent qual-ities in developing full learning and achievement potential.

Because external stimulants associated with the home environment are directly related to success, we will discuss two categories of external stim-ulants: family/parental influences and home environment.

Family/Parental Influences

The family may begin to influence a child's attitude toward reading as soon as the child is able to respond to language because oral language is the base of the reading process. To encourage development, parents need to talk to their children as soon as they are born to provide them with models of language use. Through the physical act of holding a baby snuggly and securely while showing him or her the pictures in a book, parents and other family members begin to develop the notion that reading is a plea-surable experience.

As children mature, parents can begin reading to them, holding the book so that they can see the pictures as well as the print. The intent here is not to initiate reading but to begin to be aware that there is a relationship between the print and spoken language. As parents discuss the ideas in the material they read with their children, this interaction introduces new words that children may incorporate into their vocab-ularies.

Modeling. Many studies have shown that children who view their par-ents reading, who are read to, and who have books and educational toys succeed at prereading tasks. Although most modeling research is not spe-cifically related to readiness for reading, Durkin (1966, 1972) found that modeling was an important predictor of reading success in her studies of early readers.

Verbal Interaction Between Parent and Child. Anderson and Lapp (1979) postulated that the degree of verbal and reading efficiency was depen-dent on the frequency and quality of a parent's contact with the child. Also, Hess and Shipman (1965) suggested that a child's performance on cognitive tasks is associated with the "teaching style" of the mother. This maternal teaching style is particularly evident in reading episodes be-tween parent and child.

Reading Aloud. Whether it is classic children's stories that are read chapter by chapter, or a favorite comic book read until the reader and the child know every word, being read to is not only a joy to both parties, but beneficial to the young reader. There is an extensive body of nor-mative literature suggesting that reading to young children enhances lan-guage development (Templin, 1957; MacKinnon, 1959; Durkin, 1983;

Through the physical act of holding a baby while showing him the pictures in a book, parents and other family members begin to develop the notion that reading is a pleasurable experience. (Photo by Linda Lungren.)

Bullock, 1975) and is related to reading success (Almy, 1958; Durkin, 1980, 1983).

In addition, there is a great deal of support for the idea that children should be read to during the school day. Chapparo (1975) maintains that "Storytime reading to children should be an integral part of every reading program—children need models." Durkin (1983) argues in favor of reading to young children on the premise that an oral reading episode "can be a vehicle for learning about children's readiness for reading."

There is little empirical research on the effects of style of reading to young children and cognitive growth. One of the few studies in this area was reported by Swift (1970) when he explained the success of a parent training program called *Get Set*, which first presented the value of reading to young children. A study by Flood (1977) found that parents can enhance their children's experiences by following these four steps during a reading episode:

1. Prepare children for the story by asking warm-up questions.
2. Interact with the child during the story by asking and answering many questions.
3. Reinforce the child during the episode in a positive manner.
4. Finish the episode by asking evaluative questions.

"Littering the Environment with Meaningful Print." In discussions of children's language, DeFord and Harste (1982) advocated "littering the environment with meaningful print" (p. 595). Although aimed at classroom environments, the suggestion also applies to the home environment. Parental contact may be the most important factor in establishing a rich atmosphere for developing interest and skill in reading for the young child, but other factors in the home environment also are significant to the reading readiness task. The chief factors are educational materials and television.

Books and Materials

There is also an extensive body of normative literature suggesting that children need to have books and other educational materials available to them in the home to prepare more successfully for reading (Berstein, 1976; Beck, 1973; Durkin, 1983). Materials may include such items as chalkboards, magnetic letter sets, toys that utilize the alphabet, children's magazines, paper, pencils, and a desk or table where the child can "work," "study," or play school. This kind of supportive home environment allows children to combine learning with playing in the most natural of settings, the home.

Television

For decades people have been trying to assess the influence of television viewing upon reading, language, and cognitive skills. As early as 1957, Templin argued in favor of periodic studies about children's language because of the influence of television on changing norms of language ability. Seventeen years later, Leifer (1974) reported, "To date we understand little about the combined roles of television, the home, and the school in influencing child development" (p. 74). While some have feared that television might lead to a state of illiteracy, others such as Steinberg (1983) suggest that "TV is the most important promoter of reading" (p. 510), and others have shown that cognitive understanding of story is related to the understanding of television "stories" (Indrisano and Gurry, 1984). While the debate continues, it is clear that the greatest single nonhuman environmental influence on a child's language ability and cognitive ability (including reading ability) is television. There is no longer a question of whether or not educational TV shows are effective.

"Sesame Street."   The popular children's show "Sesame Street," a joint venture of the Carnegie and Ford Foundations and the U.S. Office of Education, turned public attention to the positive educational aspects of television. The show was fine-tuned by extensive pretesting and observation of the viewers' responses. As a result, the proposed format of the show underwent some changes. Vocabulary, letter names, and beginning sounds were taught through rhythm, puppetry, songs, stories, and direct instruction.

"The Electric Company."   "The Electric Company" was designed to pick up where "Sesame Street" left off—that is, to supplement the reading of 7- to 10-year-olds.
    Roser (1972) noted that the show was designed to emphasize the following:

1. The left-to-right sequence of print corresponds to the temporal sequence of speech.
2. Written symbols stand for speech sounds. They "track" the stream of speech.
3. The relationship between written symbols and speech sounds is sufficiently reliable to produce successful decoding most of the time.
4. Reading is facilitated by learning a set of strategies for figuring out sound-symbol relationships. (p. 684)

Finally, the undisputed fact that television is here to stay has led many educators (e.g., Probst, 1983; Ploghoft and Sheldon, 1983) to suggest curricular means of capitalizing on children's television viewing. Television cannot and should not be ignored as a vehicle of potential for children's learning.

Suggested Readings Related to Goals.   We encourage you at this time to review the goals at the beginning of this chapter. If you feel you would like to explore one or more of these areas in greater depth, please refer to the cross-indexed bibliography at the end of the book.

3 Reading as a Part of the Integrated Language Arts

We have witnessed the birth and growth of human systems of communication, chief among which is language. The nature of speech and writing are no longer closed books to us. The fundamental purpose and function of speech have become clear. We have seen what language and languages consist of. We have observed the intimate connection of language with all basic human activities.

[Mario Pei]

Goals

To help the student understand
1. The importance of integrating all the language arts
2. Listening skills
3. Speaking skills
4. Writing skills

"Communication is language in action . . ." (National Council of Teachers of English, 1982, p. 186), and language is the foremost means of communicating our ideas and feelings. Language is a code system through which we express ourselves. For example, in speaking and writing, we *encode* our thoughts; we *decode*, or extract meaning, while listening or reading.

Children are able to communicate their thoughts through the language arts. "Language arts" describes our communication processes as well as a major portion of the school curriculum. The *development* and *integration* of the language arts of *listening, speaking, reading,* and *writing* is a crucial task for you, the teacher.

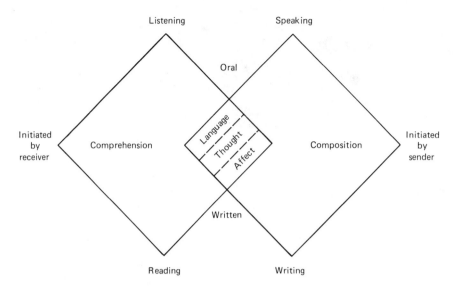

Figure 3–1. Relationships among the language arts, with an emphasis on comprehension and composition. (From "Reading and Writing Revisited" by Roselmina Indrisano, Number 18 of the *Ginn Occasional Papers,* 1984.)

Teachers and researchers have argued for years that the interrelations among the language arts need to be fully understood in order to develop an integrated, coherent reading curriculum. In recent years, we have come to understand more fully the dependency relationship between oral language and reading/writing achievement; for example, Menyuk (1984) and others stress the need for developing oral language in its many forms as the basis for learning to read and write. Researchers have also begun to examine the relationships between reading and writing, stressing their similarities; for example, Tierney and Pearson (1984) have suggested that reading and writing involve both composing and comprehending.

Indrisano (1984) presents the relations among the language arts, emphasizing comprehension and composition, in Figure 3-1. In almost any situation involving listening, speaking, reading, or writing you use more than one of the language arts simultaneously. From this perspective, it is natural to view the act of communication as an interrelated process. Loban's (1976) research findings support this view; he states that students who have low abilities in oral language also have difficulty in reading and writing. He further suggests that the inverse of this interrelationship is true: students with adequate language abilities show little, if any, difficulty in acquiring other communication skills.

Classroom teachers must not only integrate the language arts among themselves but also throughout the entire curriculum. According to Cazden (1983),

> Language arts must be integrated into all curriculum areas. . . . The purposeful use of those [language] skills can be provided most powerfully outside the language arts and in the service of the subject areas of literature, science, social studies, and mathematics. (p. 122)

In any content area classroom, a student listens to instruction or ideas; she shares her ideas by speaking; she reads content materials and writes detailed reports to express her thoughts. Obviously, language arts cannot be isolated in a single, separate, 40-minute-a-day period. Cazden (1983) further reminds us that "the language arts are the curriculum area that cannot stand alone. Only linguists have language as their subject matter" (p. 122).

Perhaps by now your tasks as a reading/language arts teacher seem overwhelming. You may have questions such as these:

1. What specific information will I need to know about each of the language arts?

In any content area classroom, a student listens to instruction or ideas; she shares her ideas by speaking; she reads content materials, and writes detailed reports to express her thoughts. (Photo by Linda Lungren.)

2. Which communication skills are appropriate for the students at a given stage of development?
3. How can I teach all of the language arts in conjunction with all of the content area skills?
4. Are there activities I can use to facilitate learning these skills?
5. Where do I begin?

No one ever knows all there is to know about teaching. Whenever a teaching task seems overwhelming, it is important for you to stop, pose the questions to which the answers will solve your dilemma, and then set out through reading, thinking, student observation, or chatting with your colleagues to answer your queries. As you teach, you will continuously pose new questions/problems and then seek to answer them. This chapter is designed to serve as a model to aid you in answering your questions about the teaching of three of the language arts—listening, speaking, and writing—and how to integrate them, along with reading, into your total program.

The Language Arts

Listening

Consider for a moment how much time people, and particularly students, spend listening every day. For example, a 1950 study of elementary school children by Wilt estimated that 57.5 percent of a student's day is spent in listening. Yet, after a comprehensive review of the literature and research on listening, Pearson and Fielding (1982) reached this conclusion: "For too long we have neglected listening as a part of our language arts curriculum" (p. 626).

Of course, the development of listening skills begins in the home. Children are exposed to sound from the very earliest moments of life. By the age of 4, the young child is silent for only 19 minutes a day (Brandenburg, 1915). The earliest listening patterns are developed in the home, and the degree of listening activity reinforcement supplied by the home affects the development of beginning listening skills (Feldman, 1967).

Care must be exercised not to confuse *listening* with *hearing;* hearing is only part of the listening process. Listening involves first hearing information and then processing, reflecting, and responding to it.

Part of your job as a classroom teacher will be to try to identify children with hearing disabilities rather than poor listening skills. Detecting these problems is not always easy; through observation, however, you may notice that a student

1. Is abnormally inattentive or abnormally attentive
2. Relies on gestures when speech would be more effective
3. Is behind in speech development

4. Strains to hear what is being said
5. Gives inappropriate answers to your questions
6. Ignores a speaker with whom he or she does not have direct eye contact
7. Has difficulty relating sequences to that which he or she has listened
8. May be unable to reproduce consonant phonemes
9. Has difficulty repeating long, detailed sentences
10. Evidences voice production (pitch, stress, rhythm) difficulties

In addition, be particularly alert to any student who may exhibit one or more of these signs when you have knowledge of the student having any of these medical complaints:

1. Frequent colds or ear infections
2. Allergies
3. Measles, mumps, or rubella

   If you suspect that a student is suffering from a hearing difficulty, make the appropriate referral to a speech and hearing specialist or school doctor. If, after a checkup, the student is diagnosed as having no hearing loss, you will have to plan curricula to facilitate the progress of these underdeveloped listening skills. Pearson and Fielding (1982) suggest that research has proven that direct instruction in listening can improve listening comprehension. They also note, "The key, though, is that instruction occurred in a listening, *not* in a reading, mode and that the children were aware that they were receiving listening instruction" (p. 619).

OTHER FACTORS RELATED TO LISTENING

Teachers must be careful not to confuse linguistic variations in speech patterns with hearing impairment. You may observe omissions, additions, distortions, and substitutions in the speech patterns of your students that are an outgrowth of dialect rather than a function of hearing difficulty. If you are working with students whose dialects differ from your own, be careful not to diagnose their listening/language needs incorrectly.

   Attitudes toward listening may also vary depending on a student's culture. For example, some cultures prohibit the male from listening to female commands; others restrict the singling out of an individual for the purpose of a compliment; and still others may limit the frequency of child-adult conversations.

   As you begin to select from commercially prepared programs or as you begin to develop your own curricula, be careful to remember the following developmental and environmental constraints:

> It is not uncommon, however, for children to have to listen far beyond their reasonable attention spans. This they must do while lawn mowers clatter, other children shout outside the window, people walk on noisy flooring, and they sit in sweltering temperatures—in short, they encounter every imaginable kind of inhibition to attention. (Lundsteen, 1979, p. 32)

IN YOUR CLASSROOM

In the following section, we will discuss some of the ways in which you can begin to integrate listening activities through your curriculum.

Classroom Environment.   You can increase your students' receptiveness to what they hear by implementing these simple suggestions:

1. Arrange the students' seats in such a way as to focus attention on the speaker. A semicircle, for example, will allow students to see and hear each other better.
2. Speak clearly and loudly enough to be heard. Don't "talk to the chalkboard." Whenever possible, be animated!
3. Emphasize concrete, not abstract, ideas, for example, "Hancock Elementary School" not "school."
4. When you speak, use contrast to keep shifting the students' attention so they continue listening to you.

In addition to planning an environment that facilitates productive listening, be sure to plan situations that encourage positive listening attitudes and habits.

Developing Positive Listening Attitudes.   You can help your students to develop positive listening habits by

1. Discussing with your children the importance of listening
2. Beginning each lesson by establishing a specific purpose
3. Encouraging children to listen and share ideas
4. Reinforcing good listening habits
5. Being a good listener yourself

Sharing Sounds.   The following activity has several advantages. Not only will it help your students learn to listen effectively, it will allow them to practice speaking and it will help you to learn about your students. Ask the students to share the sounds of their personal world by describing

1. The sounds they hear on the way to school
2. The sounds of emotions (happiness, sadness, amazement, etc.)
3. The sounds of things they enjoy most
4. The sounds of seasons
5. The sounds of home and family
6. The sounds of a quiet, relaxed time
7. The sounds that remind them of school
8. The sound of the voice of someone they love

Creating Sound.   Children of all ages enjoy producing sounds from such objects as metal lids, water taps, paper, and other materials that are easy to collect. Provide a large cardboard box where "sound machine makers" may be stored. Each time a student devises a new sound, encourage him or her to share it with others. Keep your curriculum flexible enough to accommodate new developments.

Adding Purpose to Listening.   One of the facets that differentiates hearing from listening is inferring meaning from what is heard. You may encourage the development of comprehensive listening by planning lessons that

---

1. Illustrate sequencing (numbers, letters, directions).
2. Encourage the students to listen and anticipate what may follow. For example, read the children a story or poem and omit some obvious words. Encourage the children to listen for context clues that will help them to supply missing information.

   Mary was going to the _____ to get a book. She _____

   Harold on Palm Street. _____ decided to _____

   with her.

3. Encourage the children to infer meaning from what they have heard. This may be done by reading short paragraphs or stories followed by questions such as

   Why do you think . . .? How would you feel . . .? What would you do . . .? How do you know . . .?

4. Encourage children to answer questions. This may be accomplished by reading a passage similar to

   Anita and Linda were spending the summer with Grandmother. Anita awakened early one morning and tiptoed into Grandmother's kitchen. As she crept around the corner of the pantry feeling for the cookie jar, she jumped with fright! A shadow! Someone else was in the kitchen. She momentarily forgot about the cookie jar and groped for the light. There was Linda also inching her way toward the cookie jar.

After reading the passage, ask

   1. At what time do you think the story occurred?
   2. How did Anita know Linda was in the kitchen?
   3. How many girls stayed at Grandmother's?
   4. What were the girls doing in the kitchen?

It is valuable to ask a wide range of questions because answering such questions encourages the students in various thinking activities.

Student Self-evaluation.   Encourage your students to evaluate their strengths as listeners. They may do this by observing if they

1. Direct their attention toward the speaker
2. Listen until the speaker has completed his or her statement
3. Think carefully about the message being sent
4. Listen for the organizational style of the speaker
5. Determine the validity of the statement
6. Think of appropriate responses
7. Weigh the value of their response

Stammer (1981) has suggested the following four-step method (MAPP) that may aid you in developing curricula to ensure that your students will develop more effective listening behaviors.

1. *Modeling*—Students will use you as a role model, so be sure you are a good listener.
2. *Assessment*—To assess your students' listening comprehension, you must understand the listening process.
3. *Preparation*—Plan your lessons (particularly giving directions) in a manner that will encourage productive listening.
4. *Practice*—Allow students to practice careful listening by planning activities that will foster and promote listening skills.

Speaking

Language is the foundation of communication. Yet communication is an ongoing problem because parents and teachers tend to emphasize "correct" communication rather than determine the extent to which correct communication encourages effective communication. Before we discuss communication, however, we must go back to the beginning: sound.

A child is exposed to sound and is encouraged to speak from the very earliest days of life. Children listen to sounds, attempt sounds, and combine and experiment with the production of speech sounds. The child eventually strings these unintelligible sounds together, continually receiving ample positive reinforcement from the adults and siblings of his or her family. Eventually, the words and word strings acquire comprehensibility. These early language patterns soon begin to include sentences so that "after the age of six there is relatively little in the grammar or syntax of language that the average child needs to learn, except to achieve a school imposed standard of speech or writing to which he may not be accustomed in his home environment" (Carroll, 1971, pp. 200–211).

Some believe that speech, one of the most commonly used communication processes, begins as early as five months after conception (Wilkinson, 1971), whereas others believe it begins with the child's first cry at birth. Most children utter their first intelligible word sometime in the second six months of life (Bellugi and Brown, 1964). Regardless of the age of acquisition, each child progresses through stages of cooing, babbling, single words, word commands, phrases, sentences, and the mastery of grammatical rules.

By the age of 5 or 6, most children have learned the basic structures of language and they have developed extensive speaking vocabularies, approximately twenty-five hundred words. In addition, children develop language "habits," which are determined by age, socioeconomic group, and geographical region. Once acquired, these language habits are difficult to alter. The concept of "correct" language is impossible because of pronunciation, word collection, phrasing, and construction variations.

Given the fact that most children come to school with language and the desire to communicate, why is there so often a communication breakdown in the classroom? Perhaps it is because that "instead of carefully building new strengths on top of old ones, traditional schooling has all too often denied the linguistic strengths students already possess" (Meier and Cazden, 1982, p. 505). Furthermore, studies by Loban (1976) suggest that the dichotomy between correct language (the language of the school or teacher) and effective language (the language of the child) can lead to student failure.

The elementary school curriculum is designed in such a way that you can build on the early language structures of children. As you attempt to implement such curricula within your classroom, it is important that you understand the comprehensiveness of any individual's language usage.

Language is a unique way of *expressing the self*. From simple sounds like crying to more sophisticated forms of language, we use language to convey our needs, desires, and emotions. The language of self-expression is seldom neutral because it conveys the essence of human sensations. As classroom teachers, you must encourage the use of the language of self-expression through a climate of acceptance. A student will interpret rejection of her language or her ideas as personal rejection, rejection of the self. One of the functions of life is the continual identification of self in a constantly changing environment of social interaction. Encouraging and accepting students' self-expression will help them during these formative years and in their later lives.

Young children's language is often *egocentric* in nature. As a student is engaged in group situations or when she must listen to others to complete a task, this egocentric language will lessen. As the student becomes involved in more sender-receiver exchanges, her language becomes more *expository*, which ultimately enables her to receive a wider variety of messages. Language is a means of acquiring information as well as a means of self-expression.

Other means of acquiring information are through *gestures, graphics,* and *mechanical codes.* There is a wide range of sources and activities that can be utilized to help children become familiar with these symbols. Role-playing and pantomime activities can help children with the interpretation of gestures. Graphic messages are received by interpreting traffic signs, advertisements, books, and other printed materials. The interpretation of mechanical messages can come to the receiver through traffic lights, flashing lights on a police car or ambulance, and train crossings. These unspoken expositions of language offer a wide range of facts and ideas.

Finally, you can give your students an opportunity to expand their oral language skills by planning such activities as reader's theater, giving formal and informal speeches, interviewing, role playing, storytelling, creative dramatics, puppetry, and choral speaking. These activities are not only valuable tools for building oral language skills but they are fun for teachers and students alike.

STYLES OF LANGUAGE

Students need to encounter a variety of language styles so that they acquire the necessary experience to respond to each type of situation with the appropriate language style. As Joos (1967) suggests, *informal* situations shared with intimate friends allow us to exhibit our private language styles. This style is often comprised of one-word or one-phrase utterances. The receiver is so well aware of our thinking patterns that she can anticipate what we will say almost before it is said. *Casual* situations shared with friends who are not quite as intimate may still allow us to use our private language; however, our utterances may need to be more explanatory. The *consultative* style of language is one that is used to convey factual information. The speaker may use this style when she is expressing her ideas to an audience of people who are not members of her private community. The need arises for an alternate style of language, a more public language, that will be shared and understood by most of the audience. Certain contexts require *frozen* styles of language, such as written messages or speeches to colleagues that often depend heavily on the use of an extremely formal language. It will become obvious that the development of various dialects must receive some attention in your classrooms if you are to prepare students to accommodate the multilanguage interactions that they will experience throughout their lives.

Writing

"Writing, like speaking, is a real-life way of thinking things through—of clarifying, exploring, and growing" (Langer, 1982, p. 340). Similarly, Murray (1968) states that "writing is the process of using language to discover meaning in experience and to communicate it" (p. 27). Initial writing involves inventing, devising, selecting, eliminating, and arranging one's ideas. Proofreading, editing, and correcting one's ideas are laborious but critical tasks in the writing process.

Some educators distinguish between "creative" and "practical" writing experience by referring to stories and poems as acts of creativity. Although we understand their rationale, we believe that anytime a person conveys her thoughts through written language, regardless of the form,

Initial writing involves inventing, devising, selecting, eliminating, and arranging one's ideas. Proofreading, editing, and correcting one's ideas are laborious but critical tasks in the writing process. (Photo by Linda Lungren.)

she has engaged in an act of creativity. Throughout this chapter, we will avoid a distinction between creative and practical writing.

THE WRITING PROCESS

For many students (and some teachers) writing is an unpleasant task—a task to be avoided if at all possible. Foley (1981) suggests that classroom writing problems may be traced to risk taking. She states,

> One reason that students do not learn to write easily is because they are not taught to take risks. Similarly, some teachers do not teach writing easily because they feel uncomfortable or uncertain about the process. Instead of risking

failure, they reduce writing instruction to thoughtless drill in grammar and mechanics. (p. 4)

In the following section, we will discuss the writing process and some ways for you, the teacher, to become comfortable with writing instruction in the classroom.

THEORY

Many educators have examined the components of the writing process and have generated models to describe it (Petrosky and Brozick, 1979; Hayes and Flower, 1980; Foley, 1981). In this traditional approach, Foley suggests that the teacher is constantly in control of the writing process. "The result is that the teacher evaluates his own work, in effect, because he is evaluating how closely the writer followed what he was asked to do on the corrections the teacher included" (1981, p. 74). Lapp and Flood (1985) found that the teacher's attitude about self as a writer is related to the teacher's view of the students as writers.

In recent years, writing instruction has received a great deal of attention from educators and researchers. Current theories of writing instruction tend to emphasize writing-as-process rather than writing-as-product. Within this framework, writers are not only concerned with correctness of form, but also with learning, generating, and discovering through writing (Flood and Salus, 1984). A successful writing program will probably take on a form similar to the following:

1. Develop the assignment.
    a. Establish the purpose of the writing
    b. Identify the intended audience
    c. Allow the students to develop their topics while the teacher guides and supports them. Children "write best about what they know." (Foley, 1981)
2. Discuss and plan for writing.
3. Prewrite.
4. Discuss.
5. Write.
6. Share.
7. Edit and rewrite.

Any given writing assignment may extend over several days. Additionally, many educators suggest that children should have a particular time each day set aside for writing. This writing can be in a journal or it can be any other form of writing the student chooses. Lapp and Flood (1985) found that after being given instruction in how to teach writing, teachers adjusted the allotted classroom time given for writing to include more time for the processes of writing than the mechanics of writing.

Although the content and form of writing may differ between the elementary school student and the intermediate-level student, the *process* remains the same. In the following sections, we will provide you with more specific suggestions and activities for your student writers at each grade level.

THE PRIMARY YEARS

Quite often during the early school years writing is the result of listening and speaking experiences. You will find that children love to listen to and create stories. When encouraged, young children will freely engage in

My Dog Had A Cold

Once upon a time there was a dog named (Muffen.) he was so cute. one day we went Outside . he began To sneeze then. I ran down to the (docter's.) he said that (Muffen) had the flu. (Muffen) was very scared so I said (Muffen) your/(you're) lucky. I broke my finger. you better hurry and get better so you can come To my Birthday Monday. all/(I'll) have the doctor give you a shot. arrrr said (Muffen.) you have to have a shot it's the only way To get better for my Birthday Monday. The next morning was

TEACHER COMMENT

This sentence is a little too long.

a (desaster.) I took (Muffen) to the (docter) and then the stuff began. (Muffen) bit the (docter's) leg bit my hand and he didn't get a shot he got a (Spanken) instead.

The
End

by
Shannon
(age: 8)

TEACHER COMMENT

Shannon,
    Don't forget to start a new sentence with a capital letter. Also, each sentence should end with a period. Please check the spelling of the words I have circled. I hope Muffin was able to come to your birthday party!

storytelling. You can capitalize on these situations by recording their stories and having the students listen to their own stories while creating illustrations for them. An activity such as this may serve as the basis for an entire writing curriculum.

It is important that the students' writing gives them some degree of satisfaction. This can be accomplished by displaying it in the classroom. In addition, Sealey, Sealey, and Millmore (1979) note that the writing examples you display should have a readily understood purpose.

The attitudes toward writing that children develop in the primary grades may last a lifetime. Be flexible with your assignments and remember that there are many ways to complete any task. Through early language discussions, you will be able to encourage students to believe that they have many things to write about. Correct style, form, and spelling may need to receive secondary attention during these writing attempts. Any device that encourages children to *talk*, and eventually to turn that talk to *writing*, can be viewed as a positive motivational device.

Shannon, a second-grade student, wrote the story about her dog after she had "talked" it through with her teacher. At this early age, narratives are frequently a reflection of the student's experiences rather than an exercise in creativity.

We recommend that you don't correct every error in these early writing attempts; this may discourage the child. Note that Shannon's spelling errors are all phonetic representations of the words she chose to use. After she checks the proper spelling of these words, she will realize that not all words are spelled phonetically. This can be a valuable part of the writing experience for a young child.

Your language and writing programs will be closely intertwined during the early primary grades. The following activities may be used or adapted to foster successful writing experiences in your classroom:

1. Provide various sensory experiences, such as
   a. Smelling (orange, perfume, onion)
   b. Touching (sandpaper, velvet, clay)
   c. Seeing (pictures, cartoons, books)
2. After the sensory exposure, encourage the students to share their reactions verbally.
3. Make recordings of their shared reactions.
4. Encourage the students to listen to the recordings and then illustrate their thoughts.
5. Help the students add descriptive words or phrases.
6. Encourage the students to edit their work. Editing may be an arduous task, but point out that it is a necessary task that is engaged in by all writers. Too often the editing process is not explained to students. The student thus incorrectly assumes that a successful writer/author produces a finished piece of prose after only one attempt. When the student/writer is not able to do the same, she views herself as being punished when she engages in the editing process. Because the student feels she has failed when she is asked to edit, many students view

themselves as poor writers and consequently never explore themselves as writers.

7. Finally, share the written product aloud with the other students. The students may share their work with their family by writing a note or a letter to accompany it.

Activities such as these integrate the language arts (listening, speaking, reading, and writing) through stories, poems, letters, and notes.

You will probably soon notice that the best student stories are often shared accounts of in-depth perceptions. It is very important to plan activities that will heighten the sensory awareness of your students. The following activities can serve to encourage students' awareness of their world while extending language development:

1. Ask the students to describe the face of someone they love.
2. Have the students close their eyes and listen to a variety of sounds. Then have them describe the sounds.
3. Let the students try to identify objects by touch. A variety of objects can be placed in paper bags.
4. Ask the students to describe pleasant or frightening odors.

THE INTERMEDIATE YEARS

As students move on to the intermediate grades, there are ever-increasing opportunities to engage them in the writing process. It is important to emphasize writing in your curriculum because writing activities (1) provide students with an opportunity for self-expression, (2) provide an additional channel for extending language development, and (3) arouse students' interest in literary materials.

Note the wry humor and imagination displayed in the following science fiction story written by Eric, a fifth-grade student.

Missy Martian's Mission

One day a very, very small spaceship came out of the sky. It looked like a beer can. It even opened like one. I know that because I saw it.

A little person came out and said, "La ba." I said, "Ha ha". She said, "Oh, that's the launguge" you speak." "Yes, it is," I said. "I have been taught to speak all langues on the planet Earth.

"What planet do you come from?" "Ram Bam," she said. "Will you say T.V. in your language," I said. "Boob tube, by the way, what is T.V.?" "It's a picture that flashes on a box." "Oh, then what does picture, flash, and box mean?" "Never mind."

"What is your name?" "Missy! What is yours?" "Charles." "My mission is to bring back a human being. Will you come?" "How long will it be?" "Only about a nagratriairn." "How long will that be in my time?" "Oh, only about ten minuts." "Ok, I'll go." Caboom and we were there. "What was that, double light speed?" We came down out of the sky and landed on a landing pad. I was taken for test.

"Hey, that's a needle!" "We are going to test your blood." "Ouch!" "Hey, your blood is red, ours is green! We're ready to take you back." Caboom and we were home. We said goodbye to each other and then of to Ram Bam she flew again.

by Eric (age: 11)

**T.C. Eric,
your story is very good and very creative. Each time a new character (person) speaks you should begin a new paragraph. Please check the spelling of the circled words before you turn in your final copy.

**T.C.
Eric,
your picture
add a lot
to your
story!

**T.C. = TEACHER COMMENTS

Eric's story exemplifies how children are influenced by their experiences. Eric very willingly shared his fascination with *E.T.*, *Star Wars*, *Raiders of the Lost Ark*, *Gremlins*, and other science/space adventures. Because his teacher encouraged conversation and writing, he gladly shared his ideas through a fictional piece.

Suggested Readings Related to Goals.   We encourage you at this time to review the goals at the beginning of this chapter. If you feel you would like to explore one or more of these areas in greater depth, please refer to the cross-indexed bibliography at the end of the book.

4 Aspects of Reading Readiness

I think the necessity of being ready increases.—Look to it.
[Abraham Lincoln]

Goals

To help the student understand
1. The history of readiness practices in the United States
2. The nature of reading readiness
3. The components of model prereading programs in preschool and kindergarten
4. Assessment instruments that measure aspects of readiness

When Is a Child Ready to Read?

Educators have asked (and answered) this question in a variety of ways through the years. It still remains a controversial subject. A brief historical overview of the issues will demonstrate how difficult the question is to answer.

Setting the Precise (Mental) Age: History

Until 1931, learning to read and beginning school were almost simultaneous events in the United States. For most children then, reading instruction began around the age of 6, and few educators questioned the acceptability of this practice. Huey (1908) specifically spoke against the

When is a child ready to read?
Educators have asked this ques-
tion in a variety of ways through
the years. (Photo by Linda Lun-
gren.)

practice and seemed to favor a more spontaneous approach: "[the child] is concerned about the printed notices, signs that come his way, and should be told what these things say when he makes inquiry" (p. 28).

After two researchers (Holmes, 1927; Reed, 1927) reported that many children failed first grade because they were not ready to read, the question of reading readiness began to be examined more carefully. Many researchers, including Holmes, concluded that children entering first grade were not ready to learn to read. Frequently, relevant variables such as teacher preparation, instructional methods, materials, and class size were not examined in these investigations; however, readiness programs began to emerge throughout the country.

Theories regarding readiness came from many quarters. Gesell (1940), a physician, believed that children were not ready to learn to read at 6 years of age and that instruction should be postponed until they were "readied." Since his position stemmed from his interest in neural maturation, he looked for an explanation of biologically determined developmental stages from the point of view of intrinsic growth, neural ripening, and unfolding behaviors. He was convinced that the ability to read occurred at one of these stages. The prevailing psychological trends of the time, which placed great importance on the "natural" development of the child, may in part account for why his views were so widely accepted.

Determining a Reading Readiness Age

Since public opinion favored exactness of measurement rather than vague notions of stages of development, educators and psychologists set out to determine the exact age at which reading instruction should begin. In the 1920s, group intelligence tests had become available to the educational community. The numerical equivalent of a child's mental age provided by these tests became the catalyst for pinpointing the moment at which a child would be capable of beginning reading instruction. The commonly accepted formula for determining mental age was

$$\text{Mental age} = \frac{\text{Intelligence quotient} \times \text{chronological age}}{100}$$

The results of many studies in the 1920s showed a high correlation between reading achievement and intelligence. Arthur (1925) concluded that a mental age of 6.0 to 6.5 was "necessary for standard first-grade achievement." The study that was the most famous and that had the most profound effect on beginning reading instruction was one conducted by Morphett and Washburne and reported in 1931. They stated unequivocally that 6.5 was the proper mental age to begin reading instruction, although their study was conducted on children using only *one* method of instruction in *one* school system (Winnetka, Illinois). The conclusion of this report read, "Mental age alone showed a larger degree of correlation with reading progress than did intelligence quotient or the average of mental and chronological age" (p. 502). This report became the foundation for reading readiness programs for the next 30 years.

Objections to 6.5 M.A. Advocates

It didn't take long for educators to begin to question the wisdom of the mental age concept of reading readiness. In one report, Gates (1937) stressed the importance of individual strengths and weaknesses on beginning reading instruction:

> This study emphasizes the importance of recognizing and adjusting to individual limitations and needs . . . rather than merely changing the time for beginning reading. It appears that readiness for reading is something to develop rather than merely to wait for . . . (p. 681)

In addition, he suggested that "the age for learning to read under one program with the method employed by one teacher may be entirely different from that required under other circumstances."

The concept of reading readiness gradually began to focus on aspects other than a precise mental age for beginning reading instruction. MacGinitie (1969) summarized Durkin's theory that readiness and beginning reading instruction should not be viewed as two separate entities in his concise statement, "When a child is taught a little, he is then ready for a little more." Along with Gates (1937), Durkin (1980) suggested that rather than inquire about the correct age for beginning instruction, the researcher should ask, "Is the child ready to succeed with this particular kind and quality of instruction?" Furthermore, Calfee and Hoover (1973) suggested that programs and teaching methods that are not individualized to meet the needs of beginning readers will not be effective.

Assessing Reading Readiness Potential

Many reading readiness tests were developed from the 1930s through the 1950s, and they attained some measure of popularity. However, criticisms of such tests ultimately led educators to search for other methods of predicting reading success. Such criticisms included the following:

1. They do not adequately assess potential reading ability.
2. The competencies measured by the tests are not directly related to reading.
3. Visual discrimination tasks are often too difficult.
4. Total reading readiness programs are built on the results of diagnostic tests, the components of which may not have measured later reading success.

Teachers and researchers began to look for alternatives, tests that could predict the potential of a child to be able to learn to read. An assessment of four prereading skills (alphabet recognition, vocabulary, whole-word recognition, and visual discrimination) can help you to identify students who will probably succeed in reading and those who may experience some difficulty.

ALPHABET RECOGNITION

A great number of studies (Monroe, 1935; Durrell, 1958; Weiner and Feldman, 1963; Silvaroli, 1965; Silberberg, 1968) suggest that children's ability to name the letters of the alphabet can be a potential predictor of later reading success. In fact, Bond and Dykstra (1967) and Jansky and DeHirsch (1972) indicated that letter naming was the single greatest predictor of later reading success.

Although there seems to be a strong link between letter naming and reading success, studies by both Olson (1958) and Muehl (1966) indicate that the relationship is not a *causal* one. That is, letter-name knowledge (or its lack) alone does not cause high or low reading achievement.

One researcher (Samuels, 1972) reported that two separate studies failed to support the assumption that letter-name knowledge facilitates reading. However, in a partial replication of Samuel's study, Chisholm and Knafle (1975) found opposite results; they discovered that letter-name knowledge was highly predictive of reading achievement.

As a whole, these studies suggest that the quickest way to predict reading success is alphabet recognition and that this knowledge is probably essential to learn to read English (Calfee, Chapman, and Venezky, 1972; Carswell, 1978). It bears repeating, however, that there is no cause-effect relationship between letter-name knowledge and reading success. Alphabet recognition can be used as an efficient, useful predictor of reading success, but not as a method of instruction.

VOCABULARY

Reading achievement and intelligence have been shown to be closely related. For example, Lohnes and Gray (1972) concluded, "The best single explanatory principle for observed variance in reading skills was variance in general intelligence" (p. 60). In turn, the most common component of IQ tests is the vocabulary subtest.

In an effort to assess the predictive efficiency of certain standardized readiness tests, Almenoff (1979) conducted a study of second-grade students on whom complete kindergarten testing data was available. One of the three best kindergarten predictors of second-grade reading achievement was found to be the Vocabulary subtest of the Vane Kindergarten Test. Almenoff also found that two of the three "most efficient predictors of second grade reading achievement" were the Vocabulary subtest of the Vane Kindergarten Test and the Word Meaning subtest of the Metropolitan Readiness Test. It must be noted, however, that complexity and range of vocabulary are closely related to experience; therefore, we may once again be measuring exposure rather than potential.

WHOLE-WORD RECOGNITION

Several researchers have shown that word recognition and reading are closely related. Gavel (1958) and DeHirsch, Jansky, and Langford (1966) found that recognition of words that a child has been taught was highly predictive of reading achievement at the first-grade level. Examples of these words include a child's full name (for example, Mary Agnes Cunningham), or a date (July 4, 1776), or words with special meaning for the child (Big Bird, candy, monster).

Richek (1977–78) tested kindergarten children on seven reading readiness tasks and two word-learning tasks. The word-learning tasks were similar to a sight-word and a sound-symbol method of initial reading instruction. Richek found that a large proportion of the students scored higher on the sight-word than on the sound-symbol word-learning task.

VISUAL DISCRIMINATION

Visual discrimination is often cited as a necessary reading readiness skill, but its predictive value is very controversial.

Both Goins (1958) and DeHirsch et al. (1966) found that matching two- and three-letter sequences is highly predictive of reading achievement. For example,

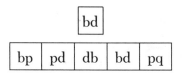

The directions for this task might be, "Color the box in the second line that contains the same letters as the box on the first line."

To test the ability of kindergarteners to process the features of patterns, Kak (1980) used computer-generated alphanumeric characters (A, N). Kak's data suggest that students with reading problems may process elements (e.g., line lengths, angles) less efficiently or less accurately.

Many researchers (Wilson and Fleming, 1960; Bryan, 1964; Barrett, 1965) have reported that visual discrimination ability in young children correlates highly with later reading achievement. However, Calfee, Chapman, and Venezsky (1972) were unable to demonstrate that visual discrimination was an adequate predictor of reading achievement.

In short, alphabet recognition, vocabulary knowledge, word recognition, and visual discrimination *may* be useful as predictors of later reading success. They may also help you to identify children who would be appropriate candidates for early reading programs.

Early Reading Readiness Programs

The question still remains: "When should a child be taught to read?" *When* cannot be pinpointed to an age or a time; it will vary with each child. But when a child exhibits an interest in printed material, that child is demonstrating an interest in learning to read.

Farr and Roser (1979) remind us that a child's literacy development begins very early. A child who grows up in a literate society is developing the basic structure of literacy long before the beginning of school instruction. As Goodall (1984) suggests, children today are constantly exposed to print in the form of books, magazines, television, advertisements, billboards, and household product labels. When a child asks, "What does that say?" he is asking for reading instruction. When he can say, "That says Wheaties," he is indeed reading.

To answer the important question, "When should a child be taught to read?" with the relatively simple answer, "When he or she indicates an interest in printed material," avoids the question to a degree. If we are talking about formal instruction and educational strategies, a more sophisticated answer seems necessary. We need to examine the meaning of "readiness."

Readiness

At one time, readiness test scores were used to determine when a student was ready for reading instruction. However, some educators focused too strongly on test scores and too little on the student as an individual with a unique history and individual needs.

A definition of readiness suggested by Ausubel (1959) is "the adequacy of existing capacity in relation to the demands of a given learning task." In other words, he suggested that the "when" of reading instruction depends on the student, the instruction, and the specific components of what is being taught. Students with the same chronological age may range from those who are "ready" to learn that their name begins with "J" to those who are able to "read" a short sentence. The students in the latter group have already learned to decode some words and have committed them to their sight vocabularies. As classroom teachers, you must be cautious not to infer or assume that these differences in "readiness" are caused by intelligence differences among the students. Rather, you should recognize that their readinesss preparation is merely at different stages of development.

There is no "proper" age at which to begin reading instruction; readiness varies from student to student. This is recognized in some other countries where reading instruction begins much earlier than in the United States. At about 5 years of age, students begin reading in the United Kingdom; students in Israel often begin instruction at 4 years of age.

A related area of interest is the phenomenon of early reading. Many researchers have investigated the effects of early reading programs; we will examine some of these data in an effort to determine whether early reading is a help or a hindrance.

Early Reading

Durkin (1966) conducted a study on early reading for six years in New York City and Oakland, California. Some of the children read before first grade and before receiving any formal reading instruction. Durkin concluded that early reading was not necessarily a function of socioeconomic status, ethnicity, or intelligence. She further reported that the early readers achieved higher reading scores during their entire elementary school careers.

Durkin later conducted a similar study in Illinois with 4-year-old children, but she did not reach the same conclusions. In this study, early readers who had been trained in a special two-year preschool language arts/reading program scored significantly higher than did their nonearly reading classmates on standardized reading tests in grades 1 and 2, but the differences between the two groups were not statistically significant in grades 3 and 4.

As a possible explanation, Durkin suggested that one very likely explanation for the reversal is that the characteristics of a family that fostered preschool reading ability would continue to foster achievement, with or without an instructional program in school. Another possible explanation may lie in the analysis of test data. Durkin's original data analysis did not take into account the phenomenon of increased variance in the scores of the upper-grade students; a reanalysis of the data might indeed show that the early readers did outperform nonearly readers even in the later grades.

While such studies may provide insight into the *effects* of early reading, many questions remain unanswered as to its causes. For example, "What type of environment (if any) is conducive to early reading?" "Which home factors contribute to the success of early reading?" "How much influence does a parent have on early reading?" In an attempt to address similar issues, Vukelich (1984), who has emphasized the significant role of the parent in the early reading process, suggests many family activities that may enhance this process.

Finally, we must add a cautionary note about early reading. Despite stories and anecdotes to the contrary, young children do not learn to read by themselves (Durkin, 1966, 1983; Flood and Lapp, 1981). However, interviews with parents of early readers have uncovered these common characteristics:

1. Parents of early readers conversed a great deal with their children.
2. Early readers tend to ask many questions.
3. Parents of early readers took the time to answer questions.
4. A very common question is, "What's that word?"

You will occasionally hear criticisms of early reading attempts, but we believe that the major objections can be easily countered. Following is a brief discussion of common objections.

Objections	*Comments*
1. Early reading will hurt the child's vision.	There is little evidence to support this position. On the contrary, children's own activities seem to indicate that a child's vision is ready for reading by 4 or 5 years of age. Many children are writing by this age, an activity that requires similar visual acuity.
2. Parents are not qualified to teach reading.	Parents may not have taken formal reading and/or education courses, but there are many activities that they can do with their children to foster and encourage an interest in printed materials.
3. Early readers will be bored in school.	Children will only be bored with reading if they have to start over again. If classroom programs are tailored to the individual needs of each child and personalized to ad-

4. Childhood is a time for play, not academics.

dress the strengths and weaknesses of each child, there will be no room for boredom.

Reading can be a playful and enjoyable activity for children. If children could spend as much time on reading activities as they seem to want, the concern about introducing too much academics seems unwarranted.

Early Intervention

Some educators feel that prereading or early reading programs are unnecessary or even counterproductive, despite a lack of evidence to support this position. On the other hand, many researchers argue that there is a great need for early programs. They believe that high-risk, potentially handicapped children need to be identified when they are very young; then remediation can begin before the problems are overwhelming. As in medicine, we have now entered the age of prevention in education. We must examine preventive measures to avoid later serious education problems.

The case for early intervention often stems from the position that the causes of reading failure can be found in a child's earliest stages of development (Hallgren, 1950; DeHirsch, Jansky, and Langford, 1966; Ingram, 1970; Owens, Adams, and Forrest, 1968; Silver, 1971; Satz and van Nostrand, 1973; Goetz, 1979; Flood and Lapp, 1981; Zirkelbach, 1984).

Early intervention advocates argue that very young children are frequently more receptive to remediation than older children. For example, Caldwell (1968) stated, "There is some evidence to suggest that the child may be more sensitive to environmental stimulation (for example, remedial intervention) during that period in which maturation of the brain is evolving and when behavior is less differentiated" (p. 220). Research also indicates that basic language ability in children develops between birth and the age of 5 or 6 (Menyuk, 1963). This evidence, too, suggests that the amelioration of reading difficulties in elementary school children might best be accomplished through intervention during the preschool years.

In the next section we will discuss one linguistic theory that some use to oppose early intervention—the critical period for the acquisition of reading theory.

Critical Period for Language Acquisition

Basically, this theory suggests that there is a developmental, biologically determined *critical period* for the acquisition of reading. Proponents of this theory suggest that to tamper with this biological clock is unnatural and will have an adverse effect on the child. While there is some evidence to support the notion of a critical period in language acquisition, some educators have extended it to the reading process as well.

The critical period can be defined as a nonchronological period or stage in which the human organism is especially sensitive to the specifics of language development (phonology, syntax, morphology, semantics). It is possible that there are certain periods that foster the development of each of these components. These periods of heightened sensitivity might parallel psychophysiological theories (Menyuk, 1971, 1984) of the rate of growth in the human brain, which closely parallel Piaget's (1963) stages of cognitive development. The perception of a critical period as a sensitive stage, however, merely means that there are periods of sensitivity to language development, *not* that there are terminal points after which language development will not occur.

Most educators reject the theory of a critical period for the spontaneous acquisition of reading, largely because it is not generally agreed that there is a critical period for the acquisition of language. However, related research on cognitive development suggests that there may be a critical period in which to *begin* reading instruction. This theory suggests that initial reading instruction should take place between 4 and 6 years of age, a time when the student is rather sophisticated, having acquired most of the rules of English syntax.

Traditionally, reading has been taught when a student is 6 to 8 years old. Piaget described this as a time when the student is involved in "concrete operations." For the student who is experiencing difficulty in learning to read, it may be that the repetitive drills involved in beginning reading are interruptive. Another partial explanation of the problem may be a mismatch between the student's cognitive development and beginning reading instruction.

There is also a major change in skill performance between the ages of 5 and 7. This change may be due to

1. General level of intellectual functioning and/or language
2. Improved organizational abilities
3. Changes in attention, that is, duration and fixation

The best answer to the question of when to begin reading instruction seems to come from Gates (1937), Calfee and Hoover (1973), Flood and Lapp (1981), and Zirkelbach (1984), who have suggested that instruction should match the needs of the child.

Model Programs

The best way to evaluate a prereading or early reading program is to determine the extent to which it meets the needs of each individual. As Brubaker and Keiser (1982) suggest, a model program guides children yet allows them to progress at their own rate. It also provides a rich language environment. Haley-James (1982) also encourages early writing efforts "which can also benefit . . . learning to read" (p. 462). Finally, while there is probably no causal relationship between environmental factors and success in reading, Teale (1978) suggests that the following factors be considered:

1. A range of printed material should be available in the environment.
2. Children should read in the environment to promote the idea that print is meaningful.
3. The environment should facilitate contact with paper and pencil.
4. Those in the environment should respond to what the child is trying to do.

Some linguists (e.g., Menyuk, 1984) and some cognitively oriented psychologists (e.g., Piaget, 1963) maintain that children acquire language by generating rules, testing them, and reinforcing them. From this perspective, teachers must make reading an accessible adventure for their students. A rich variety of materials must be made available to students for them to be able to extract letter-sound relationships. Students must see books and other printed materials; they must hear the words read over and over. Only in this way will they be able to generate and test hypotheses about letter-sound correspondences.

Objectives and Strategies for Early Reading Programs

Successful early reading programs do not just happen—they must be carefully planned and organized. As with any goal, it is necessary to identify your objectives and to plan your classroom strategies to meet these objectives. The following chart lists 14 objectives we consider essential in a good prereading program along with strategies that can be implemented to meet these objectives.

General Objectives	*Strategies*
1. Improvement of general language ability: phonology, morphology, syntax, semantics, and pragmatics. For bilingual and non-English–speaking students, there should be support for language development in the students' native language to provide opportunities for the acquisition of English as a second language.	Language experience approaches. Students who show interest in beginning reading instruction will be afforded the opportunity to begin a personalized language experience reading program. These students can make word cards and will be taught to "read" single words.
2. Enjoyment of books and an understanding of books as re-	Reading to students individually and in small groups, in other lan-

sources. Books represent a wide variety of cultural and linguistic backgrounds. Students whose first language is not English should have the opportunity to be read stories in their own languages.

guages (where appropriate) and in English. Asking questions relating to the story and encouraging students to retell it in their own words. Consider having picture books readily available to students in a reading corner, showing films of familiar stories, and taking trips to libraries and museums and other neighborhood places of interest.

3. Comprehension of material related orally such as in understanding simple directions or a story that has been read.

Listening experiences via records and tapes of stories, songs, and nursery rhymes. Provide listening experiences that result in following simple directions, for example, musical listening, singing and movement experiences.

4. Appreciation of the relationship between oral and written language.

Language experience approaches. Students who show interest in beginning reading instruction will be afforded the opportunity to begin a personalized language experience reading program. These students can make word cards and can be taught to "read" single words.

5. Confidence in their ability to create written materials, for example, stories dictated to a teacher.

Taking down students' dictated stories and helping students to make their own books. Opportunities for dramatic play.

6. Recognition of the alphabet.

Games and other manipulative materials (felt letters and felt board; magnetic letters and magnetic board; alphabet Bingo) that develop alphabet recognition and letter-sound association.

7. Sight vocabulary that is familiar and important to the student, such as the student's name and the names of frequently used classroom materials (for example, door, window).

Use of labels in the classroom to indicate names of things and places for their storage; use of students' names on lockers, or tote boxes, and art work.

8. Letter-sound associations, particularly initial phonemes, consonants, and recognition of familiar sounds.

Phonics training for those students who show interest and who, it appears, will profit from such a program.

9. Recognition of rhyming words.

Phonics training for some students who show interest and who, it ap-

10. Introduction to and/or development of effective viewing of educational television.

pears, can profit from such a program.
Use of educational television in selected classrooms.

11. Ability to communicate about concrete objects.

Use of referential communication games.

12. Recognition of sequence.

Use of recipe charts for cooking activities. Use of sequencing materials, for example, puzzles, stories (some without endings), and picture cards.

13. Simple categorization.

Work with students on visual discrimination skills (for example, matching letters, shapes, and designs).

14. Acquisition of directionality.

Exercises and games on directionality (left-right, up-down, etc.).

Sample Lesson Plan

The following lesson plan is presented as an example of how you might use the suggested strategies to implement one of your objectives. This lesson could be used to teach sequencing (objective 12).

Use of children's names on lockers is a good strategy for teaching a sight vocabulary. (Photo by Linda Lungren.)

Objective/Goal

Recognition of sequence.

Behavioral Objective

Given three different pictorial sequences, the student will be able to choose the one that accurately represents the events from the story.

Materials

Book or story, cardboard, pictures, or illustrations.

Strategy and Implementation

1. The teacher reads a story to the students.
   (Alternative: The student can listen to a story the teacher has recorded and "follow along" in the book.)
2. The students and teacher discuss the events in the story.
3. Using pictures, illustrations, or even appropriate cartoons, the teacher arranges the characters or pictorial events in three different sequential arrangements.
4. The student is asked to select the pictorial arrangement that correctly depicts the story.

You can see that the instructional techniques and activities listed in the previous section fall into four major categories: letter recognition, whole-word techniques, phonics techniques, and language experiences. In the next section we will examine each of these areas separately.

Letter Recognition.   As soon as a student has exhibited an interest in print, you should capitalize on this interest by beginning letter-recognition activities. Most 3-year-olds, having been exposed to shows such as "Sesame Street," are capable of recognizing the letters of the alphabet. The needs of the student must determine the type of letter-recognition that is employed, and these activities fall into three categories:

1. Matching the same letter shapes from two groups of letters
2. Using an auditory modality
3. Teaching students the letters of their names

Reinforcement activities might include (1) tracing letters from stencils, (2) drawing letters in sand or clay, or (3) writing letters on the chalkboard with water and watching them "mysteriously" disappear.

Whole-Word Techniques.   Often, the first word a student will memorize is his or her own name. You can encourage this whole-word recognition by allowing students to put name labels on such items as desks, lockers, lunch boxes, or cubicles.

You can foster whole-word recognition by planning lessons that emphasize common everyday words such as days of the week, weather words, or dates. For example, you may have a chart where the student is asked to choose the correct day and put the name in a slot:

Today is	Thursday	Sunday

Monday
Tuesday
Wednesday

Friday
Saturday

or you may have a sign describing the daily weather with a spinwheel:

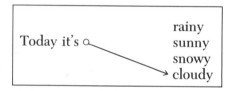

Each student may take a turn pointing the arrow to the word describing the weather that day.

A birthday bulletin board such as this one is always a good way to help students with sight words:

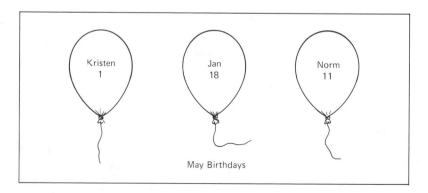

Labeling objects and assigning student tasks in the classroom will help children with whole-word recognition and categorization. (Photo by Linda Lungren.)

Another excellent idea is to label objects or areas in the classroom. Not only will this help students with whole-word recognition, it can also acquaint them with categorization, a useful technique for beginning readers. You may label parts of the classroom: Reading Area, Play Corner, Coats and Hats, Library, Tapes and Records, and so on. Shelves or materials may also be labeled: Puzzles, Games, Toys, Books, Paints, Crayons, Newspapers, Paste, and so on. In addition, signs can be useful for teaching sight words:

It's lunch time.	It's snack time.	It's milk time.
Doctor is in.	Mailbox	Toy Department

Phonics Techniques. Most young children love to rhyme, and this is an excellent way to introduce students to working with sounds. Ask your students to rhyme as many words as they can with these words: hill, way, cot. Children also enjoy playing "Name of the Day." Pick a child's name and say, "The name for today is John—Who has a name that begins with the same sound as John?" You can also use such activities to help you determine which children seem ready for more phonics activities.

Language Experience Techniques. As Mallon and Berglund (1984) suggest through their posing and answering of recurring questions, the language experience approach is a very popular and successful method of reading instruction because it uses the actual language of the child as its foundation. The key to this activity is participation. You might begin by asking, "Beth, what is your favorite color?" On a large piece of construction paper (or on the chalkboard) write

Beth's favorite color is yellow.

Next you should elicit related statements from the other students by asking, "Chris, can you think of something yellow?"

A lemon is yellow.
Bette's house is yellow.
Ray is wearing a yellow shirt.
Peter has a yellow banana.

You can then end with something like

Many things are yellow.

You can encourage the children to draw pictures to illustrate these charts or to use pictures clipped from magazines. Sometimes the illustrations alone create great interest for the children.

Language experience charts like the next one can be constructed for special occasions:

We are going to have a Halloween party.
We will wear costumes.
Robin is going to be a clown.
Margaret is going to be a farmer.
Michael is going to be an owl.
Sharon is going to be a swan.
Jimmy is going to be a ghost.
Anthony is going to be a monster.
Frank is going to be a pirate.
Lena is going to to be a rabbit.
Tony is going to be a cowboy.
We will have candy and cookies.

Initially, you may have to read the entire chart to the students. Later, each student can read his or her own entry. Eventually, they will be able to read the entire story themselves.

Assessing Reading Readiness: Observations and Checklists

As a teacher, you will want not only to assess students' readiness skills, you will also want to measure student growth. There are two common methods of achieving these goals: (1) observation of children using a checklist of characteristics known to be important to success in reading and (2) reading readiness tests. The best measure of a student's readiness involves a combination of both.

In the next section, we will provide samples and examples of assessment instruments in order to acquaint you with these tools.

Your most valuable tool in fostering reading success may be your own observations. After making observations, record some brief notes about each child's progress. Portions of three checklists that you may decide to use are included here: (1) Russell's Checklist, (2) the Prereading Rating Scale, (3) an informal teacher checklist. You may also want to examine the Santa Clara County Inventory of Developmental Tasks, an observation instrument.

RUSSELL'S CHECKLIST

Russell's Checklist (1957) can help teachers to organize the knowledge they have acquired about a student or group of students. The checklist contains fifty items covering four readiness aspects: physical, social, emotional, and psychological. In the display following, we have included the first measure from each of these sections.

CHECKLIST FOR READING READINESS*

Physical Readiness

		Yes	No
1. Eyes			
a. Does the child seem comfortable in the use of his eyes (does not squint, rub eyes, hold materials too close or too far from eyes)?	1.	☐	☐
b. Are the results of clinical tests or an oculist's examination favorable?	2.	☐	☐

Social Readiness

1. Cooperation			
a. Does he work well with a group, taking his share of the responsibility?	12.	☐	☐
b. Does he cooperate in playing games with other children?	13.	☐	☐
c. Can he direct his attention to a specific learning situation?	14.	☐	☐
d. Does he listen rather than interrupt?	15.	☐	☐

Emotional Readiness

1. Adjustment to task
   a. Does the child seek a task, such as drawing, preparing?   24. ☐ ☐
   b. Does he accept changes in school routine calmly?   25. ☐ ☐
   c. Does he appear to be happy and well adjusted in schoolwork, as evidenced by relaxed attitude, pride in work, and eagerness for a new task?   26. ☐ ☐
   d. Does he follow adult leadership without showing resentment?   27. ☐ ☐

Psychological Readiness

1. Mind set for reading
   a. Does the child appear interested in books and reading?   30. ☐ ☐
   b. Does he ask the meanings of words or signs?   31. ☐ ☐
   c. Is he interested in the shapes of unusual words?   32. ☐ ☐

*Abridged and adapted from *Manual for Teaching the Reading Readiness Program of The Ginn Basic Readers*, Revised Edition by David H. Russell et al., © Copyright, 1957, 1953, 1958, by Ginn and Company (Xerox Corporation). Used with permission.

Not all of the items in Russell's Checklist will pertain to any one child. However, you will help students to make a good start by watching the behavior of the students related to the overlapping categories of their physical, social, emotional, and psychological readiness.

PREREADING RATING SCALE

The Prereading Rating Scale is also a checklist used by the teacher to assess abilities in the following areas:

1. Facility in oral language
2. Concept and vocabulary development
3. Listening abilities
4. Skills in critical and creative thinking
5. Social skills
6. Emotional development
7. Attitude toward and interest in reading
8. Work habits

The test manual describes the use and interpretation of this twenty-eight–question scale in detail.

INFORMAL TEACHER CHECKLIST

You can make your own informal checklist:

INFORMAL TEACHER CHECKLIST

Student's name ————————————
Date: ————————————

Skill	Definitely Yes	To a Degree	No	Comment
a. Can recognize letters				
b. Can rhyme				
c. Has memorized alphabet				
d. Can describe actions and pictures				
e. Can sound out words				
f. Can tell story about picture				
g. Can hold a pencil				
h. Can match objects that are the same or different				
i. Knows that written words mean spoken words				
j. Can put pictures in order				
k. Can write letters of alphabet				
l. Knows numbers				
m. Can write numbers				
n. Can name the colors				
o. Knows words about time (before, after, until)				
p. Can "read" simple stories				
q. Knows abstract words (happy, brave)				
r. Knows words about space (front, back, above)				
s. Knows common nouns (dog, lake)				

Teachers should be certain that a student is not experiencing visual or auditory difficulties before assessing specific cognitive competencies. You can initially assess auditory and visual acuity through observation.

Vision. Reading is primarily a visual act; therefore, vision is obviously an essential component of reading. Seeing is central to reading because the printed stimulus enters the mind through the eye. Spache and Spache (1977) described the visual aspect of the reading process in this way:

> His eyes hop or glide from one stop to the next, from left to right. He does not read in a smooth sweep along the line but only when the eyes are at rest in each fixation. During the sweeps or swings from one fixation to the next, the reader sees nothing clearly, for his eyes are temporarily out of focus. Each fixation, during which reading actually occurs, lasts from about a third of a second in young children to about a quarter of a second at the college level. In all probability most of the thinking that occurs during reading is done during this fractional part of a second, for a number of studies show that the duration of the fixation often lengthens if the reading material is very difficult. The fixations are the heart of the visual reading act, for they occupy about 90 per cent of the time for reading, while interfixation and return sweeps account for the rest.
>
> If the reader fails to recognize what he sees in a fixation, or to understand the idea offered, he tends to make regression. That is, he makes another fixation at approximately the same place or he swings backward to the left to read again. He may regress several times until the word is recognized or the idea comprehended before resuming the normal left-to-right series of fixations. Then near the end of each line he makes one big return sweep to a fixation close to the beginning of the next line. (p. 9)

As a classroom teacher, you are in an excellent position to detect students' vision problems. Any of the following behaviors may be a clue that the reader is experiencing visual difficulty: tilting of the head, facial contortions, thrusting the head forward, books held too closely to the face, body tension while observing distant objects, tension during visual work, excessive hand movements, avoidance of close visual work, poor sitting positions, frequent rubbing of eyes, or loss of place while reading.

Hearing.   Auditory acuity may also be viewed as a reading readiness base. Both language development and reading may be adversely affected by even the smallest hearing impairment. To what degree the lack of auditory ability may impede the reading process is unknown. We do know, however, the child's ability to hear small sound units and add meaning to the units is a word analysis skill that is essential to reading. Readiness programs should provide tasks that help students perceive partial- as well as whole-word utterances.

In an effort to identify students who may be experiencing hearing difficulties, be alert to common symptoms such as an inability to discriminate like or unlike sounds, slurred or inaudible language, cupping one's ear when listening, turning one's ear toward the speaker, requesting that sentences be repeated, interchanging words with similar sounds, frequent colds, earaches, and unnatural tonal quality of voice.

SANTA CLARA UNIFIED SCHOOL DISTRICT INVENTORY OF DEVELOPMENTAL TASKS

This checklist was developed by the Santa Clara Unified School District in Santa Clara, California, to assess vision and hearing and lan-

SAMPLE SHEETS FROM GUIDE*

Visual Memory   *Level II*   *Task 5.8*

5.8   Reproduce a sequence of two pictures from memory.
      Material: Five picture cards, three flashcards
      Procedure: Show student a flashcard for 5 seconds. Say: "First
                   this, then this." Remove card from view. Say: "Make
                   one just like mine." Student reproduces the se-
                   quence seen on the flashcard by arranging two pic-
                   tures in the proper order.

Scoring Procedure
      Scoring:

0	1	2
Student has two or more errors.	Student has one error.	Student has all correct.

Visual Memory   *Level II*   *Task 5.9*

5.9   Reproduce designs from memory
      Material: Three picture flashcards
      Procedure: Say: "I'm going to show you a card with a drawing
                   on it. After I turn the card over, you draw one just
                   like the one on the card." Show student the card for
                   5 seconds.

      Scoring:

0	1	2
Student cannot re-produce two or more designs	Student fails to reproduce one design.	Student can re-produce the three forms accurately.

Visual Memory   *Level III*   *Task 5.10*

5.10 Reproduce a sequence of three pictures from memory.
      Material: Five picture cards and three picture flashcards.
      Procedure: Show student a flashcard for 5 seconds. Say: "First
                   this, then this, then this." (point left to right.) Re-
                   move card from view. Say: "Make one just like mine."
                   Student reproduces the sequence seen on the flash-
                   card by arranging three pictures in the proper order.

      Scoring:

0	1	2
Student has two or more errors.	Student has one error.	Student has them all correct.

*Santa Clara Unified School District, Santa Clara, California.

guage/thought development. It can also be used to assess certain aspects of readiness.

This instrument is extremely comprehensive and should be examined in terms of the authors' approach and objectives. It has been described in terms of sequential and hierarchical skills; a taxonomic approach was used in its creation. In addition, each of the skills is ordered by ascending difficulty.

The sample items illustrate the comprehensiveness of this inventory, along with scoring procedures.

STANDARDIZED TESTS

Along with personal observation and informal checklists, you may also want to use standardized reading readiness tests for assessment purposes.

Some of the common readiness tests include Clymer-Barrett Prereading Battery, Gates-MacGinitie Readiness Skills Test, Harrison-Stroud Reading Readiness Profiles, Macmillan Reading Readiness Test, and the Metropolitan Readiness Test. Most of these include subtests that check vocabulary, knowledge of the letters of the alphabet, visual and auditory discrimination, and hand-eye coordination. Evaluation of a student's performance on these tests can also give the teacher insight into the student's attention span and ability to listen to and follow directions.

First-grade intelligence tests may be used in some school districts. These are similar in some ways to readiness tests, although readiness tests are believed to provide a better prediction of beginning reading success.

Some or all of the following tasks are included in most formal reading readiness tests: sentence comprehension, associating words and pictures, copying, counting and writing numbers, visual discrimination, auditory discrimination, word recognition, and drawing a human figure.

In special cases, you may desire a comprehensive evaluation of a student's language development. The Illinois Test of Psycholinguistic Ability (ITPA) will meet this need; however, you should be aware of these factors:

1. The ITPA is administered individually.
2. It has many subtests and requires a considerable amount of time to administer in total.
3. Considerable practice is required for effective administration and scoring.

For these reasons, it is usually administered by a speech and language specialist.

Future Trends

In this chapter we have presented a blend of historical insights, research and theory, and practical curricular considerations. Many issues remain unresolved regarding reading readiness and early reading. However, we believe that if you focus on the strengths and needs of the student as an individual, you can sow the seed early that reading is a fun, challenging, and valuable experience. In fact, Gentile and Hart (1983) believe that there is a "critical relationship among play, learning to read, and early reading achievement" (p. 436). Help your students to play, and help them to learn to read.

Suggested Readings Related to Goals.   We encourage you at this time to review the goals at the beginning of this chapter. If you feel you would like to explore one or more of these areas in greater depth, please refer to the cross-indexed bibliography at the end of the book.

3 *The Reading Process*

5 Decoding: Word Analysis Through Phonics

In a perfect language, every simple sound would be expressed by a distinct character; and no character would have more than one sound. But languages are not this perfect; and the English Language, in particular, is, in these respects, extremely irregular.

[Noah Webster]

Goals

To help the student understand
1. The relationship between the visual mode and reading
2. The relationship between the auditory mode and reading
3. The components of phonics
4. How to establish a phonics instruction program

An important part of teaching students to read is helping them to decode the written symbols of a language they already know and understand. Shimron and Navon (1982) cite the idea that "a straight-forward view of the reading process is that reading is a matter of translation from the visual signs of the text to the auditory signs that compose words the reader has already learned" (p. 212). However, when faced with their own language in this written "code," many children fail to understand that they *already know* what is on the page.

Some educators believe that children have several vocabularies: speaking, listening, writing, and reading vocabularies. A child first acquires a listening vocabulary, followed closely by the development of a speaking vocabulary. Most people auditorially comprehend a far greater range of

A child first acquires a listening vocabulary, followed closely by the development of a speaking vocabulary. (Photo by Linda Lungren.)

language patterns than they use in their spoken text. Listening vocabularies also exceed early reading and writing vocabularies. It must also be noted that a knowledge of the language of any one of these vocabularies does not necessarily ensure transfer to knowledge of any other vocabulary.

By the age of 4 most children have acquired a basic understanding of the syntax of their language. By the time they begin formal reading instruction, students can discriminate between most of the sounds of the English language, and they have acquired substantial listening and speaking vocabularies. You can help children make the transition from listening and speaking vocabularies to a reading vocabulary by capitalizing on these natural abilities.

In this chapter we will discuss and explain the phenomenon of decoding and its application to beginning reading instruction.

The Visual Mode: Perception

Visual perception can be defined as the ability to "take in" objects in the environment. Most physiologically normal children are adept at visual perception by the age of 4; not only can they perceive objects, but they can also discriminate among fine details.

Letter Discrimination

Look at the following pairs of letters:

bd   qg   mn   oc
EF   JT   RP   QO

Even competent readers will admit that the differences between the letters in these pairs are very subtle, so it is easy to understand why students cannot always see these differences. Difficulty with visual discrimination of letters becomes even more obvious by reading the following sentences quickly:

> The old man made a mold out of gold.
> The bold boy ran home and said he wanted
> to buy a gold mold. "Gold is cold," his
> mother told him, "and gold is not sold
> in a mold." The bold boy told the old
> man he could not buy his gold mold.

Gibson and Levin (1975) suggest that children use *distinctive features* to discriminate among abstract visual symbols. Students attend to four distinctive features:

1. *Straight-line segments.* In the Roman alphabet, there are several letters that are made up of this type of visual symbol:
   E   F   H   I   L   T
2. *Curved segments.* In the Roman alphabet, the following letters are examples of curved segmental visual symbols:
   C   O
3. *Symmetries.* The following alphabetic letters are examples of symmetries:
   M   W   X
4. *Discontinuities.* Several alphabetic letters are examples of discontinuities:
   K   B   G   J

Students use these distinctive features to try to identify letters. For example, one student might look at the letter J and see straight-line segments and curved segments. A second student may see only the top part of the letter J, which looks like T; he may fail to perceive the curved line segments and to attend to both stimuli. To avoid such difficulties, teachers can help students to learn letter discrimination by using a developmental strategy similar to the following:

Step 1: Ask students to look at single letters.
   1.   a   d
   2.   d   b

3. b b
4. b a

Step 2: Ask children if each pair of letters is the same or different.
Step 3: Ask children to look at sets of letters and decide if the sets are the same or different.

ad ba db ad

Step 4: Ask the children to examine sets of words and determine if they are the same or different.

| bat | pat | | fall | ball | | cow | cow |

At this point, explain to the students that any word can be written at least five different ways:

BED Bed bed *Bed* *bed*

Some of your students may be ready to progress to this step.

Step 5: Ask children to examine the following pairs of words and to determine if they are the same or different:

BED *Bed* bed bed *bed* bed

Letter-Name Knowledge

In Chapter 4, we discussed the importance of letter-name knowledge to reading readiness; in addition, Durkin (1974) argues convincingly that knowledge of letter names is helpful in initial reading instruction. Murphy and Durrell (1972) use a letter-naming system similar to the following for initial phonics instruction:

G: | *Initial* | *Medial* | *Final* |
|-------|---------|-------|
| get | agree | frog |
| green | begin | bag |
| goat | against | fog |

Since the advent of "Sesame Street," most students arrive in school knowing the names of the letters of the alphabet. Letter names are relatively easy to learn, and the experience may, through general transference, facilitate the more difficult task of letter-sound associations.

The Auditory Mode: Perception

Children are capable of perceiving almost all of the sounds in their environment by the age of 4, although they may not be able to produce all the sounds of English until they are 8 or 9 years of age. An inability to produce all sounds does not, however, necessarily interfere with the ability to begin reading.

Auditory Discrimination

Young native English-speaking children cannot only perceive sounds, they can also discriminate between English sounds (e.g., sit, hit; man, pan). They can also match sounds; for example, *dog* begins with a /d/ sound. Which of the following words begins with the same sound?

---

may   say   day   ray   way

Your goal as a teacher is to help each student "break the code" by helping the student see the relationship between letters and sounds. Your students have language—syntax, vocabulary, and phonology—and they can visually discriminate between many different symbols. Most students know the names of the letters of the alphabet and can discriminate between them. What your students need now is the knowledge of the code, the link between sounds and letters.

Letter-Sound Correspondence (Grapheme-Phoneme Correspondence)

The following chart shows consonant and vowel correspondences in various positions within words. The list represents most of the sounds of the English language and can be very useful in teaching students how to analyze words.

The phonemes in this list, written between slash marks (e.g., /t/) are symbols for the English sounds. Each single symbol stands for only one sound.

Any student who can read all of the correspondences in meaningful contexts in Table 5-1 and Table 5-2 can probably be considered a competent decoder.

Discriminating Among Words

If you were beginning to read in Chinese, you would probably see sentences like these:

日日有明月

秋季末森林内村人採木材

TABLE 5-1

Consonant Correspondence in Various Positions—Letter-Sound (Grapheme-Phoneme) Relationships

Phoneme	Grapheme	Phoneme in Initial Position	Phoneme in Medial Position	Phoneme in Final Position
/b/	b	bake	cabin	tub
/k/	c	cat	become	zinc
	k	kite	making	work
	ck		tracking	back
	x		complexion	
	ch	charisma	anchor	monarch
	qu	queen	racquet	bisque
	cc		account	
/s/	s	suit	insert	porous
	ss		massive	miss
	c	cite	pencil	face
	st		gristle	
	ps	pseudonym		
	sc	scissors	Pisces	
/č/	ch	cherry	lecher	such
	t		picture	
/d/	d	dish	body	hard
	dd		middle	odd
/f/	f	fish	safer	roof
	ff		raffle	muff
	ph	phonograph	telephone	graph
	gh		roughness	tough
/g/	g	good	rigor	bag
	gh	ghetto ghost		ugh
	gg		trigger	egg
	gu	guest	beguile	rogue
/ǰ/	g	gin	wager	
	du		schedule	
	j	jug	prejudice	raj
	dg		dredger	hedge
	dj	djinn	adjoin	

TABLE 5-1 *(continued)*

Phoneme	Grapheme	Phoneme in Initial Position	Phoneme in Medial Position	Phoneme in Final Position
/h/	h	horse	behead	
	wh	who		
/l/	l	long	bailer	boil
	ll		falling	doll
/m/	m	moon	hamper	dream
	mb		tombstone	dumb
	mm		drummer	
/n/	n	nest	diner	pin
	nn		thinner	
	gn	gnat	signing	assign
	kn	knight		
	pn	pneumonia		
	mn	mnemonic		
/ŋ/	ng		stinger	song
	n		think	
/p/	p	point	viper	hip
	pp		hopping	
/r/	r	rat	boring	tear
	rr		merry	purr
	wr	write		
	rh	rhyme	hemorrhage	myrrh
/š/	sh	shadow	crashing	dish
	s	sure	nauseous	
	ci		precious	
	ce		ocean	
	ss		obsession	
	ch	chic	machine	
	ti		motion	
/t/	t	test	water	cat
	tt		letter	putt
	pt	ptomaine		receipt
	bt		debtor	debt
/θ/	th	thin	ether	wreath
/ð/	th	then	either	bathe
/v/	v	violet	hover	dove
/w/	w	will	throwing	how
	ui		sanguine	
/ks/	x		toxic	box
	cc		accent	
/y/	y	yarn	lawyer	day
/z/	z	zipper	razor	blaze
	s		visit	logs
	zz		drizzle	fizz
	x	xanadu xylophone		

TABLE 5-1 (*continued*)

Phoneme	Grapheme	Phoneme in Initial Position	Phoneme in Medial Position	Phoneme in Final Position
/ž/	z	Xanadu	azure	
	su		treasure	
	si		allusion	
	g	genre	regime	decoupage
gz	x		exhibit	
	gs			digs

TABLE 5-2
Vowel Correspondences

Sound Label	Vowel	Letter Label	Example
Unglided or short	/æ/	a	an
		au	laugh
Glided or long	/ey/	a.e*	pane, bake
		ai	rain
		ea	steak
		ei	feign
		ay	tray
		ey	obey
		ua	guard
Unglided or short	/e/	e	pen
		ea	lead
		eo	jeopardy
		ei	heifer
		ai	stair
		ie	friendly
Glided or long	/iy/	e.e*	mete
		e	he
		ea	heat
		ee	tree
		ei	conceive
		ie	believe
Unglided or short	/i/	i	hit
		ui	guild
		y	gym
		u	business
Glided or long	/ay/	i.e	write
		uy	buyers
		ie	tries
		ai	aisle
		ia	trial
		y	spy
		i	find

TABLE 5-2 *(continued)*

Sound Label	Vowel	Letter Label	Example
		ei	height
		igh	night
Unglided or short	/a/	oo	not
Glided or long	/ow/	o.e	shone
		oa	goat
		ow	snow
		o	no
		ew	sewing
		ough	dough, through
		oo	floor
		eau	beau, bureau
		oe	hoe, doe
Unglided or short	/ə/	u	nut
		oo	flood
		ou	enough, curious, pretentious
		ough	rough
		o	hover, cover, come
Glided or long	/yuw/	u.e	yule
		eau	beauty
		ew	dew
Unglided or short	/u/	oo	good
		u	put
Unglided or short	/ɔ/	a	walk
		au	maul
		o	frog
		aw	saw
Unglided or diphthong	/aw/	ow	down
		ou	cloud
Glided or diphthong	/y/	oy	boy
		oi	loin

*The dot stands for omitted letter.

However, even competent adult readers of English might say that all words in Chinese look the same to us. In English, these two Chinese sentences mean

> Every day the moon is bright.
> At the end of autumn, the villager gathers wood in the forest.

Students who are beginning to read feel much the same way about English words as you may feel about these sentences—the words all look alike. Teachers must be very patient with students who are beginning reading instruction to make sure that they can distinguish between each separate word.

Competent readers have no difficulty discriminating one word from another. This proficiency is the result of a great deal of exercise, practice,

Teachers must be very patient with children who are beginning reading instruction to make sure they can distinguish between each separate word. This puzzle is helpful in practicing sight words. (Photo by Linda Lungren.)

and experience. Most students in the first grade are able to distinguish the letters of the English alphabet in a relatively short period of time and with little practice, but it is not uncommon to hear a young child say, "I have trouble reading the little words." This might mean that young children have difficulty in quickly identifying words such as *in, and, on, an, for, from, form,* and *foam.*

Regarding our example from Chinese, you may also find it interesting to note that some educational researchers are now investigating the role of phonology in reading by comparing alphabetic systems (such as English) with nonalphabetic writing systems (such as Chinese) (see Shwedel, 1983, pp. 707–713). While the results are as yet inconclusive, such cross-cultural studies may provide us with valuable information in the future.

Phonics Instruction

Once students are able to discriminate between words, they are ready to learn to *decode* words. Through decoding, students attach meaning and concepts to written words; one of the many decoding strategies students use is a phonics strategy.

From Phonology to Phonics

Phonetics is the study of speech sounds; a phonetician studies the physiological and acoustic aspects of speech sounds. The study of the sound system of a language is *phonology*. The phonologist seeks information about the relevant sounds of a language. Educators have taken the analysis of the relevant sounds of English and used them to set up letter-sound correspondences to aid in the teaching of reading. The educator has taken the most useful parts of this knowledge for the teaching of reading and has attempted to develop a body of knowledge called phonics. This subset, phonics, includes the most common sounds of English and the most frequently used letters or strings of letters that record these sounds.

Early Phonics Instruction

Prior to phonics instruction, which commenced in the 1890s, beginning reading instruction consisted of memorizing and reciting the alphabet. Eventually, emphasis began to shift from exercises in naming letters to exercises in naming the sounds of the letters. Phonics exercises were unrelated to meaning. Children would recite "phonics"; for example, they would practice the following drill:

da	ra	pa	sa	la	na	ma
di	re	pi	si	li	ne	me

Rebecca Pollard's Synthetic Method was introduced to schools in 1890. In this method she advocated the following practices:

1. Articulation drills in single letters before reading instruction began
2. Drills for each consonant; each consonant had the sound of a syllable: /bə/, /kə/, /də/, /fə/, /gə/, /lə/, /mə/, /nə/, /pə/, /rə/, /sə/, /tə/
3. Drills on phonograms: bill, pill, mill, drill, trill; back, pack, sack, track
4. Drills on diacritical markings in sentences: the lamb ate the grass at night
5. Drills on phrases in sentences: The dog/sat/on his tail,/and/he yelped

Syllabication

One of the many controversial areas in reading instruction is the teaching of *syllabication* as a decoding strategy. (For a discussion of this controversy, see Groff, 1981.) There is research to suggest that teaching vowels out of the context of the syllable has little meaning for the beginning reader. You may, therefore, wish to begin phonics instruction with the introduction of the syllable. But what is a syllable?

Syllables are usually determined by the existence of a vowel; the phonological features in a syllable are a vowel and, often, a consonant; together, they result in emphasis on one part of the word. Gibson and Levin

(1975) found that some students use such units rather automatically when they are decoding; instruction in the visual recognition of larger letter units facilitates many students' word-recognition abilities. The visual identification of letter sequences for pronunciation can facilitate the decoding process.

In his discussion of the syllable, Groff (1971) points out that English is a "stress-timed language"; therefore, it is easy to identify the number of syllables in a given word, but it is very difficult to determine syllable boundaries. The syllable presents a problem similar to that of a cartographer deciding exactly how much of the valley between two hills belongs to each hill.

To teach and apply phonics strategies, you must have a basic understanding of syllables and stress. The following generalizations may be helpful; remember, however, that they are subject to exception.

1. All syllables have a vowel sound: try, e-rase.
2. When a final *e* appears as a vowel in a word, it usually does not add another sound: make.
3. When there are two consonants between two vowels, a syllable division usually exists between the consonants: stam-pede.
4. When there is a consonant between two vowels, a division occurs between the first vowel and the consonant: e-mit.
5. If the single consonant preceded and followed by vowels is *x*, the *x* and the preceding vowel are in the same syllable: ex-it.
6. When a word ends in *le*, preceded by a consonant, the consonant and le make up a new syllable: stum-ble, han-dle.

Stress Points and Phonics

Words in English contain stress points (some call them accents) that are essential to pronunciation and meaning. Knowledge of English stress point rules will give students one more tool to help them decode unfamiliar words. The following is a brief set of rules you may find helpful as a part of your phonics program:

1. If a root has two syllables, the first is usually stressed: flipper, dragon.
2. If a root has two syllables and the second syllable contains a long vowel, the syllable with the long vowel is stressed: canteen, exceed.
3. If the first vowel in a multisyllabic root is a short vowel and it precedes two consonants, the first syllable is stressed: missionary, mastery.
4. If the first vowel in a multisyllabic root is a long vowel and it precedes two consonants, the syllable that contains the long vowel is stressed: library, patriot.
5. If a final syllable contains *le*, it is not stressed: preamble, grumble.

Although stress is an important component in learning to read, it is extremely difficult to write an exhaustive compilation of rules that does not generate a long list of exceptions. Most students, however, who have heard a word spoken will be able to find the stress pattern while they are de-coding the constituent parts of the word. If the student decodes con-sti-tu-tion, he will be able to match the stress to his knowledge of the spoken word.

Consonants

Before we discuss consonant sounds, we recommend that you *not* teach students the actual technical terminology used to describe sounds in En-glish (cluster, digraph, diphthong, etc.). Research indicates that while many students accurately use sound-letter correspondences, they may have dif-ficulty understanding the terms used to explain these sounds. Examples often are easier to cope with than definitions (Tovey, 1980).

Students must understand the differences between sounds and letters and the correspondences (or lack of correspondences) among them. Sev-eral consonant letters have only one sound in English, while others have a variety of sounds. In the next few pages we will introduce you to a se-ries of rules that govern the pronunciation of consonant graphemes.

The beginning sounds in the following words are representative of the most common consonant sounds. Each of these sixteen graphemes (let-ters) usually has only one sound in the initial position in English words.

b	*ball*	l	*lamp*	s	*sand*
d	*date*	m	*most*	t	*tall*
f	*fall*	n	*nap*	v	*vote*
h	*house*	p	*pet*	w	*wax*
j	*jam*	r	*roll*	z	*zoo*
k	*kite*				

We have not included the consonants *c, g, q,* and *x* in this list for the following reasons: *c* and *g* have two sounds, hard and soft; *q* and *x* do not have sounds of their own.

C

Hard sounds: The *hard* sound of *c* is heard in words such as *cat, candy, cape, coat, cuff, cough, calf, fabric,* and *picnic.* The hard sound of *c* is heard as /k/.

Soft sounds: The *soft* sound of *c* is heard in words such as *city, cell, cent, cigar,* and *face.* The soft sound of *c* is heard as /s/.

When the consonant *c* is followed by *a, o, u, r,* or *l,* the sound of /k/ is often heard. This is also true when *c* appears at the end of a word. When *c* is followed by *e, i,* or *y,* the sound of /s/ is often heard.

G

Hard sounds: The *hard* sound of *g* is heard in words such as *goat, gulp, gate, begin, again, cog,* and *bag.* The hard sound of *g* is heard as /g/.

Soft sounds: The *soft* sound of g is heard in words such as gentle, gym, gin, courage, and badge. The soft sound of g is heard as /j/.

In many words when the consonant g is followed by *e, i,* or *y,* the sound of /j/ is heard; when g is followed by *a, o, u, r,* and *l,* the hard sound of /g/ is heard. This is also true when g appears at the end of a word. This principle is not as reliable in its application to g as it is in application to *c.*

Q

The consonant *q* is always accompanied by the vowel *u.* Together they represent the following sounds:

qu as the /k/ sound: antique, queue, statuesque
qu as the /kw/ sound: quack, quail, quarrel, queen, quiz, quote

X

The letter *x,* like the letter *q,* represents no sound of its own, and is used to represent the following sounds:

x as the /z/ sound: xylophone, xenon
x as the /ks/ sound: taxi, box
x as the /gz/ sound: exist, exotic

W AND Y

The letters *w* and *y* are unique because they can function as both consonants and vowels: *saw, say.*
    The letters *w* and *y* function as consonants only when they appear as the initial letter in a syllable.

w: *went, wonder, subway*
y: *yard, yellow, canyon*

CONSONANT CLUSTERS (CONSONANT BLENDS)

When two or more consonants appear in succession in a word and are both pronounced or are blended when pronouncing the word, they are referred to as consonant blends. The following examples represent a sample of consonant blends in the initial position:

bl	*blow*	fl	*flip*	pr	*pry*	sn	*snip*
br	*bring*	fr	*free*	sc	*score*	st	*stay*
cl	*cloud*	gl	*glow*	scr	*screw*	str	*straw*
cr	*crow*	gr	*grab*	sk	*skin*	sw	*sway*
dr	*draw*	kr	*kraut*	sl	*slow*	tr	*train*
dw	*dwell*	pl	*play*	sm	*small*	tw	*twin*

The following words represent examples of consonant blends in the final position:

-ft	-ld	-lm	-lp	-lt	-mp
lift	cold	calm	gulp	felt	bump
raft	held	palm	help	salt	lamp

-nd	-nk	-nt	-sk	-sp	-st
end	bunk	ant	desk	gasp	best
sand	sink	bent	mask	wisp	fast

CONSONANT DIGRAPHS

When two consonants appear together in a word and form one sound, they are referred to as a *consonant digraph*. The following words contain examples of consonant digraphs: *ch*: chair; *th*: them; *ng*: ring.

In the case of the digraph *th*, it is necessary to distinguish between the voiced and voiceless sounds:

Voiced: *they*, *that*, *breathe*
Voiceless: *think*, *thimble*, *bath*

The following lists contain examples of consonant digraphs in the initial and final positions:

Consonant Digraph	Initial	Final
/č/		
ch	chain	bunch
	chin	march
/š/		
sh	shell	dish
	shine	wash
/ð/		
th (voiced)	that	smooth
	there	
/θ/		
th (voiceless)	thank	bath
	thing	wrath

In addition, the consonant digraph *wh* is often found in the initial position: *whale*, *wheel*. The consonant digraph *ng* is often found in the final position: lo*ng*, stro*ng*.

Vowels

The vowel sounds of English are often complex for students learning to read because each vowel letter may represent several sounds. In the next few pages we will introduce you to English vowels, their orthographic representations, and the rules governing them. It is extremely important for you to familiarize yourself with these rules to adapt these principles to your reading instruction program.

The following letters represent vowel sounds in English:

a   e   i   o   u   (y, w, h)

These alone and in combination are used to represent the fourteen vowel sounds of English. Every vowel has a long and a short sound:

Long Vowel Sound	Short Vowel Sound
a able	apple
e evil	elephant
i ice	igloo
o ocean	octopus
u universe	umbrella

The long vowel sounds can be marked with a macron (ˉ):

ā cāme	ē bēlow	ī bīke	ō hōme	ū fūse
gāte	prēfix	līme	ōld	ūse

For students who need work on vowel sounds, we recommend that you make flashcards or word lists with words having long vowel sounds in the intial and medial positions. You can expand on lists similar to these:

Long Vowel Sound	Initial	Medial
ā	acorn	cake
	age	face
	April	pane
ē	Egypt	begin
	equal	Pete
	even	remind
ī	ice	bike
	item	mile
	ivy	nine
ō	obey	cone
	ocean	nose
	Oklahoma	stove
ū	ukelele	cube
	uniform	fuse
	use	mule

The short vowel sounds can be marked with a breve (˘):

ă căt	ĕ bĕd	ĭ mĭll	ŏ cŏt	ŭ bŭs
săt	rĕd	pĭt	hŏp	rŭn

Short Vowel Sound	Initial	Medial
ă	after	bad
	am	fan
	apple	map
ĕ	egg	fell
	enter	help
	escape	sled

ĭ	igloo	hill
	ill	pig
	itch	ship
ŏ	odd	fox
	on	mop
	octopus	rock
ŭ	ugly	club
	under	duck
	usher	jump

You may find the following rules useful to help you introduce vowel usage.

SHORT VOWELS

1. A vowel grapheme represents a short vowel when it is followed by a consonant unit (closed syllable), for example, fat, crab, pet, pit.
2. A vowel grapheme represents a short vowel when it is followed by a compound consonant unit, for example, dg/j/ or -x/ks/: badge.
3. A vowel grapheme represents a short vowel when it is followed by a cluster of consonants, for example, *tt* or *st* as in fast.
4. A vowel grapheme represents a short vowel when it is followed by a double consonant, for example, little, ball, bottle.

LONG VOWELS

1. A vowel grapheme represents a long vowel sound when it is followed by a consonant, which in turn is followed by *l* or *r* and another vowel, usually a final *e*, for example, cradle, table, ogre.
2. The vowel graphemes *oi* and *oy* represent the gliding sound /y/ in boil and boy. The vowel graphemes *ou* and *ow* represent the gliding sound /aw/ in bout and how.
3. When the vowel grapheme occurs as the last unit of a syllable and when it is preceded by a consonant unit, the grapheme will represent the long vowel (open syllable) sound, for example, Jimmy, tree, knee.

SCHWA SOUND

The schwa sound /ə/ appears often in unaccented syllables of polysyllabic words, and in many recent dictionaries, the symbol appears in some accented syllables. The schwa /ə/ is illustrated in the following words:

alone	(ə lōn')
system	(sis' təm)
easily	(ē' zə lē)
gallop	(gal' əp)
circus	(sur' kəs)

As you can see, the schwa sound may be represented by any vowel letter if the letter is found in an unaccented syllable. The schwa may also represent the short *u* sound and the vowel sound in er, ir, and ur.

Y AS A VOWEL

The letter *y* generally represents the short *i* sound when it appears within a syllable not containing another vowel letter.

    lymph   myth   system

The letter *y* generally represents the long *ī* sound when it appears as the final sound in a one-syllable word.

    cry   sky   try

The letter *y* generally represents the long *ē* sound when it appears as the final sound in a multisyllabic word.

    berry   dairy   very

The letter *y* generally represents the long *ī* sound when it appears as the final letter of a syllable that is not the last syllable in a multisyllabic word.

    asylum   cycle   dynamo

Y can also be heard as *r* controlled: Myrtle.

VOWEL DIGRAPHS

Two consecutive vowel letters that represent the equivalent of *one* vowel sound are called a vowel digraph. Here are a few examples:

b*ai*t	c*ou*gh	l*oa*n
br*ea*d	f*ie*ld	rec*ei*ve
c*au*ght	f*oo*d	s*ou*p

VOWEL DIPHTHONGS

A vowel diphthong consists of two vowel letters in one syllable, *both* of which are sounded. The first vowel is strongly sounded, while the second becomes a glided or semivowel sound.

Examples of vowel diphthongs in English are

Diphthong	*Example*
oi	boil
oy	boy
ow	howl
ou	count

GENERALIZED VOWEL RULES

The following rules may be of help to you when you introduce your students to the concept of vowel sounds:

1. When a single vowel in a syllable is followed by the letter *r*, the vowel is affected or influenced by it.

chart	dollar	mark	for	work
cart	her	first	fort	curl

2. When the letter *a* is followed by *ll* of *lk* in a syllable, the *a* represents the sound of *ou* or *au* as in *aw*ful.

all	wall	enthrall	walk
ball	call	chalk	talk

3. When the letter combinations *gn, gh, ght, ld,* or *nd* follow the single letter *i* in a syllable, the *i* represents a long vowel sound.

sign	tight	mild
sigh	light	mind

4. When the letter combination *ld* follows the single letter *o* in a syllable, the letter *o* generally represents a long vowel sound.

cold	fold	mold
told	old	behold

5. When the letter combination *re* follows a single vowel in a syllable, one generally hears an *r* sound.

core	tire	bore	lure
here	tore	cure	sure

6. *E*'s at the end of a monosyllabic word usually make the first vowel a long sound. This is sometimes called the Magic *E* Rule.

cape	time	dote	huge
hate	wine	tone	mute

Phonics is one of the most difficult and important strategies for a student to learn. However, it is one thing to understand the theoretical principles behind phonics instruction and quite another to know how actually to use phonics strategies to help students develop meaningful decoding skills. While the controversy over how much phonics to teach continues, some professional opinion now seems to be swinging back in favor of more intensive phonics programs (Fulwiler and Groff, 1980).

Of course, every teaching situation is unique, based totally on the teacher and the students involved. You, as the instructor, must be knowledgeable and comfortable with phonics strategies to generate enthusiasm and comprehension in your students. We hope to answer some instructional questions that teachers of reading often ask, reemphasizing the fact that *every situation is different.* The instructional answers provided here are only guidelines for you as a teacher. You will have to implement the teaching of phonics in your own way to meet the specific needs of your students.

No one strategy can meet the needs of all your students. Phonics, like other word analysis strategies, is merely a means to the goal of comprehension. If we lose sight of comprehension as the end of all reading instruction and begin to emphasize only phonics strategies, we may never reach our goal. Phonics strategies are *aids* that help students with comprehension.

How to Begin

The most frequently asked question about teaching phonics strategies is, "What should I teach first?" This question implies an effective introductory sequence for teaching consonant and vowel correspondences. The answer to this question is complex, but recent research has offered us a number of reasonable suggestions:

Suggestion 1:   Offer vowel instruction early in the program. Many teachers and publishers of packaged programs have delayed teaching the vowels because they believed that all the consonants needed to be taught first. They argued that the regularity of the letter-sound correspondence of the consonants helped the child to learn to read. This view failed to consider the high correlation between the letter-sound correspondences of many vowels and the importance of the ability to decode vowels in order to read independently without adult guidance. Most children can clearly articulate vowels by the ages of 4 or 5, and most children have had some experience in decoding vowels, such as when they memorize certain sight words like *Hanna* or *Happy Birthday*. The early introduction of vowels will help students to become involved independently in the reading process from the beginning of instruction.

Suggestion 2:   Structure vowel sequence on decibel rating. A logical question follows: Which vowel sounds should be introduced in the early stages of instruction? Fairbanks's (1966) work may provide us with some meaningful answers. He found that the vowels in the following words have different decibel levels:

Vowel		Decibel Levels
cap	/ae/	4.5
talk	/ɚ/	3.8
shop	/a/	3.7
choke	/ow/	3.0
check	/e/	2.2
coop	/yu/	1.9
cup	/ə/	1.1
cheek	/iy/	1.0
cook	/u/	0.3
pit	/i/	0.0

These findings suggest that children can discriminate vowel sounds with the highest decibel ratings. This natural phenomenon should dictate the sequence of instruction.

Suggestion 3:   Present visually contrastive pairs (e.g., *d* and *b*) very early in the program. In the past, teachers have been encouraged not to introduce two letters simultaneously that are easily confused with one another, such as *d* and *b*. However, the current opinion is that the introduction of contrastive pairs like *d* and *b*, *q* and *g*, and *m* and *n* has instructional value because the student has to focus on the distinctive features of each of the letters within a specific context (dog, bog). Researchers argue that this initial struggle will reduce later confusion for the student.

Suggestion 4:   To teach the first consonants, use the /f/, /s/, /v/, and /m/ sounds in words. Coleman (1967) maintains that students find *continuants*, consonants that are produced by the constant release of air, like /s/, easier to blend with other sounds than consonants that are formed by stopping the air flow, like /t/. He suggests that the continuants are easily learned and should be among the first consonants which are taught to the beginning reader. Continuants include

/s/   sat
/f/   fat
/v/   vat

Suggestion 5:   Introduce students to variations in letter-sound correspondences. One criticism of the linguistic method of reading instruction, which is described in detail in Chapter 10, is that students begin to expect one-to-one letter-sound correspondence (pan, man, can), and they find it difficult to transfer their phonics strategies to new words that do not fit the pattern. These findings suggest that students should be introduced to variations in letter-sound correspondence from the very beginning, such as *tap* and *tape*, in order to prepare them for later reading.

Suggestion 6:   Make good use of natural order strategies. Marchbanks and Levin (1965) maintain that it is also important to note that students use definite order strategies when they are decoding. First they look at the initial letter(s), then they look at the final letter(s), then the middle letter(s), then the configuration of the word. This phenomenon underlines the need for students to learn independent phonics strategies so that they will be able to cope with new and unfamiliar words.

Suggestion 7:   Introduce students to word families through phonograms. Teachers often use word families or phonograms to teach phonics. For example, ask your students to write as many words us they can with *b*, *s*, *r*, and *t* as the initial letter. You can use these lists to create games or other activities for students.

Suggestion 8:   Practice new words by verbalizing. Kibby (1979) found that words learned by the phonics method were best retained when practiced in the production mode or by verbalization. Using the concept of phonograms in oral games or employing the tape recorder may facilitate retention of words learned phonetically.

Based on these suggestions, the following questions and answers will help you to develop a sequential, effective, phonics teaching program.

1. Q. Should consonants or vowels be introduced first?
   A. They should be introduced simultaneously, taking into consideration the information we have acquired about continuants (/f/, /s/, /v/, and /m/), visually similar graphemes (*b* and *d*), and decibel loading for certain vowel sounds.

2. Q. Should short vowels or long vowels be introduced first?
   A. Short vowels should be introduced in the order presented in the decibel loading chart. Long vowels should be introduced as contrasts to short vowel sounds, using words that have become part of the child's sight vocabulary, such as cap and cape. When you are introducing graphemes and graphemic patterns, you should tell the children that graphemes represent sounds, not that graphemes make phonemes.

3. Q. Should I reinforce vowel correspondence by teaching vowels within words, such as *cat, bat, rat?*
   A. Definitely. Children should be introduced to the concept of syllable and word meaning from the beginning of their reading programs.

4. Q. Should I emphasize the sound of initial consonants within the word?
   A. Yes. Consonants should be introduced within CVC (consonant-vowel-consonant) words (e.g., *pan, bat, sun*). Do not stress the sounds; instead, emphasize each sound within the context of the word.

5. Q. Should I be concerned about dialect variations in my children's pronunciation?
   A. Dialect variation will result in different sounds for letter-sound correspondences. However, this should not concern you because your students will develop letter-sound equivalents that reflect their own dialect.

Syllable Strategies

Syllabication can be a valuable decoding skill for students to learn. In some ways, this is an easy task because students already understand the principles of syllabication. An inductive method of teaching can be used by asking students to pull apart words that they have in their sight vocabulary, such as hap-py and birth-day. Then ask them to read words like

mis - chief	Tues - day	to - day
ap - ple	sun - shine	re - port

The following rules may be helpful when you are teaching your students the principles of syllabication:

1. Look at the word. Ask yourself if it is a compound word. If it is, name the parts that make up the word, such as base · ball.
2. Look for affixes in the words and look for tense markers like *-ed* and *-ing*. Look for familiar word parts such as *-ness*. If there are word parts that you know, separate them from the word and read the rest of the word—this will be the root word, for example, good/ness. Now put the stress on the root, *good*, and read the whole word: goodness.
3. Look in the midst of the word for a cluster of consonants or for a consonant digraph. If there is a cluster of two consonants, try to separate the word into two parts between the two letters of the cluster: ras · cal. If the cluster has three consecutive consonants, separate after the second of the three consonants: shing · le. If there is a consonant digraph, divide the word after the digraph. Put the stress on the first syllable: thatch' · er.
4. If no cluster of consonants exists within the middle of the word, you might want to try the following. Separate the word after the consonant that comes after the first vowel in the word and read the word by making the vowel in the first syllable a short vowel and putting the stress on the first syllable: can · ard. Vowel sounds in the second syllable will usually be a schwa sound /ə/. If you still do not know the word, separate the first vowel after the first vowel digraph, such as *ai* in raisin, and read the first syllable as a CV (consonant-vowel) word. Give the vowel a long sound and put the stress on this syllable.

Reteaching Phonics

It is often difficult to know how much formal phonics instruction is necessary before you are reteaching or overteaching this strategy. Some students may have a working understanding of phonics without being able to use the rules accurately all the time. For example, if the student looks at this sentence

> *Ellen Lewis hit the tennis ball out into Rochester Park.*

and reads

> *Ellen Lewis hit the*

and stops, your strategy would be to say, "Let's break the word apart; you know the parts of the word: ten-nis." Then you might tell him to read the next word, "ball," and ask him to guess the preceding word. When he has succeeded in decoding the word, he may continue the sentence:

> *ball out into*

and stop again. You may continue with the same technique:

> Ro-ches-ter (Rochester)

One final suggestion may be crucial in establishing an effective reading program: If a student reads the sentence "Senator Lawrence Darrell of California voted in favor of the bill" as "Senator Lawrence Dar of Connecticut voted for the law" and answers the comprehension question "Did Senator Darrell oppose the legislation?" with a "no," then understanding may have taken place and further phonics instruction may not be necessary for this sentence. In fact further phonics instruction may be counterproductive; it may interfere with the student's progress. However, the student must be encouraged to read carefully, since word substitution *may* result in comprehension errors.

Finally, these general guidelines may be helpful when establishing your reading program:

1. Phonics is one means of decoding. If it is too confusing for the student, try another strategy.
2. Try to break words into parts for the student using syllabication rules.
3. If the student cannot decode the word and you sense that frustration is overwhelming him, tell him the word.
4. Phonics is a means to an end: comprehension. When phonics decoding hinders comprehension, it is no longer useful. Decide just how many words the student can struggle through in each sentence before there is serious comprehension loss and structure your teaching accordingly.

Suggested Readings Related to Goals.   We encourage you at this time to review the goals at the beginning of this chapter. If you feel you would like to explore one or more of these areas in greater depth, please refer to the cross-indexed bibliography at the end of the book.

6 Strategies for Vocabulary Development

The elements and structure of a language do not themselves have meaning. They are only symbols, sets of symbols, cues that cause us to bring our own meanings into play, to think about them, to rearrange them, etc.

[D. Berlo]

Goals

To help the student understand
1. How to use sight-word strategies as a word-recognition skill
2. How structural analysis can be used as a word-recognition skill
3. How to use contextual analysis as a word-recognition skill
4. How to teach vocabulary

In Chapter 5 we discussed phonics skills and strategies; in addition, you will want to instruct your students about other word analysis strategies they can use to help them decode unknown words. Three valuable skills for students to acquire in order to ensure continued vocabulary development are *sight-word analysis*, *structural analysis*, and *contextual analysis*.

> One's facility with vocabulary is a major factor in comprehending; it is unlikely that a reader could understand a passage that contains numerous unknown words.

While this statement may seem acceptable, it has not received total agreement. Anderson and Freebody (1979) suggested that knowledge of vocabulary may not be causally related to reading comprehension. Sup-

Children are able to recognize many words prior to beginning reading instruction. (Photo by Linda Lungren.)

porting Anderson and Freebody's research are Jenkins, Pony, and Schreck (1978) who present further evidence that vocabulary instruction is not causally related to comprehension.

However, other researchers have found that instruction in vocabulary does improve reading comprehension; for example, Draper and Moeller (1971) used a standardized test to measure comprehension gains after a vocabulary program had been initiated for a complete school year. Graves and Bender (1980) and Barrett and Graves (1981) also found vocabulary instruction to be causally related to improvement in comprehension.

While there appears to be a need for continued research on this topic, it is our opinion and that of Graves (1984), Calfee (1981), and Stotsky (1976) that students of all grade levels need to be engaged in systematic programs of vocabulary development and expansion in an effort to enhance their overall reading comprehension.

Classroom time is so precious that many teachers wonder when and how to integrate vocabulary instruction with reading and content area instruction. We believe that vocabulary development is so essential to learning that a portion of most lessons should be devoted to vocabulary instruction.

Instruction should be designed to expand student knowledge of

1. *General words:* Those words that comprise the major portion of our lexicon are used for general communication, for example, silence, weather, school, hospital. The list of connectives in Table 6-1 and the Heritage Word List (Table 13-1) are also examples of general words.
2. *Multiple meaning words:* Those words that change meaning according to context, for example, squash, drill, mass, flake.
3. *Specialized words:* Those words related to a specific content area, for example, uranium (science), noun (English), subtraction (math).

One way to teach these words is through sight-word analysis.

Sight-Word Analysis: Strategies

Whole Words

The sight-word (sometimes called "look-say" or "whole-word") approach to beginning reading is often used with high-frequency words to begin a basal reading program. By using such high-frequency words, students are able to respond to and participate in the reading process immediately.

Most students are able to recognize some words even before they begin reading instruction. These words are usually words that they see often (e.g., walk, stop), words that have special meaning for them (e.g., her name, Happy Birthday), and words that name frequent interactions (e.g., bike, candy).

You may help your students build or expand their sight word vocabularies by using "organic" words (Ashton-Warner, 1963) or "key" words (Veatch et al., 1979). These are secret words that have a personal or special meaning for each student. Ask the students to tell you a secret word, then write it on an index card, and let them keep the cards in their special files.

Review these words periodically with each student, and use them as catalysts for storytelling, language experience charts, or play productions. The language experience approach to teaching reading (see Chapter 10) uses students' experiences, expressed in the language the students already know and use, to begin instruction. Allow the students to study their private words and share them with classmates. Through these activities, students develop sight-word recognition of words that are important to them; also, the interaction of the students helps to develop a classroom atmosphere that is very congenial and conducive to learning (Brown, 1981).

Some basal reading programs present sight words in such a way that students can compare and contrast new words with previously presented words. For example, initial stories might introduce a phonogram like *an*, and later introduce *can, Dan, fan, man,* and *ran*.

Skilled readers utilize many clues when they are reading, including word shape and word length (Haber et al., 1983). For example, if you were told that you were looking for the name of a state that begins with the letter "I" and ends with the letter "a," both word shape and word length could help you determine which was Iowa and which was Indiana:

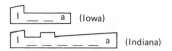

The importance of word shapes to the overall reading process is still being debated, but research seems to indicate that word shape information may be useful in word recognition (Rayner, 1976, 1978; Haber and Haber, 1981; Haber and Schindler, 1981; Haber et al., 1983).

As a teacher, you must be aware of a phenomenon called "first-letter guessing." A student realizes [ran] means ran; she is introduced to [man] and is told this says *man*. What sometimes happens is the following. The student internalizes this information: ran = *ran*. When she sees the word "run" in a sentence, she recognizes the *r* and "guesses" that the word says "ran." In other cases, the student who has learned ran = *ran* might even say "ran" when she comes across such words as rooster, rabbit, rye, or rough.

It is important for you to choose appropriate words to teach as sight

TABLE 6-1
The "Top Twenty" Connectives*

Grade 12	
Geography	but, when, however, although, because, so, thus, as, if, also, while, for example, then, therefore, since, yet, where, that is, perhaps, in fact
History	but, while, although, thus, if, as, even, however, because, since, until, when, then, yet, in fact, therefore, meanwhile, whether, perhaps, despite
Chemistry	but, if, since, for example, however, when, thus, if so, also, as, because, although, therefore, while, so, perhaps, yet, that is, until, such as
Biology	but, if, however, thus, for example, since, as, because, when, while, although, even, then, therefore, such as, also, yet, perhaps, that is, so
Physics	if, but, because, when, therefore, as, then, however, for example, also, although, since, while, thus, so, in other words, so that, on the other hand, consequently, furthermore
Grade 6	
Science and social studies combined	but, if, when, because, as, then, even, also, perhaps, however, although, while, for example, since, yet, so that, such as, too, until, whether

SOURCE: Denis Rodgers, "Which Connectives? Signals to Enhance Comprehension," *Journal of Reading*, 17 (March 1974), 462–466. Reprinted with permission of the author and the International Reading Association.

words so that your students' memories do not become overtaxed. Some students who have not had exposure to long words may need help learning long words such as *imagination* and *chimpanzee* as sight words. Concentrate instead on each student's name and on words that have convenient visual referents (e.g., red, door, one).

You may find it valuable to base your sight-word instruction program on one of the lists that have been compiled on high-frequency words (e.g., Dale, 1931; Dolch, 1936; Harris and Jacobsen, 1972). These lists include high-frequency functional words that students are likely to encounter as they begin reading instruction. Repetition is the key to helping students learn a sight-word vocabulary, especially as many high-frequency words defy phonetic generalizations (e.g., guess, know, through).

Contractions

It is desirable to teach contractions as sight words because the inconsistency of their pattern formation often causes problems (e.g., will not: won't; is not: isn't). You can help your students to recognize contractions by teaching them this rule: When two or more words combine to form a new shorter word, an apostrophe (') is substituted for one or more letters in the new word.

A lack of correspondence between spelling and pronunciation in words that students encounter throughout the school years makes it important to continue teaching both whole words and contractions as sight words even beyond the initial reading instruction level. More difficult and less frequently used words that may be effectively taught as sight words include *pneumonia, phlegm,* and *mnemonic.*

In addition, many words have come into common usage in English that have been borrowed from other languages. The spellings of such words are often unusual and are best taught as sight words. Examples include *kayak* (American Indian), *bureau* (French), and *pinochle* (German) (Ruddell, 1974).

Guidelines for Sight-Word Instruction

You will be introducing and reinforcing sight-word skills regardless of the grade level or content area in which you are teaching. The following rules will help you to assist students to develop sight-word vocabularies.

1. Use pictures to illustrate the word being taught when it is appropriate. Encourage students to study the picture and the number of words on the page and try to predict what is being said in the passage.
2. Ask the students to look at the words as you read them. This helps them to decide if their guesses are correct.
3. Point to the picture and reread the passage while the students follow along.

4. Encourage the students to read the passage with you.
5. Ask individual students to read the sentence while their classmates follow the story visually.
6. After reading a sentence, point out the individual words you are introducing.
7. Discuss the meaning of each word. Explain that some words serve as helpers to complete sentences, such as *the*, *is*, and *am*.
8. "Tell" students certain words that have extremely irregular patterns: *sight, of, who, laugh, though, the,* and *should.*
9. While framing each word, assist students in recognizing the length and configuration, initial letters(s), and ascending letter features.
10. Finally, encourage students to reread the sentence with you.

Structural Analysis: Strategies

Another important strategy for unlocking the memory of unknown words is through analyzing the structure of the word. Structural analysis, breaking words into their smallest parts, is a useful decoding skill for a student to know when she encounters words that are not part of her sight vocabulary. Finding meaning in parts of words may not only help in decoding them, it may also help in understanding their meanings. A student who knows that *in = not* and *able = capable* can unravel a word like *indefinable* and arrive at the meaning "not capable of being defined." A thorough knowledge of the rules of *morphology* will help you to establish the structural analysis segment of your word analysis program.

Morphology

The smallest unit of meaning in any language is a *morpheme*. A morpheme is not necessarily a word, as a word may have a single morpheme (e.g., venture) or several morphemes (e.g., ad · venture · some). "Free" morphemes are uninflected and can stand alone as a word (e.g., mix); "bound" morphemes cannot stand alone (e.g., -ing as in mixing). Free morphemes are often found as root words while bound morphemes are usually *affixes* (prefixes and suffixes). For example, in the word *previewing*, *pre* and *ing* are bound morphemes, while *view* is a free morpheme.

AFFIXES

Knowledge of how words are constructed is an important step in knowing how to unlock word meanings. To do so, students must be introduced to English affixes. Affixes are bound morphemes; they include prefixes and suffixes.

Affixes can be found in four major classes of words: nouns, verbs, adjectives, and adverbs. Examples are histor*ian*, *en*liven, ador*able*, sweet*ly*.

New affixes are constantly being added in English. Many of these pass

TABLE 6-2
Key to 100,000 Words

Prefixes	Other Spellings	Meaning	Master Words	Root	Other Spelling	Meaning
1. de		down or away	detain	tain	ten, tin	to have or hold
2. inter		between	intermittent	mitt	miss, mit, mis	to send
3. pre		before	precept	cept	cap, capt, ceive, ceit, cit	to take or seize
4. ob	oc, of, op	to, toward, against	offer	for	lat, lay	to carry, bear
5. in	il, im, ir	into or not	insist	sist	stat, sta, stan	to stand endure or persist
6. mono		one or alone	monograph	graph	gram	to write
7. epi	op	over, upon, beside	epilogue	log	logy	speech or science
8. ad	a, ab, ac, af, ag, al, am, an, ap, ar, as, at	act to or to-ward	aspect	spect	spec, spi spy	to look
9. com um	co, col, con, cor	with or together	uncomplicated	plic	play, plex, ploy, ply	to fold, twist or intervene
10. non ex	o or of	not out, formally	nonextended	tend	tens, tent	to stretch
11. re pro		again or back forward or in favor of	reproduction	duct	due, dult	to lead, make, or fashion
12. dis	di or dif	apart from	indisposed	pos	pon, post, pound	to place or put
13. over sub	suc, suf, sug, sup, sur, sus	above, under, supporting	oversufficient	fic	fac, fact fash, feat	to make or do
14. mis tran	tra, tran	wrong or wrongly, across, beyond	mistranscribe	scribe	crip, criv	to write

SOURCE: Leonard A. Stevens, "Fourteen Words That Make All the Difference," *Coronet*, 40 (Aug. 1956), 80–82.

quickly from the language, but some remain in general usage. For example, from *hamburger,* we derive *burger,* and *cheeseburger* can be created.

A prefix is an affix at the beginning of a word that changes its meaning. Many common English prefixes will be valuable for your students to learn; see Table 6-2, for example.

Examples: inter   (between)   :   interstate
                  un   (not)   :   unhappy
                 sub   (under)   :   submarine

The meaning of a word can also be modified by a new ending, a suffix that is also an affix. Thorndike (1932) listed the five most common English suffixes:

-er   as in   long*er*
-ion   as in   educat*ion*
-ity   as in   pur*ity*
-ness   as in   salt*iness*
-y   as in   rain*y*

There are also many other suffixes you can help your students to learn and recognize.

INFLECTIONAL ENDINGS

There are few inflections remaining in English because English has evolved into a word order language. Those that still exist are used for forming plurals, possessives, marking tenses, and comparatives. All of the commonly used tenses are included in the following listing:

1. *Plural, Possessive, and Third Singular Verb Markers*

    a. If the word ends in any of these phonemes (/s/, /z/, /c/, /j/), the inflectional ending is /ə/ plus the phoneme.

        mass /mez/   masses /mezəz/
        garage (gəraj/   garages /gərajəz/

    b. If the word ends in a voiceless consonant, the appropriate ending is /s/.

        bit /bit/   bits /bits/
        sip /sip/   sips /sips/

    c. If the word ends in either a voiced consonant or a vowel, the appropriate ending is /z/.

        crib /krib/   cribs /kribz/
        rid /rid/   rids /ridz/

2. *Tense Markers*

    a. Past tense and past participle
    Both of these forms use the same rules to produce their appropriate endings.
        (1) If the verb ends in /t/ or /d/, the ending is /əd/.
            rate /ret/   rated /retəd/
        (2) If the verb ends in a voiceless consonant, the ending is /t/.
            dip /dip/   dipped /dipt/

(3) If the verb ends in a voiced consonant or a vowel, the ending is /d/.

rib /rib/   ribbed /ribd/

  b. The progressive

When the progressive is used, for example, *ing,* as in "He is going," /lŋ/ is added to the verb form, following *be,* to form the present participle.

he will sell   /hi wll sel/

he will be selling   /hi wll bi sellŋ/

3. *Comparatives*

When forming the comparative or the superlative of many adjectives, *-er* and *-est* are added, respectively.

	Comparative	*Superlative*
fresh	fresher	freshest

Compound Words

Most students are able to identify and decode compound words easily because of their familiarity with the words that combine to form compound words. Gleason (1969) conducted a study of children's definitions of compound words and discovered the following definitions for the words *airplane, breakfast,* and *Friday.*

> They knew what the words referred to and how to use them, but their ideas about the words were rather amusing. One little boy said that an airplane is called an airplane because it is a plain thing that goes in the air. Another child said that breakfast is called breakfast because you have to eat it fast to get to school on time. Several subjects thought that Friday is called Friday because it is the day you eat fried fish.

During beginning reading programs, students may be taught to identify many compound words as sight words (e.g., stepchildren, grandmother). Because many of these words will be part of the students' spoken vocabularies, they can be used as a base for forming generalizations about other compound words. Some examples of other common compound words frequently found in basal readers are *airplane, cowboy, sidewalk,* and *birthday.*

Structural analysis skills give students one additional tool to help them recognize and understand words. Understanding morphology rules allows students to analyze complex words with ease.

The following guidelines may help you to implement your structural analysis program:

1. Encourage students to analyze the ending of each word, such as *s, ed,* as tense markers, *s* as possession, and *s* as a plural marker.
2. Encourage students to split words into parts with which they are already familiar, for example, re/view/ing.

3. Encourage students to guess the pronunciation of a new word by looking at the parts of the word that are familiar to them.
4. Encourage students to make their own "new" compound words. This
will help them to better understand how compound words are formed.

An understanding of structural analysis will help your students to deal
with many new words. Structural analysis, like phonics and sight-word
strategies, is only one way of helping students learn to decode words. Each
strategy is useful only as an aid to learning—no strategy can substitute for
learning.

Contextual Analysis: Strategies

Word meaning is also often dependent on the context in which it is used;
for this reason, skill in utilizing clues in the surrounding text to arrive at
word meaning is an essential skill for all readers. In addition, "context
may sometimes facilitate the identification of words with difficult letter-
sound patterns" (Juel, 1983, p. 307). You can expose students to all of the
available clues for understanding unknown words by instructing them not
only to examine the unknown word, but also any *contextual clues* that
may be provided.

Some of the more common contextual clues students may encounter
are these: definition statements, synonyms, antonyms, summaries, examples, similes, appositions, and groupings. We will examine each of these
clues in greater detail in the following section.

Definition Statements.   Authors monitor the introduction of new
words in beginning readers' textbooks. One common way of presenting
a new word is to introduce and *define* it in the same sentence: The *cor-
nea* is the transparent outer coating of the eyeball.

Synonym.   Students can often infer the meaning of a new word by
relating it to an already known word: Brett *yearned* to visit Ireland; it
was his greatest *desire.*

Antonym.   Sometimes the meaning of a word is made clear through
an antonym, a word with an opposite meaning: The harbor was usually
so *placid* it was a shock to see the *raging waves.*

Summary.   A summary in the form of a brief listing of the qualities
or characteristics evoked by a word can clarify a new word for the reader:
This report contains many *redundant* words and ideas. The extra words
are not needed, and you state the same idea over and over again.

Examples.   Using examples is a clear and useful method for illustrating the meaning of a new word: Circus clowns are *jocular.* They
wear funny clothes and tell jokes to make people laugh.

Simile.   A simile is a figure of speech that uses *like* or *as* to make a
comparison: The diamond glistened *like* a bright star; the young ball-
player was *as* tenacious as his idol, Willie Mays.

Apposition.   An apposition is a word or phrase that is equivalent to the subject. It is usually adjacent to the subject and may or may not be set off by commas: The Statue of Liberty, a famous New York City landmark, was awe-inspiring.

Groupings.   When an unfamiliar word is grouped in context with other words to depict similarities, the meaning of the word is more readily recognized by the reader: The balloons were yellow, blue, red, orange, and *magenta.*

Several other types of contextual clues can be beneficial to readers: *italics, capitalization, quotation marks, boldface type, parenthetical statements,* and *footnotes.* In addition, you can instruct your students how to use *picture* clues, *lexical* (word and sentence meaning) clues, *relational* (word order) clues, and *interpretation* clues:

Picture Clue:
    The _____ was quietly eating a banana.

Lexical Clue:
    Ripe, round, red, and juicy, the _____ crunched as Pat took a bite.

Relational Clue:
    Sue jumped over the _____ so her shoes did not get wet.

Interpretive Clue:
    The spider spun its filmy _____ in the dark corner.

The role of contextual analysis in the decoding process is somewhat controversial and is still being investigated (see Biemiller, 1979; Juel, 1980). However, as Spache and Spache (1977, p. 497) point out,

Apparently most context clues demand some degree of inferential thinking. As a result, some teachers assume that contextual analysis is not much more than guesswork and therefore should not be promoted. The truth is that such inferential thinking is an essential part of the reading process at all maturity levels and should be strongly encouraged.

You may look upon contextual analysis as another *aid* to unlocking word meanings and developing reading comprehension. Encourage your students to pay attention to the context of a passage. When they are stumped by an unfamiliar word, tell them to ask themselves the following questions:

1. Are there clues to the meaning of this word in the surrounding words?
2. Will I understand this word if I continue to the end of the sentence?
3. Have I examined the pictures for clues to the meaning?

The following instructional guide is designed to help you teach unknown words. It may be supplemented with any learning cues suggested throughout this chapter and Chapter 5.

Preparing for Vocabulary Instruction, Assessment, and Expansion

1. Read the students' texts and select the words that are not part of their oral/aural vocabulary. These may be general, multiple-meaning, or specialized words.
2. Separate these words into two categories.
   a. Those that are critical to passage comprehension
   b. Those that are not critical to passage comprehension
3. Select for instruction a limited number (four or five) of the critical to passage comprehension words.
4. Prepare instructional examples of these five words. These examples should clarify the meaning of the unknown word either through a *synonym* or a *definition*. The words used in the definition must be commonly understood by the students. Be careful not to define the unknown word by using its derivative. (Negative example: *Silence* means the act of being *silent*. Positive example: *Silence* means no noise.)

It may be helpful to use a student's dictionary for these examples. As you prepare to teach the word *silence*, you should not present it to your students as *silence—the state or act of keeping silent* (derivative) because comprehension of the unknown word is based on one of its derivatives, or as: *silence—refraining from speech or from making noise*. Yes, you would not present it in this form because the student would need to know the difficult word *refraining*.

It would be appropriate for you to use the following example:

silence—no noise; quiet.

5. Prepare more detailed examples in which the unknown or target word is used in a context that clarifies its syntactic and semantic meanings. The following example is correct because it presents the syntactic and semantic meaning of the word *silence*.

   ex. All of the students worked quietly at their desks. There was no noise. The teacher could not even hear their pencils move. The students worked in total silence.

6. Prepare examples and nonexamples to be used for evaluation. If the student comprehends the target word, he or she will be able to discriminate between examples and nonexamples. The target word should not be used in the context of these examples, and there should be only minimal difference between examples and nonexamples.

   ex. Tom and Pete sat in the library. They quietly read their books and looked at magazines.

   nonexample: Tom and Pete sat in the library. They watched a film about animals and talked about their favorite animals.

7. Once you have made adequate preparation for instruction and assessment, you will need to develop practice activities that will ensure retention and expansion of new words. The following are examples of such activities:

   a. Sentence substitution

   There was no noise in the church.

   There was _____ in the church.

   The student is asked to supply the missing word in the second sentence.

   b. Sentence generation

   Say to the student; *There was silence.*

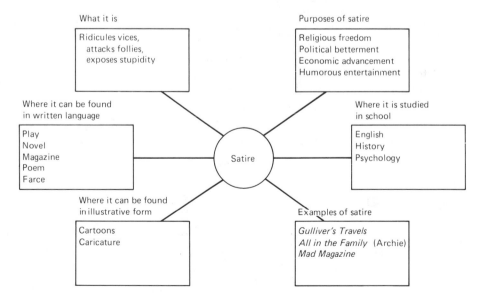

Figure 6–1. Semantic mapping: satire

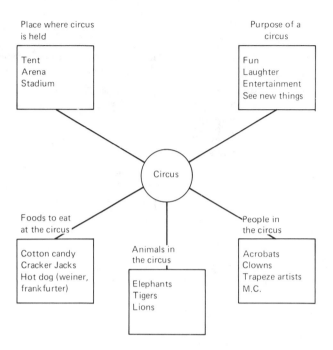

Figure 6–2. Semantic mapping: circus

Ask the student to repeat the sentence and to generate context which is a semantic expansion.

There was silence. You could hear a pin drop.

Everything around us was still.

c. Semantic mapping

The development of a semantic map enables the student to develop word categories. Present the target word (satire, circus) and together with your students generate the categories (see Figures 6-1 and 6-2). This happens by asking the students, "What do you know about _____ ?" Write all answers on the board; then work together to determine groupings.

d. Semantic feature analysis

This technique enables the reader to comprehend similarities and differences among words. You can generate the target words and categories and then discuss similarities and differences with the students.

	Vegetation	*Animal*	*Hot/humid*
Jungle	+	+	+
Forest	+	+	−
Garden			

	Vegetation	Animal	Hot/humid
Glass			
Cup			

Once you have selected the appropriate examples you are ready to begin instruction assessment.

Vocabulary Instruction and Assessment

1. Present the unknown word with the selected synonym or definition.
   ex. The word is silence. *Silence* means no noise.
Ask your students to tell you what the word means. When they have answered, "*Silence* means no noise," reinforce the example by saying, "Yes, *silence* means no noise."
2. Present the target word in expanded context that is designed to clarify semantic and syntactic meaning.
   ex. Tom and Pete sat in the library reading their books. They didn't talk or get up from their chairs. They read in silence.
3. Present examples and nonexamples that have minimal difference.
   ex. Jason walked down the forest path. He listened to the water rush by in the stream. He heard his dog bark at a squirrel.
After presenting this example, ask the students, "Was there silence in the forest? How do you know?"
   ex. Jason continued down the forest path to a clearing. He could hear nothing; not even birds chirping.
Ask, "Was there silence in the forest? How do you know?"
4. Present expansion activities and emphasize word synonyms, categories, similarities, and differences. It is through these activities that vocabulary is developed.

Suggested Reading Related to Goals. We encourage you at this time to review the goals at the beginning of this chapter. If you feel you would like to explore one or more of these areas in greater depth, please refer to the cross-indexed bibliography at the end of the book.

7 *Understanding Comprehension*

An adequate and comprehensive theory of reading needs to encompass and interrelate all of the relative cognitive, emotional, behavioral and environmental factors.

[N. Lueers]

Goals

To help the student understand
1. The processes involved in reading comprehension
2. Schema theory development
3. Text structures and textual cohesion
4. Instructional practices that help students acquire comprehension strategies

Reading Comprehension: An Overview

In its broadest sense, reading comprehension is the acquisition of information from printed materials. If information is not processed, if comprehension has not taken place, then reading has not occurred. Reading *is* comprehension.

There are many divergent points of view regarding the exact nature of the comprehension of written discourse. For an extensive review, see Flood (1984). Briefly, the "bottom-up" theorists believe that reading takes place in two stages: (1) decoding of words and (2) reading for meaning. This viewpoint implies that reading takes place in the following way: letter identification, letter-sound correspondence, the putting together of sounds, and lexical search for word meaning. The meaning of each word in a group is used to comprehend the meaning of the group. The inverse point of view is held by "top-down" theorists. They believe that higher-order cognitive structures are used to comprehend lower-order morphemic (word) and phonological (sound) information. A third viewpoint, and one held by many theorists (Menyuk and Flood, 1981; Rumelhart, 1984), is a parallel processing or interactive viewpoint. These theorists claim that letter-sound correspondences, letter-sequence correspondences, and syntactic structures are used in parallel to arrive at the meaning of a string of words. This third view is the most reasonable position—it is based on the premise that readers must be aware of what they are doing; that is, readers must bring their knowledge of language to conscious awareness to be able to derive meaning from texts.

The process of reading becomes automatic when students become experienced readers, and when the material is lexically and structurally familiar to them. However, unfamiliar (lexically or structurally) material forces readers consciously to employ all of their world knowledge to make sense of the text.

Different reading tasks utilize different levels of language, as illustrated by Menyuk's (1984) diagram:

Type of Language Processing	*Reading Task*
Phonological decoding	
	Reading at the word level
Word retrieval	
Phrase analysis	
	Reading at the sentence level
Sentence analysis	
Integration of information Across sentences	
	Reading at the passage level
Across passages Memorial processing	

You can see that the reading process includes the following: (1) all linguistic categorizations are brought to conscious awareness in the initial acquisition of reading in the translation process, (2) materials that are structurally well within the grasp of the reader are read automatically (i.e., from page to mind), and (3) material that contains structures that are in the process of being mastered require conscious processing. Each written word is categorized phonologically and lexically; the words in a phrase or sentence are initially made comprehensible to the reader in an explicitly

Reading comprehension is the acquisition of information from printed materials. If information is not processed, if comprehension has not taken place, then reading has not occurred. (Photo by Linda Lungren.)

conscious way. Once this has been done, they are related automatically. The processing of written language, like spoken language, takes place in a parallel fashion; that is, all levels of language are referred to, when needed, to determine meaning.

Comprehension: What Is It?

At this time, researchers are not positive about every aspect of reading comprehension, but they are certain that the student who comprehends a story or text is the one who is actively involved in the written material. Reading is not a passive process; it demands active participation. The reader has to decode, search his memory, and think, think, think while processing a text.

Proficient readers perform many operations while reading; this interaction between the reader and the text, the processing of the written material, is an indivisible whole. The reader's interaction with and processing of the text occurs in the reader's mind in a moment. However, the time that it takes may not be the critical element in the reading process; the critical element may be the active participation of the reader. You can influence the active participation of your young readers in three essential ways:

1. *Motivation*—by providing interesting materials and provoking interest by setting clear, worthwhile goals.
2. *Strategies development*—by providing readers with the strategies that are necessary for comprehending stories and texts. These strategies must exist within the reader before he or she can become a full participant in reading.
3. *Concentration*—by providing teacher-generated activities that foster concentration and observation by the young reader. The activities can help your students to "zero in" on the materials that they are reading.

Reading Comprehension: Theories

Although we know that reading comprehension has to be an active process—the reader must work—we still do not have a totally adequate explanation of how reading comprehension works. In recent years, many researchers have attempted to explain the processes involved in comprehending written discourse.

As explained previously, there are three positions that are held on the nature of the reading process. Each is a point on a continuum, stressing one particular facet of the process. The continuum stretches from one end where it is believed that reading is essentially text-based (that is, the text defines the act of the reading) to the other end where it is believed that reading is essentially knowledge-based (in the mind of the reader); this view has been called the schema view of reading, based on Bartlett's (1932) notion that we have cognitive schema operating during the reading process. The text-based position is frequently referred to as a bottom-up process view of reading; that is, the text is the starting point of the reading act. The schema or knowledge-based position is frequently referred to as a top-down process view of reading.

In the middle of the continuum there is a third view of reading, one that suggests that reading is both text-based (bottom-up) and knowledge-based (top-down). This position is called the interactive process view of reading.

In the next few pages, we present models of the theories of several views of reading. Each of the designers of these theories espouses an interactive view of reading, although each can be placed on the continuum in approximately the following places:

Gough; LaBerge and Samuels	*Rumelhart; Frederiksen*	*Smith*
Text-based or bottom-up view of reading	Interactive view of reading	Knowledge-based or top-down view of reading

In studying current theories, it is extremely important to attempt to understand as much as we can about the nature of reading comprehension to plan appropriate reading curricula.

Gough's Model

Gough's model (1972) of reading is serial in nature, a chain reaction that is touched off by the initial visual fixation when the eye first focuses on a body of print. From this purely physiological function, an icon or direct visual representation of the print is transmitted to the brain. The letters in the icon are then identified and converted to phonemic (sound) representations.

Once a word has been identified, it is, in essence, put on "hold" in the primary memory, which serves as a repository for successive words until it can be ascertained whether, according to the structure and content of the sentence it is in, the first meaning found for the word is correct.

It is at this point that Gough's "wondrous mechanism" (aptly named *Merlin*) works its magic on the words in the primary memory. By sorting out the deep structure or grammatical relationships of the fragments on "hold," *Merlin* provides a semantic interpretation of the words and comprehension is achieved. At that juncture the whole, now understandable, contents of the fixation are relegated to the final memory register, the charming TPWSGWTAU (The Place Where Sentences Go When They Are Understood).

After all this has transpired and phonological rules provide the necessary instructions for pronunciation, speech is achieved and reading has been accomplished.

Gough might suggest that reading instruction should begin with letter-by-letter teaching and then progress to words. He might argue that lexical meanings are grouped into meaningful units and interpreted by the reader in conjunction with the syntactic and semantic knowledge that he or she possesses. According to Gough, the reader does not "guess" at words (as will be suggested in other models); rather, the reader "plods" along, step by step. Higher levels of comprehension (such as inferences) are not included in Gough's model.

LaBerge and Samuels's Model

The key concepts of this model are *attention* and *automaticity*. Given the limited nature of attention capabilities, LaBerge and Samuels believe that a reader can attend only to multiple tasks simultaneously when no more than one task requires full attention. For example, when decoding is an automatic task, then the reader's attention can be totally concentrated on comprehension.

The process involved for achieving comprehension as seen by LaBerge and Samuels has four components, all of which are linked with a feedback loop that interconnects. This allows for complex strategies of information processing, depending on the ability of the reader and the difficulty of the material. The four stages are

1. *Visual memory.* In this first stage of information processing, the eye transmits to the brain various pieces of orthographic information for use in letter and word recognition.
2. *Phonological memory.* The second stage involves the mapping of sounds to letters and words through both acoustic (how they sound) and articulatory (how they are formed for speech) cues. Information to accomplish this stage may be supplied from any of the other components, even as feedback from the semantic memory. This is especially true of difficult words recognized from the meaning of the context.
3. *Semantic memory.* The main function of this component is to derive meaning from the information provided by the previous two stages.
4. *Episodic memory.* This is the "optional" stage that goes to work when there is difficulty in any of the normally automatic word-recognition processes. In essence, this phase provides "booster" attention to a code, momentarily diverting full attention from the comprehension or semantic memory stage.

LaBerge and Samuels view reading as a serial acquisition of skills that are testable, sequential, and teachable. The basic skills of reading are to be "overlearned" to the point that they become automatic. One of the main ways to achieve this automaticity is by repetition and reinforcement of the skill in question.

Rumelhart's Model (1976)

Using computerized language processing as a base, Rumelhart has devised a theory of reading comprehension that utilizes the principle of interactive stages. There are no fixed steps through which a reader must progress to arrive at comprehension; rather, Rumelhart conceives of a "message center" or "pattern synthesizer" that is bombarded with information from various independent "knowledge sources." These sources represent various components of the reading process and provide information simultaneously to the message center, which generates hypotheses or expectations about what is being read. Thus information from any level of the reading process (i.e., feature, letter, letter cluster, lexical, syntactic, and semantic levels) can advance or nullify any hypothesis under consideration at a given moment.

This constant input and evaluation of information from stage to stage produce the uniquely interactive nature of Rumelhart's theory. It is both a top-down and bottom-up process. While Rumelhart's theory is predicated on the belief that a reader will begin with graphemic input and advance through the other stages to comprehension, it does allow the reader to begin at any point and work in any direction. Thus, if a reader arrives at understanding by using semantic knowledge to formulate a correct hypothesis, the top-down process is at work.

Frederiksen's Model

Another theory of comprehension was presented by Frederiksen in 1977. This model is flexible because it operates from both the top-down (the reader begins with the high-level skills of comprehension and progresses to the low-level skills of decoding) and bottom-up views, thus agreeing with Rumelhart's interactive theory.

In addition, Frederiksen accounts for the higher-level comprehension skills by generating a taxonomy of text-based inference that describes classes of comprehension operations. These classes range from the most basic lexical operations to the complex inferential task of determining the truth or value of a text. Using Frederiksen's theory, it is possible to determine the relationship between the actual elements of a piece of discourse and its comprehensibility (Marshall and Glock, 1978–79). The fact that text structure affects comprehension has important ramifications in such areas as school text selection and beginning reading instruction.

Frederiksen based his model on these assumptions:

1. A skilled reader's comprehension is based on the interaction between the high- and low-level skills in a top-down manner.
2. If a reader encounters difficulty in decoding or other low-level skills, he or she will revert to the bottom-up technique.

In addition, Frederiksen extends his theory to the act of writing by assuming that the thought process used in writing begins where the reading process ends—that is, with "knowledge structure" or area of comprehension. Starting with this broad network of what is known about the topic, a writer then decides what to put down on paper by selecting the most important information and the most effective words to convey that information.

Based on his assumptions of the comprehension act, Frederiksen believes that early reading instruction should be oriented toward achieving two main goals:

1. Teaching children to process written material in the same manner as they process oral language
2. Teaching decoding skills so the reader is not bound by the bottom-up mode

Smith's Theory

Smith's theory (1978) rejects the notion that reading is a decoding of printed words to spoken language. Smith believes that comprehension must take place first and that the indentification of individual words comes second. As an example of this phenomenon, he uses the following sentence: "We should *read* the *minute* print on the *permit*." None of the italicized words can be articulated until they have been understood in context. He believes that a reader sees four to five words ahead of and behind the actual word that he or she is reading. Research has shown that, when lights are turned out on an oral reader, the reader is able to recite the next four or five words of the passage that he or she is reading. Smith reasons that this occurs because the eye is ahead of the voice by four or five words.

Central to Smith's theory is the concept of "nonvisual information" or a previous familiarity with the manner in which words connect to form meaning. Smith believes that when the material is familiar to the reader, it is quickly comprehended. On the other hand, when the material is more unfamiliar and the vocabulary is more complex, the reader has difficulty comprehending the passage.

The main limitation of this view, however, is that it does not account for three well-known phenomena:

1. Students who have never seen most of the words that they have in their spoken vocabularies
2. Fluent readers who encounter words that they have never seen before
3. Second language learners whose aural/oral repertoire exceeds their visual repertoire

Story Schemata

In recent years, educational literature has abounded with information about students' understanding of stories and the relationship between story elements and such understanding. Marshall (1983) states, "Central to these studies is the assumption that comprehension is organized and that the closer the reader's organization is to that of the text, the greater comprehension is likely to be" (p. 617).

Stein (1979) reviewed the state of the art and reported that researchers have maintained that there is a prototype grammatical structure for all stories. She suggests that listeners recognize the structures of stories they hear (or read). Marshall (1983) reiterates that "children as young as 5 are aware of the basic story organization" (p. 616). The ultimate questions in this research are, "Does a particular structure exist in the listener (reader) or in the story itself?" "Does the structure exist in both the reader and text and does comprehension occur when the two match each other?"

Bartlett (1932) argued that a story structure ("an active organization of past reactions and experiences which are always operating in any well-developed organism") would be affected by the listener's schema when the story structure was beyond the experience of the listener and that prototypical structures exist primarily in the mind of the listener.

According to Stein and Glenn (1977), the acquisition of schematic story structures is the result of having stories told or read to the young child. The child who is read to frequently is able to generate rules about story structures, and this child is able to change the actual story in such a way that it fits with his or her schema for stories.

Schema Theory

The primary focus of recent comprehension research is on what the reader brings to the text (Wilson, 1983). This research demonstrates that schema, organized prior knowledge, plays a vital role in comprehension. Comprehension is an active process; it depends on a dynamic interactive memory structure or set of structures—schemata—used to organize and interpret what is heard or read. Dehn (1984) states, "The problem of reading comprehension . . . is one of constructing an internal conceptual representation of the story, or recognizing how the story being read relates to prior concepts and mental structures" (p. 85). What we remember, and consequently infer from a passage, seems to be affected not only by linguistic cues and semantic content, but also by the knowledge that we bring to a passage. Schema theory seems to account, in part at least, for some of the inferences we draw from our memory stores.

While the idea of schema theory has been traced to the philospher Kant, it was reintroduced to the educational community in the works of Bartlett (1932), and its definition has undergone a number of transformations in later psychological works (Rumelhart and Ortony, 1977; Winograd and Johnston, 1980).

Rumelhart (1984) defined schema as representations of all one's knowledge, from situations to events, from actions to a sequence of actions, from objects to a sequence of events. If you accept this definition, it must follow that readers have mental images for almost all their life experiences, ranging from the concrete to the abstract. Thus, when we read the word "flower," we actually have a schema for the concept of flower. This schema may include types of flowers, our experiences with flowers, and the properties of flowers. Events may be similarly encoded in our minds; therefore, when we read, we may be constantly referring to prototypic experiences that allow us to make sense of the text. For example, if we read about going on vacation, proponents of schema theory would argue that our comprehension results from our relating the book experience to our own "going on vacation" schema. Some theorists and researchers have also attempted to identify types of schemata.

Housel and Acker (1979) categorized schemata into content schema and relational schema. Content schema is "receiver stored knowledge about objects and events" (p. 14). The schemata are not specifically related to other people. Examples of this type of schemata are knowledge of historical events and mathematical theorems. Relational schema is the "expectations for the different ways people relate to one another" (p. 14). Examples of relational schemata include one-upmanship, competition, love, and hate.

Calfee (1980) suggests that one may acquire schemata through experience and/or training. Once schemata are encoded in one's memory, they result in a set of expectations; once we discover that "x" follows "w," we begin to presume "x" will always follow "w."

Along with prior knowledge, making *inferences* is a critical component of reading comprehension. Carr (1983) points out that "information that can be logically assumed may be omitted [by authors]. The reader uses information from the explicit text, plus knowledge of the world, to infer the missing information" (p. 518). Inferences are generated by matching up internal representatives encoded in the memory with the reader's existing prior knowledge (schemata). When a match occurs and an inference is generated, comprehension results. In this way, readers draw on a broad range of world knowledge, spontaneously integrating the information, making inferences, assumptions, and "best guesses." Existing schemata provide the basis for the identification and organization of the critical semantic elements of a message.

Not all researchers accept the notions of schema theory. The concept of "scripts" (Schank and Abelson, 1977) and the script elaboration model challenge schema theory advocates. Reder (1980) describes scripts as a series of causal scenes, with each action helping the next action; they capture the essence of a stereotyped sequence of actions for a familiar situation. For example, based on one's expectations of going to a market, Schank and Abelson argue that people have scripts for going to the market and that readers use their scripts to make sense of the text and to make appropriate inferences. The difference between the script and script elaboration model is the degree of emphasis placed on elaborative processing. For example, Reder claims that readers employ not only past experience to understand a current situation, but also add more information to the memory representation of the event. In the elaboration model, a "going to the market" script would also stimulate individual "idiosyncratic" embellishments of going to the market; they may include more elaborate descriptions of the script. Reder argues that this elaboration actually increases retention.

Many researchers have used the constructs of schemata, scripts, and script elaboration to explain the reader's use of prior knowledge in the reading process. For Rumelhart (1984), reading is really a reader's searching for a schemata that "offers a coherent account of the various aspects of the text." The readers are merely using their prior knowledge to make sense of the text. When comprehension fails on the part of the reader (as opposed to a lack of skill on the author's part), it may be due to a schemata deficiency wherein the reader has no experience at all with the subject, or it may be that through inattentive reading, the appropriate schemata, although existing in the reader's mind, is not summoned up to make sense of the text.

Analysis of Text

Several researchers have examined texts in an attempt to extract the structures that underlie them, giving them cohesion and making them meaningful.

Most textual structure research begins with the assumption that there are two major structural categories for prose: *narration* and *exposition*. Although this is a controversial position, it is useful in understanding the research to date. In addition to prose structures per se, researchers have also investigated the issue of text cohesion. Both issues, text structure and cohesion, are discussed in the pages that follow.

Narration

Calfee (1980) described narrative text as episodic sequential prose. Elaborations of this definition have been discussed in the literature on story grammars. Tierney and Mosenthal (1980) define story grammars as "internalized story structures"; McConaughy (1982) says that a story grammar "describes general categories for the components of a well formed story text and describes rules for the way these components are organized" (pp. 582–583). Guthrie (1977) identified common elements of narratives (setting, theme, plot, resolution) and rules that govern these elements. Other researchers have identified different types of stories. For example, Stein (1979) has classified stories as simple and multiple episodic narratives. For Stein, simple stories consist of setting and episodic structure. The multiple-episode stories consist of sequential, causal, or simultaneous happenings. In addition to conducting research on the elements and types of story grammars, researchers have attempted to identify the internal relationships of story grammars. Mandler and Johnson (1977) identified the relational terms that signal structural relations within stories; they maintain that such words as *and* and *then* signal the reader to elements in the story.

While these researchers have focused on the *what* of narrative structure, other researchers have examined the question of *how* structures are encoded. Stein and Glenn (1977) maintain that most people acquire "internalized story structures" through the telling and retelling of stories that contain such structures. As a result of familiarity with these structures, the reader or receiver uses information for hypothesis formation and testing. Flood and Lapp (1981) argue that "children and adults expect specified types of information to be explained in a fixed order within the framework of the story" (p. 36).

Story Grammars

Summers (1980) illustrated three different story grammars designed by Rumelhart, Thorndyke, and Stein and Glenn. The story *Bernie, the Bear* will serve to illustrate each grammar. Each grammar includes several categories of elements within a story; each of the grammars is slightly different.

The sentences in the *Bernie, the Bear* story are numbered. In each of the three diagrams that follow, the numbers that are included in the diagram refer to the sentences in the *Bernie, the Bear* story.

BERNIE, THE BEAR

1. Once upon a time there was a big brown bear named Bernie.
2. He lived in a dark hole deep in the forest.
3. One day, Bernie was wandering through the forest.
4. Then he spotted a big glob of honey on the stump of a tree.
5. Bernie knew how delicious honey tasted.
6. He wanted to taste it right away.
7. So he walked very close to the tree.
8. Then he licked the honey with his tongue.
9. Suddenly, Bernie was surrounded by swarming bees.
10. He had been stung by the bees.
11. He felt sad and hurt.
12. Bernie wished he had been more careful.

Rumelhart's Grammar

Rumelhart includes two major categories in his grammar: syntactic structures and semantic structures.

Syntactic Structure Categories

Action—activity by a being or by a natural force
Application—attempting to carry out a plan or desire
Attempt—formulation and application of the plan
Change of state—event of one object changing state
Consequence—outcome of the action
Desire—internal response in which one wants something and will probably try to get it
Emotion—an internal response; usually an expression of feeling
Episode—an event and reaction
Internal response—a mental response to an external event
Event—a change of state or action
Overt response—willful reaction to external event
Plan—creating a subgoal that will accomplish the desire
Preaction—activity done to allow planned action
Reaction—response to prior event
Setting—introduction of characters and conditions
State—condition of an object or stable relationship
Story—structural discourse that centers around the reactions of one or more protagonists to events
Subgoal—a goal developed in service to a higher goal

Semantic Structure

And—simultaneous relation
Allow—enabling relation
Initiate—relation between external event and reaction
Motivate—relation between internal response and action
Cause—causal relation
Then—temporal relation

His grammar is illustrated in the following diagram:

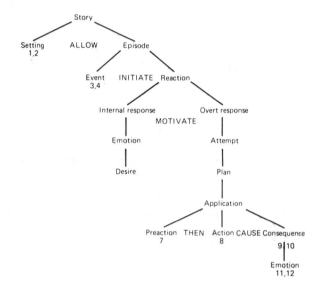

Thorndyke's Grammar

Thorndyke includes nine categories in his grammar:

1. Story—setting + theme + plot + resolution
2. Setting—character + location + time
3. Theme—stated event and goal or implied goals introduced by events leading up to and justifying goal
4. Plot—x number of episodes (cluster of actions in attempts to achieve goal)
5. Episode—subgoal + attempt + outcome
6. Attempt—event or episode
7. Outcome—event or new state
8. Resolution—final result (event) or final state
9. Subgoal and goal—desired state

His grammar is illustrated on the next page:

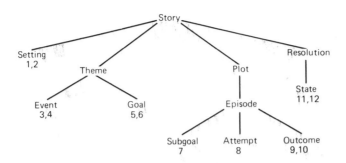

Stein and Glenn's Grammar

Stein and Glenn's grammar includes three major elements: story, setting, and episode.

Categories

Story—setting + episode
Setting—describes social and physical context
Episode
Episodic structures include five elements:

1. Initiating event—change in environment that prompts character to respond
2. Internal response—character's internal reaction including goals, effective states, and cognitions
3. Attempts—behavior motivated by internal response
4. Consequence—attainment or nonattainment of goal; results of behavior
5. Reaction—character's response to consequence; generally describing feelings and thoughts.

Their grammar is illustrated below:

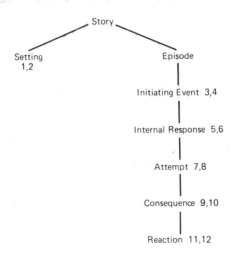

Exposition

Calfee (1980) described expository prose as an object/descriptive approach to writing. The importance of deciphering the structure of this approach has become quite important because educators realize that it is expository texts that are used to "educate" postprimary-grade students in most educational settings.

Research on the structure of expository prose has a history of working from the inside out. Rather than beginning with an overall story grammar examination of the elements and types of exposition, a review of the research shows that researchers first focused on the internal relations within the text.

Niles (1970), a pioneer in expository structural analysis research, identified four organizational patterns of internal relationships for expository writing:

Type	Example
1. Cause and effect	In history texts, causes and effects of revolutions
2. Comparison-contrast	In science texts, a comparison of planets in our solar system
3. Time-order relations	In history texts, chronological description of events
4. Simple listing	In mathematics texts, the steps in solving word problems

One of the ways that you can help your students to read expository text effectively is to help students to identify the author's organizational pattern of writing. Vacca (1973) suggests that signal words within texts announce to the reader/listener the type of organizational pattern used by the writer or speaker. In his scheme, the word "because" is tied with the cause-and-effect pattern, "however" is tied to the comparison and contrast pattern, "when" with time order, and "to begin with" with simple listing. This work is similar to the previously discussed story structure research of Mandler and Johnson (1977) and Rumelhart (1976).

In developing a grammar for exposition that is analogous to the narrative construct of story grammar, Meyer (1975) took these organizational patterns and placed them into broader categories called *content structures*.

The content structure of a passage can be pictured as a tree, with the overall shape of the tree determining the type of text. In Meyer's scheme, there are three different levels to a content structure:

Level 1   Main ideas (macropropositions)
    2   Supporting details
    3   Specific details

Expository structure research has focused on the significance of the research as well as its definition and classification. In her recent work, Meyer (1984) has summarized much of the research that validates the content structure framework. The gist of her argument is that reading comprehension is enhanced when the reader is cognizant of the structure. Meyer cites the work of Taylor (1980), Meyer (1975, 1980), Meyer and Rice (1981), Bartlett (1978), and Armbruster and Anderson (1981), in asserting that there are five basic research findings that emerge from examining the relationship between the content structure of prose and what people remember after reading it:

1. Major ideas found in the upper levels of the content structure are better remembered than are those found at the bottom.
2. The type of structure of expository relationships affects recall more when they occur at the upper levels of the content or tree structure than at the lower levels.
3. Different types of relationships have different effects on memory.
4. People skilled at identifying top-level structures have better recall.
5. People can be taught to identify different top-level structures.

In view of the research findings stating that comprehension is facilitated when readers understand the patterns of text organization, the following discussion will detail the four types of organizational patterns delineated by Niles (1970) and how they may be effectively used for reading instruction.

Cause and effect. This pattern of text organization answers the questions: "What is the cause of _____?" and "What are the effects of _____?" Cause-and-effect text organization is found in many content area materials.

Classroom application: To help students differentiate *cause* from *effect*, point out that

1. A cause may have one or more effects.
2. An effect may have one or more causes.
3. The cause must always precede the effect.

Comparison-contrast. By determining how things are alike and how they are different, comparison-contrast discourse goes beyond simple descriptions to present relationships between and among topics. Text patterns of this sort provide answers to the questions of "How are _____ and _____ alike?" "How are _____ and _____ different?" and "How are these things related to each other or yet another factor?"

Classroom application: After reading a passage that utilizes comparison-contrast as the organizational pattern, have students

1. List the differences (contrast)
2. List the similarities (comparison)
3. List any shared qualities

Time-order relations (chronology). Very often found in history texts, this discourse pattern uses sequencing of events to organize information. The obvious questions answered by chronologies are "What happened first? second? third?" and "What is the consequence of these events?" Time-order relation texts are among the easiest to recognize and comprehend because of their straightforward, time-line style of organization.

Classroom application: The following activities will help students to recognize and understand time-order relations:

1. Have the students list, in order, the events detailed in a historical passage.
2. Provide a time line that supplies only the appropriate dates. Have the students fill in information of various sorts relevant to the historical period.

    For example, fill in the blanks with the description of a typical activity for each date given.

Before 1 A.D.	A.D. 79	1709	*Mid-* 1700s
___	___	___	___
___	___	___	___
___	___	___	___
___	___	___	___

3. For a variation of activity 2, students may be encouraged to provide a pictorial time line, create a dialogue between two people of a town in each historical period, or write a newspaper headline or column that is representative of life in each period.
4. To reinforce the time-order relation text pattern further, students may wish to write a chronology or draw up a time line of their own lives, the history of their town, school, state, and so on.

Simple listing (taxonomy).   Description and classification of characteristics are typical of the listing style of text organization. This format provides information about the subject in a taxonomic structure progressing from its most general aspects to the more detailed ones. Pertinent questions concerning a taxonomic pattern of discourse are "What kind of thing is _____ ?" "What makes it so?" and "What varieties of it are there?"

The "tree" or "branching"-style outline is useful for demonstrating the relationships among the attributes of subjects discussed in a listing-style format. For example, the following "tree" diagram might illustrate a passage about the piano:

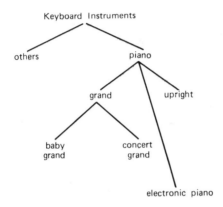

Classroom application. You can help your students to understand and utilize the simple listing format in the following ways:

1. Provide students with an incomplete outline of a listing passage and ask them to fill in the blanks.
2. Ask the students to elaborate on the simple tree diagram by answering such questions as, "What makes it so _____ ?" (popular, important, expensive, etc.) "What are the characteristics of the _____ ?"
3. In preparation to writing an original essay in the listing format, ask students to organize their information in a taxonomic diagram before they begin writing.

By encouraging the students to become familiar with text structures, you will be providing them with valuable tools for attacking many types of content discourse that might otherwise be overwhelming due solely to the complexity of the information discussed. The ability to reduce the discourse to an elemental outline form may provide the key to unlocking its meaning.

Text Cohesion

Chapman (1984, p. 266) defines cohesion as "the characteristic that makes a text a text rather than a haphazard collection of sentences." Halliday and Hasan (1976) maintain that cohesion is the relations of meaning that exist within a text. For them, cohesion occurs when the interpretation of any item in a text requires reference to other items in the text.

We have made indirect references to cohesion throughout this chapter; Niles's organizational patterns, Vacca's signaling terms, and Meyer's rhetorical relations are direct and/or indirect examples of cohesion. Halliday and Hasan add more specific descriptions to these internal relations. In their scheme, the reference device is defined as referring the reader back to a prior definite thing. Substitution refers to the replacement of one thing by another. It must be noted, however, that cohesion is more of an interpretative aid than an addition to content. As Halliday and Hasan (1976) assert, "It is the continuity provided by cohesion that enables the reader or listener to supply all the missing pieces, all of the components of the picture that are not present in the text but are necessary for its interpretation" (p. 16).

Literal, Inferential, and Critical Reading Comprehension

Many practices in the teaching of comprehension are based on the idea that there are three levels of comprehension; these levels are usually called *literal* (on the line) comprehension, *inferential* (between the lines) comprehension, and *critical* (beyond the lines) comprehension. This distinction has been useful in the past because it divided the whole world of comprehension into three manageable categories. However, many problems arose from this design because educators began to think linearly about these three levels, assuming that they represented three levels of difficulty. It was assumed that these three levels were ordered hierarchically and that literal comprehension was easier than was inferential comprehension, which in turn was easier than critical comprehension.

This idea was probably the function of reading educators' attempts to model comprehension processes in a manner similar to the way that Bloom modeled levels of cognitive functioning. Figure 7-1 illustrates the way in which reading educators attempted to create a taxonomy of reading objectives based on Bloom's notions:

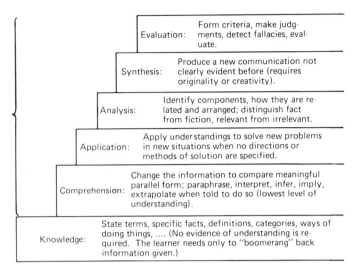

Figure 7–1. Bloom's taxonomy of educational objectives.

Bloom's taxonomy presents learning as a developmental process in which each category of the hierarchy became progressively more difficult. Mastery of one category may be dependent upon the preceding category.

Some reading educators have suggested that Bloom's taxonomy of educational objectives is closely related to the hierarchy of learning that encompasses the comprehension processes. In the past, researchers in reading have based reading comprehension taxonomies on Bloom's taxonomy. These schemata were similar to the following:

Levels of Cognitive Development	*Reading Comprehension*
Knowledge (recall)	Text explicit information (literal comprehension) Identifying sounds, letters, phrases, sentences, paragraphs Recognizing and recalling details, main ideas, sequence, comparison, cause-and-effect relationships, character traits, patterns
Comprehension (understanding)	Translating ideas or information explicitly stated: classifying, generalizing, outlining, summarizing, synthesizing
Application (abstracting)	Text implicit information (inferential comprehension) Realizing of one's experiences and textual exposures Inferring details, main ideas, sequence, comparisons, cause-and-effect relationships, character traits
Analysis (analyzing)	Predicting outcomes
Synthesis (production)	Interpreting figurative language, imagery, character, motives, and responses Synthesizing convergently and divergently

Levels of Cognitive Development	*Reading Comprehension*
Evaluation (judging)	World knowledge information (critical comprehension) Making evaluative judgments of reality or fantasy, fact or opinion, adequacy and validity, appropriateness, worth, desirability, and acceptability Valuing Detecting propaganda euphemisms, fallacy of reasoning, statistical fallacy (maps, charts), stereotyping, oversimplification
	Appreciation Emotional response to content Identification with characters or incidents Reactions to the author's use of language Reactions to the author's word pictures

Sources of Reading Comprehension

Because the three-part division of literal, inferential, and critical comprehension is still used by many publishers of reading comprehension tests and reading texts, it may be useful for you to think of this categorization scheme as an attempt to divide the sources of reading comprehension into three very important components:

1. *Literal comprehension*—extracted from text explicit information
2. *Inferential comprehension*—extracted from text implicit information
3. *Critical comprehension*—extracted from world knowledge (experience)

There are two major objections to a three-level (literal, inferential, and critical comprehension) classification scheme:

1. It is assumed that there is a linear progression of difficulty in these three levels of comprehension, and it is assumed that tasks that measure comprehension can be labeled correctly as literal, inferential, or critical.
2. The scheme only takes the source of comprehension into consideration. It does not take into account the dynamic active process of comprehension in which the reader participates. The operations of the learner during the reading process are ignored in this three-level scheme.

The first objection—the assumption that there is a linear progression of difficulty in these three levels of comprehension that can be labeled literal, inferential, or critical—stems from certain current discoveries. Let us try to determine the level that each of the following questions are measuring:

TEXT

(1) Zoe and Zeke, two talented masons, were building an internal fire-place for a cantankerous architect. (2) The architect was inflexible with his blueprints, insisting that the measurements had to be absolutely per-fect despite his annoying habit of altering the plans every 20 minutes. (3) After 3 hours of utter frustration, Zoe and Zeke thought they understood the plans. (4) As they started to lay the foundation, the architect decided he wanted an external fireplace and announced, "I think your work is unprofessional. You're fired." (5) Zoe and Zeke, quite flabbergasted, said, "Sir, you are a poor excuse for an architect and the bane of all crafts-men. Your sense of professionalism is a sham."

L, I, C

_____1. *How many times did the architect alter the plans while Zoe and Zeke were working?*

_____2. *Why did the architect tell the masons that they were unprofessional?*

_____3. *What was the masons' reaction to being fired?*

_____4. *When did the masons understand that the architect was troublesome?*

The entire passage is straightforward and comprehensible. The details of the story are explicit, and the characterizations of the architect and the masons are direct and thorough (for interpreting the author's point of view). However, the four questions, while easily answered, are quite difficult to label as literal, inferential, or critical. The source for the answer to each question is in the text, thereby making the question appear to be a test of literal comprehension, but the exact answer is not in the text. For ex-ample,

Question: *How many times did the architect alter the plans while Zoe and Zeke were working?*

Text Source: *The architect was inflexible with his blueprints, insisting that the measurements had to be absolutely perfect despite his annoying habit of altering the plans every 20 minutes. After 3 hours of utter frustration, Zoe and Zeke thought they understood the plans.*

Operation: *Convert 3 hours into 180 minutes. Divide 20 minutes into 180 minutes to arrive at the answer: 9 times.*

The answer is not stated explicitly in the text; the reader is called upon to perform certain arithmetic operations beyond the text. Therefore, you may be tempted to label the question inferential. However, it is clear that the reader has to operationalize previous knowledge (arithmetic computation) to answer the question. Does this straying from the text qualify the question for the label critical comprehension?

The difficulty of assigning the correct label is at once apparent and unnecessary. We have carefully explained the entire process of answering the question without giving the question a label. This strongly suggests that we should be investigating the *processes* involved in answering the question (in comprehending) and that we may be wasting our time by fighting over inappropriate and misleading labels.

Operations During Reading Comprehension

A second objection to a three-level classification scheme proposed by some reading educators is that it only takes the source of comprehension into consideration. This is a reasonable objection because this scheme does not account for the multiplicity of operations in which the reader participates. Let us illustrate this point by analyzing several operations that are involved in answering these seemingly literal questions:

Question: *What did Zoe and Zeke do for a living?*
Text Source: *Two talented masons*
Operations: a. *The reader has to understand apposition:* <u>Zoe and Zeke,</u>
                       <u>two talented masons</u> *means that Zoe and Zeke are two*
                       talented masons.
                    b. *The reader has to process synonymy: step 1, "do for a*
                       living" = occupation/job; step 2, occupation/job = ma-
                       sons.

While the question is easily answered, the sophistication and complexity of the operations suggest that a facile label such as "literal comprehension" is an inadequate descriptor for the entire process of comprehension. Rather, it seems important to examine each of the steps involved in the processing of the original story, the processing of the question, and the formulation of a correct answer.

It is extremely important to begin to unravel some of the processes involved in proficient comprehension. An appropriate way to begin this unraveling is to examine the operations of the reader during reading episodes. We know the following facts about readers:

1. Readers process propositions, not sentences. A proposition is a relational structure established by a predicate term and one or more argument terms; for example, in the sentence "Sharon's daughter, Johanna, is an intelligent girl," there are at least six propositions.
   Sharon is a mother.
   Sharon has a daughter.
   Her daughter is Johanna.
   Johanna has a mother.

Johanna is a girl.
Johanna is intelligent.

These propositions are not articulated consciously by the reader. In this view of reading, it is suggested that the reader is ready to accept anything that follows logically from these propositions, such as Johanna can count backward, but the reader is also prepared to examine carefully new information that does not logically follow from these propositions, such as Johanna is a boy.

2. All readers process (infer) regardless of memory demands (Flood and Lapp, 1977).
3. Readers attend to certain semantic and/or syntactic elements in the initial propositions of texts (Flood, 1978; Trabasso, 1972). An example of this phenomenon was reported by Flood (1978) when he asked proficient readers to supply the second sentence for two passages that began in the following ways:

Passage A   *Passage B*
Christmas always meant   *One of the oldest drinks*
going to Grandma's house. *known to man is milk.*

In Passage A, all readers wrote in a personal narrative (reminiscent) style, supplying a second highly descriptive sentence about the event of Christmas. In Passage B, all readers supplied a second data-filled sentence using a formal, nonnarrative style.

All proficient readers seem to participate in similar operations during comprehension. Most proficient readers, after being exposed to the following two sentences

Josie is laughing, smiling, and squealing.
She is hugging the master of ceremonies.

will probably infer something like "Josie is happy because she won the prize." The operations in which the reader participates can be described in the following way:

Type	*Example*
1. Clarification of anaphoric referent	she = Josie.
2. Superordination of strings of lexical items	laughing, smiling, squealing = happy.
3. Inferring causality	Josie is laughing, smiling, and hugging the master of ceremonies *because* she won the prize.

Although we are only at the threshold of our understanding of reading comprehension, we are coming to some agreement that we need to specify the operations that the readers must perform if they are reading with proficiency. The following system, designed by Flood and Lapp (1977) and shown in Table 7-1, is an attempt to create a scheme that is based directly on data collected from readers' processing of texts. These data were collected from readers of three age ranges (12 years old to adulthood; Flood and Lapp, 1977).

TABLE 7-1
Text Processing

Category	Text	Recall
1. Generating text identical information	soda	soda
2. Generating macro- and microstructures	couch	sofa
a. Synonomy: a narrowly defined category; traditionally acceptable synonyms. This category assumes a high degree of rater reliability. Synonyms can be conventionally acceptable such as couch/sofa (thesaurus) or text specific		
b. Colloquial (figurative) synonym: acceptable synonym within a specific context	dollar	buck
c. Superordinate: recall of the larger unit to which text belongs	bear	animal
d. Subordinate: recall of smaller unit of which text element is a part	flower	daisy
e. Categorization: generation of larger concept that encompasses several text elements	uniforms, drums, batons, marching people	parade
3. Generating cause		
a. Text proactive: extracting previous information from text that explains events as effects of causes	Jason was a lawyer. He became a dentist.	Jason realized that he had made a mistake.
b. Text retroactive: extracting subsequent information from text that explains an event as a cause	Jason liked Chicago. Jason moved to Cheyenne where he enjoyed his business	Jason moved from Chicago to Cheyenne because he didn't like his job in Chicago.
c. Experience proactive: presumptions about events that preceded and caused the existing event	Jason's business was successful.	Jason's family gave him a great deal of money.
d. Experience retroactive: assumptions about events that succeeded the existing event	Jason's business was successful.	Jason was successful as a lawyer after he sold his business and converted his business assets into client contacts.

Category	Text	Recall
4. Generating dimension		
a. Space: placing an event in space (metric or nonmetric)	Jason practiced law.	Jason's business was transcontinental, stretching from urban to rural communities.
b. Time: placing an event in time (metric or nonmetric)	Jason studied law.	In the autumn, Jason studied law.
c. Motion: recalling movement	Jason's business was transcontinental.	Jason flew from coast to coast to help his business.
d. Manner: recalling specifiable characteristics	Jason studied.	Jason studied assiduously.
5. Accommodating referents		
a. Conjunctive: joining two elements	Jason was an architect. His fellow engineers praised him.	Jason was an architect and an engineer.
b. Syncretic: merging diverse elements into a single element	Jason was an architect. His fellow engineers praised him.	Jason was an architectural engineer.
c. Disjunctive: recall of one selected element	Jason was an architect. His fellow engineers praised him.	Jason was an engineer.
d. Episodic: sequencing events in a temporally fixed, irreversible order	Jason was an architect. His fellow engineers praised him.	Jason was an architect but stopped being an architect. Then he became an engineer.
e. Additive: creating two sources to accommodate diverse information	Jason was an architect. His fellow engineers praised him.	One Jason was an architect. Another Jason was an engineer.
f. Anaphoric: establishing a referent.	They praised him.	The engineers praised him.
6. Generating case frames (traditional case grammar relations)	Jason learned law.	Jason was taught law by the faculty of Tulane Law School.
7. Generating attributes		
a. Actors	Jason studies law.	Mild-mannered Jason, the bookworm, studied law.
b. Events: attributing qualifications to events	Jason led the parade.	The parade was the grandest show in Dublin.
c. Place: adding specificity to places	Jason studied in Louisiana.	Jason studied in the humidity of the South.
d. Dimension: attributing characteristics to dimensions	He moved to Chicago.	He moved very far from Tulane.
8. Generating text erroneous information	Jason, once a lawyer, became an accountant.	Jason studied architecture, but practiced nothing.
9. Generating text external information	Jason was a lawyer.	I don't know why Jason was what he was.

SOURCE: Flood and Lapp (1977)

Instructional Strategies

As a teacher, you are probably wondering where to begin to help your students develop reading comprehension skills. Many suggestions will be presented in this chapter. For a complete review of current recommendations, see J. Flood (1984).

As a first step, we suggest that you analyze the text for difficulties that your students may encounter. Ask yourself, "Is the passage written clearly? Does it make sense?" If there are severe problems, you can (1) abandon the text and select an alternate text that is more clearly written or (2) rewrite the text, correcting it to clarify potentially troublesome areas. For example, if the text says "Dan and Dee are playing basketball, but Don is not. Don and Del are roller skating," you may want to

1. Change the names to avoid confusion.
2. Make the unclear reference to Don in the second sentence less ambiguous.

The reader could rightly wonder if the Don in the second sentence is the Don in the first sentence.

A corrected, more readable version of the text that adheres closely to original intent might be "Jay and Dee are playing basketball, but Jeffrey is not because he is roller skating with Marge."

Questioning Strategies

In addition to clarifying unclear texts, you can direct students' reading by developing comprehension tasks. The most frequently used task is *questioning*. There is an extensive body of research literature that demonstrates the importance of directing and focusing students' reading through teacher questions. It is absolutely critical for you to understand that a question is a useful tool, a stimulant for learning.

Too often in the past, teachers have fallen into the trap of thinking that a question automatically produces a certain type of thinking (a specific mental operation). The operation is done by the reader in his or her thinking processes, not by the question; the question is merely a device that may or may not stimulate the type of thinking that is desired by the teacher. We have spent a great deal of time and effort labeling questions as literal, inferential, and critical (evaluative). Much of this time and effort has been futile; we should turn our attention to examining the processes and operations that are involved during reading, remembering that questions can merely serve as *stimulants* to thinking, not as substitutes for it.

Because questions are sources for thinking, it seems obvious that we should ask our students many different types of questions to stimulate many different mental operations. It seems equally obvious that students interpret questions in many different ways; it is possible that a question that the test maker intended to elicit recall of explicitly stated information may not serve the purpose for some students. For example,

Ken Baxter, who was 15 years old, wore a costume that was far too young for him. He came as a bunny rabbit.

Question:	*What costume did the boy wear?*
Intended answer:	*A bunny costume.*
Possible answers:	*1. He wore a babyish animal costume.*
	2. His costume is appropriate only for young children to wear to parties.
	3. He was the laughingstock of the party.

Each of the possible answers is relatively correct; each strays farther from the text and the actual question, but we must be ready for interpretive answers like number 3, "He was the laughingstock of the party," if we want to fully understand the way our students make sense of texts.

Questions as Stimulants for Thinking

You may also look at questioning as a tool for ordering thinking, for putting the pieces of a puzzle together. When a student misinterprets or miscomprehends, as demonstrated by getting the single crucial question wrong, what do we know? We only know from the answer that something went awry; we need to go back to the passage and discover, with the student, the pieces of the puzzle that he or she does not understand. This retracing procedure can be done through systematic questioning that is based on the logical propositions within the text or story. The following example is based on the beginning of the children's book, *Where the Wild Things Are:*

1. *The night Max wore his wolf suit and made mischief of one kind*
2. *and another*
3. *his mother called him Wild Thing!*
4. *and Max said "I'll eat you up!"*
5. *so he was sent to bed without eating anything*

Let us suppose that you asked your readers to answer this question: "Why did Max's mother send him to bed without eating?" The answer that you might expect from your students would be similar to "Max was sent to bed without eating." To arrive at the desired response, the reader has to (1) attend to the text and (2) perform numerous mental operations simultaneously.

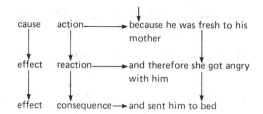

Table 7-2 illustrates that complexity of the question by listing some of the operations (processes) that a student must perform and the text source for extracting the information needed to answer this question.

If the student is unable to answer the question correctly, you, as the teacher, can retrace the reader's steps by asking logically ordered questions that require fewer operations than the original text. This set of questions may aid you to assist the reader in reconstructing the text:

Question 1:   *What did Max's mother call him on the night he made mischief of one kind and another?*

Question 2:   *Why did Max's mother call him Wild Thing?*

Question 3:   *What did Max say to his mother when she called him Wild Thing?*

TABLE 7-2
Information Processing

Operation	Text Source	Explicit	Implicit	World Knowledge
		Type of Information Processing		
1. Vocabulary: "fresh" means the reader has extracted a. tone (Max's intent) b. dialogue rules c. mother's intention in her reply	and Max said "I'll eat you up!"			x
2. Joining facts together: and = so, therefore (cause effect)	his mother called him Wild Thing and (so, therefore) Max said		x	
3. Transformational grammar deletion rule	"I'll eat you up!" (to her)	x	x x	
4. Figuring out anaphoric referents	(to her) = (his mother)		x	
5. Establishing cause	(so his mother said "Go to your room without eating anything") so he was sent to bed without eating anything			x

Question 4:   *What do you think Max's mother thought of that?*
Question 5:   *Then what did Max's mother say/do?*

Leading students through the text in this step-by-step manner may be a productive procedure for helping them to understand the interrelatedness of the entire text. The following example will help you to design similar curriculum for middle-school readers.

THE DIRECTED READING ACTIVITY

In addition to establishing an effective questioning program, you may want to use a comprehensive teaching method, the *directed reading activity*.

1. During the first stage, encourage involvement with the subject matter by calling upon your students' prior knowledge of the subject. This use of prior knowledge is the calling up of one's schema.
2. During the second stage, introduce key vocabulary terms. This stage helps students to develop schema.
3. During the third stage, springboard questions are used by the teacher to provide the student with a guide for searching for the *key* content.

The following DRA entitled "Your Heart and How It Works" by the American Heart Association, was designed by Jan Patterson to be used with a ninth- and tenth-grade coed physical education class involved in a lesson on the circulatory system. The students will be studying not only the circulatory system, but also the effects of exercise, nutrition, smoking, stress, and so on on that system. Preceding this lesson, the students saw a film called *I am Joe's Heart* about a man having a heart attack. This physical education period is 90 minutes long.

Background

Teacher: Remember that last time we were together we saw a film about an older man having a heart attack? How many of you thought that this really did not apply to you? Well here is the bad news and the good news. All of you have at least the initial stages of heart disease with cholesterol building up in your arteries. The good news is that during this unit, I am going to tell you how you can change all this. However, first we need to know how our circulatory system works.

1. Teacher draws a picture of a valentine-type heart on the blackboard and asks:
    What is this a picture of?
    Is this what your heart looks like?
    What do you know about the heart?

2. Show the film *Work of the Heart*. It lasts 19 minutes and is distributed by the American Heart Association. This film discusses the heart as the pump for the circulatory system and also shows an open heart surgery in which a valve is replaced. Answer any questions from the students after the film.
3. Have the students make a fist and hold it to the left of their sternums. Tell them
    a. Your heart is about the size of your fist.
    b. From the film we know the heart is mostly muscle and that it uses every fiber when it contracts or pumps blood.
    c. Now I want you to gently squeeze your fist (still at chest level) 25 times. Teacher counts.
    d. Now squeeze your fist as *hard* as you can 25 times. Teacher counts. Is your hand getting tired? If it isn't, you may not be squeezing hard enough.
    e. Imagine, your heart beats 70 to 90 times in 1 minute, 4,000 times in 1 hour, and about 100,000 times in 1 day.
4. Have the students listen to their own heartbeats with stethoscopes. Ask where else they can "hear" their heartbeat (carotid, neck, and wrist). Have them calculate their resting heart rate—count pulse for 15 seconds and multiply that by 4.
5. Students will then do a 3-minute step test, elevating their heart rate and checking one another's pulse from the carotid. Ask students
    What happens to your heart rate during exercise?
    What do you think is happening to your heart? blood? and lungs? during that exercise.

Vocabulary

We are going to find out just how your blood circulates and is pumped through the body, but first we need to understand some terms: "pulmonary," "atrium," "ventricle," "artery," and "vein" are written on the blackboard.

Pulmonary

Example

1. In referring to some parts of the lungs or something to do with the lungs, the word *pulmonary* is used.
2. The name of the artery carrying blood to the lungs is called *pulmonary*.

Practice

1. The doctor found a lump in John's lung. Was this a pulmonary lump?
2. There is a blood vessel that carries blood away from the lungs. Is this a pulmonary vessel?

3. The doctor lectured on a chamber of the heart. Was this a pulmonary chamber?
4. The heart was beating fast while the athlete ran. Was this a pulmonary beat?
5. There is a sac around each lung. Is this a pulmonary sac?

Atrium

Example

1. The heart is divided into four chambers; the top right and left chambers are called *atriums*.
2. The section of the heart where the blood first enters is called an *atrium*.

Practice

1. After the blood enters the heart, it is pumped into a vessel. Is this vessel an atrium?
2. The bottom section of the heart pumps blood out of the heart. Is this called an atrium?
3. The lungs receive blood from the heart into small sections along their sides. Are these called atriums?
4. The upper left chamber of the heart receives blood from the pulmonary vein. Is this an atrium?
5. Used blood from the feet and legs enters the upper right side of the heart. Is this an atrium?

Ventricle

Example

1. The two right and left heart chambers below the atriums are called the *ventricles*.
2. Blood is pumped out of the heart to the rest of the body from the *ventricles*.

Practice

1. The lower left heart chamber pumps blood to the brain. Is this chamber a ventricle?
2. There are two upper heart chambers that receive blood. Are these ventricles?
3. The doctor replaced a heart valve in the chamber that allows blood out of the heart. Did he operate in the ventricle?
4. There are two chambers on the right side of the heart. Are they ventricles?
5. Used blood that is pumped to the lungs for new oxygen comes from a ventricle. Yes or No?

Artery

Example

1. A blood vessel that carries blood away from the heart and to the rest of the body is called an *artery*.
2. A blood vessel that carries red blood full of oxygen and food to body cells is called an *artery*.

Practice

1. Is the blood vessel that carries blood to the heart called an artery?
2. There is a blood vessel that carries blood to the brain. Is this an artery?
3. An athlete needs a lot of oxygen during exercise. Does he rely on arteries for that oxygen?
4. The doctor replaced a blood vessel carrying blood away from the left ventricle. Was this an artery?
5. Is the blood vessel that carries blood from the legs to the heart called an artery?

Vein

Example

1. A blood vessel that carries blood away from the body cells to the heart is called a *vein*.
2. A blood vessel that carries bluish blood full of waste gas or carbon dioxide away from body cells is a *vein*.

Practice

1. Is blood that contains carbon dioxide carried by a vein?
2. Do arteries and veins carry the same kind of blood?
3. Through a microscope, Jim saw a blood vessel carrying blood away from a body cell. Did he see a vein?
4. Does blood travel to the lungs from the heart through a vein?
5. Is blood that contains food for body cells carried by veins?

Springboard Questions

1. How does blood get to the heart? Where does it originate?
2. How does blood travel through the heart?
3. What are the functions of the heart chambers, heart valves, and lungs?

Reading Done Aloud by the Teacher

"Your Heart and How It Works" (Figure 7-2 and Figure 7-3 from the American Heart Association, 1979)

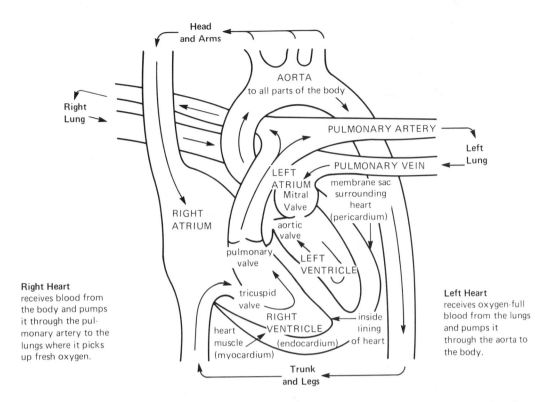

Right Heart
receives blood from
the body and pumps
it through the pul-
monary artery to the
lungs where it picks
up fresh oxygen.

Left Heart
receives oxygen-full
blood from the lungs
and pumps it
through the aorta to
the body.

Figure 7–2. *Your Heart and How It Works.* Your heart weighs well under a pound and is only a little larger than your fist, but it is a powerful, long working, hard working organ. Its job is to pump blood to the lungs and to all the body tissues.

The heart is a hollow organ. Its tough, muscular wall (myocardium) is surrounded by a fiberlike bag (pericardium) and is lined by a thin, strong membrane (endocardium). A wall (septum) divides the heart cavity down the middle into a "right heart" and a "left heart." Each side of the heart is divided again into an upper chamber (called an atrium or auricle) and a lower chamber (ventricle). Valves regulate the flow of blood through the heart and to the pulmonary artery and the aorta.

The heart is really a double pump. One pump (the right heart) receives blood which has just come from the body after delivering nutrients and oxygen to the body tissues. It pumps this dark, bluish red blood to the lungs where the blood gets rid of a waste gas (carbon dioxide) and picks up a fresh supply of oxygen which turns it a bright red again. The second pump (the left heart) receives this "reconditioned" blood from the lungs and pumps it out through the great trunk-artery (aorta) to be distributed by smaller arteries to all parts of the body. (© Reproduced with permission. American Heart Association.)

Assessment Questions

Explicit

1. The heart is about the size of a _____.
   Process: Fact retention; long-term memory recall.
   Found: First paragraph, line 3.

2. Which side of the heart receives the blood from the feet and legs? _____

                 Process: Fact retention; long-term memory recall.

                 Found: Upper left paragraph, line 1, under illustration.

YOUR HEART AND HOW IT WORKS CROSSWORD PUZZLE

ACROSS:

2. The valve between the left atrium and the left ventricle
3. The heart is classified as a ____
6. Blood vessel which carries blood to the heart
8. The heart is a little larger than your ____
10. ____ regulate the flow of blood through the heart
12. One function of the heart is to ____ blood to the lungs
14. The tough, muscular wall of the heart
16. Upper chamber of the heart
17. From the right side of the heart blood goes to the ____
18. Lining of the heart
19. Waste gas: carbon ____
20. Warning of a heart attack: pain may radiate down the ____
21. Blood vessel which carries blood from the heart

DOWN:

1. The valve between the left ventricle and the aorta
4. The valve between the right ventricle and the pulmonary artery
5. The heart pumps blood to each body ____
6. Lower chamber of the heart
7. Fiber-like bag surrounding the heart
9. Wall which divides heart cavity down the middle
11. The valve between the right atrium and the right ventricle
13. The artery/vein connecting lungs and heart
15. ____ is pumped through the body to nourish all of the tissues
16. Great trunk artery which receives blood from the left ventricle

Figure 7–3. *Your Heart and How It Works* crossword puzzle. (© Reproduced with permission. American Heart Association.)

3. Another name for the heart wall is the _____.

Process:	Fact retention; long-term memory recall; synthesis of information in two sentences.
Found:	Second paragraph, lines 1 and 2.

4. The section that divides the heart in half is called the _____

Process:	Knowing the definition of wall, "down the middle," and using them synonymously with section, and "divide in half"; fact retention; long-term memory recall.
Found:	Second paragraph, lines 5 and 6.

5. The upper two heart chambers are called _____.

Process:	Fact retention; long-term memory recall; synthesis of information within two sentences.
Found:	Second paragraph, lines 1 and 2.

Implicit

1. From which part of the body does the blood receive oxygen?

_____

Process:	Synthesis of information; inference, deduction, and recall.
Found:	Paragraph 3, lines 5 to 10.

2. When performing a physical activity, from which side of the heart does the blood come to deliver the oxygen? _____

Process:	Synthesis of information about the left side of the heart; inference and deduction.
Found:	Upper right paragraph, lines 1 to 6.

3. The mitral valve allows blood out of which heart chamber?

_____

Process:	Understanding the illustrated heart; retention of information about ventricles; fact recall.
Found:	Illustrated diagram of the heart (Figure 7-2).

4. During strenuous physical activity, the heart beats fast to bring in used blood and deliver "new" blood to body cells. What word best describes the action or job of the heart? _____

Process:	Understanding the effects of exercise on the heart; knowing the job of the heart; fact recall; knowing the meaning of the word "pump."

Found:	Paragraph 1, lines 4 to 6; paragraph 3, lines 1 to 6.

5. From which part of the heart does the aorta come? _____

Process:	Understanding the illustration; understanding the sections of the heart; synthesis of information; fact recall.
Found:	Illustration, upper right paragraph, lines 5 and 6; paragraph 3, lines 3 and 4.

ReQuest

Another useful questioning technique for helping students to understand texts is called ReQuest. The ReQuest technique can be used as a replacement for the first two stages of the directed reading activity format. The technique involves teacher-student question-and-answer sessions. The technique begins with both the teacher and student silently reading the first sentence of a passage. The teacher reads the entire passage, but the student does not; then the student asks as many questions as he or she desires. The teacher answers the questions as completely as possible. After the student has asked as many questions as desired, the teacher begins to ask questions and the student has to answer. Through this procedure, the student gains insight into the questioning process as both a participant and observer of the teacher who acts as a role model. The procedure continues until the student is capable of answering the question, for example, "What do you think is going to happen in the rest of the selection?" This procedure or technique results in the development and retrieval of one's schemata and concepts.

To illustrate the ReQuest technique, we turn now to the topic, "Spiders." The beginning of the fifth-level Laidlaw basal reader is "Many people think spiders are insects" *(Exploring Science)*. To begin the ReQuest procedure, encourage the student to ask the teacher as many questions as possible about the first line. The student may ask, "What do most people think spiders are like?" or "Why do many people think that spiders are insects?" The teacher responds with appropriate answers. At this point it would also be useful to indicate to the student the type of mental processes involved in answering the questions. This could demonstrate the process of schema formation and information retrieval (i.e., the use of prior knowledge to answer questions). The teacher could follow the student's questions with a question such as "Do you think that spiders are insects?" This procedure could be repeated with each succeeding passage until the student feels comfortable.

It should be noted that this technique can be used as a partial substitute for some of the stages of the directed reading activity, for it naturally provides help with background information as well as vocabulary words. This process, in turn, serves as a springboard question exercise.

Concept Development

Many researchers consider schema and concepts as synonymous; therefore, concept development can be seen as a form of schema development. Reading effectiveness can be enhanced through concept formation development.

Flood and Lapp (1981) suggested two ways in which concept formation can be encouraged. One technique is to share with students a broad general experience. Once the students have shared a common experience, they are asked to group the components of the experience. This involves their becoming aware of the common properties of their groups. After the categories have been established, it is recommended that the students address the issue of labeling the categories. In this manner, the students are trained in organizing concepts and, as such, schema development.

A second technique is called question initiating. The technique begins, once again, with a shared experience. From this point, the student is asked to invent as many questions as possible that result from the experience and his or her reactions to that experience. The questions are listed and categorized. In both techniques, once the categories have been established, it is necessary to discuss why items belong in a category.

To exemplify the concept formation process, we will use a lesson from a third-grade social science text (*Communities and Social Needs*, King, Bracken, and Sloan, 1977). The particular lesson that we have chosen deals with community government. To develop schema awareness through concept formation, we begin with a shared experience such as meeting with a member of city government, visiting city government, or seeing a film on city government. Then the teacher asks the students for a list or lists of what they have seen. The students may list the following: *councilmen, councilwomen, typists, visitors, security officers, discussions on police, money, fire, trash, big building, fancy offices, people working hard, people not working hard, people voting, people discussing, people arguing.*

From this list, the teacher asks the students to set up categories. They may categorize these words in three lists like the following:

Category A	Category B	Category C
big building	discussions	money
fancy offices	arguments	fire
security officers	votes	trash
councilmen	people working hard	police
councilwomen	people not working hard	
typists		

After the categories have been designed, ask students to label the categories. For example, category A could become *Things and People We Saw*, category B could become *What Government Workers Do*, and category C could become *What Government Workers Talk About*.

Once the categories and labels have been determined, a discussion regarding the similar characteristics of each item in each category can follow. This leads to a discussion on organization and the specific concepts (in this case) of the physical setting of government, the activities of government, and the functions of government.

Prediction

As previously stated, comprehension is an *active* process. As part of this process, many educators suggest that you encourage students to make predictions about a text to integrate the text into prior knowledge (Hansen, 1981; Blachowicz, 1983). Based on studies with second-graders, Hansen (1981) recommends the following procedure to stimulate this integration:

1. Prior to having the children read a story, select a few of the ideas that you, the teacher, find important.
2. Write two questions for each idea, one concentrating on previous experiences that relate to the idea and one that requires the students to make a text-related prediction.
3. Ask the students to write their answers and predictions.
4. Discuss the students' answers and predictions.
5. Ask students to read the passage.
6. Ask students to answer the follow-up questions (using both literal and interpretive questions).

To demonstrate this prediction strategy, we will use the topic of "Spiders" again. One idea that may be developed is "the functions of spider webs." To promote the comprehension of this concept, the teacher needs to ask two questions, one to stimulate prior knowledge awareness and one to encourage predictions. To stimulate prior knowledge awareness, you could ask for a list of characteristics of spider webs that students have seen. To promote predictions, you could ask children to speculate on why spiders make webs. Next, ask the students to write their lists, read the material, and answer follow-up questions.

Functional Literacy

Once you have instructed your students in concept formation, you have begun to ready them for the task of reading. However, the demands of comprehension are so complex and varied in today's world that it is important for you to go beyond this preparatory process. Let us presume that you have effectively introduced your students to a new concept and that you have prepared appropriate questions for stimulating thinking. Now it is your task to help them through new, varied, lifelike materials that require the transfer of the reading strategies that they have acquired.

The 1981 National Assessment of Educational Progress* surveyed the reading strengths of American students. Discussing the results of this assessment, Micklos (1982) stated, "Schools appear to be having difficulty instilling in older students the higher level reading skills needed for complex reading tasks" (p. 762). The findings may suggest that we as teachers need to expand our curriculum to include the teaching of comprehension strategies through materials that are relevant to older readers. The importance of such a curriculum expansion becomes obvious because we are surrounded daily by discussions of literacy. What is literacy? Who is literate? How is literacy related to reading comprehension?

Let us begin by defining functional literacy. It is obvious to most of us, as teachers, that a person considered literate by the standards of one culture may be unable to meet the literacy demands of another culture. Therefore, literacy tests must be suitable to assess the competencies of the general population with regard to life-coping tasks rather than only being applicable to a small part of the population. Once this issue has been addressed, it becomes necessary to ask, "Literacy for what purpose?"

The *advancement of literacy* is a basic goal of American education. The success of achieving this goal is often questioned as America continues to become an ever more *visual* nation, where films often replace rather than supplement books and television supplants general newspapers and journal reading. At this time, when Americans appear to be spending less time with reading materials, we are witnessing an increase in both political propaganda and marketing advertisements. Every day consumers are required to make decisions regarding insurance, taxes, applications, credit loans, personal purchases, and government organizations. Can a person be considered literate if he or she can perform only academic tasks? If the answer is yes, one wonders why so many students have evidenced success in school subjects, yet seem to have difficulty with high-level comprehension tasks.

Consider the following examples:

A program designed to foster literacy is extremely complex because it must include the development of language arts and computational skills as well as provide application strategies necessary in making decisions in life-coping situations. The following outline is presented in an attempt to explain this duality further:

I. Do you have the academic skills of literacy?
    A. Language arts
        1. Spoken language

---

*The National Assessment of Educational Progress (NAEP) is an information-gathering project that surveys the educational attainments of 9-year-olds, 13-year-olds, 17-year-olds, and adults (26 to 35) in ten learning areas: art, career and occupational development, citizenship, literature, mathematics, music, reading, science, social studies, and writing. Information regarding any such surveys may be obtained by writing to NAEP, Suite 700, 1860 Lincoln Street, Denver, Colorado 80203.

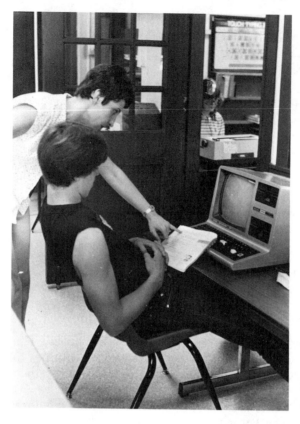

A program designed to foster literacy is extremely complex because it must include the development of language arts and computational skills, as well as provide application strategies necessary in making decisions in life-coping situations. (Photo by Linda Lungren.)

Are you able to communicate in the dominant language of the culture?
2. Written language
   Can you express yourself through the written language of the dominant culture? (syntax, semantics, spelling)
3. Reading
   Can you critically comprehend the printed materials of the dominant culture? (perceive, infer, evaluate, apply)

B. Computation
   Can you add, subtract, multiply, divide, compute fractions and percentages, interpret graphs and thermometers?

II. Can you apply these skills to life-coping situations?
   A. Personal
      1. Restaurant functioning
      2. Driver's license application
      3. Transportation schedules
      4. Instructional manuals
      5. W2 forms
      6. Grocery slips
      7. Bank slips
      8. Insurance forms

      9. Savings accounts
     10. Home purchases
  B. Career
    1. Employment ads
    2. Pension plans
  C. Health
    1. Medications
    2. Health care
  D. Civic responsibilities
    1. Community resources
    2. Consumer economics
    3. Environmental issues

A curriculum designed to produce literate citizens must stress the *application* of basic academic skills to life-coping situations. To accomplish this task, students must be introduced to a common set of materials that is used by all people when they are involved in their daily functions.

Persuasion

Students need to be introduced to the art of persuasion to comprehend texts fully. They have to be able to ask themselves such questions as, "What is the author's point of view?" "Is this a biased accounting of the facts?"

The theme of persuasion, the art of persuasion, and the art of persuading are certainly not new. Throughout history, people have attempted to *influence*, or persuade, others. Persuasion, which can utilize a variety of techniques, often uses forms of *propaganda* to promote products, ideas, and people. Propaganda involves one person or group's deliberate attempts to persuade another person or group of people to accept a differing point of view or action. The base of propaganda is heavily laden with syllogism.

SYLLOGISTIC REASONING

A *syllogism* is an argument whose conclusion is supported by two premises. One of these premises, the major premise, contains the *major* term, which is the *predicate* of the conclusion. The other, the *minor* premise, contains the *minor* term, which is the subject of the conclusion. Common to both premises is the *middle* term, which is excluded from the conclusion.

A common example of syllogistic, or deductive, reasoning is the following:

        A is B
        B is C
        therefore
        A is C

In this instance,

$$A \text{ is } B \quad \text{(major premise)}$$
$$\downarrow$$
(major term)

$$B \text{ is } C \quad \text{(minor premise)}$$
$$\downarrow$$
(minor term)
$$\qquad B \quad \text{(middle term)}$$
$$A \text{ is } C$$

Consider the following examples:

A. All people are human.
B. Sean Livingston is a human.
C. Therefore, Sean Livingston is a human.

Is this conclusion correct? Yes, when the *major* and *minor* premises are true, the conclusion is true.

However, consider the following:

A. All redheads have a gift for music.
B. Larry Johnson is a redhead.
C. Therefore, Larry Johnson has a gift for music.

Although this is syllogistic reasoning, the conclusion is false because the major premise is false. Critical readers (and listeners) must learn to distinguish between *valid reasoning* and *truth*.

In an attempt to influence one's intended audience, it is a common device to present an argument in a manner that is *valid* but then to use major and minor premises that are false. If one is not a critical *thinker*, *reader*, and *listener*, it is quite easy to be fooled by what appears to be a logical argument or syllogistic reasoning.

Remember, *all* persuasion is not *negative*; neither does it all contain *falsehoods*. Some persons or groups may be interested in persuading us to do good, happy, enjoyable, and morally sound things. Therefore, the reader or listener must be trained to detect the underlying *message within the message*. The critical reader or listener engages in an evaluative process that makes possible the determination of written or spoken propaganda. As readers and listeners, we are confronted daily with persuasion, or propaganda, from newspapers, magazines, textbooks, radio, movies, and television.

Consider these examples:

A. You're in good hands with Allstate.
B. Four out of five dentists surveyed recommend sugarless gum for their patients who chew gum.

Aren't the statements in these advertisements the major premises or syllogisms? For example,

A. You're in good hands with Allstate.
B. I want to be in good hands.
C. I should get Allstate insurance.

or

A. Four out of five dentists surveyed recommend sugarless gum for their patients who chew gum.
B. I want to follow the recommendation of four out of five dentists.
C. I ought to chew sugarless gum.

The basic line of each of these advertisements is a *major* premise within syllogistic reasoning. The reader/listener must be alerted to propaganda's appeal to his or her emotions, interests, needs, desires, fears, and prejudices. The questions posed by the critical reader are virtually the same as those needed for propaganda detection. Critical reading involves students posing and answering such questions as

What do you think happened next?
Why do you think this happened?
What other things might have happened?
How would you have acted differently?

Critical thinking requires an understanding of the many ways in which other people or groups attempt to influence our thinking. Propaganda techniques are easily detected in advertisement. The following are common forms of propaganda that are used to influence consumers. We have selected one product—cereal—to illustrate how a noncritical thinker/reader/listener can be influenced to buy a particular product. Although these examples are designed to exert positive influence, the same techniques can be used to effect negative outcomes. You may wish to present these techniques to your students because they are the primary audience for whom cereal commercials are designed.

PROPAGANDA TECHNIQUES

Bandwagon

COAST TO COAST, MORE MOTHERS BUY *RINGOS* THAN ANY OTHER CEREAL.

Although the bandwagon approach attempts to convince you that the vast majority of consumers prefer a particular product, it fails to alert you to the options.

Prestige

GOLD MEDAL WINNER PAT PUSHTON EATS *CRINKLES* CEREAL.

The prestige approach implies that you might be more like this famous personality if you were to use this product.

Testimonial

> WALT DRIVER, GOLF PRO, SAYS, "I EAT *TOGGLES* CEREAL EVERY MORNING AND YOU SHOULD, TOO."

The testimonial approach not only implies that you will be like the golf pro, but it also tells you what this famous personality believes is good for you.

Repetition

> REMEMBER, *STARS AND BARS* IS NOT JUST FOR BREAKFAST. IT'S SO GOOD YOU'LL WANT TO MUNCH, MUNCH, MUNCH *STARS AND BARS* FOR LUNCH, LUNCH, LUNCH.

Repetition creates a catchy jingle that is easily repeated.

Plain Folks

> THE PRESIDENT OF *AWAKE* CEREAL WAS ONCE A GARDENER. SHE STILL ENJOYS COFFEE CLUBS WITH NEIGHBORHOOD MOTHERS.

This type of propaganda implies that the president is just one of the family; therefore, she would never cheat or sponsor an unreliable product.

Snob Appeal

> ALL THE FAMILIES IN ROLLING HILLS ESTATES EAT *MORNING STARS.* DO YOUR KIDS EAT *MORNING STARS?*

Snob appeal suggests that if you want to be considered a member of the upper class, your children must be Morning Star eaters.

Emotional Word Appeal

> MOTHERS WHO CARE BUY *SWEETO* CEREAL FOR THEIR CHILDREN.

This approach certainly implies the criterion necessary for successful motherhood.

Authority

> MOST DOCTORS AGREE THAT *MEGAVIT* CEREAL IS BETTER FOR YOUR HEALTH.

Not only are you not informed as to what Megavit is better than, but you are also influenced by the fact that physicians have attested to its value.

Transfer
Although words may not be used to influence you, a picture is presented of a healthy child holding a box of Megavit cereal. You are encouraged to draw the conclusion that your child can be just like this if she eats Megavits.

Labeling
A catchy label such as ZAP easily becomes part of your vocabulary. You look for it at the grocery store.

Ego Building

ARE YOU BRIGHT ENOUGH TO BUY *SUNNY DAY* CEREAL?

Is there any one of us who is not anxious to be labeled bright? We have the incentive to be readily persuaded.

Image Building

EAT *IRON BUILDERS* CEREAL AND YOU'LL BE LIKE ATLAS.

Again for the many, many people who wish to be a powerhouse of physical or emotional muscles, this becomes the perfect persuasive gimmick.

Oversimplification

EATING *STARLIGHT CEREAL* MAKES YOU FEEL HEALTHIER AND HAPPIER.

How easy life is if only one follows the reasoning presented in this method of persuasion.

Buckshot
This persuasive method utilizes many approaches in a direct attempt to strike as many individuals as possible.

Smith (1963) suggests that, to help children learn to analyze propaganda, they should be trained to ask and answer the following questions:

1. Who is the propagandist?
2. Whom is he (or she) serving?
3. What is his (or her) aim in writing on this subject?
4. To what human interests, desires, emotions does he (or she) appeal?
5. What technique does he (or she) use?
6. Are you or are you not going to permit yourself to be influenced through the tactics of this propagandist? (pp. 276–277)

One procedure that acquaints students with types of propagandists, as well as aids them in developing a questioning habit regarding propaganda, is to designate a specific wall chart, scrapbook, or bulletin board as a propaganda center. Students then collect propaganda statements found in ballads, public speeches, posters, leaflets, journals, reports, newsletters, pamphlets, textbooks, newspapers, novels, radios, conversations, and button slogans. Categorizing statements by propaganda type will provide students with practice in answering the questions posed by Smith. Eventually this process of analysis will become automatic.

In addition to asking high-level questions and alerting students to propaganda techniques, you may need to offer demonstrations that will supply students with needed conceptual information. Experimenting with manipulating liquids, clay, and beads often encourages intellectual developmental processes. The selection of activities is dependent on the developmental stages of your students. Demonstrations may aid learning for some students who have reached a particular developmental stage, but it may be ineffective for those without sufficient "readiness." You must be *sensitive* to the developmental stages at which your students are operating.

Although many sociopsychological factors affect a student's learning, studies by Crossen (1948), McKillop (1952), Groff (1962), and Johnson (1967), have emphasized that the student's *attitude* toward a particular topic affects his or her ability to draw inferences from the materials. Merritt (1967) suggests that it is the primary job of the classroom teacher to sequence instruction in reading to elicit desired comprehension behaviors. Merritt further cautions us that competency in reading comprehension can be developed *only* when materials are used in sequence according to the experiential readiness of the student.

As you attempt to implement any type of instruction designed to further the development of your students' reading/literacy and comprehension skills, keep in the mind the following points:

1. Students must be able to decode and understand the words in context before they can critically evaluate the validity of their content.

2. Students must be able to gain needed information through interpretation of *all* graphic aids pertaining to the material that they are being asked to read.

3. Students cannot critically evaluate beyond their experiential and reasoning capacities.

4. Students must be encouraged to suspend judgments based on personal experience until they fully understand the presentation of the reading passage.

5. Students may need to be introduced to prereading activities that will expand their experiential backgrounds. Such expansions may be a must if you are asking them to draw conclusions that rely heavily on personal experiences.

6. Students are better able to accomplish a reading task if the objectives of the task have been clearly defined.

7. Students may be better able to react critically to a written passage if the author is somehow similar to the child in age or ethnic background.

Lesson Guidelines

When you actually plan a lesson that is intended to foster comprehension development, you must

1. *Establish a purpose.* Ideally, the purpose of the lesson should be closely tied to the students' lives (planning the arrangement of the classroom, selecting a new game, discussing a classroom activity). Although your topic cannot always be totally related to the students' lives, it can be presented so that it establishes a new interest or capitalizes on an existing interest. Plan questions that will tap appropriate types of comprehension.

2. *Select materials.* The materials being selected should lend themselves to the teaching of a specified skill. Fiction, nonfiction, games, workbooks, and high-interest/low-vocabulary materials are only a few examples of the extensive resources that are available to you. Remember that the selected materials should help you to accomplish the purpose of the lesson.

3. *Plan experiences.* Through questions, materials, and follow-up activities, you will need to provide each student with opportunities to develop skill in finding main ideas, finding supporting details, detecting the organizational plan of the material, detecting sequential arrangements, adjusting reading rate, and critically evaluating work.

The ability to comprehend printed material involves myriad skills that are not acquired as a once-and-for-all process. To learn and continue to comprehend requires continuous attention. As classroom teachers you must continuously supply activities and questions that help students in the developmental process of comprehension.

Materials

Any written document is a potential source for teaching students how to comprehend texts. Any story, poem, essay, newspaper article, diary entry, or timetable can be used to help students to improve their comprehension.

Many publishers have designed extremely effective comprehension development materials. *Comprehension Plus* was developed by Flood and Lapp (1983) to provide supplementary materials for teaching comprehension. Each lesson in the six grade-level series (A–F) is a self-contained instructional unit. The student is introduced to the focus skill before he or she is expected to use it in comprehending a text. Special emphasis is given to vocabulary development and using the newly learned strategy in context. A sample lesson on distinguishing fantasy from reality is provided on the following pages.

Suggested Readings Related to Goals.   We encourage you at this time to review the goals at the beginning of this chapter. If you would like to explore one or more of these areas in greater depth, please refer to the cross-indexed bibliography at the end of the book.

LESSON **18**

Look at the picture of Tina. Is Tina really a queen? No. Tina is **imagining** that she is queen.

You can imagine many things that are not real. When you imagine something, it doesn't really happen. It happens only in your mind.

Read the story below. Draw a circle around each sentence in the story that tells something that could not be real.

Harry did not like to drink milk. One day his mother said, "If you drink your milk, you will grow big and strong." Harry drank his milk. Then Harry said, "I am growing as tall as a mountain. I am so strong that I can pick up a big truck. I am going to drink some more milk. Then I will be able to touch the moon!"
Harry could see himself grow bigger and bigger. He imagined himself touching the moon.

Here is a **tip**.   Sometimes the people in a story imagine things that are not real.

Read the story below. Can you tell what is real and what Tommy imagined?

Too Much TV?

Tommy Dale's mother was taking him to the <u>dentist</u>. Tommy wanted to stay home and watch TV.

"Now I won't know how the <u>space</u> show ended," Tommy said to his mother.

"That's all right," she said as they walked into the dentist's office. "They all end the same way. The good guys and the bad guys shoot at each other with their ray guns."

"And the good guys win," Tommy said.

"That's right," his mother said. "Now hurry. The dentist is waiting for you. I'll be right here in the waiting room."

Tommy went into the office. He sat in the chair and looked up at the dentist. The dentist told Tommy to open his mouth so he could shoot some X-rays.

As Tommy looked up, he saw a green spaceman holding a ray gun. "Oh, no, you don't!" Tommy shouted. He jumped out of the chair and ran out of the room. "Mother! Mother! He's trying to shoot me! He isn't a dentist. He's from space. He told me to open my mouth. And I did. Then he said he was going to shoot some X-rays. He was going to shoot me in the mouth with a ray gun!"

"Oh, Tommy! You have been watching too much TV," said his mother as she walked him back into the dentist's office.

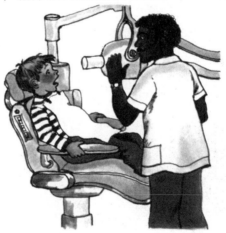

Word Hunt

Write the underlined word from the story to finish each sentence.

1. Tommy watched a TV show about places that are not on

Earth. It was a _____ show.

2. Tommy went to the _____ to have his teeth checked.

3. _____ are pictures of your teeth.

Something to Think About

Draw a line under the sentence in each pair that tells what Tommy imagined.

1. The dentist was from space.
Tommy liked to watch space shows.

2. Tommy sat in the dentist's chair.
The dentist was going to shoot Tommy.

3. The dentist was a green spaceman.
The dentist was going to take pictures of Tommy's teeth.

4. The dentist had a ray gun.
The dentist used an X-ray machine.

Something More

Look at the picture below. Write a sentence about it that could be real. Then write a sentence about it that could *not* be real.

Could Be Real

_____

_____

Could *Not* Be Real

_____

8 *Essential Study Skills*

If the goal is to help students learn from text, there is a need for major changes in our expectations for students and instructional support, regardless of the changes or improvements to text.

[R. Tierney]

Goals

To help the student understand
1. The importance of teaching reading study skills
2. Individual reading study skills

Reading study skills can be viewed as *tools* that help students to gather information or knowledge in a particular area or field of study. Lamberg and Lamb (1980) define *study skills* as "procedures, strategies, or techniques used by students to consciously direct their academic performances" (p. 407). Shepherd (1978) asserts that "the goal of the study skills is the student's total independence to gain information for himself" (p. 112). By helping students to acquire and use study skills, we are helping them become *independent learners.*

The reader's ability to use study skills to expand learning is referred to as metacognitive monitoring. Flavell (1976) described metacognition as

one's knowledge concerning one's own cognitive processes or products as anything related to them, e.g., the learning of relevant properties of information or data. For example, I am engaging in metacognition (meta-memory, metalearning, metaattention, metalanguage) if I notice that I am

167

having more trouble learning A than B; if it strikes me that I should doublecheck C before accepting it as fact; if it occurs to me that I had better scrutinize each and every alternative in any multiple-choice type task situation before deciding which is the best one; if I sense that I had better make a note of D because I might forget it. (p. 232)

Many study skills are applicable to all content areas; some are more specifically related to a particular area of study. For this reason, the topic of study skills will be analyzed twice in this text. In this chapter we will discuss generally those study skills that are needed by students to experience success in learning in all content areas, and in Chapter 9 we will explore the interpretation of these same study skills within specific content areas of study (math, science, social studies).

Organization

Primary Years

For most children, a sense of order or organization begins to develop at home (e.g., "Please hang up your jacket"; "Put the book back on the shelf"). Because success in using organizational skills depends on the ability to perceive relationships, this early organizational training is promoted in school.

Grouping items of the same size, shape, or color is a simple starting point for developing organizational skills. These skills are refined by grouping objects of varying shades of the same shape, but different sizes, from largest to smallest, or vice versa.

CATEGORIZING

First-grade children are ready to advance to organizing words and sounds. You might ask them to classify words that have the same beginning, medial, or ending sounds, for example,

camp	fill	bag
coat	sit	rug

Children can also categorize words that have related meanings; for example, you might ask them to group all the words that name actions or all the words that name types of jobs.

The order of organization, *sequence*, is an important skill with which students should become familiar early on. Younger students particularly need guidance in organizing their thoughts and ideas. One enjoyable activity is arranging pictures or cartoons in a logical sequence so that they "tell a story." Another way to guide young students in developing a sense of sequence is to solicit ideas for a group story. You do this by encouraging them to consider the appropriate sequence of events. Once the story is composed and recorded on a chart, it may be cut into sentence strips

You can use the organization of materials in your classroom to foster the development of organizational skills. (Photo by Linda Lungren.)

so that students can read the sentences and then reconstruct the original story.

Students must be able to see relationships among ideas to develop organizational skills. For example, after hearing or reading a story that takes place in a foreign land, ask them to identify the things in the story that indicate the setting of the story. Another approach is to have them write ideas about two characters (R2D2 and Luke Skywalker) from a story they know; you can then mix them up and ask the students to regroup the ideas that relate to each character.

You can use the organization of materials in your classroom to foster the development of organizational skills. Through classroom discussions, students help to plan the organization and placement of these materials. Then individuals or small groups of students (on a rotating basis) can be responsible for returning items to their proper location.

SUMMARIZING

Summarizing is a skill that people use throughout their lives (What was the movie about? Why did you enjoy that book?). Summarizing requires the ability to select the most significant points in a story, incident, or report and to relate them in a sequential order. Summarizing should be introduced during the primary years and refined in the later grades. Taylor (1983) suggests that "teachers should probably spend more time on summaries at all levels of schooling" (p. 527). Furthermore, Brown, Campione, and Day (1981) remind us that "the ability to provide an adequate summary is a useful tool for understanding and studying texts." You can ask primary students to tell about some event or story in their own words. Even at these early levels you can begin building organizational skills with students through examples and discussions. We suggest that you

1. Encourage students through questioning to observe the structure of the material being read by having them ask themselves
   a. Am I reading an essay within a book or a total book?
   b. What clues do the pictures give me?
   c. What clues does the title give me?
   d. What do the subtitles give me?
   e. Is there a summary?
2. Survey lessons with students to determine the language clues that enable the student to better understand the author's organizational structure by asking
   a. Are there clue words that add to the total idea?

in addition	since	moreover
and	furthermore	too
another	otherwise	as well as
also	likewise	plus
again	besides	after all

   b. Are there clue words that emphasize the concluding idea?

finally	in conclusion	thus
in sum	consequently	in the end
in brief	hence	then
at last		

   c. Are there clue words that emphasize reversing, qualifying, or modifying ideas?

but	on the other hand	in contrast
nevertheless	either-or	even if
still	conversely	however
opposed to		

   d. Are there clue words that indicate thought emphasis?

| because | as |
| like | for instance |

   e. Are there clue words that indicate relationships in time, space, or degree?

last	here	many
now	there	more
later	close	little
after	for	some
previously	by	best

following	away	all
meanwhile	under	fewer
at the same time	above	greater
before	across	above all
immediately	beneath	worst

3. Encourage awareness of the headings and subheadings of the material being read.
   a. Position on page
   b. Type of print
4. Discuss the informational clues offered through headings, subheadings, and organizational pattern.
5. Read materials with students and ask questions that focus on organizational structure.
   a. What are the major headings? subheadings?
   b. Were time relationships evidenced through headings?
   c. Were irrelevant subheadings included?
   d. Were more subheadings needed?
   e. Was a summary provided?

6. Develop note-taking skills.
   a. Begin reading a story.
   b. Stop when the emphasis of the story shifts.
   c. Write a sentence that summarizes what was read.
   d. Write a phrase containing the main points of the sentence.
   e. Continue reading and repeat this process each time the emphasis of the story shifts.

Intermediate Years

As students enter the intermediate school years, they encounter materials that present more complex ideas that are written in more complex forms and writing styles. At the intermediate level, the emphasis is on expanding the organizational skills developed in the early years to help students deal with more difficult materials. The development of organizational skills helps students to realize relationships among facts. Once a student has identified the organizational structure of the material, he has an operational base from which he can synthesize, compose, and evaluate newly learned facts.

Students must learn to recognize the way an author structures ideas and fits information together. Vacca (1981) points out that "the perception of organizational patterns-relations in single sentences, in paragraphs, and in long text passages has been considered basic to comprehension by many authorities in the field of reading" (p. 141). This study skill enables the reader to follow the author's plan by recognizing organizational patterns, major ideas, and details. The common organizational patterns used by authors include time order, enumeration, comparisons, contrasts, and cause-and-effect relationships.

You can help your students to recognize common organizational patterns by pointing out that they are often suggested by the author's choice of signal words. Examples of signal words are

Time order	before, after, when, on (date)
Enumeration	first, next, finally, then
Comparison	like, similarly, as well as
Cause and effect	because, since, therefore, as a result

OUTLINING

Outlining can be a difficult skill to master if its foundation—organization—is not taught throughout the primary grades.

The basis for success in outlining lies in being able to understand the content that one is trying to outline and in being able to grasp the relationships among the ideas involved. The foundation for development of this skill is found in the primary skills: classifying (grouping ideas) and summarizing.

Friedland and Kessler (1980) reported that they were successful in teaching outlining to intermediate-level students through the use of a practical exercise. They introduced the concept of outlining (without naming it) by asking students how they could best arrange the contents (everything from clothing to pencils to gum wrappers) of a messy dresser. The next exercise was preparing and organizing a classroom inventory. Only then did the students advance from classifying items to classifying ideas: "from the simple and concrete to the complex and abstract."

The concept of outlining can be developed easily and naturally if you make a list of related ideas into a simple format. These lists may have the more important ideas set off by numerals and the supporting ideas indicated by letters. Move first into the use of major ideas, with supporting ideas indented, and then add letter and number designations.

As more formal outlining is practiced, a few basic principles of outlining should be taught. They are illustrated in the following form:

Topic

I. A Major Idea
  A.
    1.
      a.
        (1)
          (a)
          (b)
        (2)
      b.
    2.
  B.

This simple outline form goes as far, and perhaps farther, than the majority of elementary students will be able to go in understanding and outlining material. Ultimately, the student needs to understand that the purpose of outlining is to help him or her identify main ideas and supporting ideas in some body of information. The students must understand that the author has already designed an outline for the material; they have to interpret and use the outline as a clue for comprehension.

One of the easiest ways to help your students identify topics and subtopics is to provide them with an incomplete outline of a text excerpt. You provide the main topics and have the students supply the missing topics and subtopics. For example, give your students a text excerpt such as the following, which discusses two types of water pollutants:

> Chemical pollutants come mainly from industrial plants. In fact, industry—factories, mills, and mines—accounts for more than half of all water pollution. Insect sprays and artificial fertilizers used in agriculture are also responsible for the chemical pollution of water. There are other forms of chemical pollution. For instance, many detergents we use contain substances called phosphates. These phosphates make detergents act more quickly. However, they also pollute the waters in much the same way fertilizers do.
>
> Sewage comes mainly from cities and other communities that dump waste, including that of humans, into lakes and streams. Water pollution also comes from sewage treatment plants and septic tanks. (Hartley and Vincent, 1983, p. 500)

After reading the passage, ask students to complete an outline similar to the following:

Water Pollutants

Topic I.   There are several types of chemical pollutants.

Subtopic   A.
Subtopic   B.
Subtopic   C.

Topic II.   Sewage from cities pollutes the water.
Subtopic   A.
Subtopic   B.

The following activities can also help students to understand the significance of main headings and subheadings:

1. After students have read only chapter headings and subheadings, ask them to discuss the information they expect to be contained in each.
2. Encourage students to write a story summary using only the information provided in story headings and subheadings.

3. Ask students to read several paragraphs and develop a heading for each paragraph.
4. Select several newspaper articles. Remove the titles. Ask students to read the articles and select the appropriate title.

In addition to main topics and subtopics, students need to understand (1) the format of an outline and (2) the different types of outlines.

Format

Some students experience difficulty with outlines because they do not understand the relationships presented in the organized text structure. A student must be taught that in an outline, he does not use a "I" unless he has information for "II." He may continue on through "III," "IV," "V," and so on, but unless the information can be broken into at least two parts of equal importance, he does not break the idea away from the preceding heading of greater importance. Therefore, if he has "I," he needs "II;" if he has "A," he needs "B"; if he has "1," he needs "2," and so on.

Types

The two basic types of outlines are the sentence outline and the word or phrase outline. The type of outline chosen is determined by the student's own needs and the complexity of the material. If a great deal of time is going to elapse between development and use, the student may want to use the sentence form because it will be easier to remember later. The word or phrase outline is very useful for study purposes or when giving an oral review of printed materials.

Sentence Outline

Birthday Events

I. The morning of my birthday we went to the zoo.
   A. We saw many unusual animals.
   B. Some of the animals performed tricks.
II. In the afternoon I had a party.
   A. Mom got me a blue skateboard.
   B. Everybody ate cake and ice cream.

Word or Phrase Outline

Birthday Events

I. Zoo in morning
   A. Unusual animals
   B. Animal tricks
II. Party in afternoon
   A. Blue skateboard
   B. Cake and ice cream

Most educators recommend that the different forms not be mixed, especially when the skill is first being learned. After a student becomes more skilled, she may find a mixture more satisfactory when preparing an outline for her personal use.

NOTE TAKING

Taking notes is a valuable study skill, particularly as students begin to encounter content area materials. Rickards (1980) discusses two possible functions of note taking:

1. Note taking may facilitate comprehension and recall of facts through "encoding" of material.
2. Note taking plus reviewing notes may be productive of recall.

You will find some students who resort to paragraph lifting in the name of note taking. These students particularly need your help to make use of different clues and cues in the text. Reemphasize focusing attention on topics and subtopics. Then have the students read the material accompanying their topics and subtopics and make notes in a form that they can understand and reuse. The notes should paraphrase the most significant information in the material. To take good notes, the student must

1. Be able to pick out the important points and related ideas
2. Realize the value of listening or reading before summarizing or paraphrasing
3. Write notes in his or her own words
4. Write brief notes
5. Use structural clues: *first, most important, finally*
6. Invent an independent abbreviation code
7. Be consistent
8. Develop a topical note filing system that includes a bibliographic reference to topic, date, and purpose of notes

As a class activity, you might read a selection with your students and then discuss which ideas should be recorded as notes. Be sure that students understand that notes should include who, what, when, where, why, and how.

Students who have difficulty with note taking may not have mastered the skill of summarizing. You may wish to reteach or review summarizing and plan activities that help students to identify main ideas of paragraphs and passages.

SUMMARIZING AND SYNTHESIZING

In the intermediate grades, students begin to get involved in projects such as report writing, which require synthesizing and restating information gathered from many sources. This process is related to locational skills as well as to the ability to organize. Synthesizing requires the use of note taking, outlining, and summarizing skills.

The student must be able to

1. Identify sources of information
2. Use these sources effectively
3. Synthesize the information into meaningful, logically ordered whole

As a student becomes competent in the use of a few sources, the number can be gradually increased. Students must also have a knowledge of suitable sources from which information may be gathered.

Summaries and synthesizations are both similar to outlines in that they all contain major facts and minor details in the student's own words. A summary presentation may take the form of a paragraph, a listing of events, or a record of procedural steps. To help develop these skills, you might have students read a text excerpt that contains a summary; then ask them to

1. List the main ideas and important details.
2. Discuss their reasons for including these ideas and details.
3. Determine if these bits of information are contained in the summary.
4. Analyze the different styles used to present major and minor points in the text and in the summary.

Graphic Aids

Graphic aids include pictures, charts, graphs, maps, and tables; they can be valuable tools to enhance learning. Hawkins (1980) particularly encourages the use of graphs in the classroom: "Graphs can make astronomical numbers understandable. Statistical data can be presented in simple and interesting forms through these devices. Comparisons can be made. Relationships which are not readily grasped from tables or statistics or narratives can be shown and clarified" (p. 1). Educational research also supports the use of graphic aids. In a study on the effect of pictorial aids, Truman (1981) reported that students learn better with pictures than without pictures.

You can help students to recognize the value of graphic aids by preparing materials that have an obvious relevance to their lives. Some examples might be

1. A table showing the number of students in the school according to grade
2. A map of the area around the school
3. A chart illustrating the height of each student
4. Diagrams showing how to use classroom audiovisual equipment
5. A picture file depicting each student's hobby

As students encounter graphic aids in texts, review the material with them and explain the illustrated concepts in detail. By continually using and emphasizing pictorial aids, you will encourage your students to use these aids as they attempt to understand printed materials.

Primary Years

You can help children to develop skill in remembering by helping them to set purposes for listening, reading, or watching films. If you state these purposes in broad terms, students will not focus too much attention on details to the exclusion of larger concepts.

One of the oldest and most frequently used means of checking recall is question asking. Our purpose here is not to discuss techniques of question asking; rather, it is to point out the various ways in which students can provide answers to questions. Answers to questions may be given orally or through demonstration, the carrying out of some direction, or role playing. Answers may also be shared through media, art, music, and dance.

Finally, we urge you to encourage students to verify information that they have recalled as an aid to accuracy as well as recall. This is particularly valuable if a difference of opinion exists as to the facts being recalled. Too often, the teacher simply supplies the correct answer and the issue is resolved. Although it may involve more time, let the students with differences of opinion reexamine their sources and discuss their differences. In the long run, this will be time well spent.

Intermediate Years

QUESTIONING

As suggested in the Primary Years section, questions may be generated by the teacher or placed at the beginning, middle, or end of the text throughout the reading process. Our purpose here is not to discuss the techniques of question asking or placement since these are addressed in Chapter 7 but, instead, to explain the use of instructional strategies that will result in the student's ability to generate appropriate questions during the reading process. Andre and Anderson (1978–79) suggest that during the self-questioning technique, the reader must "(a) pause frequently, (b) deal with an understanding question, (c) determine whether or not comprehension has occurred, and (d) decide what strategic action should be taken" (p. 620). The reader's ability to implement steps (a)–(d) is an example of metacognitive monitoring or using effective study strategies. The following question guide was developed and used with students as an instructional technique designed as an example of the primary and supporting questions that one could generate to monitor one's own understanding of the text. We have also listed the possible thinking processes the reader would engage in while answering these questions.

The following text selection was used by a middle-school teacher as part of a unit on health and personal hygiene (Tuten et al., 1983):

The Muscle Fiber

1. The basic unit of the muscular system is the muscle fiber, and
2. there are basically two types of muscle fibers. One type is re-
3. ferred to as slow-twitch fiber because it is slow to contract but
4. has the ability to continue contracting for long periods of time.

5. The slow-twitch fibers have a rich blood supply and high level of
6. myoglobin and are important for endurance-type activities such
7. as marathon running and long distance swimming. Because
8. they have a high mitochondrial content, they are able to make
9. good use of oxygen for the production of energy.
10.   The second major type of muscle fiber is the fast-twitch fiber
11. which is best suited for fast, short-term contractions. However,
12. there are two different categories of fast-twitch fibers: fast-white
13. fibers and fast-red fibers. The fast-white fibers are not as well
14. supplied by blood vessels, have a lower content of myoglobin
15. and mitochondria and, therefore, a reduced capacity for pro-
16. cessing oxygen. These fibers are utilized in fast, short burst
17. activities like sprinting and shot putting. The fast-red fibers have
18. a better blood supply and a higher content of myoglobin and
19. mitochondria which enables them to process oxygen a little
20. better. They are used in activities of high intensity but moderate
21. duration such as middle distance running. The fast-red are still
22. not the equal of the slow-twitch fibers in usefulness during a
23. long-term physical effort.
24.   Each individual varies in the number of fast-twitch and slow-
25. twitch muscle fibers in their muscle tissue. The particular ratio
26. you have is determined at birth and cannot be altered. There-
27. fore, it is clear that those who inherit a predominance of slow-
28. twitch fibers have an advantage in the performance of
29. endurance-type activities and a greater potential for the devel-
30. opment of superior cardiorespiratory fitness. They will, of
31. course, have a disadvantage in activities requiring speed and
32. power sports. Individuals who have a predominance of fast-
33. twitch fibers will not perform as well in long-term efforts which
34. require superior aerobic capacity. Their potential for a high level
35. of cardiorespiratory fitness is also reduced.*

As the teacher presented the text, he posed the following problem, "After you have read pages 42 and 43, name the two types of muscle fibers and list the differences between them. Also discuss the capabilities the individual would possess if he had a higher concentration of either type."

As the reader reads, she needs to employ a monitoring system to collect the information needed to solve this problem. Readers can be taught to generate questions that enable them to solve such problems. The following is an example of the questions this teacher generated with his students as he worked to make them independent monitors.

Also listed are the possible thinking strategies that would be required to answer each question. The section of the text that must be understood to answer each question is also noted.

---

*From *Weight Training Everyone* by Tuten, Moore, and Knight, pp. 42–43. Copyright 1983 by Hunter Textbooks, Inc., Winston-Salem, N.C. Used by permission.

Questions	Processes	Text Line No.
Paragraph I		
Primary		
1. What is a slow-twitch muscle fiber?	Recall of slow-twitch muscle fiber. Then the reader will give a definition of the slow-twitch muscle fiber.	1–9
Supporting Questions		
2. What is the basic unit of the muscular system?	Thought process, the muscular system? Then the reader will give a definition of the slow-twitch muscle fiber.	1
3. How does the slow-twitch fiber get its name?	The reader would recall the slow-twitch muscle fiber. This will enable the reader to determine how it got its name.	2–3
4. The slow-twitch muscle fiber is slow to contract but has an important ability. Name that ability.	The thought process would be on the slow-twitch fiber's contracting ability.	4
5. What types of activities are the slow-twitch fibers important for?	The reader would recall the definition of the slow-twitch muscle fibers and describe the activities best suited for this type of muscle fiber.	5–7
6. What is the advantage of having a high mitochondrial content in the slow-twitch muscle fiber?	The reader would recall the advantage of having a high mitochondrial content and describe why.	8–9
7. There are two important aspects that make the slow-twitch muscle fibers valuable for endurance-type activities. Name them.	The thought process would be on two important aspects: endurance and slow-twitch muscle fibers.	5–6
Paragraph II		
Primary		
1. Explain a fast-twitch muscle fiber.	The reader's thought process would be to give a definition of a fast-twitch muscle fiber.	10–23
Supporting Questions		
2. What is the fast-twitch muscle fiber best suited for?	Reader would describe its primary usefulness.	10–11
3. Name the two types of fast-twitch muscle fibers.	Reader would recall fast-twitch muscle fibers and describe its two types.	12–13
4. Why do the fast-white fibers have a reduced capacity for oxygen?	Thought process would be on what types of individuals possess fast-white fibers.	13–16
5. In what type of activities are fast-white fibers utilized?	Recall would be in the types of activities individuals are involved in who possess these factors.	16–17
6. The fast-red fibers have a better blood supply and a higher content of myoglobin	Reader, given all the information needed in the question, would then determine the answer.	17–20

and mitochondria than do the fast-white fibers, which in turn enables the fast-red fibers to do what?

7. In what types of activities are the fast-red fibers utilized?

Thought process would be on what type of activities individuals are involved in who possess these fibers.

20–21

Paragraph III

Primary

1. What types of activities would be advantageous to an athlete with a higher concentration of fast-twitch fibers and an athlete with a higher concentration of slow-twitch fibers?

The reader's thought process is on advantageous activities for the athlete with high concentrations of both types of fibers.

24–35

Supporting Questions

2. Is it true that each individual varies in the number of fast-twitch and slow-twitch fibers in his muscle tissue?

Thought would be on whether the question is true and, if so, why.

24–25

3. When is the ratio of fast-twitch to slow-twitch muscle fibers determined in your body?

Recall: At what time in one's life does this take place?

25–26

4. Athletes who possess a high number of slow-twitch fibers have an advantage in the performance of what type of activity?

The reader would weigh three aspects of this question to determine the outcome: (1) the athlete, (2) advantage of fibers, (3) the type of activity.

26–30

5. Endurance activities help to give the athlete a greater potential for developing what?

The thought process would be on endurance-type individuals versus what type of muscle fibers.

29–30

6. What is a disadvantage of having slow-twitch muscle fibers?

The question would be answered by determining the type of individual who possesses the slow-twitch muscle fiber.

30–32

7. What is a disadvantage and advantage of having fast-twitch muscle fibers?

Recall would commence on the fast-twitch muscle fibers, then the disadvantages and advantages.

32–35

While we have presented a detailed list of questions for monitoring this text, students should be encouraged to ask only enough questions to ensure, not disrupt, comprehension. Self-monitoring is a skilled process that one employs to aid, not impede, one's own comprehension. Emphasis must be on comprehending, not on posing questions. As teachers, we must help students to maintain this delicate balance.

While this system was used with expository text, Singer and Donlan (1982) designed a self-monitoring questioning strategy to be used when reading narrative texts. Their monitoring strategy encourages the reader to first ask himself questions drawn from his general knowledge about the characteristics of a story. Questions of this type would include

1. *Who is the main character?*
2. *What is the main character trying to accomplish?*
3. *What problems are stopping the main character from accomplishing the desired goal?*
4. *How did the primary character overcome the problems?*
5. *Is this story based on fantasy or reality?*

These questions are referred to as schema-general since they are general questions derived from the reader's schema or prior knowledge of story structures, for example, the characters, dialogue, sequence, plot. These questions may be applied when reading any narrative.

As the story gets more complex the reader should be helped to answer story-specific questions that apply to the story being read. A sample of such questions to be used when reading *Sylvester and the Magic Pebble* by Steig might include

1. *Is this story about magic or fantasy?*
2. *Did Sylvester believe the pebble was magic?*
3. *Will Sylvester always believe in magic?*

Techniques such as these are essential since during the middle school years, students encounter more factual and more complex materials. They sometimes experience difficulty recalling the amount of information that is required of them. Another very useful metacognitive strategy that students can learn is the SQ3R technique.

SQ3R

SQ3R stands for survey, question, read, recite, review. This method helps students to understand and recall what they read through an organized, well-planned approach to reading. Let us examine each of the steps in this process.

Survey.
Students survey the text or material to get a general idea of the content and organization. Surveying involves glancing over such items as chapter titles, main headings, subheadings, graphic aids, tables of contents, introductions, summaries (when provided), italicized words, introductory sentences, numbered points, and chapter exercises. This sets the stage, or provides a framework, for subsequent steps.

Questioning.
Questioning relates to the major headings. The students can use the headings to pose questions that they believe the text will answer. This gives the student a purpose for reading—a question to answer. For example, if the heading is "Transportation in the Nineteenth Century," the student might pose the following questions:

1. *What forms of transportation did people use in the nineteenth century?*
2. *How did these forms of transportation differ from modern methods of transportation?*
3. *What effects did these forms of transportation have on the people's lives?*

Read.
The students are now ready to read the selection, keeping in mind the questions they have formulated. Encourage them to look for the main idea and supporting details.

Recite.
The fourth step, the second R, is reciting the answers to the questions. This will aid comprehension and enhance recall of the material. Students must ask themselves if the answers make sense; if they do not, they may want to go to another source to check the same information.

Review.
Finally, students review what they have read. Explain that reviewing is similar to surveying, but with the details filled in. Students can review the information in their minds, or they can write down notes or an outline.

Encourage your students to learn and use the SQ3R method of reading and studying. They will find it is a useful strategy that aids comprehension and facilitates recall of material.

Locating Information

Primary Years

Developing locational skills is absolutely essential for helping students to become independent learners. Locational skills provide students with the necessary means to secure information and to identify and use appropriate sources of information. The first skill each student must acquire is the ability to *alphabetize*.

ALPHABETIZING

Students must be able to alphabetize letters and words in order to use dictionaries, encyclopedias, indexes, glossaries, and other reference materials. We suggest you begin teaching alphabetizing in a manner similar to the following:

1. Introduce the letters of the alphabet in sequential order.
2. Write the alphabet on the board and ask students to supply the missing letters:

    a, b, ___, ___, e, ___, g, h, ___, ___, ___, l, ___, n, ___, p, ___, ___, ___, ___, u, ___, w, x, y, ___

3. Supply word lists and have students alphabetize them by the first letter, for example, the, and, fun, beg, you.
4. Supply word lists that will have to be alphabetized by the second letter, for example, frog, fish, fun, float, fell.
5. Supply word lists that will have to be alphabetized by the third and fourth letters, for example, bank, back, bandit, barn, barber.

DICTIONARIES

An ideal way to reinforce alphabetizing skills while introducing dictionary usage is through a picture dictionary. Single-picture dictionaries arrange words according to some common relationship: animals, clothing, food. Words in the groups may be alphabetized and illustrated with pictures. Students may begin with these simple dictionaries and gradually advance to using standard dictionaries.

PARTS OF A BOOK

A student's first lesson in using a book should be through the introduction of the *parts of a book*. During the primary years, students may not need to use *all* the parts of a book, but they need to be aware of the existence of the many components of a book.

Have your students examine the cover of a book and note its title. You might ask such questions as

1. What do you think this book is about?
2. Why do you think the author chose this title?
3. Is there a picture on the cover? If so, what does it show? How do you think this relates to the contents of the book?

Following this, students can be introduced to the *table of contents*. Discuss the author's purpose for including a table of contents and how it can be helpful. You can demonstrate that a table of contents can be used to locate major parts of a book, but it may not contain a complete listing of all headings and subheadings. Explain that the table of contents is in numerical order from the beginning to the end of the book. Students need to begin finding pages by number as soon as they can read numbers.

The table of contents is the foundation for text usage. Once the students are knowledgeable about using it, they should be introduced to classroom reference materials such as the almanac, atlas, and encyclopedia.

REFERENCE MATERIALS

You can capitalize on children's natural curiosity by encouraging them to explore atlases, almanacs, and encyclopedias. We recognize that very few primary-level students will be able to use these reference materials independently, but many may be ready to profit from having information read to them. Others may be able to read material in some of these references if they have help initially in locating the information. Even the youngest of children should be introduced to these reference tools and encouraged to view them as additional sources of information.

If you explain that most reference books arrange information alphabetically, it will also serve to reinforce the importance of alphabetizing skills. You may have some students who are ready to explore the use of an index; however, because this is not common, index usage will be discussed for intermediate-grade students.

You can introduce your students to classroom reference materials by

1. Discussing the type of information contained in each resource
2. Comparing and contrasting the purpose of each type of resource
3. Demonstrating that the text contents appear in alphabetical order
4. Selecting questions that will provide practice in using the materials, for example,
   a. Where is the highest mountain in the United States?
   b. Who was the president in 1960?
   c. Where might you find a guanaco?
   d. Name a province that borders Alberta, Canada.
5. Surveying materials with the students to determine which is the most suitable for answering each question

You may prefer teaching the use of reference materials as part of the library unit; if so, be sure to enlist the aid of your librarian or resource specialist.

LIBRARY SKILLS

By introducing students to the library at an early age, you may encourage them to develop reading habits that last a lifetime. Several library skills can be developed at the primary level: proper care of books, appropriate

You can capitalize on children's natural curiosity by encouraging them to explore atlases, almanacs, and encyclopedias. (Photo by Linda Lungren.)

library behavior, knowledge about types of materials in the library, and a general understanding of the arrangement of library materials.

Explain to the students that appropriate library behavior is based upon respect for the rights of others. Library users are asked to be quiet (not silent) so that everyone in the library can read, work, or study without noisy distractions. You can help students to recognize the type of atmosphere that makes their use of the library most pleasant and productive and to realize that they have responsibility in helping create this atmosphere for others as well as for themselves.

As soon as you feel confident that your primary-grade students understand the need for library courtesy and taking care of library materials, you may want to introduce them to the card catalog. For more specific information, refer to a later section of this chapter, "Using a Card Catalog," page 189.

Intermediate Years

Throughout this chapter we have emphasized that at the intermediate level the focus is on expanding skills developed at the primary level. You can help students to extend their awareness of locational skills by developing a thorough understanding of the parts of a book.

PARTS OF BOOKS

Students should be aware of the parts of a book, the function of each part, and how to find and choose the material suited to their needs. An effective way to teaching this information is through a class activity using a textbook. Point out and discuss the function of items such as these: preface, table of contents, index, foreword, glossary, publication data, and title. In this way, students will learn that every part of a book is a potential aid, not merely a "filler."

USING THE INDEX

An excellent way to teach students about using the index is to contrast it to the table of contents, a book part with which they are already familiar. You can begin by pointing out that a table of contents lists the contents of the book progressively, from beginning to end. An index, however, is arranged alphabetically by topic. The index can provide the reader with more in-depth information about the topical relationships within the text than can be found in the table of contents. The index also synthesizes all references to a single topic by precise page numbers.

Examine and discuss an index with your students. You should explain that some books contain more than one index, for example, a subject index and a name index. You can also point out that an index usually includes names, places, events, cross-references, and topics.

GLOSSARY

Glossaries are often not included in primary-level books. However, as intermediate-grade students begin to read content area materials, they begin to use the glossary, which contains words, definitions, and explanations that relate to the special contents of a book.

Nullify   *To set aside or disobey a law.*
Overseer   *A person who supervised slaves at work.*
Pioneer   *The first person to go into an unsettled land.* (Brady and Brady, 1977, p. 511)

APPENDICES

Many content area texts include an appendix. Appendices may have varied content, but their purpose is to supply, in a condensed form, supplementary information that is related to the textual content. For example, in a social studies text, you might find any of the following: maps, Declaration of Independence, Bill of Rights, U.S. Constitution, capsulized chronological lists of significant dates, and so on. Appendixes are listed in the table of contents, and information included is indexed, as is other text information.

DICTIONARY SKILLS

At the intermediate level, mastery of dictionary skills should be continuously emphasized because the ability to use a dictionary correctly to help unlock word meanings and pronunciation is a skill needed by students at all levels. In fact, a student's mastery of the many skills usually categorized as dictionary skills will strongly affect his or her success in using many other reference books. To help students develop this skill, you will need to provide instruction related to these areas: finding words, word meanings, and word pronunciation.

Finding Words.
To use a dictionary successfully, a student must be able to

1. Recognize letters
2. Differentiate between letters
3. Put the letters of the alphabet in the proper sequence
4. Alphabetize words by first, second, third, and eventually all letters

Students learn to use a dictionary quickly and efficiently by developing a sense of letter location. You can begin by pointing out that the letter "M" is approximately the middle of the alphabet. Next, have the students open a dictionary in the middle and note which letters are on the pages that fall to the left and right. Then ask them to divide each half so that they can note the letters in each quarter of the dictionary. The students should now be ready to look for the page where a particular letter begins. Ask them to open a dictionary to the place where they anticipate finding the first letter and then go forward or backward to the correct page.

You should also explain that guide words are valuable tools to help determine if a particular word is included on a given page. They can also be used to help a student searching for a word determine if he or she should turn forward or backward in relation to the place where the dictionary was originally opened.

Word Meanings.
The words students know and use have meaning for them based on their past experiences. Encourage students to use the dictionary to validate the meanings of their language and to promote vocabulary development.

When using a dictionary, students will often encounter a variety of information. Sometimes they will have to examine several definitions in order to select the one that seems to fit the context in which it was used. To help students understand the meanings of some words, scale drawings are sometimes used and students need to learn how to use and interpret them. Also, synonyms and antonyms are included as part of the definitions of many words, and students must understand what synonyms and antonyms are for this information to be helpful in unlocking word meanings.

Pronunciation.
An important function of a dictionary is to provide a key to interpreting spoken language. For a student to use the dictionary for this purpose effectively, she needs to have an understanding of syllabication and phonics.

In most dictionaries, the pronunciation of a word is included as part of the dictionary entry. Students need instruction in using a pronunciation key to develop pronunciation skills. Your lessons on how to use a pronunciation key should include

1. *Phonetic respellings*
2. *The use of accents*
3. *Diacritical markings*
4. *Syllabication*
5. *The schwa (ə)*

Developing pronunciation skills is also aided by an understanding of prefixes, suffixes, and plurals. We urge you to include these in your lessons on pronunciation skills.

LIBRARY SKILLS

At the intermediate level, students need to learn additional library skills. These skills include (1) library organization, (2) use of the card catalog, and (3) extended knowledge and use of reference materials.

Library Organization.
Libraries may have different types of organization, so it may be appropriate to gear your lessons to your own school library. Some common organizational patterns include arranging books according to

1. Fiction (These books may be further subdivided. For example, picture books may be separate from other fiction books. Frequently, too, paperback books are separate from hardback books.)
2. Nonfiction
3. Biographies
4. Reference books
5. Periodicals

Explain that the books are filed different ways within each section. Fiction is arranged alphabetically by the *author's* last name. Biographies are usually filed alphabetically by the last name of the person the book is *about.* Frequently, there is no special arrangement of periodicals, although they, too, may be in alphabetical order by title. Reference books may be shelved according to the Library of Congress System or the Dewey Decimal System, or they may simply be grouped together in one area.

Since most schools still use the Dewey Decimal System of classification for nonfiction books, you must explain the system to your students. In this system, all subject matter is divided into ten main classes and assigned particular numbers. Books are filed *numerically* according to content; for example,

700–799	Arts and Recreation
800–899	Literature

Each class can be subdivided several more times according to content. For example,

700–799	Arts and Recreation
790	Recreation
796	Athletics and Sports
796.52	Mountain Climbing

Have your students think of a topic and try to decide into which of the ten main classes their topic would likely fall. This will provide an opportunity for you to introduce the use of the card catalog.

Card Catalog.
In most card catalogs, a book will have three cards: a *title* card, a *subject* card, and an *author* card. Students need to learn how to read each type of card and to understand when they would use a particular kind of card.

Visiting the library and actually using the card catalog will enable students to understand that

Some card catalogs in libraries are found on microfiche and include a title entry, a subject entry, and an author entry. (Photo by Linda Lungren.)

1. Cards are arranged alphabetically by author, subject, or title.
2. Subject, title, and author cards all contain the same information.

Reference Materials.

You can encourage the use of reference resources by the type of lessons and activities you plan. For example, students can use reference books to acquire additional information on topics currently being studied. You should attempt to ask questions that encourage children to consult many sources. ("What were some of the effects of the 1906 San Francisco earthquake?")

Students need to understand and practice how to match a particular general reference book with the information they are seeking. For example, to find the pronunciation and definition of a word, a dictionary can be used. If an extensive explanation of a particular word is desired, an encyclopedia may be the desired reference. If the student needs more specialized information related to a geographic area, a type of plant, or a scientific phenomenon, a specialized reference book is needed.

Extended library skills are necessary for intermediate-grade students to pursue an area of interest or to research information for a paper or a report. Encourage them to use *The Reader's Guide to Periodical Literature* to locate current magazine articles to supplement material from other sources. *The Reader's Guide* provides references to 190 periodicals; its entries are arranged alphabetically according to topics, along the lines of an index.

Parapsychology
>   Scientists, gamblers, & magicians [claims of the paranor-
>   mal] R. Dietz. il por *Humanist* 43:9–11+ Mr/Ap '83

Parasites
>   *See also*
>   Trypanosomes
>   Getting the message across [combining family planning
>   and parasite control] M. Jones. il *World Health* p22–4
>   F/Mr '83

Parchomenko, Walter
>   The Soviet Union's hidden minority. *America* 148:296–8
>   Ap 16 '83   (*Reader's Guide*, 1983, p. 1145)

Students will need instruction on how to read each entry and how to interpret the abbreviations. Point out to them that in the front of each *Reader's Guide* there is an explanation of all abbreviations used. Once students have located a magazine article, their success in interpreting the material will depend to some degree on their reading flexibility.

READING FLEXIBILITY

There is a slight shift in the focus of reading instruction at the intermediate level. The reading program must still emphasize the development of word-recognition and comprehension skills *(learning to read)*. In addition, content area reading instruction *(reading to learn)* should encourage the development of flexible reading techniques. Students must learn

1. When to read slowly and carefully
2. When to read quickly
3. How to skim materials
4. How to scan materials

One of the ways to help students become flexible readers is to encourage them to always examine their *purpose* for reading before they begin reading. The purpose for reading determines the appropriate *rate* of reading. For example, when students are reading to learn, they are attempting to

1. Comprehend the author's message
2. Answer questions
3. Synthesize information
4. Make generalizations
5. Identify important facts and supporting details

With these goals in mind, students must read more slowly and carefully than if they were reading for recreation or enjoyment.

You can help students to adapt their reading rates to the purpose for reading by presenting them with factual text excerpts and several purposes for reading:

For enjoyment
For determining the general study topic
For finding a specified bit of information

After completing this, discuss with the students how they have altered their reading rates and techniques according to each new purpose.

Skimming is a technique used when the reading purpose is to acquire a general impression of the material content. When a student skims a passage, she should be encouraged to note headings, subheadings, and topic sentences. Skimming is a very selective reading process; if the student needs more detailed information to answer questions, skimming may not be appropriate.

Scanning is also a valuable tool for flexible readers. Hoffman (1979) suggest that the objective of scanning "may be to locate specific information in a body of text without attempting to deal with the content as a whole" (p. 324). Students should be encouraged to look for clue words or phrases that may indicate the location of the answer the student is seeking.

Practice activities can help your students to develop the ability to scan. You might begin by asking them to determine answers to very simple questions:

1. Where *was the nova discovered?*
2. When *did the volcano last erupt?*
3. Which *world leaders attended the Yalta Conference?*

After posing the questions, refer the students to the passage containing the information. Ask the students to move their eyes quickly across each line of text until the clue word for their answer becomes obvious.

1. Place, nova
2. Date, volcano
3. Names, Yalta Conference

Next encourage the students to read the sentences immediately preceding and following the one in which they found their answer. These sentences may contain information that will add exactness to the information being sought.

Practice with a *purpose* is the key to developing skimming and scanning skills. Proficiency in using these skills frequently has a valuable by-product: increased reading rate. Flexibility in reading allows students to increase reading rates naturally.

FOLLOWING DIRECTIONS

From the very beginning of schooling we ask students to *follow directions*. Yet, too often, teachers expect students to be able to follow directions even though they may not have received instruction in this area.

Young students have some maturational limitations that affect their ability to follow directions. In the early years, the maxim "Keep it short and simple," is appropriate. Long strings of instructions can only lead to confusion. At the primary level, most directions are given orally; therefore, it is a good idea to concentrate on developing effective listening skills. Be aware, also, that students soon recognize and respond to the teacher's patterns for giving directions. The teacher who habitually repeats directions three times may soon find that students tune in on round three, if at all, and even then they may listen very ineffectively.

Due to the increased maturational level of intermediate-grade students, they can recall a longer list of directions for a longer period of time. At these levels, increased ability to reason and see relationships should enable students to make mental connections that facilitate the ability to follow directions.

An effective way to help students develop skill in following directions is by organizing directions as clearly and concisely as possible. You may also find the following suggestions helpful:

---

1. Start by giving one-step directions:
   a. Circle the correct answer.
   b. Number each item.
2. Move to two-step directions only after the child has mastered the concept of one-step directions:
   a. Underline all nouns and circle all verbs.

   b. Review the information in the text and then develop a graphic aid
      to illustrate the data.
3. Introduce three-step directions only after the child has mastered the
   concept of two-step directions:
   a. Read the story, draw a picture to illustrate it, and share the story
      and illustration with a friend.
   b. Eat your lunch, clean up the classroom, and go out to play.
4. Introduce activities that involve multistep directions:
   a. Assemble the model.
   b. Complete the experiment.

The study skills we have discussed have limited value in isolation; students need instruction and practice to master these skills and techniques. Remember that reading study skills can have a significant effect on a student's academic success. These skills are developmental. Each student deserves to be introduced to them and to be helped to recognize their purpose and value. Students need multiple opportunities to develop and refine their command of them. Most of these opportunities will be developed through learning pursuits that interrelate study skills with such content areas as math, science, and social studies, but that should not deter the primary-grade teacher from introducing skills appropriate for his or her students.

Suggested Readings Related to Goals.   We encourage you at this time to review the goals at the beginning of this chapter. If you feel you would like to explore one or more of these areas in greater depth, please refer to the cross-indexed bibliography at the end of the book.

9 Content Area Reading

A crucial issue in content area reading instruction is how to instruct students so that they are able to study and learn from their texts. Text learning skills are needed at all grade levels, once content area instruction has begun.

[D. Moore and J. Readence]

Goals

To help the student understand
1. The role of reading in the learning process
2. The importance of reading in social studies
3. The importance of reading in mathematics
4. The importance of reading in science
5. The importance of reading in music and art

Reading and Learning

The ability to read a text is one of the most important skills a student must acquire. Reading is a process that has no specific content but is essential to the mastery of all content areas. Jenkinson (1973) reminds us that "reading is not a subject. . . . It cannot be taught separately. . . . It is part of every other subject" (p. 39). Nonetheless, too often reading is taught only in the context of a basal reading program.

In light of this, it may be appropriate to question the role of university teacher-training programs. Lapp et al. (1978) studied the dichotomy between universities espousing teaching reading in the content areas without providing *models*. They found that preservice teachers were only able to implement instructional strategies relating to content area reading when the cooperating teacher modeled or demonstrated these strategies. Some universities are attempting to correct this deficiency by emphasizing teaching models in which reading is viewed as a *process* necessary to master all content area learning.

Basal Reading Programs and Content Area Teaching

Basal reading programs emphasize word-recognition and comprehension skills, skills that are necessary for students encountering content area texts. Word-recognition skills enable the student to recognize and analyze new lexical items. Whether the material is narrative (as in most basal readers) or expository (as in most content area texts), comprehension skills are needed for students to recognize literal facts, infer unstated meaning, and evaluate author intent. These skills initially acquired through basal reading in the primary grades continue to help the intermediate and advanced reader encountering content area materials.

You can incorporate content area texts into your classroom curriculum as soon as students have demonstrated mastery of such readiness skills as letter and sight-word recognition. These content area materials should be considered a *supplement* to, not a replacement for, the basal reader. A basal reading program is a good foundation for successful content area learning. However, it is not safe to assume that there will be a transfer of learning from the largely narrative basal to a fact-specific content area text without instructional aid.

As Flood, Lapp, and Flood found (1984), some percentage of basals at all grade levels are comprised of narrative text, but the major portion of the reading material in the primary grades is narrative. Not surprisingly, this type of reading may not be adequate preparation for content area reading. Intermediate-grade students who have exhibited little, if any, difficulty with narrative materials, often demonstrate a limited understanding of content area materials. As Tierney and Lapp suggest (1979), National Assessment data indicate that many students are experiencing problems making a transition between narrative texts and materials that contain synthesized facts and a concisely stated, often terse, style of writing.

The following excerpts, taken from intermediate texts, illustrate the differences in content and writing styles that are encountered by the intermediate-age student who is required to read narrative and factual materials. Both excerpts deal with the topic of weather and seasonal changes.

> "Oh boy! It'll snow! And tomorrow is Christmas!" Eddie flipped his furry cap into the air, missing Mom's reading lamp. It landed among the potted plants Willa Mae was watering.
> "Cut it, Ed!" she cried. "And be sure to stay right with Jason. Mom said for you boys to be home before the snow gets bad."

*Reading is a process that has
no specific content but is
essential to the mastery of
all content areas.
(Photo by Linda Lungren.)*

"Okay, we'll make it home" Jason promised. "It isn't snowing yet. Come on, Eddie, I've got our money all counted."

Eddie slammed the front door. They clattered down the stairs fast.

"Is there enough money for the lamp shade, Jay?" Eddie asked to make sure. "And what will we get for Willa Mae?"

"We'll find something. There'll be enough."

It wasn't long before they caught their first sight of the fountain in the park.

"It's frozen!" Eddie gasped. He pulled Jason toward it. The water in the fountain must have frozen while it was still bubbling down. Now the statue animals—the turtles, frogs, and swans—had frozen into strange, icy shapes. It was lovely, like fairyland.

"Hm . . . snow's starting," Jason said, sniffing the air. A few flakes were blowing lightly over the ice. He looked up at the gray, tumbling sky. "We'd better get downtown for our shopping," he said. (*Clymer, 1970, pp. 42–43*)

If you live in a place where the leaves change color, you probably have noticed that the color display is never quite the same from one year to the next. One year the leaves may be very colorful, but the next year their colors may be dull. Several things seem to affect how bright or how dull the color change will be—the amount of water in the ground during the summer, the amount of nitrogen in the soil, the amount of light reaching the leaves, the amount of sugar stored in the leaves, and the night temperatures during autumn. Strong light and cold nights, for example, seem to help certain pigments form in leaf cells.

In some way we do not yet fully understand, toward the end of summer the chlorophyll pigment of the leaf cells begins to break down. As more and more chlorophyll is broken down, the yellow and orange pigments are unmasked. At the same time, new yellow and orange pigments are being made. The leaves begin to change color.

Meanwhile, other pigments are being made in the leaf cells. How much they show up depends partly on weather conditions during the summer. It also depends partly on weather conditions while the leaves are changing. Brown pigments begin to form when the chlorophyll breaks down. So do the flaming red, blue, and purple pigments. When the brown pigments form, they blend with orange and yellow and give oak leaves their typical orange-brown color. The red pigments seem to reach their peak when the outflow of sugar made in the leaves slows down and the sugar then collects in the leaves. (*Asimov and Gallant, 1973, pp. 33–34*)

Which passage do you think would be more difficult for a fourth- or fifth-grade student to read and comprehend? The selections are approximately equal in length, and both deal with the same topic. The second passage, however, contains more difficult, more technical, vocabulary (pigment, chlorophyll). Another vocabulary stumbling block may be the use of familiar words in unfamiliar ways (color, leaves). Reading either passage requires the use of word recognition and comprehension skills; however, like most content area materials, the second selection also requires the student to be competent in several of the following general study skills:

1. Establishing a purpose for reading
2. Noting simple clues to organization of selection: definitions, context, numbered ideas, cue words indicating order
3. Skimming for general concepts
4. Scanning for minute details
5. Differentiating fact from opinion
6. Recognizing main ideas
7. Using dictionaries, glossaries, and footnotes to determine meaning
8. Adjusting reading rate to suit reading purpose and type of material

Study Skills

Let us examine the development of study skills by continuing to use the two preceding passages. One way to foster readiness for reading content-specific material would be to present a narrative story about weather information along with a factual-type story format. Through questions and discussions you can guide the students in recognizing that topical material can be presented in a variety of genres.

Younger students often need instruction and practice in differentiating fact from opinion. The language experiences of your students can provide an excellent opportunity for teaching this study skill. After eliciting several *opinion* statements from the students, you can encourage and assist the students in changing these to *factual* statements. For example,

Opinion	*Fact*
Pat: "I have more fun in the summer."	"There is more time to play outside in the summer."
Jan: "I like to plant a garden."	"Different seasons and climates are needed for gardening."

You can provide additional practice in differentiating fact from opinion by having students examine advertisements, newspapers, magazines, and classroom reading materials. (For a more comprehensive examination of study skills, refer to Chapter 8.)

Content Area Reading and Study Skills

Successful content area reading lies in the application and extension of study skills. "Study skills can and should be taught in the context of content learning, and in fact, many educators see study skills as synonymous with learning skills" (Lamberg and Lamb, 1980, p. 88). Teachers of all grades must be concerned with study skills because you cannot assume that all of the skills will be developed and refined in any one grade. As Flood, Lapp, and Flood (1984) suggest, the early school years focus on instruction in basic reading skills. Reading instruction in the intermediate grades emphasizes

1. *Refining* basic reading skills
2. *Extending* comprehension skills
3. *Expanding* reference study skills
4. *Strengthening* metacognitive strategies
5. *Exploring* specific content area materials in order to extend concepts and to clarify generalizations

Planning Considerations

The teachers today just go on repeating in rigamorole fashion, annoying the students with constant questions and repeating the same things over and over again. They do not try to find out what the students' natural inclinations are, so that the students are forced to pretend to like their studies; nor do they try to bring out the best in their talents. As a result, the students hide their favorite readings and hate their teachers, are exasperated at the difficulty of their studies, and do not know what good it does them. Although they go through the regular course of instruction, they are quick to leave when they are through. This is the failure of education today.

Confucius, c. 551–479 B.C.

Teachers must make every effort to alter the instructional conditions described by Confucius nearly twenty-five hundred years ago. The following principles can be used as guidelines when you plan for reading in any content area lesson.

Students

1. Students need to have a purpose for learning, a purpose that is related to the concerns and interests of the students.
2. Students need to be motivated to learn. "Attentive, involved students will learn more, remember longer, and usually make better use of their learning" (Tonjes and Zintz, 1981, p. 27).
3. Students learn most effectively when they have a positive attitude. Having a purpose for learning along with interesting, challenging activities helps to foster positive attitudes.
4. Students comprehend by relating their school experiences with their life experiences. "The more experience a student has that relates to a topic the better that student will be able to understand the reading content" (Roe et al., 1978, p. 145). You must determine how much is known about a particular topic and then begin instruction at the student's level of readiness.
5. Word-recognition, comprehension, and study skills are necessary to learn through reading.
6. Students learn in many ways. By offering a variety of learning activities, you will be able to meet the needs of *all* of your students.
7. Students learn at different rates. Setting a time limit can be counterproductive unless your purpose is to measure rate.
8. Students must be active participants in the learning process, for learning is not a passive process.

Teachers

1. Teachers must have a thorough understanding of the material they are teaching.
2. Teachers must have some knowledge about the students they are teaching. (Refer to Chapter 11.)
3. Teachers need to plan activities that will encourage growth of *all* students. (Such activities are included throughout this text.)
4. Teachers must have a thorough understanding of the various methods designed to teach reading through content area subjects. (Refer to Chapter 10.)
5. Teachers should make proper adjustments for word-recognition, comprehension, and study skills application for effective teaching of reading in any content area (as discussed throughout this chapter).
6. Teachers need to understand the practical application of learning theory, for example, How do children learn? Does their rate of learning coincide with their physical and social growth? (Refer to Chapter 2.)

7. Teachers should be well-versed in evaluative techniques. (Refer to Chapter 15.)
8. Teachers must remember that there is not one set of unique skills related to learning a specific content area (as discussed throughout this chapter).

Reading in Social Studies

Social studies draws its content from several fields, including anthropology, civics, geography, psychology, sociology, and economics. It is quite common to find passages with information integrated from several disciplines in social studies texts. Social studies stresses the role of the individual in society and encourages the study of the interactions of people.

For your students to explore successfully the vast amount of knowledge included in social studies, they will need to learn not only the factual content but also the skills that are needed to become independent learners of this information. In the following pages, we will provide you with a thorough understanding of the skills relating to reading in social studies and discuss the processes for implementing these skills in the classroom.

Social Studies Vocabulary

As in other content areas, students reading a social studies text may encounter two areas of difficulty: *concepts* and *vocabulary*. A *concept* is a mental construct of the common characteristics or components of something. Shepherd (1978) notes that "vocabulary in the social studies represents the concepts by labeling them" (p. 206).

Dupuis and Snyder (1983) recommend that concepts be taught in as concrete a manner as possible. Hands-on activities, bringing objects to class, field trips, and even movies or slides can help students to understand concepts. Special attention must also be given to social studies vocabulary because "in many content areas, mastering the new vocabulary, those new words or phrases which label the parts of the material to be learned, is equivalent to mastering the concept" (Dupuis and Snyder, 1983, p. 299).

The potential vocabulary difficulties in social studies are common to all content areas. They are (1) technical vocabulary (words unique to the content area), (2) specialized vocabulary (common words that have a specific meaning in the content area), (3) words with multiple meanings, (4) abbreviations, and (5) acronyms. Some examples of these vocabulary problems are

Vocabulary	*Examples*
1. Technical vocabulary	socialism, republic
2. Specialized vocabulary	court, third world

For your students to explore successfully the vast amount of knowledge included in social studies, they will need to learn not only the factual content but also the skills that are needed to become independent learners of this information. (Photo by Linda Lungren.)

3. Multiple meanings   state, cycle
4. Abbreviations   sq. mi.; r.p.m.
5. Acronyms   NATO, UNESCO

In addition, Marksheffel (1966) points out that the people who write text books "understand so well the materials about which they write that they appear to forget that the student has but a meager knowledge of the vocabulary and concepts necessary for understanding" (p. 174).

The following suggestions can help your students to develop the language/reading skills necessary to master social studies vocabulary.

1. Discuss word derivations and forms of words. For example, democracy comes from two Greek roots (*demos*, people; *kratos*, rule): Democrat, democratic, democratization, democratically.
2. Examine new words as they appear in the text. The students can learn the meanings of such words through contextual analysis, using the glossary, or using a dictionary.
3. Use supplementary materials such as pictures, maps, globes, models,

films, recordings, and exhibits to demonstrate and reinforce vocabulary and concepts.
4. Introduce social slogans, figures of speech, and slang:
     End the Draft!
     Uncle Sam Wants You!
     It's a bummer.
5. Have the students categorize words according to historical periods, for example, Whigs, carpetbaggers, pharoahs.
6. Develop word histories of key words to use as mnemonic devices (something that helps you to remember something). For example, if you were teaching the word *mnemonic*, point out that Mnemon was a companion of Achilles who functioned as Achilles' memory.
7. Point out words that involve the concepts of distance, space, or time, for example, beyond, age.

Graphic Data

Social studies texts are often replete with maps, pictures, charts, tables, diagrams, time lines, and graphs to supplement printed information. Too often teachers assume that these graphic aids are self-evident, when in fact they frequently require instruction for the student to be able to comprehend them. Students are likely to encounter

1. Tables (Figure 9-1)
2. Charts and graphs (Figures 9-2 and 9-3)
3. Diagrams (Figure 9-4)
4. Maps

Many texts present graphics but do not require students to use them or fail to explain them sufficiently so they can be used. You should point out to your students that graphics can help them to understand concepts and facts presented in the text. To ensure that each student is able to

Balance of Trade: 1975–1980
(In billions of dollars)

YEAR	EXPORT	IMPORTS	
1975	107.1	98.0	+ 9.1
1976	114.71	124.0	– 9.3
1977	120.8	151.7	–30.9
1978	142.0	175.8	–33.8
1979	182.1	206.3	–24.2
1980	220.7	240.1	–19.4

Figure 9–1. Table. (From W. Hartley and W. Vincent, *American Civics*, 4th ed. New York: Harcourt Brace Jovanovich, Inc., 1983, p. 426.)

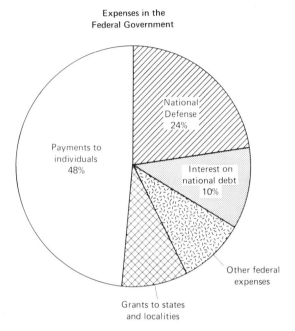

Expenses in the
Federal Government

Figure 9–2. Pie chart or circle graph. (From
U.S. Bureau of Management and Budget, 1980.)

analyze the information being presented, ask these questions about each
illustration:

1. *What is being illustrated?*
2. *What is the purpose of the illustration?*
3. *What information is provided by the caption?*
4. *What information is provided through the key, symbols, or scales?*

Maps are probably the graphic aid most frequently found in social studies texts; therefore, we will examine map skills very carefully.

Map Skills

To read a map, students must be taught to

1. Determine the author's purpose for including it
2. Use the scale and key
3. Determine latitude and longitude
4. Determine how directions are portrayed
5. Compare distances

The following activities can help your students to develop skills that are
necessary for interpreting maps.

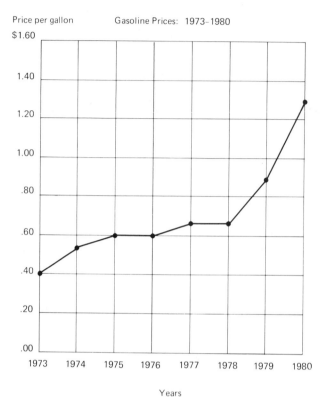

Figure 9–3. Line graph. (From W. Hartley and W. Vincent, *American Civics*, 4th ed. New York: Harcourt Brace Jovanovich, Inc., 1983, p. 380.)

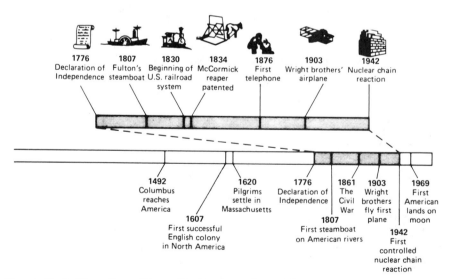

Figure 9–4. Time line. (From H. Gross et al., *Exploring World Regions: Western Hemisphere.* Chicago: Follett Publishing Co., 1975, p. 233.)

1. Have the students analyze the parts of the maps: type of map, scale, dates.
2. Provide activities that require the students to analyze climates, trade routes, currents, and topography.
3. Ask students to compare information from two (or more) maps and to note relationships.
4. Plan activities that require the students to utilize maps and to demonstrate their understanding of the parts of a map.
5. Discuss the importance of captions.

Several comprehension skills are needed when reading social studies materials. These include cause-and-effect relationships; making comparisons; detecting propaganda; differentiating fact from opinion; sequencing; and conceptualizing time, space, and place relationships.

Cause and Effect

Frequently, facts, events, and interactions in social studies texts are depicted through cause-and-effect relationships. Students must be taught to recognize cause-and-effect relationships and to identify the cause(s) and the effect(s). Several teaching suggestions are included in Chapter 7 that you may find valuable for teaching cause and effect.

Propaganda

Students are generally taught to recognize propaganda in English and social studies classes. As we discussed in Chapter 7, children may be influenced by many types of propaganda. Students must be made aware that not all propaganda is so obvious as that found in advertisements, political speeches, and historical slogans. Subtle uses of propaganda in writing that appears to be more informative than persuasive is more difficult to detect. Social studies materials can be used to encourage students to

1. Examine an author's purpose
2. Determine key words used to introduce propaganda
3. Note the use of persuasive words
4. Evaluate the facts provided by an author to convey an issue
5. Evaluate historical slogans as to their origins, applications, and persuasive appeal

Comparison/Contrast

Social studies materials lend themselves well to having students note similarities (comparison) and differences (contrast) among historical periods, countries, governments, customs, climates, and people. To help students note these relationships, you can plan classroom activities appropriate to the students' interests, ability levels, and particular textual content. For example, you may have students compare historical documents from different countries (Magna Carta and Bill of Rights) or have small groups of students compare the customs and culture of several different countries. (You may find other teaching examples in Chapter 7.)

Sequencing

"History evolves chronologically with the passing of time. One of the understandings students will need to acquire is the large movements of history and the overlap of historical movements" (Shepherd, 1978, p. 216). You can encourage students to develop a chronological perspective by

1. Discussing present-day occurrences while identifying historical factors.
2. Developing historical time lines.
3. Reviewing historical occurrences that have repeated themselves more than once in history: assassination, war, treason. What is the nature of man that he continues to perpetuate these behaviors? What societal factors contribute to his nature?

Fact vs. Opinion

As we discussed in Chapter 7, being able to differentiate fact from opinion is an important reading skill for students of all ages in all content areas. Students must develop this skill to enable them to become wise consumers and independent decision makers. Too often, children have the notion that if an adult makes a statement or if something can be found in printed material, "it must be true." Students should be encouraged to evaluate supporting premises.

Some ways by which you can help your students to differentiate fact from opinion are

1. Help students become aware that such words as *perhaps, think, in my opinion, maybe, one possibility,* or *my beliefs suggest* often indicate statements of opinion.
2. Have students use reference materials to verify the accuracy of information that may be fully or partially based on opinion or conjecture.
3. Provide paragraphs or short selections that the students can use to practice distinguishing fact from opinion.
4. Encourage students to examine the author's point of view.

Conceptualizing Relationships

Students must be able to conceptualize *time, space,* and *place* relation-ships to understand and appreciate social studies information. The follow-ing activities are useful ways of helping students to understand these con-cepts.

1. Have students compare different aspects of their city today with how it was fifty or one hundred years ago.
2. Discuss the implications of advanced technology with respect to trans-portation and communication.
3. Illustrate variations in life-span expectancy and world-time evolution.
4. Have students compare old or ancient maps of regions with modern maps.
5. Have students develop a time line showing important dates and events in their lives.

Teaching Social Studies

Your teaching approach, of course, must be based on the content of the material and your students' needs. We have included suggestions in this chapter that will be helpful in teaching individual skills. We also recom-mend that you use the directed reading activity (DRA) discussed in Chapter 7 for introducing and implementing a new lesson.

Through the motivation part of a DRA, you may add to a student's background knowledge and integrate what is already known about the topic. Preteaching difficult vocabulary will free the student to concentrate on the *content.* The springboard questions will give students a purpose for reading, and the comprehension questions will help you judge the effec-tiveness of the lesson. Using a directed reading activity is an excellent way of putting educational theory into classroom practice.

Reading in Mathematics

Of all the content area subjects, it is in mathematics that reading is prob-ably most neglected. Mathematics is a great deal more than basic com-putation. The reading and studying of mathematics requires both an un-derstanding and a development of specific concepts and principles. Mathematics instruction should have a twofold purpose:

1. To enable students to develop an understanding of the patterns that are used to formulate concepts and principles
2. To enable students to solve problems

To accomplish these objectives will ensure *both* problem mastery and conceptual understanding.

Mastery of the language of mathematics is essential to accomplishing these objectives. The language of mathematics is composed of words, numbers, and symbols. As Roe, Stoodt, and Burns (1978) point out, "The reader of mathematics must be able to read symbols, signs, abbreviations, exponents, subscripts, formulae, equations, geometric figures, graphs, and tables as well as words" (p. 264). As with other new languages, the student hears, explores, discusses, experiments, uses, and tests words that might be part of the conceptual framework of this language.

To meet the dual objective of *understanding* and *solving*, students must have some competence in reasoning, a process that involves a student's ability to reorder known data to derive new relationships. *Reasoning* is closely related to comprehension because both entail the ability to detect problematic clues, to hypothesize, and to evaluate conclusions. Finally, in an attempt to accomplish the specified objective of understanding and to solve problems, the student must be able to estimate and to compute.

A review of reading/mathematics literature (Corle, 1972) suggests the following:

1. Certain intellectual capabilities are essential for mathematical achievement. According to Piaget, these are competence with the concept of conservation of number, quantity, length, volume, and weight; the achievement of the concept of reversibility; and the maturation of logical abilities. Piaget stated that a child must be able to comprehend the fact that a number is the synthesis of two logical entities: class and asymmetrical relations, before he can achieve in mathematics. He contended that these capabilities are achieved when a child has matured sufficiently to comprehend them.

    Bruner, while accepting a developmental sequence in mathematical capability, contended that a child's environment can be changed so that it is consistent with his intellectual development. Piaget allowed considerable age-range for the development of the intellectual behaviors of children, and Bruner believed that environmental factors modify the learning rate of a child. Perhaps these amount to the same concept. In any event, both maturation and environment should be considered by teachers of elementary mathematics.

2. Certain reading skills are necessary for success in solving verbal arithmetic problems. According to Corle and Coulter (1964), the three most important reading skills are vocabulary development, literal interpretation of the problem, and selection of the proper solution process (reasoning). It is also noted that listening skills seem to be related to mathematical ability, primarily through their relationship to reading achievement.

3. Success in mathematical problem solving is greatly influenced by certain mathematical prerequisites and reading skills, but it is also affected by other variables. Among these are motor abilities, verbal abilities, personality characteristics, and physical conditions. It is also influenced by the arrangement of data within a mathematics problem.

4. Textbook readability is a major consideration in a child's mathematical success because in many classrooms textbooks are the only resource provided for mathematics instruction. Therefore, the vocabulary, both general and quantitative, the difficulty of nonverbal items such as symbols and graphs, and

the interest level of the text should be evaluated carefully to insure that the material is suitable to the child's ability and grade level. (pp. 87–88)

Mathematical Language

Reading a mathematics text requires the interpretation of two types of language. The first is the printed word, through which mathematical concepts are explained. The second involves interpretation of signs and symbols.

Shepherd (1978) identified four types of vocabulary within the printed language of mathematics:

	Examples
1. Technical words peculiar to some area of mathematics	Geometry: arc Algebra: polynomial
2. General words with mathematical meanings	prime, radical, square
3. Words that signal a mathematical process	times, difference, subtract
4. General words that can determine a student's comprehension	after, compare, over, each, than

Students must learn to recognize and understand various mathematical terms. You can facilitate this process by (1) providing concrete *and* abstract examples, (2) defining terms, or (3) discussing concepts.

An understanding of the printed word is necessary as students encounter story or word problems. It is not uncommon for students who have previously exhibited computational competence to have difficulty solving word problems. Cunningham and Ballew (1983) liken the relationship between computation and word problem solving to the relationship between word identification and reading comprehension. Computation should be the means to an end: problem solving.

Students should be taught to analyze word problems and should be encouraged to

1. Read the problem carefully and begin to conceptualize
2. Reread to decide what problem is posed
3. Reread to detect the clues given for solving the problem
4. Determine procedures for solving the problem
5. Solve the problem
6. Check the results

These steps are illustrated in the following problem:

Kelly is three years older than Pat. Pat is nine years old. How old is Kelly?

1. Ages?   (Problem conceptualization)
   Pat (nine years old)
   Kelly (three years older)

2. How old is Kelly?   (Problem posed)
3. 9 years old   (Clues)
    9 years old +3
4. Addition   (Procedure)
5.   9 years old   (Solve)
     + 3
     ─────────────
        12 years old
        Kelly is 12 years old
6.   12   (Check)
     -   3
     ─────
         9

In addition to vocabulary words and story problem concepts, the student of mathematics encounters such symbols and signs as $=$, $\times$, $+$, $-$, $\div$ that represent words such as equal, times, plus, minus, and divide. Encourage your students to think of these symbols as mathematical shorthand.

Reading Tables, Graphs, and Pictorial Data

Mathematics texts often require students to read and interpret tables, graphs, and other pictorial data. Figures 9-5, 9-6, and 9-7 are examples

AREAS OF STATES
■ = 100,00 km^2

Alaska	■ ■ ■ ■ ■ ■ ■ ■ ■ ■ ■ ■ ■ ■ ■
California	■ ■ ■ ■
Montana	■ ■ ■ ■
New Mexico	■ ■ ■
Texas	■ ■ ■ ■ ■ ■ ■

Figure 9–5. Data given by graphs. A geography class made this pictograph. It shows the areas of the five largest states. Each area is rounded to the nearest 100,000 square kilometers (km^2). In the pictograph, each ■ represents 100,000 km^2. (From J. Forbes, T. Thoburn, and R. Bechtel, *Macmillan Mathematics*, Series M, Book 7. New York: Macmillan Publishing Co., Inc., 1982, p. 388.)

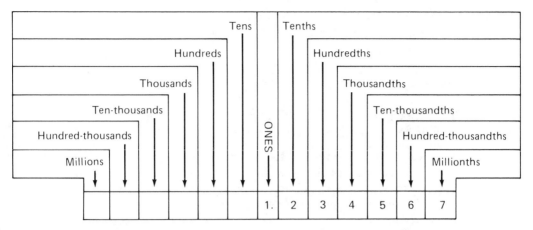

Figure 9–6. Data given by graphs. (From J. Forbes, T. Thoburn, and R. Bechtel, *Macmillan Mathematics*, Book 8. New York: Macmillan Publishing Co., Inc., 1982, p. 68.)

of types of visual representations that might be found in mathematics texts. To understand such visual data, students should be encouraged to

1. Read descriptive phrases that tell what the table or graph represents.
2. Carefully study any given numbers or letters or words to determine what has been measured.
3. Read any column of data presented to gain a clearer understanding of what is being represented.
4. Analyze any pictorial representations and convert them to numbers.
5. Compare and draw conclusions, if requested.

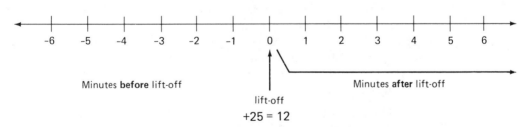

Figure 9–7. Problem solving: Using number scales. A number scale can be used to show numbers that are measures. An important time or position is labeled "zero" and other measures are given as "below or before zero" and "above or after zero." In this example, a countdown started 13 minutes before lift-off. It continued for 25 minutes. How long after lift-off did the countdown stop? A number scale can be used to show times before and after rocket lift-off. The countdown stopped 12 minutes after lift-off. (From J. Forbes, T. Thoburn, and R. Bechtel, *Macmillan Mathematics*, Series M, Book 7. New York: Macmillan Publishing Co., Inc., 1982, p. 362.)

Students will have a better understanding of bar, line, circle, and picture graphs and tables and histograms if they analyze them using the five preceding steps.

Teaching Mathematics

The following guidelines will help you to teach students to *understand* as well as *solve* mathematical problems.

1. Students need intense practice in *reading, speaking,* and *computing* the succinct language of words and symbols in mathematics.
2. Design activities to reinforce the technical terms, labeling processes, and symbol representations of mathematics.
3. Students must be encouraged to read for the purpose of the problem because the purpose of the problem is intrinsic to solving it.
4. Encourage students to view symbols as mathematical shorthand. Begin by asking them to write formulas in longhand and to restate them in symbols.
5. Students must be encouraged to employ both analytical and computational processes in solving story problems. Encourage them to read a problem and picture it in their minds. Then ask them to reread the last sentence to determine what they are being asked to do. Next, have them reread and determine the process, estimate an answer, and then attempt to solve the problem.
6. Practice and opportunity must be given students to design tabular, graphic, and pictorial representations. Students should be encouraged to read the table or graph and determine its purpose. Next, they should analyze the vertical columns to determine their meaning. Finally, they should read all bindings and additional notes. If they are reading a graph instead of a table, they will need help in noting the quantity or units of measurement.
7. Students must be given practice in following directions. Ask them to read or listen to the directions to gain an overview of the task. Next, have them reread each separate phrase of the directions while thinking about the exact application. Then, have them synthesize or combine all parts of the directional task and proceed.
8. Practice in reasoning, estimating, generalizing, and computing are part of a successful math program.

The following is a directed reading activity designed by Larry McCullough for use with his sixth-grade class.

DIRECTED READING ACTIVITY

Background Experience

Material required: Text, road atlas or pilot's navigation map.
Application: Use the distance/driving time chart in the atlas or the pilot's navigation map to begin the discussion of points and lines. Recom-

mend using the atlas as the students will probably never have seen the navigation map, but they will have seen a road atlas somewhere.

Question: How many of you have ever seen a road atlas? (Hold up atlas.)

Question: Have you ever seen this page? (Show students the distance/driving chart in atlas.)

Question: How would you describe what you see on this page?

Answer: (Looking for answer "point/dot" and "lines.")

Question: How would you describe the page itself?

Answer: (Looking for the answer "plane"; if no response, give answer.)

Discussion: On maps most small cities and towns are usually represented by a dot or point and the roads by lines. (At this point write the words and symbols "Point," "Line," and "Plane" on the board and draw the symbol for each.)

Question: What are some other things that you could use to describe a point, line, or plane? (Get the students to develop their own list of items for each symbol.) Ideas: stars, far-off lights, airplane vapor trails, telephone and power lines, surface of walls, desk tops, panes of glass.

Question: How would you define or what would you call the point where two lines come together? (Use picture on board or the construction lines of the room.) That point is the "Intersection" of two lines. Two lines intersecting will always define a single point.

Question: Two planes "Intersecting" will always define what?

Answer: A line. (Write "Intersection" on the board. Ask students to give examples.) Ideas: Street intersection, corner of a building.

Question: If a water pitcher has water in it, we may say that the pitcher holds water or what is another word for hold?

Answer: (Looking for the word "Contain"; if no response, give the answer.) In geometry we say a line contains a point and that a plane contains a point or a line. However, points lie on lines and planes and lines lie on planes. Example on the board: line "l" containing point "A" lies on plane "M."

Vocabulary

A. *Points:* Points have no size and are labeled by capital letters. (Label the point on the blackboard.)

B. *Lines:* Lines have no thickness or width and in geometry will be straight lines. Lines are labeled using a lowercase letter. Lines can also be defined by two points (capital letters). (Label line on the blackboard.)

C. *Planes:* Planes have no thickness and each individual plane is developed in only two directions. Another way to say that is to say that a plane is drawn in two dimensions. They are represented by drawing a four-sided figure, such as this. Planes may be defined by three points on the plane that are not in a straight line, such as this. Planes are labeled by capital script letters. (Label the drawing.)

D. *Intersections:* Lines or planes or lines and planes intersect if they have points or lines in common. (Demonstrate.)

E. *Contain* and *Lie on:* Lines contain points. Planes contain points and lines. Points lie on lines and planes. Lines lie on planes. (Demonstrate).

Springboard Questions

A. Why is it important to have an understanding of the definitions for point, line, plane, intersection, contain, and lie on?

B. Do those terms have anything to do with the world about you?

Silent Reading

Now read the following page in class to yourself:

A Study in Geometry: Points, Lines and Planes

A point has no dimension

A position or a tiny nail hole suggest the idea of a point. Points have no size or dimension. Points are usually illustrated by dots and are named by capital letters.

A line has one dimension

A geometric line means a straight line

The idea of a line is suggested by an airplane path or a very tight string. Lines have no specific length since they extend indefinitely. They also have no thickness or width. Lines are illustrated by arrows on both ends and are named by, a lowercase letter. The name of a line is also determined by using the letters of the two points.

A plane has two dimensions

A table or a wall surface suggest the notion of a plane. A plane also has no thickness and extends indefinitely in two directions. Planes are named by capital script letters and are represented by four-sided figures. Planes can also be named by three points of the plane, but these points cannot be on the same line.

WX intersects YZ at A. The intersection of WX and YZ is A. Lines and planes can also intersect if they have points in common.

Remember:
1. lines contain points
2. planes contain points and lines
3. points lie on lines and planes
4. lines lie on planes

Look at the figure on the left. All of the information pertains to that figure: all the points of $\overline{KL}$ are also points of $\mathscr{D}$. It can also be stated that $\mathscr{D}$ contains $\overline{KL}$ and lies on $\mathscr{D}$. K lies on $\overline{KL}$ and lies on $\mathscr{D}$. Both $\overline{KL}$ and $\mathscr{D}$ contain K.

Main Questions

If the students are unable to answer the main questions, the teacher should ask the supporting questions.

A. Name the math symbol we have been discussing that is identified by a capital letter; a lowercase letter.

    1. What is the size of a point?
    2.. What is the width of a line?
    3. Which symbol helps to define the other?
    4. What is the length of a line?
    5. Does a grain of salt define a point or a line?
    6. Does the edge of a box define a point or a line?
B. What is the math symbol that extends in two directions?
    1. What is its thickness?
    2. How is a plane identified?
    3. What is the symbol we use for a plane?
    4. According to the reading selection three _____?_____ define a
    plane.
    5. What thing in the world about you suggests a plane to you?
C. What is the point called where two lines or a line and a plane or
   two planes come together?
    1. What is the point where two lines cross called?
    2. What is the intersection of two planes called?
    3. What is the intersection of a plane and a line called?
    4. Can two lines intersect more than once?
    5. Can two planes intersect more than once?
D. What is the difference between the terms "Contain" and "Lie on"?
    1. What does a line contain?
    2. What does a plane contain?
    3. What does a point contain?
    4. What does a point lie on?
    5. What does a line lie on?
    6. Suppose P and Q are two points. How many lines lie on P and Q?

Reading in Science

Elementary science texts include information from all the sciences—
geology, biology, physical science, botany, and chemistry. The emphasis
is on *involvement* through observation, inquiry, and discovery. You can help
your students to discover the world of science by presenting information
through many types of media, including films, pictures, observations,
models, and a variety of reading materials. Try to plan activities that will
allow your students to *experience* scientific phenomena through all the
senses in addition to listening, talking, and reading.
    Language and reading skills are essential to a student's mastery of sci-
ence materials. Students use these skills to discover scientific data, interpret factual material, and formulate generalizations. You must guide your
students in developing the language and reading skills that will enable
them to read their science materials successfully. Be aware that scientific
writings contain

1. A terse style of writing
2. An extremely high readability level
3. A density of facts and details
4. A multitude of difficult concepts

Many of the skills required to read science texts successfully are also common to other content areas; therefore, you can reinforce the common reading and study skills through a variety of content materials. In a science classroom especially, your instruction should enable students to

1. Understand scientific language
2. Synthesize their rates of reading with their purpose for reading
3. Utilize the parts of their text
4. Understand and utilize scientific formulas
5. Read graphic aids
6. Follow directions
7. Evaluate data
8. Make generalizations
9. Apply new data to solve problems

Scientific Language

Science vocabulary is rapidly changing and so vast that it is sometimes overwhelming to a student. For this reason, a "hands-on" approach to science has been used in many schools in an attempt to develop basic concepts before students confront the technical language of science. By using this type of approach, teachers hoped to develop in their students a positive attitude toward the study of science. Before this experience-based approach was used, it was found that the vocabulary of science often negatively affected students' listening comprehension. Students were unfamiliar with both the technical and nontechnical languages. A similar problem occurred when children read scientific materials. Mallinson (1972) suggested that this was true for the following reasons:

1. The levels of reading difficulty of many textbooks in science were found to be too high for the students for whom the textbooks were designed.
2. The differences between the levels of reading difficulty of the easiest and the most difficult textbooks analyzed in all the studies were both statistically significant and consequential.
3. In some science textbooks, whose average level of reading difficulty seemed satisfactory, there were passages that would have been difficult even for some college students.
4. Many science textbooks contained nontechnical words that could have been replaced by easier synonyms.
5. Little cognizance seemed to have been taken of growth in reading ability during the school year, since the earlier portions of some of the textbooks were difficult, whereas the latter portions were easier. (p. 139)

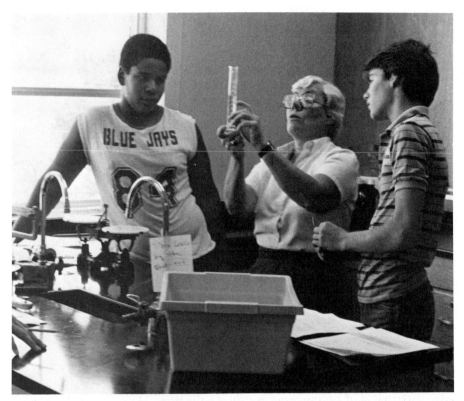

A *"hands-on" approach to science has been used in many schools in an attempt to develop basic concepts before students confront the technical language of science. (Photo by Linda Lungren.)*

Some students experience problems making the transition from reading largely narrative basal readers to reading factual material with a high concept load. One scientific selection may introduce several new concepts. The student must learn to perceive the necessary relationships, classifications, and relevance of the material. Readers of science materials are also expected to derive information from the interpretation of pictures, maps, graphs, charts, tables, and formulas—a process that may create further difficulties for some. You can reduce the possibility of language and conceptual difficulty by planning activities with the focus on firsthand observation. Such activities might include field trips, experiments, films, models, and pictures. Following are some additional suggestions for your classroom:

1. Discuss the scientific concept *before* adding the technical label.
2. Define new words and encourage students to use the glossary or dictionary.

3. Have students analyze word parts and provide them with lists or charts showing common word part meanings.

cyto   cell, hollow
logy   science, study of
hemo   blood
poly   many, much

4. Substitute common terms for technical terms. For example, *balance* may be an acceptable substitute for *equilibrium*.
5. Discuss the multiple meanings of scientific words. For example, *mass, core,* and *cell* all have multiple meanings.
6. Use visual aids to help students understand abstract concepts.
7. Encourage students to use context clues to help "unlock" the meaning of new words.
8. Develop scientific word charts that clarify and/or classify scientific terms.

<u>Heat</u>

radiation
conduction
convection

Or have students classify materials as liquids, solids, or gases.

It is particularly important for you to introduce the new vocabulary and concepts that will be encountered in a selection. Many words have multiple meanings, and each subject area contains a unique vocabulary. As a classroom teacher, you must teach the vocabulary upon which the key concepts rest.

Comprehending Scientific Data

Young children are naturally curious; therefore, many students in the primary grades are very interested in science. This interest sometimes wanes during the intermediate school years because of the difficulties students encounter in reading printed scientific material. As a classroom teacher, you may be able to lessen these difficulties by following the following procedures when you are introducing and implementing a unit of scientific study:

A. Plan for unit implementation
   1. Begin by surveying the unit of study to identify potentially difficult vocabulary.
      a. Which words contain the stems of other words?
      b. Which words may cause multiple meaning difficulty?
      c. Which words present entirely unexplained concepts?
      d. Which words can be associated with objects?
      e. Which words draw on the experiences of your students?

2. Determine which of these words contain key bits of understanding.
3. Categorize all of the remaining terms under key terms.
B. Implement the unit
   1. List the key terms on the board or on a wall chart.
   2. Present an illustration for each word. Illustrations may be made through *pictures, live specimens, slides.*
   3. Ask questions that will help students to use the new words.
   4. As the unit progresses, introduce other categories of terms in the same manner.
   5. Utilize magazines, newspapers, and trade books to supplement textbook reading.
   6. Actively involve students in the unit by having them
      a. Collect specimens or pictures of specimens
      b. Label specimens or picture displays
      c. Draw charts
      d. Develop models
      e. Perform experiments
      f. Plan field trips

Mastery of study skills is a key element in all content area reading. In science, students must be able to locate information, understand graphic representations, and interpret formulas to make evaluative judgments.

Teaching Science

LOCATING INFORMATION

One of the steps toward implementing your reading/science curriculum is to provide your students practice in locating information and in using supplementary resources. Expansion of this library study skill is particularly valuable as it relates to *scientific inquiry* because many content area science programs are based on this approach.

Have a class discussion regarding the parts of a book and the purpose of each part. Students should become familiar with using the table of contents, glossary, indexes, appendices, headings, pictures, and graphs. Once the students have developed basic competency in using these aids, introduce a variety of science resource materials. These may include encyclopedias, journals (e.g., *Scientific American*), trade books, government publications, and scientific bulletins. Dole and Johnson (1981) also recommend using fiction books with a scientific theme because "these books can provide needed background for science concepts covered in class, and they can help relate these concepts to students' everyday lives."

After the student has located a source of information for the topic being investigated, encourage him or her to survey the material to determine the main idea and to take note of all important details. When the specific information being sought has been located, the student will be able to continue his or her study. The location of new scientific data may call for the interpretation of graphic representations.

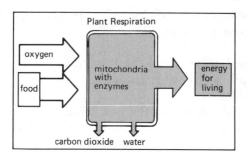

Figure 9–8. Graphic representation. (From A. Stone and L. Sherman, *Spaceship Earth: Life Science.* Boston: Houghton Mifflin Company, 1975, p. 169.)

UNDERSTANDING GRAPHIC REPRESENTATIONS

Graphic aids are intended to supplement or clarify the printed text. They are particularly valuable in exploring abstract concepts. Students should be encouraged to note titles and other identifying or explanatory information, as well as the elements of the illustration, when they encounter graphics. Students need instruction in interpreting graphic symbols because many elementary science materials contain the types of graphic representations presented in Figures 9-8 through 9-12.

CALCITE	DILUTE HYDRO-CHLORIC ACID		CALCIUM CHLORIDE		CARBON DIOXIDE		WATER
$CaCO_3$	+	$2HCl$	$\rightarrow$	$CaCl_2$	+	CO_2 (bubbles)	+	H_2O

Figure 9–9. Graphic representation.

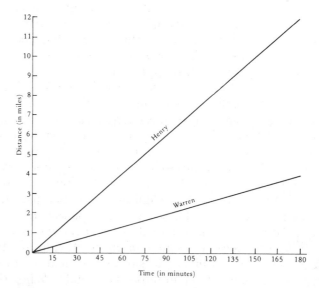

Figure 9–10. Graphic representation. (From K. Barnard and C. Lavatelli, *Science: Measuring Things.* New York: Macmillan Publishing Co., Inc., 1970, p. 35.)

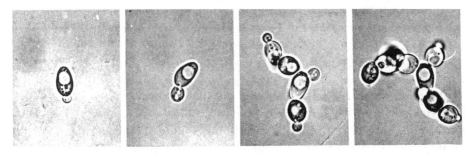

Figure 9–11. Graphic representation. Yeast cells magnified 1,000 times. Within 4 hours, the cell farthest left had began to bud; there were eight cells. (From K. Barnard et al., *Science: A Search for Evidence*. New York: Macmillan Publishing Co., Inc., 1966, p. 375.)

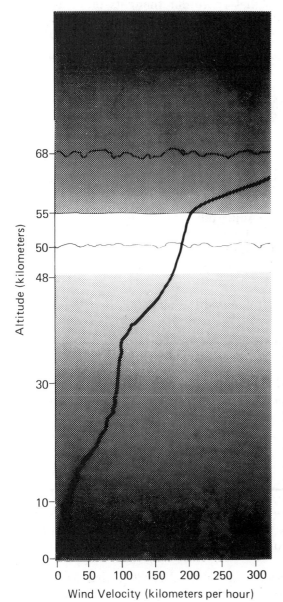

Figure 9–12. Graphic representation. The winds of Venus vary with altitude. Upper clouds whip by at 360 km an hour. But a slow breeze at the surface moves no faster than a walk. Venus is a forecaster's dream; its weather scarcely varies. In many places, Pioneer and Venera probes logged the wind speeds shown here. (From R. Gallant, *National Geographic Picture Atlas of Our Universe*. Washington, D.C.: National Geographic Society, 1980, p. 88.)

Most science texts contain graphics similar to these and others. They are intended to supplement the printed text by providing clues. Some students may find them difficult to read unless they are given careful instruction. Others may never grasp the importance of such representations unless they are alerted to their functional value. A very specific type of graphic that students encounter in science texts is a scientific formula.

INTERPRETING FORMULAS

Formulas are part of the vocabulary of science that sometimes interfere with a student's comprehension of material. Students must be taught that formulas are types of sentences that represent thoughts or ideas. The symbols within the formulas can be viewed as words:

The sentence, "Centripetal *force* is equal to the *mass* times the *velocity* squared divided by the *radius* of a circle" can be represented as

$$F = \frac{MV^2}{R}$$

The sentence equals the formula. Now let's examine each symbol, word, or numeral within the formula:

$$^2 = \text{squared}$$
$$F = \text{force}$$
$$M = \text{mass}$$
$$V = \text{velocity}$$
$$R = \text{radius}$$

After the reader *interprets* the symbol and the meaning, he is ready to evaluate the message.

As a teacher in a self-contained classroom, you may find yourself responsible for teaching art and music. Let us briefly explore the relationships between reading and the arts.

Reading and the Arts

Even if your school is fortunate enough to have music and art specialists on the staff, you should still try to incorporate the arts into the classroom. Sometimes the humanities are underrated and are not part of content area teaching.

We urge you to provide both art and music activities that will foster lifetime interest, enjoyment, and pursuit of these arts in your students.

Term	Sign	Meaning
f	forte	loud
p	piano	soft
<	crescendo	gradually getting louder
>	decrescendo	gradually getting softer

Figure 9–13. Dynamics markings. (From M. Marsh et al., *The Spectrum of Music with Related Arts*, Book 5. New York: Macmillan Publishing Co., Inc., 1980, p. 15.)

The integration of reading and the arts is similar to that of other content areas. We will briefly examine each of these areas.

Music

Although younger students do not become involved with in-depth studies of musical theory, they do encounter new vocabulary and symbols that must be read and interpreted. Music has a technical vocabulary, like other content area subjects, and an array of musical symbols that have specific meanings. Music texts often contain materials similar to those shown in Figures 9-13 and 9-14.

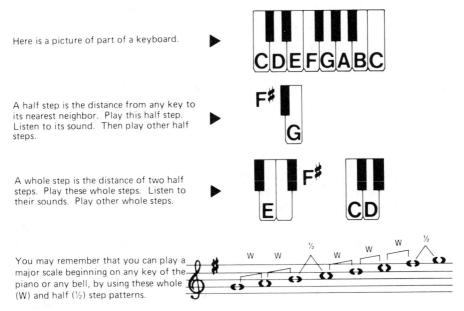

Here is a picture of part of a keyboard.

A half step is the distance from any key to its nearest neighbor. Play this half step. Listen to its sound. Then play other half steps.

A whole step is the distance of two half steps. Play these whole steps. Listen to their sounds. Play other whole steps.

You may remember that you can play a major scale beginning on any key of the piano or any bell, by using these whole (W) and half (½) step patterns.

Begin on G. Play the G major scale. It has one sharp. Which note has the sharp?

Figure 9–14. Learning step patterns. (From M. Marsh et al., *The Spectrum of Music with Related Arts*, Book 5. New York: Macmillan Publishing Co., Inc., 1980, p. 88.)

As you attempt to integrate music and reading, remember that students must be helped to

1. Perceive the technical terms and symbols
2. Interpret and understand the symbols
3. Follow performance directions
4. Evaluate music criticisms

As we have suggested throughout this text, the directed reading activity is an effective technique for content area learning. The following DRA was designed by Lori Foster for use with a middle school–aged music class.

DIRECTED READING ACTIVITY

Goal:

The students will understand different forms of music written during the Baroque period.

Rationale:

Learning about the Baroque period will help students to understand and relate some of the aspects of life to those that happened previously and will be able to make judgments for the future based on what they know about the present and the past.

Objective:

After completing the DRA, the students will be able to define and identify correctly a concerto grosso when hearing one played.

    I. Background Experience
        A. Symphony Concert
            1. Take them on a field trip to a concert.
            2. Watch one on video tape or on television.
        B. Recordings of a concerto grosso and other Baroque forms. They should write about what they hear in the recordings. Composers to listen to are
                1. Corelli
                2. Vivaldi
                3. Bach
        C. Have an oral discussion on what the students have heard.
            1. The Baroque period
            2. Multimovement music
        D. Divide the class into three groups and assign each a composer (Corelli, Vivaldi, Bach). They will read for the following information and present it to the group.

1. Birth (where and when)
2. Death (where and when)
3. Three types of music they wrote (cantatas, concerto grosso, sonatas, etc.)
4. Instruments the composers preferred

II. Introduce New Vocabulary
   A. Words, Meaning, in Context
      1. Ripieno: This means full ensemble or group. The *ripieno* is playing in contrast to the concertino.
      2. Timbre: The differences between sound of the same pitch and volume. The *timbre* of the flute is higher than the tuba.
      3. Contrast: The differences between two things. There is a large *contrast* between day and night.
      4. Texture: The makeup or structure of something. When there is only one instrument playing, the *texture* is thin.
      5. Concertino: This means a solo group. The *concertino* played the solo to the best of their ability.
      6. Pitted: To place in contest against another. The man was *pitted* in conflict against the sea.
   B. Semantic Mapping. This is an effective technique designed for vocabulary expansion. (See Figure 9-15.)

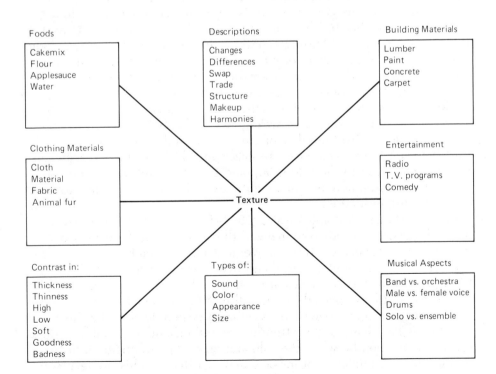

Figure 9–15. Semantic mapping

C. Semantic Feature Analysis. This is also an effective vocabulary expansion technique.

	Classification	Play Music	One Person
Group	X		
Ensemble	X	X	
Solo	X	X	X

III. Springboard Questions
    A. What are the two groups of musicians called in a concerto grosso?
    B. What techniques did composers use to contrast the two groups?
    C. What three composers wrote concerto grossi?
    D. What did Bach call his concerto grosso?
IV. Silent Reading

Concerto Grosso

The **concerto grosso** is a multimovement work for instruments in which a solo group called the *concertino* and a full ensemble called the *ripieno* (Italian for "full") are pitted against each other. In the early concerto grosso the concertino generally consisted of two violins and continuo (cello and harpsichord). The ripieno was usually a small string orchestra with its own continuo. Through contrasts in tone color, texture, melodic line and relative complexity of musical material, the solo and ensemble groups compete with each other for the listener's attention. These contrasts are the very essence of the concerto grosso.

The first important examples of the concerto grosso appeared in the works of the Italian composer Arcangelo Corelli (1653–1713). Corelli's concertos had no fixed number of movements and no set plan of contrast between the movements. He made very little distinction between the material given to the solo group and that given to the ripieno; the contrast was essentially one of weight—two violins and continuo against the full string ensemble.

Another Italian, Antonio Vivaldi (1669–1741), was the first great master of the genre. Vivaldi systematized the structure of the concerto grosso by standardizing a three-movement form. Vivaldi was a prolific composer of instrumental music, and over 450 of his concertos have been preserved. His concertos are consistently in three movements: the first is fast and long, played by the full instrumental ensemble; the second is slow and short, played by a reduced ensemble; and the third like the first, is fast, long, and written for the full ensemble. Vivaldi made a greater distinction between the solo and ensemble groups both in timbre and in complexity of musical material than did his predecessors.

Vivaldi's concertos strongly influenced Bach, who often transcribed for keyboard the works, especially the concertos, of Italian composers. Between 1714 and 1717, Bach transcribed six Vivaldi concertos for solo organ or harpsichord and orchestra. In his own concerti grossi, Bach achieved an even stronger contrast between the concertino and the ripieno in instrumental color and the degree of complexity of the music for each group.

In 1721 Bach completed six concertos for orchestra. He dedicated them to Christian Ludwig, the Margrave of Brandenburg, who had requested Bach to write some pieces for the court orchestra at Brandenburg. Although Bach referred to these works as "concertos for several instruments," they have come to be known as the *Brandenburg Concertos*. Three of them (Nos. 2, 4, and 5) follow in the tradition of Vivaldi in that they are concerti grossi that contrast a group of solo instruments (concertino) against a full ensemble (ripieno).*

V. Comprehension Questions
   A. Explicit
      1. What does concertino mean?
      2. Define ripieno.
      3. Who wrote the first concerto grosso?
      4. Name one of Bach's concerto grossi.
   B. Implicit
      1. How does a sonata compare to a concerto grosso? (comparison)
      2. Do you think Bach was stealing when he transposed Vivaldi's pieces for keyboard? (evaluation)
      3. In what ways are the ensemble and solo groups similar? (comparison)
      4. Can you think of any music written today that uses contrasts of solo and group? (comparison)
      5. Why do you think Corelli had no fixed number of movements and no plan of contrast? (implication)
      6. Listen to the following concerto grosso and count how many times the concertino is heard. (problem solving)

Art

Elementary school students rarely have art textbooks per se; rather, they often encounter reproductions of art works in content area texts, such as in social studies. These opportunities can be used to encourage children to compare artistic styles and trends and to show how art works are often reflections of the times.

Reading skills and art are related in that art has a technical vocabulary (e.g., relief, fresco, chroma) and also because following directions is very important in art instruction. For example, students must follow directions

*This passage is from Robert Hickok, *Exploring Music*, © 1979 Addison-Wesley, Reading MA, pages 147 and 148. Reprinted with permission.

in mixing paints or other art materials. Students are also often asked to evaluate works of art. In these ways, the relationship between reading and art is very similar to other content area subjects.

Suggested Reading Related to Goals.   We encourage you at this time to review the goals at the beginning of this chapter. If you feel you would like to explore one or more of these areas in greater depth, please refer to the cross-indexed bibliography at the end of the book.

SECTION **4** *The Reading Curriculum*

10 Approaches to Teaching Reading

It is easy to understand why no single program has been shown to be consistently more effective than any other. Indeed, the teacher who knows and understands a variety of programs and how they develop various reading skills supersedes the program.

[R. Farr and N. Roser]

Goals

To help the student understand
1. The historical background of reading instruction in the United States
2. The components of several methods of reading instruction
3. The necessity for formulating a personal definition of reading

"How do I teach students to read?" This is a question that has been asked and answered in many ways throughout history. The answers have undergone changes, revisions, updates, transformations, and experimentation in an effort to discover the best way to teach reading.

We will begin this chapter by presenting a brief overview of how teachers in the United States have answered this question. Such historical insights will help you to understand the advances that have been made in the teaching of reading as well as the progress that has been made in teaching in general.

Historical Perspectives

In 1965, Nila Banton Smith published a comprehensive history of American reading instruction. In it, Smith characterized each era by the influence of the times that affected the focus of instruction. We have sum-

TABLE 10-1

Eras			Approximate Date	Reading Instruction		
	Dates	Influences		Learning System	Materials	Characteristics
Religious emphasis	1607–1776	Religion	1600–1800	Alphabet spelling system	*Hornbook*	Oral reading, memorization, recitation
Nationalistic-moralistic	1776–1840	Politics	1800s	Whole-word method	*New England Primer*	Silent reading, oral reading, reading for comprehension
Education for intelligent citizenship	1840–1880	Politics and leadership		Controlled repetition	*McGuffey Eclectic Readers*	Silent reading, controlled repetition of words
Reading as a cultural asset	1890–1910	Cultural pursuits	Late 1800s	Artificial phonics system	Basic readers containing tales and excerpts from classics	Word analysis emphasis
Scientific investigation	1910–1925	Tests and measurement	Early 1900s	Look-and-say		Sight-word emphasis, testing initiated
Intensive research and application	1925–1935	Educational research		Silent reading method		Elaborate testing and measurement, silent reading emphasis
International conflict	1935–1950	Literary skills	1930s	Basal method	Student and teacher workbooks; *Dick and Jane, Alice and Jerry*	Controlled vocabulary, oral and silent reading, phonics influence
Expanding knowledge and technological revolution	1950–1965	Reading becomes a national concern	1950s and 1960s	Phonics strongly emphasized, Words in Color, individualized instruction, programmed instruction, language experience method	SRA materials	Individualization, individual language patterns, personalization
Humanistic influences on reading	1965–1973	Emphasis on individual				
Reading as information processing	1973–present	Process of reading examined	Late 1960s Mid-1970s to present	Linguistic influence Managed language/reading	*Let's Read* Use of a variety of methods and materials: *Ginn Reading Program, Macmillan R*	Patterned word units Personalization, individualization, sequential organization

SOURCE: Nila Banton Smith, *American Reading Instruction* (Newark, Dela.: International Reading Association, 1965).

marized this information in Table 10-1; in addition, we have added the instructional methods and materials that were commonly used in each era. We have also added the titles and descriptions for the periods of time since Smith's book was published in 1965. By studying this chart, you can see that reading instruction has changed dramatically through the years both by responding to the climate of the times and also by adapting to ever-increasing educational advancements.

Methodology

In America's colonial period, an alphabet spelling system was used to teach reading. Instruction was given in single-letter recognition; then combined letter-sound correspondences, such as *ab, ac,* and *et;* then parts of words, such as *tab* and *let;* and, finally, the whole word, *tablet.* Reading was almost a totally oral process in these early years because it included intensive instruction in pitch, stress, enunciation, gesticulation, memorization, and recitation.

Horace Mann, an educational pioneer, was instrumental in introducing the whole-word method of reading instruction in American schools. He advocated memorizing entire words before analyzing letters and letter patterns. His approach stressed silent reading and emphasized reading for comprehension. About this time, the *McGuffey Eclectic Reader,* which emphasized a controlled repetition of words, was introduced. Although the *McGuffey Readers* were not filled with the most interesting narrative stories, they were definitely an improvement over existing texts because of their organizational scheme: sentence length and vocabulary were controlled to match the students' current developmental level.

The next "innovation" in reading instruction occurred during the latter half of the nineteenth century. It was a phonetics method, a synthetic phonics system, similar to the programs that were discussed in detail in Chapter 5. Teachers became dissatisfied with this method because too much attention was placed on word analysis and too little attention was given to comprehension. This method was temporarily abandoned, being replaced sometime around 1910 with the new "look-and-say" method. The look-and-say method also lost favor with many teachers because the student had to learn every word as a sight word, and students made little progress in learning to read.

The rise of the silent reading method began around 1920. Teachers were now urged to abandon all oral methods of instruction and testing. Robinson (1977) states, "There were increasing demands placed on reading for meaning, instead of an oral exercise, in order to meet the varied needs of society" (p. 50). In addition, with the advent of intelligence testing and educational measurement, "research reports began to show the superiority of silent reading over oral reading for both fluency and comprehension" (Robinson, 1977, p. 50). A great deal of reading research was widely conducted (Gray, 1925–1932; Good, 1923–1953), the results of which gave rise to the extremely popular method that followed: the basal reading method, launched throughout the United States in the early 1930s.

From Basal Readers to the Present

Basal readers were at the core of most reading instruction from the 1930s onward. The basal reading program included a student text and teacher's manual as the base of the reading program. Each basal presented a controlled vocabulary and introduced levels of syntactic complexity that paralleled children's development. The basal method was dominant over other methods until the 1950s and 1960s when there was a return to *phonics*. This occurred because teachers were dissatisfied with the basal as the *only* form of reading instruction. Phonics strategies such as the Initial Teaching Alphabet and Words in Color (which will be explained later in this chapter) were used to supplement basals. Today many basal series contain a strong phonics emphasis.

In the 1960s, educational efforts were focused on meeting the individual needs of students. Techniques for individualizing reading instruction were encouraged, and programmed materials were developed to provide better classroom management techniques. The language experience method, an updating of an earlier practice, was promoted as an effective teaching method. From the late 1960s until the present, linguistic points of view have influenced the structure of many basal readers. Linguists have promoted the teaching of reading through patterned word units, for example, *Nan ran to the man.*

Very few educators would argue against the theory of a personalized reading program for each child; however, the major problem with this approach was perceived to be a time constraint. Creating an efficient, well-organized system to manage twenty-five or thirty different personalized programs daily seemed like an overwhelming task—even to some excellent teachers. This situation occurred because teachers were not trained in flexible grouping techniques, personalized contracts, and classroom management processes.

In recognition of the need for a personalized reading program, without time or management constraints, several book publishers "rose to the occasion" in the 1970s and 1980s with managed language/reading materials. These materials include elaborate record-keeping systems, basal readers, teachers' manuals, and criterion-referenced and norm-referenced tests. (These tests will be explained in detail in Chapter 12.)

This brief historical overview of reading instruction practices in the United States may shed some light on important considerations that you should examine to help you determine the best methods of instruction for your students.

Philosophy of Approaches

The goal of any approach, method, or philosophy of teaching reading has always been teaching students to read. Yet a close examination of the historical data presented shows that two different philosophies of instruction have existed throughout the history of teaching reading. The *sequential reading approach* encourages the use of materials that are systematically designed according to the developmental stages of children. The *spontaneous reading approach* encourages the development of materials related to the organic interests of the child. These philosophies have the same goal (teaching students to read) but differ in their implementation. In one sense, they can be thought of as existing on a continuum, for they encompass almost all the existing methods and influences of teaching reading.

As Matthes (1977, p. 9) points out, "there is no one miracle method that will teach all children to read." However, because of the emphasis on personalizing reading instruction, it would seem that the managed language/reading system may be the most effective method of teaching reading. We recognize that teachers' personal preferences and experiences sometimes dictate the use of a different method; in fact, most teachers do use a variety of methods in their classrooms to personalize each child's instructional program.

Figure 10-1 illustrates the embedding of existing methods of teaching reading within the sequential and the spontaneous reading approaches. The sequential reading approach is exemplified by *phonics, linguistic basals,* and *programmed instruction.* These methods clearly demonstrate that the sequential approach emphasizes decoding followed by comprehension. The spontaneous reading approach is characterized by *language experience* and *individualized instruction.* Reading for meaning from the initial stages of reading instruction is the major emphasis of this program. The diagram

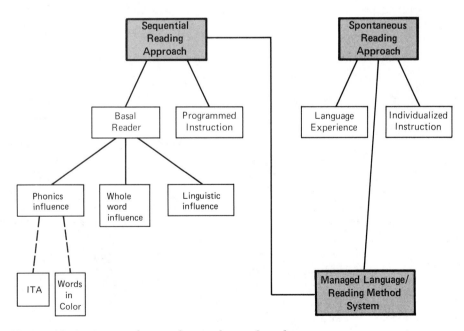

Figure 10-1. Approaches to the teaching of reading.

also shows the origins of the current *managed language/reading approach*, which integrates the strengths of both the sequential and spontaneous developmental approaches.

The strengths and weaknessess of each of the two basic approaches are readily apparent, as shown here:

Approaches	Strengths	Weaknesses
Sequential reading approach	Prepared materials, logically organized	Lack of personalization
Spontaneous reading approach	Personalized, emphasizes language base	Too time consuming, lack of manufactured materials, elaborate record keeping required

Current educational philosophy has led to the development of managed language/reading systems that capitalize on the strengths of the systems and rectify any weakness of the system. Goodman (1974) cautions us that no researcher has been able to establish any skill sequence of instruction as having 100 percent merit. Creators of these new systems acknowledge the logical developmental stages of children while providing management systems that encourage the incorporation of spontaneous development. Teachers are strongly encouraged to use the spontaneous language development of the child as the base of the reading program. The application of the managed language experience approach is thoroughly explained in Chapter 15.

Approaches, Methods, and Materials

We now explore several of the methods of teaching reading illustrated in Figure 10-1. These methods provide the basis for most of the programs currently available for classroom use.

In general, the content to be conveyed through the sequential reading approach is organized in an objective, tightly structured, and logically ordered manner. The primary focus of this material is directed toward the intellectual dimensions of the student. The philosophical parameters of this approach rely heavily on the validity of premises similar to Bruner's (1960, p. 31) idea that "knowledge is a model we construct to give meanings and structure to regularities of experience" and on other similar theories of learning. Some programmed materials and many basal reading series emphasize a sequential reading approach.

Sequential Reading Approach

BASAL READING INSTRUCTION

The premise underlying the basal reading method is that reading is a developmental task involving the acquisition of major skills and that each of these major skills is comprised of many subskills. These subskills vary in difficulty and complexity and, therefore, need to be introduced to the reader in a logical, prescribed order. Plans must also be made for integrating these subskills into an instructional program so that the reader can begin to interrelate them. If this is successfully managed, reading becomes an integrated, meaningful whole.

Most basal series are developed for grades 1 through 6, although some extend through the eighth-grade level. The materials generally include a collection of reading readiness materials, two or three preprimers, a primer, a first reader, two texts for the second and third grades, and one text for each of the upper grades. Skill workbooks, dittoes, worksheets, films and filmstrips, records, and supplementary readers may be included in the package.

A detailed teacher's manual is provided for each text in the program. In these manuals, publishers usually include a statement of the philosophy basic to the particular program, a series of story lesson plans, unit tests, lists of supplementary materials, and other related information.

One of the salient features of a basal reading program is a controlled vocabulary. The program identifies and introduces a controlled vocabulary, new words in isolation and in context. This is followed by silent and oral reading and interpretation of the material that the student has read. Subsequent activities usually involve further skill development (word-recognition, comprehension, and study skills) and enrichment activities.

Typically, an effort is made to adjust the material to the maturity level of the reader. In beginning materials, only a limited number of words is introduced, and they are reinforced through *repetition* on subsequent pages. As the student moves upward through the series, more words are introduced at each level with fewer repetitions. Some teachers' manuals provide the ratio of new words per page and the number of repetitions planned for each new word. The purpose of controlled vocabulary and planned repetition is easily understood: too many new words and too few exposures to new words can easily lead to reading difficulties.

Most basal readers, particularly those at the lower levels, are replete with pictures and illustrations. Durkin (1980) suggests that this exists for interest and also to tell the story to children who do not have the reading level of a more advanced text. In addition, most basals adjust the ratio of illustration space to print space. At lower levels, large illustrations often appear on every page or every other page. By the higher grades, illustrations may be more sparse, smaller, and more detailed.

CRITICISMS OF BASAL SERIES

In recent years, basal series have been the focus of much of the criticisms directed toward reading programs. While some of these criticisms may be justified, we feel that most of the common criticisms are in fact reflections of how basal series are *used* rather than criticisms of basal reading programs per se.

Table 10-2 lists some common criticisms of basal series along with ways of dealing with them.

You can see that basal reading programs themselves cannot bear the full brunt of all the criticisms that have been leveled against them. In some cases, teachers have misused basal series or have relied too heavily upon them. One of the most positive components of basal reading series is the teacher's manual. These manuals provide continuity for the program and security and assistance for beginning teachers. Misuse of the

TABLE 10-2
Basal Reading Programs

Criticisms	*Changes*
1. Vocabulary and sentence patterns do not match children's spoken language.	1. Since the mid-1970s, most basals reflect students' natural spoken language.
2. Content of basals is dull.	2. More recent basals have content from many subject areas in a variety of literary genres.
3. Students must read books from their *grade* level, not *achievement* level.	3. Individualizing instruction alleviates this difficulty.
4. Overuse of the teacher's manual creates sterile instruction.	4. The manual is a *guide* and should never be a substitute for creative teaching.
5. Using basals results in a uniform three-achievement-level grouping plan.	5. Flexible grouping techniques will resolve this problem.
6. Students are asked to do workbook sheets on concepts they have mastered.	6. Individualizing instruction alleviates this difficulty.
7. Basal readers provide sole source of instructional materials.	7. Creative teachers use many sources to teach content skills.
8. There is no allowance for different learning styles or modes of instruction.	8. Good teachers plan instruction based on students' needs and abilities.
9. Content often furthers sexual and class stereotypes.	9. Authors and publishers are making great strides in correcting this problem.
10. Basal series do not provide instructional procedures.	10. Instructional procedures must be geared to students and cannot be generalized successfully.

teacher's manual occurs when a teacher depends entirely on the manual or guide for classroom instruction. Matthes (1977) cautions: "A good teacher uses the guide as a guide—supplementing, enriching, and creating other experiences as the child's needs so warrant" (p. 16). Chapter 15 can also help you to personalize your basal program.

Today, all basal series are not the same (Flood et al., 1984; Schmidt et al., 1984). Some (Economy, 1983) provide a strong phonics program; others (*Macmillan R*, 1983; *Ginn Reading*, 1983) purport to be more creative than the average in their content and managed enrichment activities; still others are developed around classical literature for children. The authors and publishers of every series have attempted to incorporate activities that give the series unique characteristics. In the 1970s, some series attained uniqueness by shifting from graded to ungraded levels. Durkin (1980) cites the reason for this change as an attempt to alter criticisms leveled at a traditional graded approach. Publishers indicate increased difficulty of material through consecutive letters and numbers—for example, J, K, L, M, N. This shift is now a trend among all basal series.

In an attempt to counter the criticism that basals tend to reflect only the values and mores of white middle-class families, publishers have attempted to develop basals that contain an ethnic and economic class balance.

Basal series will probably always have their critics; however, basals can be an asset to you as a classroom teacher when used *properly*. In recent years, publishers have made serious efforts to include relevant stories and to provide technical assistance for teachers. Individualized instruction and using basal readers can be complementary methods of teaching reading. We urge you to examine a basal series for yourself and then decide if it is useful for your purposes.

Whole-Word Methodology. Whole-word instruction is a method of teaching unfamiliar vocabulary. It is often referred to as the look-and-say method, which Cheek and Cheek (1980) define as "the development of the reading skills necessary to remember words that occur most frequently in reading and that are not easily analyzed through other procedures" (p. 265). When a child encounters an unfamiliar vocabulary word, he or she can "attack" it in one of three ways:

1. Phonics: letter-by-letter, sound-by-sound analysis.
2. Structural analysis: word part (prefix, root, suffix) analysis.
3. Whole word: "What does that say?"

The whole-word method is commonly used in basal readers because students need to learn basic sight words such as *saw, was, they, under, over, it,* and *them* and because students may not have acquired word attack skills yet. The whole-word method of instruction is also necessary because English is not a perfectly alphabetic language. Twenty-six letters in the English alphabet represent approximately forty-four sounds. In many instances, it is difficult to predict through phonetic analysis the sound patterns of many irregular words. Common words such as *walk, talk, through, although,* and *lamb* as well as words derived from other languages—*chamois, hors d'oeuvre, depot, choir, vein,* and *suite*—might be taught more easily through the whole-word method. It may also be useful when teaching *homographs:*

"<u>Bow</u> down," the king growled.
There is a <u>bow</u> and arrow in the display case.
The captain of the ship is on the <u>bow</u>.

or *homophones:*

The weather <u>vane</u> is spinning.
Gloria is <u>vain</u> about her pretty formal.
The nurse drew blood from the <u>vein</u> in my arm.

Recognizing such words on sight could be more productive to the reader than engaging in an analysis of letter-sound relationships.

Remember that when you teach students whole words, you are relying heavily on their visual discrimination ability. This topic was discussed in Chapters 3 and 5; however, let us reemphasize that many studies (Durrell, 1958; Barrett, 1965; Silvaroli, 1965; Samuels, 1972) suggest that the major visual discrimination skill associated with reading success is the ability to discriminate letters of the alphabet. The necessity of having this skill becomes quite obvious when you are teaching whole words; for example,

This word is <u>did</u>.
It looks like <u>bid</u>, except
<u>did</u> begins with <u>d</u>, and
<u>bid</u> begins with <u>b</u>.

After several exposures to these words, they will become part of students' whole-word sight vocabulary. You may recall that this is the same procedure used when introducing students to the basic sight words of sight vocabulary lists.

Phonics.   The phonic approach is another method for teaching word recognition: its goal "is to give the child a key to independently unlock unfamiliar words" (Matthes, 1977, p. 44). It has been widely used since the late 1800s when educators recognized the value of letter-sound relationships as an aid to identifying unfamiliar words. Although its importance seems obvious, it is equally important to realize that phonics can only be a partial word analysis process because the English language contains twenty-six letters representing approximately forty-four sounds. English also frequently borrows words of foreign origin, words that defy English phonetic analysis. Even though such limitations are a reality, phonics instruction is quite important and has for decades been part of basal materials.

Through the years, attempts have been made to develop teaching materials that would alleviate phonic inconsistencies. Pitman (1964) devised the Initial Teaching Alphabet (ITA) to alleviate some of the confusion caused by the fact that some graphemic symbols must represent more than one sound and that several sounds can be represented by multiple spellings. The ITA, an artificial orthography, has forty-four symbols. Figure 10-2 shows examples from Pitman's ITA. However, some students have difficulty transferring reading skills learned through the ITA to traditional orthography, and many students experience spelling difficulties.

Words in Color.   Gattegno (1980) uses forty-seven colors to represent English speech sounds. Words in Color has three major limitations: (1)

Figure 10–2 Pitman's ITA alphabet.

limited supply of materials, (2) heavy reliance on phonics instruction (letter sounds and word parts), and (3) strong dependence on visual discrimination between varying shades of color.

Linguistic Influences.   Linguistics is the scientific study of language, and its influence on basal reading instruction is relatively new. Linguistics focuses on the sounds used in language, the words that result from a combination of sounds, and the meanings attached to these sounds. It also involves the structuring of words into meaningful units. Among the linguistic reading programs developed, the influence of the structural linguists seems strongest at the present time.

Since the first linguistic series was developed, *Let's Read* (Bloomfield and Barnhart, 1961), a number of other linguistic reading programs have appeared: *Merrill Linguistic Readers*, the *Miami Linguistic Reading Program*, and the *Palo Alto Linguistic Program*. These series use strict vocabulary control in beginning materials to facilitate the teaching of certain phonic principles. Students learn the sound-symbol relationships for specified consonants and the short sound of one or two vowels. Then, as many different words as possible are made from the combination of these letters. The following sentences illustrate the type of content characterizing the beginning levels of these programs:

Dan is a man.
Dan is tan.
Dan is a tan man.
Is Dan tan?

Some series do not include pictures or illustrations with stories because the authors support the theory that pictures are an unnecessary crutch and should be avoided. Others achieve a compromise by using very simple illustrations involving one or two colors.

Some linguists criticize basal reading programs because the language patterns used are unnatural—for example, "Oh, oh, oh. See Spot run." However, it is also difficult to consider sentences about "Dan, the tan man" to be reflective of natural expression. It is true, though, that as linguistic programs move to more advanced levels, sentence patterns reflect ordinary language usage. In addition, when they are compared with other basal materials on an equivalent level, the sentences in the linguistic readers often appear more complex.

Criticisms of linguistic reading programs include the following:

1. There is *one* approach to reading instruction.
2. The controlled vocabulary does not take into account the vocabulary of the children.
3. Decoding is overemphasized and comprehension is underemphasized.
4. Word-by-word reading is encouraged if teachers do not provide for practice in the normal flow of speech sounds. On the other hand, supporters of the linguistic program present these same statements as

strengths since variety of approach permits greater flexibility and in-dividualization.
5. Only words with regular spelling patterns are initially taught. The controlled vocabulary permits awareness of pattern and process before continuing to irregular spelling forms.
6. Pictures, which may stimulate interest or help with decoding un-known words, are often omitted.

PROGRAMMED INSTRUCTION

Programmed instruction, another example of the sequential reading ap-proach, is a systematic effort to take a specific block of information and divide it into small units that are organized for logical, sequential learn-ing. The organization of programmed instruction may either be branched or linear.

In a branched program, one unit (frame) of information is presented to the learner for response. If the response is correct, the student may by-pass several frames. This allows for some differentiation of instruction.

No frames are bypassed in linear arrangement. The student using the program proceeds step-by-step through each frame. Individualization is achieved through the rate at which the student moves through the pro-gram.

Perhaps the most significant aspects of programmed instruction are its immediate feedback, positive reinforcement for correct responses, and immediate correction of errors. Students constantly check the accuracy of their responses before moving on to the next segment of instruction.

The format of a program may be a workbook, teaching machine, or computer. There may also be some variety in the mode of response. Whatever the variations, the programs are designed to require individual response, immediate feedback with reinforcement (answer correct), or correction (answer wrong).

In the following section, we will discuss instructional methods that re-flect the spontaneous approach to teaching reading.

Spontaneous Reading Approach

The spontaneous reading approach integrates the cognitive and affective dimensions of students; that is, it relates to their interests as well as to their needs. Like the sequential reading approach, it is sequentially or-ganized to levels of cognitive development; however, it is also highly de-pendent on the affective domain. An interesting curriculum will help you to capitalize on students' strengths while you remediate their needs.

The two most common methods through which teachers have at-tempted to personalize reading instruction are language experience and individualized instruction. Philosophical parameters of these methods rely heavily on the validity of such premises as Dewey's famous statement (1916,

p. 125), "to learn from experience is to make a backward and forward connection between what we do to things and what we enjoy or suffer from things in consequence," and Jenkins's (1955) statement,

> Children work hard and long when they choose their own jobs. They move ahead when they have the opportunity to set their own goals. They read with greater enjoyment when they choose the material. The teacher works with the individuals and knows their interests and needs more adequately than when a group works on a single book chosen by the teacher. (p. 125)

LANGUAGE EXPERIENCE

The language experience approach to teaching reading typifies the spontaneous reading approach. It uses the already existing language of the student to develop reading, writing, and listening skills. This is not to suggest, however, that training in structural analysis, contextual analysis, or phonics analysis is unnecessary.

Proponents of the language experience approach believe that it has merit because it builds upon the interest of the student and the language that the student has already mastered. Reimer (1983) believes that language experience stories "accelerate learning by capturing the student's interest and focusing it upon the reading-writing process" (p. 396). Veatch et al. (1979) also point out that using a child's own language "provides experiences that are closely related to the child's personal and social needs" (p. 12). Perhaps, more strongly than any other approach, it emphasizes the relationships among thought, oral language, and written language.

Allen (1976) discusses the language experience approach in terms of "truths about self and language." His ten premises follow:

1. I can think about what I have experienced and imagined.
2. I can talk about what I think about.
3. What I can talk about I can express in some other form.
4. Anything I record I can recall through speaking or reading.
5. I can read what I can write by myself and what other people write for me to read.
6. As I talk and write, I use some words over and over and some not so often.
7. As I talk and write, I use some words and clusters of words to express my meaning.
8. As I write to represent the sounds I make through speech, I use the same symbols (letters) over and over.
9. Each letter of the alphabet stands for one or more sounds that I make when I talk.
10. As I read, I must add to what an author has written if I am to get full meaning and inherent pleasure from print (pp. 50–55)

Some advocates of the language experience approach encourage teachers to stress to students that reading (or written material) is "talk written down." Although it is desirable to help students make the connection be-

The language experience approach to teaching reading uses the already existing language of the child to develop reading, writing, and listening skills. Signs in the environment provide a stimulus for many language arts activities. (Photo by Linda Lungren.)

tween speech and reading, this is not a totally accurate conception of the relationship. There are some aspects of speech, such as voice inflection and rate of speaking, that will not be recorded when "talk is written down." Therefore, even though it seems highly desirable to help students to relate reading to talking, it does not seem desirable to use the idea of "talk written down" in isolation because you will not be dealing with the entire process of reading.

One of the concerns of teachers using the language experience approach to reading instruction is, Should I edit students' oral contributions? There is no one universally accepted answer to this question. Durkin (1980) suggests that whatever children say should be taken down in standard English with the spelling offered. . . . as an example. Similarly, Spache and Spache (1977) suggest that teachers should discuss word choice, sentence structure, the sounds of letters and words, but should not censor or alter the student's contribution. Veatch et al. (1979), however, allow that "Some editing is needed: pupil dictation with wrong usage is altered, and the wrong word is found and changed" (p. 46).

There may be no "right" answer to this question. Cautious editing may have no effect on one student, whereas another may perceive a "criticism" of his or her *language* as a criticism of himself or herself. You will have to decide what is appropriate for your classroom. It may be helpful to consider these questions:

1. Is the form of expression used by the student reflective of that used by the group? Do others understand what he is saying?
2. Do you consider the change you would like to make to be mechanical, an inaccurate choice of words, or a crude/rude expression?
3. Can the student's wording be changed without diminishing him or her?

You can plan a language experience that interrelates visual, oral, auditory, and kinesthetic experiences by beginning with what each student brings to school—his or her *language*. Ordinary school activities such as class projects, recess games, field trips, and art activities, as well as events and experiences from students' daily lives, can provide the basis for oral language experiences. Student's *interest* is the key.

Developing Skills Through Language Experience.   An understanding of oral language, or the listening-spoken vocabulary, is the foundation on which students build a reading vocabulary. When you record and transcribe students' statements, they see written and oral language come together. Most students come to school with spoken vocabularies of approximately fifteen hundred to two thousand words. This vocabulary can be expanded through language experiences. In this way, you can capitalize on the spoken language of the student while using the word-recognition skills needed to develop both a sight and meaning vocabulary. The central theme of this process becomes one of communication, with your charting of the students' expressed ideas. Through the development of these charts, the students see their language turn to print. Perhaps equally important, you have made reading both *meaningful* and *fun* for your students.

To teach beginning readers from a language experience approach, start by stressing the importance of sound-symbol correspondence. In this way, students begin to see that print represents ideas and that through reading, they can share ideas. Students begin to build a sight vocabulary because the words they see and hear are their words, their language. Next you can begin to introduce phonics and other word-attack skills to help them identify unknown and different words. Through this approach, word-attack skills are not being learned in isolation; rather, they are acquired more naturally through reading activities utilizing a student's own language. Furthermore, the sequential and spontaneous approaches to reading instruction begin to be integrated.

As students continually expand their sight vocabularies, we also encourage you to help them note beginning word differences and similarities. Studies of eye movement and miscues have indicated that readers concentrate more on initial and ending portions of words than on medial positions.

Initial letters: *g*ame, *g*irl, *g*o
Ending letters: ca*p*, li*p*, mo*p*
Medial letters: w*e*re, ta*b*le, bo*o*k

There are many ways by which you can extend basic lessons through language experience. For example, you may give each student a typed copy of his reaction to an experience and ask that the story be cut into words and phrases. The student begins to realize that stories consist of words and phrases that can be spoken. Now ask the student to match these isolated units with the sentence in its complete form. You can also ask the students to name and spell particular words as they paste them onto a second copy. As another activity, give paired students envelopes containing the words and phrases of their reactions and ask them to reconstruct their stories for their partners to read. Throughout this experience you may want to stress story punctuation. Ask students to consult a dictionary (with your help) to determine word meanings, pronunciation keys, and word histories.

Language experiences can also be used to enhance writing ability. Have a student lie on a large piece of kraft paper while you trace his form. Then ask him to cut out his form and color in any parts he chooses. Now give each student a typed copy of an earlier writing contribution that he will edit. When he is satisfied with his piece of writing he may paste it onto his self-portrait or copy it onto his silhouette.

Through such language experiences, children begin to acquire

1. Important phonics generalizations
2. Basic study skills
3. Extended reading vocabularies

Because they are introduced in the context of the student's own language, rather than as isolated processes, learning becomes a unified experience.

Too often students are required to spend 20 minutes on dictionary skills, 30 minutes learning new vocabulary words, 45 minutes on phonics, and 30 minutes reading their basals. Although all these experiences may be necessary, a synthesis of learning never seems to occur because we tend to ignore the language of the students rather than use it as a base foundation. Through a language experience method, you can provide the students with an opportunity for synthesizing the independent skills of the reading / thinking process.

Smith et al. (1978) also point out

> The marvelous advantage to the educator of using the student's own language is that it gives him a success base from which to build. It is akin to saying, "Your language is good. Start with your language and learn how to improve it." (pp. 47–48)

Using this formula for success, many profitable experiences can result from the language experience approach. However, we caution you to use this language structure only as a curriculum *base*. Do not fall into the same kind of faulty repetitious, uncreative patterns that many teachers do when they misuse a basal reader program. Be careful to incorporate the spontaneous expressions of your children in the initial lessons. Grammar, usage, and punctuation may be the focus of supplementary lessons.

INDIVIDUALIZED INSTRUCTION

Current trends in reading instruction emphasize individualizing reading instruction. Matthes (1977) suggests this is because "educators have agreed that children must develop at their own pace rather than be limited to group grade-leveled expectations" (p. 26). As such, individualized instruction is the base of the spontaneous reading approach.

The two key aspects of the individualized reading method are that (1) the student establishes his or her own pace and sequence for reading instruction and (2) the student selects his or her own reading materials. By allowing students to substitute interesting reading materials for the sometimes uninteresting content of basals, you can see that a definition of reading is embedded in the individualized reading method.

Within the framework of the spontaneous reading approach, reading has been described as an individualized set of process skills that are learned in social settings. Students work alone or in groups using a wide variety of materials. In this type of individualized/personalized program, the student reads materials of his or her choice, related to his or her interests. It is the intent of these programs to allow students to set their own pace for progress in materials that they have selected.

To use an individualized approach, your students will need access to a wide variety of materials. These materials must span the range of reading levels and abilities appropriate for your classroom. It is recommended that you have three to five choices available for each student at all times. If your school library does not have an adequate supply of texts, you may be able to secure materials from the public library for an extended period of time. After the selections have served their purpose, exchange them for additional books.

To implement an individualized program, you will need to be familiar with

To use an individualized approach, your students will need access to a wide variety of materials. (Photo by Linda Lungren.)

1. The reading process
2. Organizational skills
3. Sequential skill development
4. Assessment techniques
5. Reading materials
6. Classroom management procedures

One of the strongest arguments for using this method is that only by self-selection would two students be reading the same material at the same time. This dramatically reduces the likelihood of achievement comparisons. The other major advantages of this program are that the students select their own materials and set their own rate of progress. The obvious disadvantage of this method is that you could experience some initial problems with classroom management procedures because some students move at a snail's pace when they are allowed to set their own course and rate. Occasionally, there is the student who is an enthusiastic selector but a reluctant finisher. These are problems that can occur in an individualized reading program, and you must deal with each of them on an individual basis. Chapter 12 will help you to develop techniques needed to implement an individualized reading program successfully.

The most current system for teaching reading is the managed language/reading system, which has attempted to incorporate the best features of the sequential reading approach and the spontaneous reading approach.

Managed Language/Reading System

The managed language/reading system evolved from the need to provide classroom teachers with a manageable program. The system capitalizes on the strengths of both the sequential and spontaneous reading approaches. Its content, while logically organized, emphasizes an individual format of instruction. Many of the "new" programs include basals with stories that are relevant and interesting to students, along with filmstrips and tapes of the stories, dittoed worksheets, teacher guides and manuals, criterion-referenced tests, and elaborate easy-to-manage record-keeping systems. Each of these additions to the basic program is intended to help teachers individualize their program.

To provide teachers with the opportunity to individualize instruction, and also to meet the needs of each student, these new programs include intensive management systems. These management systems help the teacher to *diagnose, prescribe,* and *evaluate* a program for each student.

The following is a description of the Ginn Reading Program management system. Other programs by Macmillan, Economy, and Laidlaw closely parallel this description.

> The management system for an instructional program is neither the content of that program nor the teaching method by which content is presented to pupils. Rather, it represents a kind of framework or pattern by means of which content and teaching methods can be organized to assure that some specific outcomes occur. Usually, the desired effects of managing instruction are as follows: (1) that pupils are systematically taught at least a core set of specified educational objectives, with the exception of those pupils who have previously become proficient in certain of these objectives; (2) that evidence is generated to show whether pupils learn these objectives at a level of proficiency prespecified as desirable; (3) that provision is made for systematic reinstruction of pupils on any of the objectives for which they have failed to demonstrate proficiency; and (4) that teaching pupils to acceptable proficiency on this set of core objectives is accomplished in the minimum reasonable time.

When the core strands of the Ginn Reading Program are taught in the management mode, the foregoing outcomes can be realized. Using a management system, the teacher may select from the rich pool of hundreds of objectives those specific ones that represent the core skills of the Ginn Reading Program drawn from the comprehension, vocabulary, and decoding strands. The teacher may then build lesson plans emphasizing, or even restricted to, these core objectives and teach those students known to need them. Additional Ginn Reading Program components allow the teacher to evaluate with precision the proficiency of pupils on the core objectives. Other Ginn Reading Program resources can then be used to reteach missed objectives to just those pupils who need reinstruction. Because managed instruction focuses so tightly on core essentials and attempts to limit instruction within the core strands to that demonstrably required, whether initial or reteaching, it moves pupils with maximum efficiency toward attainment of the desired outcomes.

Implementing a management system in teaching (Ginn Reading Program) aids the teacher

In helping to select what students are to learn
In systematic planning for and provision of supplementary instruction
In individualizing instruction according to student needs
In establishing an instructional pace that is efficient yet accomplishes desired goals

The components of a successfully managed language/reading system are integrated into the existing basal program. All the component parts of the management system (e.g., activities, unit criterion exercises, record sheets, individual achievement cards) are included to make recordkeeping and instructional planning as simple and effective as possible.

A *managed* language/reading approach helps to alleviate the time constraints that were often cited by teachers as the reason for not being able to implement individualized instruction. Management of your program is discussed in greater detail in Chapter 12.

Reading: What Does It Mean?

Thus far we have examined major approaches to the teaching of reading and the various methods that have evolved from these philosophical points of view. The program that you decide to implement in your classroom will depend largely on your personal definition of reading. You must ask yourself these questions: What do I think reading is? What are my objectives in teaching a student to read?

To help you formulate your personal definition of reading, we will present several definitions of reading that reading research specialists have devised.

Formal Definitions

As you might imagine, your beliefs about the reading process strongly affect how you perceive it. Through the years, many educators have "defined" reading, yet each definition tends to emphasize different aspects of the reading process. As you read the following section, compare your ideas with those being presented.

Guthrie (1983) notes that in 1941 Gray "drew the boundaries" for the field of reading by suggesting that there were three concepts of reading: word recognition, text comprehension, and critical thinking. Robinson (1966) later expanded Gray's definition and identified five major components of reading: word perception, comprehension, reaction, assimilation, and rate, a dimension that Gray had not previously included in his analysis. According to the Gray-Robinson definition, word perception includes word recognition and the association of meanings with words. The second dimension, comprehension, involves two levels of meaning, literal and implied. The third aspect, reaction, involves intellectual judgments and emotional responses. Assimilation, the fourth aspect, involves fusion of old ideas with new ideas that now have been obtained through reading. Rate, the fifth dimension, is recognized as varying speeds depending on load of new words, the length of the lesson or time one is expected to read, and the concept load of material to be read.

Gray and Reese (1963) emphasize the *usefulness* of reading in everyday life whereas Spache and Spache (1977) focus on the *process* of reading as skill development. Tinker and McCullough (1968) have a *behavioral* outlook on reading: as new information interacts with past experiences, "modifications of thought, and perhaps behavior" (p. 8) may take place. Frank Smith's model (1978) of reading describes the process from printed words to comprehension (see Figure 10-3).

Harris (1972) points out that reading is an extension of *oral communication* that must have listening and speaking skills as its foundation. J. Smith (1973) emphasizes both *spoken vocabulary* and *experience:*

> Reading is the ability to recognize and understand the printed symbols of the child's spoken vocabulary. Printed words, as well as spoken ones, are meaningful to the young child only insofar as his field of experience overlaps that of the author of the printed text. (pp. 31–32)

Rumelhart (1976) stresses the interactive nature of the reading process:

> Reading is the process of understanding written language. It begins with a flutter of patterns on the retina and ends (when successful) with a definite idea about the author's intended message. Thus, reading is at once a "perceptual" and a "cognitive" process. It is a process which bridges and blurs these two traditional distinctions. (p. 1).

C. Smith (1978) also views reading as an interactive process, that is, as an interaction between reader and author:

> Reading then can be defined as an interaction, a communication in which the author and the reader each brings his background language, and a com-

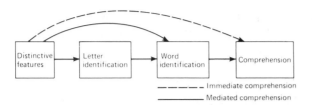

Figure 10–3. Smith's reading model. (From Frank Smith, *Understanding Reading*, 2nd ed. New York: Holt, Rinehart and Winston, 1978. Copyright © 1978 by Holt, Rinehart and Winston, CBS College Publishing. Reprinted by permission.)

mon desire to reach the other person. No matter how else one defines reading, it must involve ideas, backgrounds, common language, common interest, and a mutual point of departure. (p. 28)

Now that you have considered some of these formal definitions of reading, you should attempt to formalize your own personal definition of reading. An effective reading program must logically follow from your own personal reading definition.

A Final Definition

Reading as it has been considered in this text is the process of perceiving, interpreting, and evaluating printed material. It is one of the four major tools of communication: listening, speaking, reading, and writing. It is usually silent, and it is receptive in nature. Foundations for success in reading lie in the individual's development of skill in listening and speaking.

Reading requires the development of a meaningful vocabulary and a multiplicity of skills. The reader must be able to perceive and recognize written symbols and be able to associate concepts with written symbols. She must be able to understand both concrete and abstract ideas as they are presented in written form.

The effective reader questions that which he or she has read. She may approach written material on a literal basis, but she must progress to levels of interpretation and critical evaluation. The ability to locate needed material or information and the ability to select materials pertinent to the topic on which one reads are two very important skills in reading. In addition, the effective reader is one who can adjust rate of reading to the purpose for which reading is done.

As you continue to read and think about each of the definitions of reading that have been presented, we hope that you will be able to answer more specifically the probing questions about your individual goals as a teacher of reading. We also hope that you will generate more questions about the specific operations within each definition. Only in this way will you be able to establish an effective, managed language/reading program within your own classroom.

Suggested Readings Related to Goals. We encourage you at this time to review the goals at the beginning of this chapter. If you feel you would like to explore one or more of these areas in greater depth, please refer to the cross-indexed bibliography at the end of the book.

11 *Encouraging Reading Attitudes and Interests*

In a very real sense, people who have read good literature have lived more than people who cannot or will not read. . . . It is not true that we have only one life to live; if we can read, we can live as many more lives and as many kinds of lives as we wish.

[S. I. Hayakawa]

Goals

To help the student understand
1. Reading attitudes and how to assess them
2. Ways for teachers and parents to motivate reading
3. How to assess a student's most effective learning style
4. Ways of choosing stimulating and motivating reading materials

Why Read?

In an increasingly technologically oriented society, it often appears difficult to convince students that there are important reasons for reading. Home computers, video recordings, movies, television, and other "print-free" sources of information and enjoyment all *seem* to downplay the value of reading. While teachers are often anxious about the negative effects of media on reading, Neumann (1980) found that there is no positive correlation between reading achievement and hours spent watching television. As Neumann and Prowda (1982) and Telfer and Kann (1984) go on to suggest, teachers should capitalize on student interest in media to pro-

255

mote reading. Later in this chapter, we have suggested several ways in which you will be able to do this.

One of the most challenging goals, and perhaps the most important goal in your educational career, is to help students understand how books and other printed materials can enrich their lives. The reading habits acquired during the school years last a lifetime. The greatest gift you can give is a lifelong love of books and reading.

One of the ways to demonstrate the value of reading is to discuss the common reasons that people read. Through a class discussion, you may compile a list of reasons similar to the following:

1. To learn how to do something
2. To acquire an understanding of a concept
3. To prove a point
4. To learn more about a person or place
5. To satisfy curiosity
6. To acquire information
7. To be entertained
8. To enjoy vicarious experiences
9. To relax
10. To fill time

The teacher and the classroom environment are important factors that can influence students' attitudes about reading. Magazines can provide a wide range of interest, reading levels, and motivation for students. (Photo by Linda Lungren.)

As you can see, most of these reasons can be broadly categorized under reading for *information* or *enjoyment*. In either case, there are several factors that can affect whether or not a student *chooses* to read. The first of these is the student's attitude toward reading.

Attitudes

"A universal goal of reading instruction should be the fostering of positive attitudes toward reading" (Alexander and Filler, 1976, p. 34). Given this premise, we will examine what an *attitude* is, and how attitude relates to reading.

Attitude has been defined from many different perspectives. More than sixty years ago, Allport (1924) defined attitude in both cognitive and phy-sioneural terms as "a mental and neural state of readiness, organized through experience, exerting a direct or dynamic influence upon the individual's responses to all objects and situations in which he is related" (p. 798). Thurston (1928) called it the "sum total of man's inclinations and feelings, prejudice or bias, preconceived notions, ideas, fears, threats and convictions about any specific topic" (p. 531), while Dobbs (1947) defined attitude as a predisposition to respond to a specified object. Fishbein (1967), building on these earlier definitions, suggested that the predisposition to respond remains consistent. For example, if a child is predisposed to dislike reading, he will probably display negative behaviors each time he is engaged in the act of reading. While these reactions may demonstrate a negative attitude toward the act of reading, only the behaviors, not the attitude, would be visible to the observer. Since attitudes cannot be seen or touched, astute teachers must infer their existence from such behaviors.

Commenting on the many definitions of attitude, Epstein (1980) cited five common characteristics of various definitions:

1. An attitude is a mental construct.
2. Attitudes are learned.
3. Attitudes center on a focal object.
4. Attitudes predispose individuals to respond toward some object.
5. Attitudes are evaluative in nature.

As teachers, we are most interested in attitudes toward reading. Ciccone (1981) defines reading attitude as a system of feelings related to reading that influence a student to approach or avoid a reading situation. Since attitudes are indeed learned, they can be altered or improved upon by a teacher who examines children's reading attitudes and responds to them.

One of the most valuable ways to assess attitudes is teacher observation (Alexander and Filler, 1976), yet the difficulty of accurate measurement through observation alone is obvious. For example, three students in your classroom may exhibit negative attitudes toward reading: one may feign illness, one may misbehave, and the third student, who also has a negative attitude toward the act of reading, may be attentive to reading because he realizes that the act of reading is important to you. What determines the behavioral response? Perhaps it is a combination of the *cognitive* (development of intellect), *affective* (development of emotions or attitudes), and *conative* (development of volition) domains.

Components of Attitude

It is generally accepted that one's attitude is comprised of factors from several different domains. Since attitude is a mental construct, the significance of the cognitive (thinking) component is obvious. The affective domain is significant in forming attitudes because the affective domain is basic to the learning process. Turner and Alexander (1980) state that "how a learner feels about the information being processed affects his learning and later utilization of the information" (p. 3). This "later utilization" is reflected in Epstein's (1980) remark: "The ultimate success of a reading program's effectiveness shall be judged not solely on the basis of how well students learn to read but also in terms of whether they do in fact read" (p. 8).

Conation is discussed infrequently in the educational literature. McDougall (1921) defined conation as "the active or striving side of our nature, as the equivalent of will in its widest sense, as comprehending desire, impulse, craving, appetite, wishing, and willing" (p. 325). The conation is the original impulse that

> supplies the motive power to all the activities that are only means to the attainment of the desired end. The train of activity, supported by any one of the instinctive impulses, may become indefinitely prolonged and incessantly renewed; it may take the predominantly intellectual form of thinking, our means for the attainment of the end. (McDougall, 1921, p. 181)

Epstein (1980) states that the "[conative] component [of attitude] concerns itself with the individual's predisposition to respond to, seek out, and to approach the attitude object" (p. 16). Having examined the definitions and components of attitude, let us now examine how attitude relates to achievement in reading.

Achievement and Attitude

Roswell (1967) attempted to determine the relationship between achievement and change in attitudes toward reading of forty elementary and junior high school students, all considered disabled readers. Negative attitudes toward reading were found to be more closely related to reading achievement than to other factors, such as socioeconomic status or age. Similar findings were reported by Gardner (1972) and Puryear (1975) when studying the attitudes and achievement of fourth-graders. A study of remedial reading instruction was reported by Buerger (1968). The focus of this study was an investigation of the effect of remedial reading instruction on long-term progress and attitude. The findings indicated that the remedial reading instruction itself had no significant effect upon mental ability, vocabulary, reading comprehension, or attitudes toward reading.

Ransbury (1973) found that fifth- and sixth-grade students attributed their attitudes toward reading mainly to their ability to read. Neale, Gill, and Tismer (1970) found a positive correlation between attitude toward various subjects, including reading, and achievement in those areas.

Mathewson (1976) suggests that studies in the literature that show only a small relationship between attitude and reading achievement may be due to experiments that "measure attitude toward reading as a school course or as a school activity rather than attitude toward preferred reading content" (p. 665). This would seem to be borne out by Groff's (1962) conclusion that "the reading comprehension of an individual child as he reads is influenced to a degree by his attitude toward content type of material being read" (p. 314).

There is not currently a definitive answer as to how much reading attitudes may affect achievement. However, if further research is to provide greater insights, educators need to construct useful instruments to measure attitudes. Examples of such interest inventories will be found later in this chapter.

You may encounter some students who do not *like* to read, and others may not be convinced of the *value* of reading. In either case, the key to making students *want* to read (the conative domain) may reside in the teacher and in the classroom environment.

The Teacher and the Environment

Many students regard reading as a pleasurable activity, perhaps because of early encounters with books that they have shared with a loved one. However, some children who enter school having had pleasureable reading experiences find that school reading is an arduous task involving basal readers, worksheets, and constant teacher reprimands. Many of these students quickly develop negative attitudes toward reading. There may be other students who view reading as a means of becoming more like the adult they aspire to model, and they may realize that reading is necessary for later pleasure. But there may also be students who are unable to see the purposes of reading, and their negative behaviors may reflect this attitude.

Alexander and Filler (1976) remind us that "both the teacher (what he is and what he does) and the general atmosphere of the classroom may have effects on positive attitude development and maintenance" (p. 8). Wilson and Hall (1972) further state that

The key to developing a personal love of books is a teacher who communicates enthusiasm and an appreciation of literature through his attitudes and examples. Knowing children and their interests, and knowing literature are of great importance in promoting personal reading. Significant as these are, however, the success or failure of the personal reading program in the elementary school rests with the classroom teacher. In those classrooms where encounters with literature are an integral part of the school experience, children are more likely to become avid readers. The teacher's responsibility, then, is to provide motivation, time, and materials to stimulate personal reading. (pp. 243–244)

One of the best (and easiest) ways for a teacher to communicate enthusiasm and appreciation for literature is by being a good *model* for students. Ask yourself the following questions:

1. Do I freely choose to spend my spare time reading?
2. Do I read to my students regularly?
3. Do I reach for a book when I need information?
4. Am I knowledgeable enough about children's books to make recommendations based on students' interests and achievement levels?
5. Do I discuss my interest in reading with my students?
6. Do my personal attitudes and my classroom environment demonstrate that I value reading?
7. Am I enthusiastic and positive in my approach to reading?

The classroom itself also reflects the value you place on books and reading. Is there a reading area that is warm, attractive, and inviting? Are books and magazines prominently displayed? Do the reading materials accurately reflect the students' interests and developmental levels? Do you promote book fairs? Are there posters telling about authors and their books?

The teacher and the classroom environment are important factors that can influence students' attitudes about reading. Together, they may encourage students to read or listen to books so that "any sparks of excitement they give off in response to good books can be fanned into fires of warm enthusiasm toward reading as a meaningful lifelong habit" (Somers and Worthington, 1979, p. 6).

Reading to Students

One of the best ways you can help students learn to enjoy reading is by reading to them. Dawson (1972) suggests that "teachers should read to children every day from books that are worthwhile, appropriate in level of interest, but probably too hard for them to read themselves" (p. 37). Commenting on the value of reading to students, Spiegel (1981) also points out, "All the work is being done by the readers; the listeners can just relax and enjoy the story. As a result, children may learn to associate reading with pleasure. Furthermore, teachers are showing the audience that reading is something they enjoy and value" (pp. 29–30). The perceptive teacher will find numerous opportunities to read aloud. Students of all ages have been "hooked on reading" through this method. Reading to students provides the teacher with an opportunity to choose and help develop a taste for good literature.

Newbery and Caldecott Medal Winners

Table 11-1 supplies titles of recent award-winning books that you may want to share with your students.

TABLE 11-1
Newbery and Caldecott Medal Winners

1984 Winners	
Newbery	
Winner	*Dear Mr. Henshaw;* Beverly Cleary (Morrow)
Honor Books	*Sign of the Beaver;* Elizabeth George Speare (Houghton Mifflin)
	A Solitary Blue; Cynthia Voigt (Atheneum)
	Sugaring Time; Kathryn Lasky (Macmillan)
	The Will Giver; Bill Brittain (Harper & Row)
Caldecott	
Winner	*The Glorious Flight;* Alice and Martin Provensen (Viking Press)
Honor Books	*Little Red Riding Hood;* Rewritten and retold by Trina Schart Hyman (Holiday)
	Ten, Nine, Eight; Molly Bang (Greenwillow)
1983 Winners	
Newbery	
Winner	*Dicey's Song;* Cynthia Voigt (Atheneum)
Honor Books	*Sweet Whispers, Brother Rush;* Virginia Hamilton (Philomel)
	Homesick: My Own Story; Jean Fritz (Putnam)
	Graven Images; Paul Fleischman (Harper & Row)
	The Blue Sword; Robin McKinley (Greenwillow)
	Dr. DeSoto; William Steig (Farrar, Straus & Giroux)
Caldecott	
Winner	*Shadow;* Blaise Cendrars, illustrated by Marcia Brown (Scribner)
Honor Books	*When I Was Young in the Mountains;* Cynthia Rylant, illustrated by Diane Goode (Dutton)
	A Chair for My Mother; Text and illustrations by Vera Williams (Greenwillow)
1982 Winners	
Newbery	
Winner	*A Visit to William Blake's Inn: Poems for Innocent and Experienced Travelers;* Nancy Willard, illustrated by Alice and Martin Provensen (Harcourt)

TABLE 11-1 (*Continued*)

Honor Books	*Ramona Quimby, Age 8*; Beverly Cleary, illustrated by Alan Tiegreen (Morrow)
	Upon the Head of the Goat; A Childhood in Hungary 1939–1944; Aranka Siegel (Farrar, Straus & Giroux)
Caldecott	
Winner	*Jumanji*; Chris Van Allsburg (Houghton Mifflin)
Honor Books	*On Market Street*; Arnold Lobel, illustrated by Anita Lobel (Greenwillow)
	Outside over There; Maurice Sendak (Harper & Row)
	Where the Buffaloes Begin; Olaf Baker, illustrated by Stephen Gammell (Warner)
1981 Winners	
Newbery	
Winner	*Jacob Have I Loved*; Katherine Paterson (Thomas Y. Crowell)
Honor Book	*The Fledgling*; Jane Langton, illustrated by Erik Blegvad (Harper & Row)
	A Ring of Endless Light; M. L'Engle (Farrar, Straus & Giroux)
Caldecott	
Winner	*Fables*; written and illustrated by Arnold Lobel (Harper & Row)
Honor Books	*The Grey Lady and the Strawberry Snatcher*; Molly Bang (Four Winds Press)
	Mice Twice; J. Low (McElderry/Atheneum)
	Truck; D. Crews (Greenwillow)
1980 Winners	
Newbery	
Winner	*A Gathering of Days*; Joan Blos (Scribners)
Honor Book	*The Road from Home*; David Kherdian (Greenwillow)
Caldecott	
Winner	*Ox-Cart Man*; Donald Hall, illustrated by Barbara Cooney (Viking Press)
Honor Books	*Ben's Trumpet*; Rachel Isadora (Greenwillow)
	The Garden of Abdul Gasazi; Chris Van Allsburg (Houghton Mifflin)
	The Treasure; Uri Schnelvitz (Farrar, Straus & Giroux)

Students' Choices

In addition to the Caldecott and Newbery Award books, you may wish to share books with your students that they have listed as their favorites. For the last eight years, a complete listing of students' choices has appeared in either the October or November issues of *The Reading Teacher*. Another listing of these books has been compiled by N. Roser and M. Frith (1983).* We have included a sample for you.

---

*The following listing is excerpted from N. Roser and M. Frith, *Children's Choice* (Newark, Dela.: International Reading Association, 1983), pp. 93–119.

Beginning Independent Reading

Arthur's Eyes. Mark Brown. Ill. by the author. Atlantic-Little, Brown. 32 pp. (1980). Paperback, Avon.

The Bean Boy. Joan Chase Bowden. Ill. by Sal Murdocca. Macmillan. 62 pp. (1980).

Bullfrog and Gertrude Go Camping. Rosamond Dauer. Ill. by Byron Barton. Greenwillow. 40 pp. (1981).

Uproar on Hollercat Hill. Jean Marzollo. Ill. by Steven Kellogg. Dial. 32 pp. (1981).

We're in Big Trouble, Blackboard Bear. Marcha Alexander. Ill. by the author. Dial. 32 pp. (1981).

Younger Readers

Amanda and the Giggling Ghost. Steven Kroll. Ill. by Dick Gackenbach. Holiday. 40 pp. (1981).

Anybody Home? Aileen Fisher. Ill. by Susan Bonners. Crowell. 32 pp. (1981).

Arthur's Valentine. Marc Brown. Ill. by the author. Atlantic-Little, Brown. 32 pp. (1981).

The Day I Was Born. Marjorie Weinman Sharmat and Mitchell Sharmat. Ill. by Diane Dawson. Dutton. 32 pp. (1981).

The Discontented Mother. Ben Shecter. Ill. by the author. Harcourt. 32 pp. (1981).

Middle Grades

A Chocolate Moose for Dinner. Fred Gwynne. Ill. by the author. Windmill. 64 pp. (1977).

Cookie Becker Casts a Spell. Lee Glazer. Ill. by Margot Apple. Little, Brown. 48 pp. (1981).

Left-Handed Shortstop. Patricia Reilly Giff. Ill. by Leslie Morrill. Delacorte. 128 pp. (1981). Paperback, Dell.

The Robot and Rebecca: The Mystery of the Code-Carrying Kids. Jane Yolen. Ill. by Jurg Obrist. Knopf. 128 pp. (1981). Paperback, Knopf.

The Sick of Being Sick Book. Jovial Bob Stine and Jane Stine. Ill. by Carol Nicklaus. Dutton. 80 pp. (1981).

Older Readers

Cute Is a Four-Letter Word. Stella Pevsner. Clarion/Houghton. 190 pp. (1981). Paperback, Pocket.

From Prison to the Major Leagues: The Picture Story of Ron LeFlore. Ron Knapp. Ill. with photographs. Messner. 64 pp. (1981).

Haunted. Judith St. George. Putnam. 160 pp. (1981).

What If They Knew? Patricia Hermes. Harcourt. 132 pp. (1981). Paperback, Dell.

Who Stole Kathy Young? Margaret Goff Clark. Dodd. 192 pp. (1981).

Informational Books

Dragons and Other Fabulous Beasts. Richard Blythe. Ill. by Fiona French and Joanna Troughton. Grosset. 64 pp. (1981).

Halloween. Joyce K. Kessel. Ill. by Nancy L. Carlson. Carolrhoda. 48 pp. (1981).

Movie Stunts and the People Who Do Them. Gloria D. Miklowitz. Ill. with photographs. Harcourt. 64 pp. (1981). Paperback, Harcourt.

Ocean Frontiers. Eryl Davies. Ill. with photographs and diagrams. Viking. 64 pp. (1981).

The Sea World Book of Sharks. Eve Bunting. Ill. with photographs by Flip Nicklin. Harcourt. 80 pp. (1981).

Poetry/Verse

Alligator Pie. Dennie Lee. Ill. by Frank Newfield. Houghton. 64 pp. (1975).

Casey at the Bat. Ernest Lawrence Thayer. Ill. by Wallace Tripp. Coward. 32 pp. (1979). Paperback, Coward.

The Gobble-Uns'll Git You Ef You Don't Watch Out! James Whitcomb Riley. Ill. by Joel Schick. Lippincott. 42 pp. (1975).

Granfa Grig Had a Pig and Other Rhymes Without Reason from Mother Goose. Compiled by Wallace Tripp. Ill. by the compiler. Little, Brown. 96 pp. (1977). Paperback, Little, Brown.

Tornado! Arnold Adoff. Ill. by Ronald Himler. Delacorte. 44 pp. (1978).

Magazine Resources

It may be difficult for you to select appropriate periodicals since there are so many magazines available to children. Marian Scott and Lois Winkel have categorized some of the leading magazines for students by interest level, reading grade level, and age level.

Category/Magazine	Interest Level (Winkel)	Grade Level (Scott)
General		
Children's Digest	4–6	K–6
Child Life	4–6	K–6
Children's Playmate	1–3	K–6
Cricket	4–6	K–6
Highlights	1–6	K–6
Humpty Dumpty	K–2	K–6
Jack and Jill	2–4	K–6
Young World	6	K–9
Science		
Animal Kingdom: N.Y. Zoological Society Magazine	1–6+	K–12
Audobon	6	K–12

Category/Magazine	Interest Level (Winkel)	Grade Level (Scott)
Beaver (Canadian)	6+	K–12
Current Science	6	K–9
National Geographic	K–6+	K–12
National Parks & Conservation (Canadian)	6	K–12
Popular Science Monthly	6	4–8
Ranger Rick	2–4	K–6
Science News	4–6	K–12
Wildlife: The International Wildlife Magazine	4–6	4–6
Social Studies		
American Heritage	6+	6–12
Cobblestone	4–6	4–6
Current Events	4–12	4–12
Early American Life	6+	6–12
Sports		
Baseball Digest	6–12	7–12
Football Digest	4–6+	7–12
Sport	4–6+	K–12
Young Athlete	4–6	4–6
Fine Arts		
American Indian Art	6	4–8
Creative Crafts	6	7–9
Man & His Music	4–8	K–9
Pack-O-Fun	2–4	K–6
Plays: Drama Magazine for Young People	6	K–12
Geography		
Arizona Highways	1–6+	6–12
Alaska: The Magazine of the Last Frontier	6+	6–12
Pacific Northwest	K–12	K–12
World Traveler	4–6	K–9
Informational		
American Red Cross Youth News	2–4	K–6
Horselover's National Magazine	6+	7–9
Magazine of Fantasy and Science Fiction	4–6+	7–9
Modern Airplane News	4–6	K–12
Modern Railroader	4–6	7–12
Scott's Monthly Stamp Journal	4–6+	K–12
Scholastic News Pilot	1	1
Scholastic News Ranger	2	2
Scholastic News Trails	3	3
Scholastic News Explorer	4	4
Scholastic News Citizen	5	5

Category/Magazine	Interest Level (Winkel)	Grade Level (Scott)
Scholastic Newstime	6	6
Junior Scholastic	6+	K–12
Scholastic Search, Scope, Voice (three magazines)	7–9–12	7–9–12
Senior Scholastic	7–12	7–12
My Weekly Reader Surprise	K	K
My Weekly Reader Eye	1	1
My Weekly Reader News Reader	2	2
My Weekly Reader News Story	3	3
My Weekly Reader News Parade	4	4
My Weekly Reader News Report	5	5
Senior Weekly Reader	6	6

SOURCES: Marian H. Scott, ed., *Periodicals for School Libraries: A Guide to Magazines, Newspapers and Periodical Indexes* (Chicago: American Library Association, 1973), and Lois Winkel, ed., *The Elementary School Library Collection: A Guide to Books and Other Media*, 12th ed. (Newark, N.J.: The Bro-Dart Foundation, 1979).

Motivational Strategies

Because it may be necessary to motivate your students to read, you may find some of the following suggestions helpful.

1. Set aside a particular time each day to read to your students.
2. Choose materials with a variety of different content. Try to choose something related to the special interests of each student. This has a twofold value: reading is enhanced for the student whose interest is tapped as well as for other students who may discover a new interest.
3. Encourage students to read newspapers and magazines by having classroom subscriptions to them. Frequently, local newspaper publishers or the PTA will donate such subscriptions.
4. Have students share interesting stories or facts they have read in newspapers and magazines. This should not be strictly a current events activity; allow the students to include human interest stories.
5. Establish a reading center or corner. This can be as simple as putting a throw rug in a quiet corner, or it can be an elaborate adventure, depending on the available space and resources. It is important to make the space warm and inviting. Guidelines for the use of the corner should be designed by the teacher and the students together. The following language/reading games might be found in this reading center.

Games

Phonics We Use, learning games kit (Lyons & Carnahan).
DiGraph Hopscotch, 1 game board (Educational Board Games).
Consonant Lotto, first grade (Garrard Publishing Co.).
Faculty Cards, elementary to adult (ACO Games Division, Allen Co.).
The Happening Game, elementary to junior high (Community Makers).
Matrix Games, elementary (New Century).
People in Action, preschool to elementary (Holt, Rinehart and Winston).
Games, A Treasury of 600 Delightful Games for Children of All Ages (Jessie H. Bancroft, Macmillan).
Contemporary Games, vols. 1 and 2 (compiled by Jean Belch, Gale Research Co.).
Alphabet Soup, elementary (Parker Bros.).
Isaac Asimov Presents Super Quiz, age 12 to adult (Waddington's Games, Inc.).

6. Encourage children to seek variety in their reading selections. To facilitate this, you may want to have shelves labeled with different types of literature, such as biography, science fiction, history, science, fairy tales, and humor.
7. Have students who have all read the same book dramatize all or part of it. They can do this for their own enjoyment or to share it with classmates.
8. Purchase collections of children's drama and organize a reader's theater. Reader's theater will be discussed in greater detail at the end of this chapter. Some excellent collections include

Carlson, B. *Funny-Bone Dramatics.* Illustrated by Charles Cox. Nashville, Tenn.: Abingdon Press, 1974.
Chambers, D. W. *Storytelling and Creative Drama.* Dubuque, Iowa: W. C. Brown Company, Publishers, 1970.
Chaparro, J. L., P. Conlan-Ross, and R. Ross. *Economy Company's Reader's Theater Program.* Oklahoma City, Okla.: Economy Company Publishers, 1981.
Durrell, D. D. *Favorite Plays for Classroom Reading.* Boston: Plays, Inc. 1965.
Fontaine, R. *Humorous Skits for Young People: A Collection of Royalty-Free Short Plays and Easy-to-Perform Comedy Sketches.* Boston: Plays, Inc., 1965.
Kamerman, S. (ed.) *Fifty Plays for Junior Actors.* Boston: Plays, Inc., 1965.
Korty, C. *Silly Soup.* New York: Charles Scribners' Sons, 1977.
Olfson, L. *Classics Adapted for Acting and Reading.* Boston: Plays, Inc., 1972.

9. Start a "Recommended Books" file. In a small file, place dividers labeled with various types of literature. Invite students to write brief recommendations for books that they have read and enjoyed. The size of the file and the cards included in the file will determine the maximum length of the recommendation. Standards for these recommendations should be set up so that they will help the potential reader get an idea about the book without "giving away" the whole story.

10. Build students' enjoyment of poetry by selecting a variety of poems to read to them. Provide copies for students so that they can participate through choral reading. Have a variety of poetry anthologies available in the classroom for students to read. You might start your collection with

Random House Book of Poetry for Children, selected by Jack Prelutsky. New York: Random House, 1983.

11. Allow time occasionally for children to read something they have particularly enjoyed to other children.
12. Expand your classroom library with paperback books. If teachers coordinate the purchase of books, it is often possible to build an elaborate classroom collection through bonus books; the company from which books are published might contribute free books for every fifteenth or twenty-fifth class purchase.
13. Work cooperatively with the art teacher to plan National Book Week festivities. Students can plan and develop bulletin boards, murals, and paper sculpture to display the books that they have read.
14. Prepare crossword puzzles about books or authors or about the content of a particular book.

Animal Crossword Puzzles, grades 2–3. Wonder, Wonder Treasure Books, Inc., Division of Grosset & Dunlap, Inc., 51 Madison Avenue, New York 10010.
Beginner's Crossword Puzzles, grades 4–9. Doubleday & Company, Inc. Orders to 501 Franklin Avenue, Garden City, N.Y. 11530.
Crackerjack Crosswords, grades 4–9. Doubleday & Company, Inc.
Crossword Puzzles, grades 1–2. Wonder.
Crossword Puzzles, grades 2–3. Wonder.
Crossword Puzzles, grades 3–4. Wonder.
Crosswords for Kids, grades 2–4, by L. White. Fawcett World, Fawcett World Library, 1515 Broadway, New York, N.Y. 10036.
Junior Crossword Puzzle Books, grades 4–8. Platt & Munk Publishers, Division of Questor, Educational Products, 1055 Bronx River Avenue, Bronx, N.Y. 10472.
X-Word Fun, grades 7–9. School Book Service, Scholastic Book Services, Division of Scholastic Magazines. Orders to 906 Sylvan Avenue, Englewood Cliffs, N.J. 07632.

15. Devote one week per month to a particular book author. Learn and share information that will make the authors familiar to the students.
16. Create riddles about book characters and familiar authors. These can be organized so that they can be enjoyed by individuals, or they can be played by pairs or teams of players

Riddle Books

Cricket's Jokes, Riddles & Other Stuff. Compiled by M. Leonard and the editors of *Cricket* magazine. New York: Random House, 1977.
How Do You Make an Elephant Laugh? J. Rosenbloom. Illustrated by J. Behr. New York: Sterling Publishing Company, 1979.

Riddle Me, Riddle Me, Ree. M. Leach. New York: Viking Press, 1970.

Sesame Street Riddle Book. New York: Children's Television Workshop; and New York: Random House, 1977.

Spooky Riddles. M. Brown. New York: Random House, 1983.

Tinkerbell is a Ding-a-ling. R. Doty. Garden City, N.Y.: Doubleday & Company, 1980.

17. Literature can be used to help students solve difficult personal problems (Schwartz, 1981). When literature is used as a therapeutic measure, it is called bibliotherapy.

Schrank and Engels (1981) strongly suggest from their research that bibliotherapy is very significant in effecting attitude change and contributing to therapeutic gains in students.

The following books may be used for bibliotherapy:

Adler, C. S. *In Our House Scott Is My Brother.* Macmillan Publishing Company, 1980. 139 pp. (Stepfamily).

Angell, Judie. *What's Best for You.* Bradbury Press, 1981. 187 pp. (Divorce).

Arrick, Fran. *Tunnel Vision.* Bradbury Press, 1980. 167 pp. (Suicide).

Bates, Betty. *It Must've Been the Fish Sticks.* Holiday House, 1982. 136 pp. (Adoption).

Blume, Judy. *Superfudge.* E. P. Dutton, 1980. 166 pp. (New sibling).

Bunting, Eve. *Blackbird Singing.* Illus. Stephen Gammell. Macmillan Publishing Company, 1980. 92 pp. (Parent discord).

Chaikin, Miriam. *I Should Worry, I Should Care.* Illus. Richard Egielski. Yearling Books, 1979. 103 pp. (Moving).

Cheatham, K. Follis. *The Best Way Out.* Harcourt Brace Jovanovich, 1982. 192 pp. (Teen drinking).

Colman, Hila. *Tell Me No Lies.* Crown Publishers, 1978. 74 pp. (Illegitimacy).

Culin, Charlotte. *Cages of Glass, Flowers of Time.* Bradbury Press, 1979. 316 pp. (Child abuse).

Daly, Jay. *Walls.* Laurel-Leaf Library, 1981. 204 pp. (Parent alcoholism).

Danziger, Paula. *The Divorce Express.* Delacorte Press, 1982. 148 pp. (Divorce).

Dizenzo, Patricia. *Why Me? The Story of Jenny.* Avon Books, 1976. 142 pp. (Rape).

Dodson, Susan. *The Creep.* Four Winds Press, 1979. 218 pp. (Child molestation).

Dorman, N. B. *Laughter in the Background.* Elsevier/Nelson Books, 1980. 158 pp. (Alcholic parents).

Elfman, Blossom. *Butterfly Girl.* Houghton Mifflin Company, 1980. 146 pp. (Teen pregnancy).

Ewing, Kathryn. *Things Won't Be the Same.* Scholastic Book Services, 1980. 92 pp. (Divorce).

Feagles, Anita MacRae. *The Year the Dreams Came Back.* Atheneum Publishers, 1978. 146 pp. (Stepparents).

Garrigue, Sheila. *Between Friends.* Bradbury Press, 1978. 160 pp. (Retardation).

Hanlon, Emily. *It's Too Late for Sorry.* Bradbury Press, 1978. 222 pp. (Retardation).

Hunt, Irene. *The Lottery Rose.* Charles Scribner's Sons, 1976. 185 pp. (Child abuse).

Lee, Joanna, and T. S. Cook. *Mary Jane Harper Cried Last Night*. Signet Books, 1978. 152 pp. (Child abuse).

Levy, Elizabeth. *Come Out Smiling*. Delacorte Press, 1981. 186 pp. (Lesbianism).

Luger, Harriett. *Lauren*. Laurel-Leaf Library, 1981. 176 pp. (Pregnancy).

Mann, Peggy. *Twelve Is Too Old*. Doubleday & Company, 1980. 139 pp. (Drugs).

Moeri, Louise. *The Girl Who Lived on the Ferris Wheel*. E. P. Dutton, 1979. 117 pp. (Child abuse).

Murphy, Barbara Beasley. *No Place to Run*. Bradbury Press, 1977. 176 pp. (Peer pressure).

Neufeld, John. *Lisa, Bright and Dark*. S. G. Phillips, 1976. 125 pp. (Mental illness).

O'Neal, Zibby. *The Language of Goldfish*. Viking Press, 1980. 192 pp. (Mental illness).

Pfeffer, Susan Beth. *What Do You Do When Your Mouth Won't Open?* Illus. Lorna Tomei. Yearling Books, 1982. 114 pp. (Fear).

Platt, Kin. *The Ape Inside Me*. J. B. Lippincott Co., 1979. 117 pp. (Tempers).

Savitz, Harriet May. *Wait Until Tomorrow*. Signet Vista Books, 1981. 150 pp. (Suicide).

Shyer, Marlene Fanta. *Welcome Home, Jellybean*. Charles Scribner's Sons, 1978. 152 pp. (Retarded sibling).

Snyder, Anne. *Goodbye, Paper Doll*. Signet Books, 1980. 155 pp. (Anorexia nervosa).

Snyder, Anne. *My Name Is Davy: I'm an Alcoholic*. Signet Vista Books, 1978. 133 pp. (Teen drinking).

Sorel, Julia. *Dawn: Portrait of a Teenage Runaway*. Ballantine Books, 1977. 122 pp. (Runaways).

Sullivan, Mary W. *What's This About Pete?* Thomas Nelson, 1976. 125 pp. (Sexual identity).

Thomas, Joyce Carol. *Marked by Fire*. Flare Books, 1982. 172 pp. (Rape).

Wood, Phyllis Anderson. *Win Me and You Lose*. Westminster Press, 1977. 137 pp. (Divorce).

Yep, Laurence. *Sea Glass*. Harper & Row, Publishers, 1979. 213 pp. (Cultural heritage).

A more complete bibliography of such references may be found in *Your Reading: A Booklist for Junior High and Middle School Students* (Christensen, 1983).

Suggestions for Parents

Parents frequently want to help their children develop good reading habits, but they are not quite certain of how they can do it. You should encourage parent-child interactions in reading throughout the elementary school years. Explain that as the child matures beyond the beginning reading stages, parents can continue to provide the basis for a good attitude toward reading by reading themselves and by making good material

available for their children to read. They can encourage children to discuss things they have read, and they can discuss with each other and their
children some of the interesting things that they have read.

Nursery rhymes and jingles are particularly enjoyable for young children. In addition, picture books are designed for the young reader. Parents can acquaint themselves and their children with the children's division of the library. The young child who visits the library with a parent
and watches as the parent selects books for himself or herself is acquiring
the "library habit." Magazines and newspapers that are available in the
home make a worthwhile contribution to the child's background or foundation for becoming a reader.

You may want to share the following suggestions with the parents of
your students:

---

1. Help young children realize the fun to be found in reading. Select
   humorous poems, short stories, or magazine articles (on the child's
   level). Read some of the following books to your child and enjoy the
   humor with him or her.

Humorous Short Stories and Poems

Blume, J. *The One in the Middle Is the Green Kangaroo*. Illustrated by A. Ait-
    ken. Scarsdale, N.Y.: Bradbury Press, 1981. grades 3–5.
Fenner, P. R. *Fun, Fun, Fun: Stories of Fantasy and Farce, Mischief and
    Mirth, Whimsy and Nonsense*. Illustrated by J. Zabinski. New York:
    Franklin Watts, 1933. grades 5–6.
Hendra, J. (ed.) *The Illustrated Treasury of Humor for Children*. New York:
    Grossett and Dunlap, 1980. grades 3–7.
Riley, J. W. *Joyful Poems for Children*. Illustrated by Charles Geer. Indianap-
    olis: The Bobbs-Merrill Co., 1960. grades 3–6.
Smith, W. J. *Laughing Time*. Illustrated by Juliet Kepes. Boston: Atlantic-Lit-
    tle Brown (Toronto), 1953. grades K–3.
Wiggins, K. D., and N. A. Smith, *Tales of Laughter*. Garden City, N.Y.: Dou-
    bleday & Company, 1954. grades 5–8.

2. An excellent way for a youngster to begin to expand his or her vocabulary is by choosing books or stories with a reasonable number of
   unfamiliar words. Have the child tell you when he or she hears an
   unfamiliar word. You can record the word and return to it at an appropriate stopping place. At that time, discuss the word and its
   meaning. Any of the following books may be valuable for vocabulary
   expansion:

Alexander, L. *Westmark*. New York: E. P. Dutton & Co., 1981.
Bond, F. *Poinsettia and Her Family*. New York: Thomas Y. Crowell, 1981.
Bunting, E. *Demetrius and the Gold Goblet*. Illustrated by M. Nague. New York:
    Harcourt Brace Jovanovich, Inc., 1980.

Goldsmith, H. *Toto the Timid Turtle*. Illustrated by S. Chan. New York: Human Sciences Press, 1980.

L'Engle, M. *A Wrinkle in Time*. New York: Farrar, Straus & Giroux, Inc., 1962.

O'Dell, Scott. *Island of the Blue Dolphins*. Boston: Houghton Mifflin Company, 1960.

3. Illustrations in picture books can help children to develop an interest in reading. Encourage young readers to look at the picture and tell the story that the pictures depict. Some appropriate books might include

Crews, D. *Light*. New York: Greenwillow Books, 1981.

Freeman, D. *Penguins of All People!* New York: The Viking Press, 1971.

Lifton, B. *The Many Lives of Cio and Goro*. New York: W. W. Norton & Company, Inc., 1968.

Sendak, M. *Outside Over There*. New York: Harper & Row, Publishers, 1981.

Sharmat, M. *Gila Monsters Meet You at the Airport*. Illustrated by B. Barton. New York: Macmillan Publishing Company, 1980.

Shimin, S. *A Special Birthday*. New York: McGraw-Hill Book Company, 1976.

4. When your child has particularly enjoyed a story, choose characters from the story you can imitate or portray. As you and your child go about your daily routine, act as you think your chosen characters might act in your situation. Here are some useful references:

Bale, J. *Jango*. New York: Delacorte Press, 1965.

Buckley, H. *Too Many Crackers*. New York: Lothrop, Lee & Shepard Company, 1966.

Cowles, G. *Nicholas*. New York: The Seabury Press, 1975.

Duncan, L. *Giving Away Suzanne*. New York: Dodd, Mead & Company, 1963.

Gantos, J. *Aunt Bernice*. Illustrated by N. Rubel. Boston: Houghton Mifflin Company, 1978.

Kraus, R. *Mert the Blurt*. Illustrated by J. Aruego and A. Dewey. New York: Windmill Books/Simon & Schuster, 1980.

Levitin, S. *Journey to America*. New York: Atheneum Publishers, 1970.

Ness, E. *Do You Have the Time, Lydia?* New York: E. P. Dutton & Co., 1971.

Newman, R. *Merlin's Mistake*. New York: Atheneum Publishers, 1970.

5. The following magazines may be interesting for your students.

Boys' Life
Child Life
Children's Digest
Co-ed
Cricket
Curious Naturalist
Current Events
Daisy
Easy Home Computer

Ebony, Jr.
Family Computing
Highlights for Children
Horn Book
Humpty Dumpty's Magazine for Little Children
Information World
Jack and Jill
Junior Scholastic

Kids for Ecology
Man & His Music
Model Airplane News
My Weekly Reader Eye
National Geographic World
Nature Canada
News Explorer
Personal Computing
Popular Science
Ranger Rick's Nature Magazine
Read

Roots
Science and Children
Science World
Senior Scholastic
Senior Weekly Reader
Wee Wisdom
Wee Wish Tree
World Traveler
Young Miss
Young World
Zoonooz

6. Establish a family reading time. The type of material read is not as important as the *regularity* of the reading time.
7. The following records and "read-along" editions of good books for readers will be interesting for your students.

Drummer Hoff, Barbara Emberley (K–3)
    Film, Morton Schindel, 1969, 16mm, 5 min, color
    Filmstrip, Weston Woods, 34 frames, color w/record or cassette

European Folk and Fairy Tales
CMS Records 1968 (K–6)

Evan's Corner, Elizabeth Starr Hill (K–6)
    Film, Stephen Bosustow, 16mm, color

Mother Mother I Feel Sick Send for the Doctor Quick Quick Quick, Remy Charlip (K–3)
    Filmstrip, Look/Listen & Learn, 43 frames, b/w

The Mouse that Roared, Leonard Wibberley (7–8)
    Film, Columbia, 1959, 16mm color
    Record, CMS Records, 1970 (by the author)

Poetry Parade
    Record or cassette, Weston Woods, 1967

Where Does the Butterfly Go When It Rains? Mary Garelick
    Filmstrip, Weston Woods, 20 frames, color w/cassette or record

The Wind in the Willows, Kenneth Grahame
    Filmstrip (color), record or cassette
    Spoken Arts, Inc., 1977

The Wisest Man in the World, retold by Benjamin Elkin (K–6)
    Film, Thomas Sand, 1970, 16mm, color

The Witch of Blackbird Pond, Elizabeth George Speare
    Record or cassette, Miller-Brody Production, 1970.

8. Books make excellent gifts. Ownership has also been found to be one
   of the most important factors in encouraging reading. Some interesting books for gifts are

Blue, R. *My Mother the Witch.* Ill. T. Lewin. New York: McGraw-Hill Book
    Company, 1980. grades 4–6.
Byars, B. *After the Goat Man.* New York: The Viking Press, Inc., 1974. grades
    4–6.
Hill, D. *Mr. Pecknuff's Tiny People.* Ill. A. Daniel. New York: Atheneum Pub-
    lishers, 1981. grades 1–3.
Mazer, H. *The Island Keeper.* New York: Delacorte Press, 1981. grades 6–8.
Preston, E. *Squawk to the Moon, Little Goose.* New York: The Viking Press,
    Inc., 1974. preschool–grade 1.
Snyder, Z. *The Truth About Stone Hollow.* New York: Atheneum Publishers,
    1974. grades 4–7.

Self-concept and Reading

Many educators believe that self-concept, one's perception of self, is related to reading achievement. Quandt (1972) states that there is strong
evidence to suggest that there is a positive correlation between levels of
reading achievement and levels of self-concept. Alexander and Filler (1976)
also allow that "it is possible that there may be interactions, self-concept,
and attitudes toward reading" (p. 6).

Diagnosis of self-concept is difficult because "self-concept is a construct, not a behavior" (Quandt, 1972, p. 11). However, if an increase in
positive self-concept will result in increasing reading ability, teachers must
have an assessment instrument to determine which students may benefit
from an intervention program. Toward this end, many instruments have
been developed to assess self-concept (see Appendix in Quandt, 1972, pp.
34–35). As an example, the first six items from Gordon's (1966) *How I See
Myself Scale* are presented below.

1. Nothing gets me too mad.   1 2 3 4 5   I get mad easily and explode.
2. I don't stay with things and   1 2 3 4 5   I stay with something till I
   finish them.   finish.
3. I'm very good at drawing.   1 2 3 4 5   I'm not much good at draw-
                                            ing.
4. I don't like to work on   1 2 3 4 5   I like to work with others.
   committee projects.
5. I wish I were smaller   1 2 3 4 5   I'm just the right height.
   (taller).
6. I worry a lot.   1 2 3 4 5   I don't worry much.

After you have collected information of this type, you will be better able to select appropriate reading materials and activities that will continue to strengthen each student's concept of self.

Assessing Reading Attitude

Teachers must assess students' attitudes toward reading since these attitudes may affect the acquisition of reading skills. Epstein (1980) endorses assessing students' attitudes when he says, "If we truly desire to promote positive reading attitudes or at least reduce negative attitudes (feelings), we must be aware of students' present attitudes" (p. 9).

Teacher observation can be a valuable assessment tool; in addition, there are many attitude inventories you may use for this purpose. Examples of several appear in the pages that follow. The first is especially appropriate for young children.

READING ATTITUDE INVENTORY*

Name _____   Grade _____   Teacher _____

1. How do you feel when your teacher reads a story to you?

2. How do you feel when someone gives you a book for a present?

3. How do you feel about reading for fun at home?

---

*Paul Campbell, *Reading Attitude Inventory.* Livonia Michigan: Livonia, Public Schools, 1966.

An alternate form of the first measure follows.

READING INTEREST/ATTITUDE SCALE*

Right to Read Office, Washington, D.C., 1976

Date _____ Grade _____ Name _____

   Read each item slowly twice to each student. Ask him or her to point to the face that shows how he or she feels about the statement. Circle the corresponding symbol. Read each item with the same inflection and intonation.

A	B	C
Strongly Agree	Undecided	Strongly Disagree
(Makes me feel good)	(OK or don't know)	(Makes me feel bad)

A   B   C   1.   When I go to the store I like to buy books.
A   B   C   2.   Reading is for learning but not for fun.
A   B   C   3.   Books are fun to me.

   This second measure can be used with older students. You can read some of the following statements to your students to assess their attitudes toward reading.

READING ATTITUDE INVENTORY*

Yes   No

____   ____   1.   I visit the library to find books I might enjoy reading.

____   ____   2.   I would like to read a magazine in my free time.

____   ____   3.   I cannot pay attention to my reading when there is even a little noise or movement nearby.

*Molly Ransbury, Eckerd College, St. Petersburg, Florida.

This third measure can be used with secondary-level students.

RHODY SECONDARY READING ATTITUDE ASSESSMENT*

This is a test to tell how you feel about reading. The score will not affect your grade in any way. You read the statements as I read them aloud. Then put an X on the line under the letter or letters that represent how you feel about the statement.

SD – Strongly disagree
 D – Disagree
 U – Undecided
 A – Agree
SA – Strongly agree

		SD	D	U	A	SA
1.	You feel you have better things to do than read.	___	___	___	___	___
2.	You seldom buy a book.	___	___	___	___	___
3.	You are willing to tell people that you do not like to read.	___	___	___	___	___

---

*R. Tullock-Rhody and J. Alexander, "A Scale for Assessing Attitudes Toward Reading in Secondary Schools," *Journal of Reading*, 23 (April 1980), p. 612.

These are only a few examples of the many available instruments that purport to measure reading attitudes.

Determining a Student's Interests in Reading

Many reading authorities believe that a student's interests and attitudes are closely related. Witty (1963) defined interest as

> a disposition or tendency which impels an individual to seek out particular goals for persistent attention. The goals may be objects, skills, knowledges, and art activities of various kinds. The behavior patterns in seeking these goals may be regarded as particular interests such as collecting objects or viewing TV. They should be looked upon as acquired, although they are based upon such factors as the constitutional nature of the individual and his personality structure as affected by his unique experiences and his particular environment. (p. 331)

When applied to reading, this definition would suggest that the development of positive student interest may hinge on

1. Understanding the student's background and experiences
2. Acquiring some understanding of individual personality

There are several ways to learn about students' interests, like classroom interactions, both student-teacher and student-student. If you talk about your interests, hobbies, and activities, many students will share their interests with you. Take note of which things hold someone's interest and attention and which do not. It may also be helpful to assess students' reading interests by collecting information from an informal survey. Samples from three surveys that you may find useful are presented on the following pages. The first was developed for students in middle school, although it can be used or adapted for other levels. Such surveys can also be used to guide your selection of books and reading materials. The other two surveys will provide you with information on students' interests in general, including reading interests.

READING INTEREST CHECKLIST*

Your feelings can be shown by circling the appropriate number beside each item. For "Very little," circle the number 1. For "Very much," circle the number 5. If your "likes" are somewhere between, circle the appropriate number.

I like to read about	Very little				Very much
a. Adventures	1	2	3	4	5
b. Animals	1	2	3	4	5
c. Art/music/dance	1	2	3	4	5

---

*B. Heathington, "What to Do About Reading Motivation in the Middle School," *Journal of Reading*, 22 (May 1979), 709–713.

The following survey calls for the student to listen as the teacher reads each of these items and then respond to them orally.

INTEREST INVENTORY

Name _____ Age _____

Date _____

1. My favorite day of the week is _____ because

_____.

2. The television programs I like the most are _____

_____.

3. The most fun I ever had was when _____

_____.

INTEREST INVENTORY

Name _____ Age _____

Date _____

1. What do you like to do when you have free time?

2. How do you usually spend your summers?

3. How much reading do you do on your own?

Determining Learning Style

Each of us has a preferred learning style for every task we undertake. Some of us will say: "I'm a graphic-visual learner. I can only study by writing out the information." Others will say: "I'm an auditory learner; I need to have things spoken before I can learn." Competent adults may have a *preferred* learning style, yet they are able to use several different styles. Your students, however, may not have acquired an array of styles yet.

White (1983) notes that "while it is clear that learning style is an important consideration in educational decision making, it is equally clear that most educational programs are designed with little or no attention to it" (p. 842). You can assess students' perception of their "best" style and then decide if you want to teach to this one style or build an array of effective styles. The following is a sample of one instrument that can help you assess learning styles.

LEARNING STYLE INDICATOR

Read each pair of statements and mark the box next to the statement that *most closely* describes you.

1. I understand things better from a picture. ☐ ☐ I understand things better from someone telling me or reading about them.

2. I look at charts and diagrams before I read the written part. ☐ ☐ I read the written part before I look at the charts and diagrams.

3. I memorize things by writing them out. ☐ ☐ I memorize things by repeating them aloud.

4. I like examples first, rules later. ☐ ☐ I like rules first, examples later.

5. I usually get more done when I work alone. ☐ ☐ I usually get more done when I work with others.

6. I enjoy doing a number of things at the same time. ☐ ☐ I prefer doing things one at a time.

7. I usually ask "why" questions. ☐ ☐ I usually ask about facts.

8. I prefer working quickly. ☐ ☐ I prefer to work slowly.

9. I answer questions quickly. ☐ ☐ I answer questions carefully and slowly.

10. I take chances at making mistakes. ☐ ☐ I try to avoid making mistakes.

High-Interest Materials

Some students acquire negative attitudes about reading because they experience great difficulty with materials written at their *grade level*. It is vitally important that you select reading materials that stimulate children's interest while complementing their level of *reading competency* to attempt to reverse negative reading attitudes. The following list includes several resources that can assist you with your text selections.

MATERIALS LIST

Booklist. Chicago: American Library Association.
High/Low Report. New York: Riverside Publications.
Sarkissian, A. *High-Interest Books for Teens: A Guide to Book Reviews and Bibliographic Sources.* Detroit, Mich.: Gale, 1981.
Spache, G. *Good Reading for Poor Readers,* 10th ed. Champaign, Ill.: Garrard, 1978.
White, M. (ed.) *High-Interest Easy Reading for Junior and Senior High School Students,* 3rd ed. Urbana, Ill.: National Council of Teachers of English, 1979.

The following titles are examples of high-interest/easy vocabulary materials you may want to examine (RL= reading level; IL = interest level).

1. Eisenberg, L. *Tiger Rose.* Chicago: Children's Press, 1980. RL 1, IL 5–9.
2. Myers, W. *Brainstorm.* New York: Franklin Watts, 1977. RL 2, IL 5–10.
3. Platt, K. *Dracula, Go Home!* New York: Franklin Watts, 1979. RL 2, IL 7–9.
4. Rabinowich, E. *Toni's Crowd.* New York: Franklin Watts, 1978. RL 2, IL 7–9.
5. Salas, N. *Night of the Kachina.* Chicago: Children's Press, 1977. Rl 1, IL 7–8.
6. Sanderlin, O. *Tennis Rebel.* New York: Franklin Watts, 1978. RL 2, IL 7–10.
7. Stevenson, J. *Help, Yelled Maxwell.* Illustrated by Edwina Stevenson. New York: Greenwillow Books, 1978. RL 3, IL 2–4.

As part of your total reading program, we also recommend that you include high-interest games as part of your classroom materials. Examples of such games include

Alchoch, D. *Blendograms.* Covina, Calif: Alcoch Publishing. RL K–3, IL 3+
Balinger, W. *You and Your World,* Palo Alto, Calif.: Fenem, 1964. RL primary, IL Jr. and Sr. High.
Razzle. Beverly, Mass.: Parker Bros., 1981. Ages 8 to adult.
Scrabble Sentence Game for Juniors. Bay Shore, N.Y.: Selchow and Righter Co., 1973. Ages 6–12.

ASTROLOGY

Often, even people who claim they "don't believe" in astrology know their own astrological sun sign. Astrology, like magic, has delighted and involved audiences through the ages. A list of people born under each of the various signs should produce some interest among your students. The list can be a high-interest motivator for several reading lessons. Ask your students to

1. Determine their sign.
2. "Read" about the characteristics of their sign.

Several more advanced reading and reference skills lessons could be developed around the theme of "astrological signs." Ask students to find other famous people who were born under their sign. For example;

Aquarius (January 21–February 19)
    Leontyne Price
    Hank Aaron
Sagittarius (November 22–December 21)
    Walt Disney
    Mark Twain

As part of a cross-cultural unit, you may want to ask students to find out the symbol in the Chinese calendar for the year of their birth. They can also cross-reference people born under their sign with their Chinese character symbol.

Year of the:	Rat	Ox	Tiger	Hare	Dragon	Snake
	1960	1961	1962	1963	1964	1965
	1972	1973	1974	1975	1976	1977

	Horse	Sheep	Monkey	Rooster	Dog	Pig
	1966	1967	1968	1969	1970	1971
	1978	1979	1980	1981	1982	1983

READER'S THEATER

Many teachers have successfully used Reader's Theater to motivate students to read. Reader's Theater is the presentation of literature in which the student hears the spoken words but must *imagine* the scenery, action, and characters. Ratliff (1980) suggests that Reader's Theater may be used

1. To enhance critical study of literature and language
2. To explore appreciation and meaning of literature
3. To bring vitality and relevance to literature
4. To promote reading, writing, and listening skills
5. To enable students to publicly display their creative performance talents to an audience of peers or parents

Reader's Theater is quite different from conventional theater. The major difference is the role of the *audience;* in Reader's Theater, the audience members are *interpreters,* not merely *observers.* The goal of Reader's Theater is to establish scenes and *suggest* (not portray) characters, forcing the audience to conjure up or imagine the action. In addition, Woodbury (1979) cites five other conventions in Reader's Theater:

1. Scenery and costumes are not used or are only selectively employed.
2. Action or physical movement is merely suggested by the interpreter and is visualized in the minds of the audience.
3. A narrator, speaking directly to the audience, usually establishes the basic situation or theme and links the various segments together.
4. A physical script is usually carried by the reader or at least is in evidence somewhere.
5. There is a continuing effort to develop and maintain a closer, more personalized relationship between performer and audience. The emphasis is on aural appeal, and the audience's attention is concentrated on the literature.

Reader's Theater has advantages for many types of students. First, some students are incapable of or are reluctant to act out parts in a play. Reader's Theater does not demand physical portrayal; it asks for oral interpretation. Second, since the student who is part of the audience has to visualize the spoken word, Reader's Theater can help students develop their listening skills. Third, less capable readers can become involved in this form of reading because they have the opportunity to prepare the script. In the beginning, they can take the roles that demand less reading.

Reader's Theater is both creative and dramatic. There is no limit to what can happen in the minds of the audience. Reader's Theater is dramatic because our imaginations can soar and are not constrained by the actions on stage, as in conventional theater. Extensive rehearsal and memorization usually are unnecessary. But, as with any dramatic presentation, familiarity with the material enhances the production considerably.

Reader's Theater is also a good writing activity for students because most students enjoy rewriting literature into dramatic plays. The stories that are best for Reader's Theater scripts are those in which there is a great deal of dialogue. Actions that are visually important, but unspoken, are inappropriate for Reader's Theater—for example, Desdemona's dropping of the handkerchief.

As your students engage in a Reader's Theater production, stress that the students' role is that of *interpreter*, not actor. This is often difficult for them, particularly for young children, because they want to look at each other. It is important to discuss with students that the most important *sense* played to in Reader's Theater is not the audience's eyes, but their ears, as well as their minds and imaginations.

In Reader's Theater, part of your classroom becomes the stage. Students can be seated on stools or chairs, holding their scripts in front of them. A change in scene can be narrated by a student. Entrances and exits are handled by the characters standing or sitting, stepping forward or backward, or dropping their eyes or by any other methods that seem appropriate for a particular script. There are no rules in Reader's Theater, but the audience should not *see* the action on the stage. There should be one guiding principle: Make the audience do the work in their minds.

A FINAL NOTE

Reading is not only an essential life skill, it is a valuable way to enhance life itself. Since the reading attitudes formulated during the school years may last a lifetime, you must do all you can to foster positive interactions with printed materials. Rosenblatt (1983) summarizes this succinctly: "Reading becomes no more than an empty shell, a rote exercise, if it does not relate to the needs, interests, and aspirations of the reader" (p. 134).

Suggested Reading Related to Goals. We encourage you at this time to review the goals at the beginning of this chapter. If you feel you would like to explore one or more of these in greater depth, please refer to the cross-indexed bibliography at the end of the book.

12

Assessing Students' Strengths and Needs

We must recognize that testing students, especially with group tests, will not guarantee that we separate functionally literate from functionally illiterate students. We need to define functional literacy and create instruments that will more closely and holistically describe, diagnose, and measure the characteristics of the successfully functioning literate adult.

[Patricia Anders]

Goals

To help the student understand
1. The importance of diagnosis in the evaluation process
2. Formal and informal student assessment measures
3. Expectancy levels
4. Effective student assessment as the foundation for appropriate instruction

Each student in your classroom is an individual with different strengths and needs. To construct an instructional program that builds upon these competencies and needs, you must have tools to help you assess strengths and needs. You will probably use a combination of teacher observation, formal tests, and informal tests to help you assemble the materials needed to begin a diagnostic-prescriptive program. Your ultimate goal, of course, is to use the information you have gleaned through assessment to organize an effective, well-managed diagnostic-prescriptive reading program that will meet the needs of each individual student.

This sounds like a tall order, and it is; but it needn't be an over-

Each student in your classroom is an individual with different strengths and needs. (Photo by Linda Lungren.)

whelming task. The key is classroom management: "Good managers tend to be effective teachers because they organize the classroom to create more opportunity to learn" (Duffy, 1982, p. 365). In this chapter we will provide you with the information you need to turn your classroom into a successful environment for reading and learning.

Evaluation in the Classroom

Evaluation is a *continuous* process that you will use constantly as you set goals, diagnose student needs, and plan instructional programs. From your very first teaching experience in any classroom, it will be obvious that not all students in the same grade are reading at the same level. While this fact is common knowledge, the actual range of reading levels found in students within a single classroom can be astonishing. According to Goodlad (1966), the "broad spread from high to low achiever steadily increases with the upward movement of heterogeneous classes (relatively homogeneous in chronological age) through the school" (p. 34). He estimates that the range in levels is reflected by the number of years in the grade-level number (third grade—three years). This holds true for the intermediate grades, while in the junior high grades the range may be approximated by calculating two-thirds of the median chronological age. Goodlad further states that in subject areas that allow for outside development such as language arts and recreational reading, the range broadens to one and one-half to two times the number of the grade level. To demonstrate the significance of Goodlad's finding, look at the following example.

In a fifth-grade class, the reading ability range might be computed as follows:

Grade 5

$5 \times 1.5 = 7.5$	Grade level (5) times a spread of 1.5 for each grade level.
$7.5 \div 2 = 3.75$	Dividing spread by 2.0 determines the spread on either side of the grade level.
$5 + 3.75 = 8.75$ (high)	Adding and subtracting spread 3.75 from
$5 - 3.75 = 1.25$ (low)	grade level (5) determines the range of reading ability and grade level.

1	2	3	4	(5)	6	7	8	9
-3.75								$+3.75$

Therefore, a fifth-grade teacher might expect to have students whose reading levels range from 1.25 (approximately third month of first grade) to 8.75 (approximately sixth month of eighth grade).

Goodlad suggests that the range of reading achievement in intermediate classrooms equals two-thirds times the chronological age (CA). The following chart reflects the CA for each intermediate grade level.

Grade	CA
6.0	11.2
7.0	12.0
8.0	13.2
9.0	14.2
10.0	15.2
11.0	16.2
12.0	17.2

Now pretend that you are an eighth-grade teacher. What range of reading would be possible according to Goodlad's statement?

Grade 8

Grade 8 chronological age $= 13.2$	Information from the chart.
$13.2 \times \dfrac{2}{3} = \dfrac{26.4}{3} = 8.8$ or 9	Chronological age times $\frac{2}{3}$.
$9 \div 2 = 4.5$	Dividing total spread (9) by 2 determines the spread on either side of the grade level.
$8 + 4.5 = 12.5$ (high)	Adding and subtracting spread (4.5)
$8 - 4.5 = 3.5$ (low)	from grade level (8) determines the spread on either side of the grade levels.

1	2	3	4	5	6	7	(8)	9	10	11	12	13
			-4.5								$+4.5$	

If you computed it correctly, students in your class will range from third-grade readers to twelfth-grade readers. One of your most important tasks as a teacher is to match the student with a text at the appropriate reading level. You will have to make sure that your classroom reading materials cover an adequate range of readability levels to accommodate student differences in reading.

Readability: Computation and Caution

Readability formulas can be used to *estimate* the reading level of materials and, therefore, their appropriateness for a particular student or group of students. For example, a readability estimate of 6.0 suggests that most students who have an instructional reading level of grade 6 can comfortably read these materials. Most formulas use vocabulary difficulty and sentence length as the factors to determine the readability level of a text. Several readability formulas exist; they include Gray and Leary (1935), Lorge (1944), Flesch (1943), Dale-Chall (1948), Spache (1953), Fry (1977), and Aukerman (1972). Anderson (1983) advocates the Rix (rate index) formula that was developed in Sweden in 1968 to be used in determining the readability of English and foreign language materials. Anderson claims the Rix index is "extremely quick and easy to apply" (p. 496). The Rix estimates are calculated on a combination of word and sentence length. Word length that is based on a letter count can be expressed by number of syllables or letters.

Anderson (p. 496) suggests that this simple-to-use formula is calculated in the following way:

$$\text{Rix} = \frac{\text{number of long words}}{\text{number of sentences}}$$

Directions for Rix*

1. Select a sample of sentences from the book to be analyzed. The number of samples depends in part on the size of the book and in part on the consistency of writing. As a guide for short texts, ten samples of ten sentences each, taken regularly through the book may be sufficient; for longer works, samples of at least twice this size will probably be required. Very short texts may be analyzed in their entirety.
2. For each total sample (excluding headings, captions, etc.),
    a. Count the number of sentences. A sentence is defined as a sequence of words terminated by a full stop (period), question or exclamation mark, colon or semicolon. However, in direct speech, sequences like "Where?" he asked and "Go!" he ordered count as single sentences.
    b. Count the number of long words (i.e., words of seven or more characters after excluding hyphens, punctuation marks, and brackets). A word is defined as a sequence of characters bounded by white spaces. Thus, numbers like 1,461 and 10.2, hyphenated sequences, abbreviations (e.g., IRA, A.M.), dates such as (1981–1982), and symbols like % count as single words.
3. Determine Rix by dividing the number of long words by the number of sentences (work to two decimal places).

Interpretation	Rix Score	Equivalent Grade Level
To find the equivalent grade level of	7.2 and above	College
difficulty for Rix, locate the Rix score in	6.2 and above	12
the left-hand column and the	5.3 and above	11
corresponding grade in the right-hand	4.5 and above	10
column.	3.7 and above	9
	3.0 and above	8
	2.4 and above	7
	1.8 and above	6
	1.3 and above	5
	0.8 and above	4
	0.5 and above	3
	0.2 and above	2
	Below 0.2	1

*Consult J. Anderson, "Lix and Rix: Variation on a Little-Known Readability Index," *Journal of Reading*, 26 (March 1983), 490–496.

Using Rix as a base, Kretschmer (1984) presents a BASIC program called RIXRATE. Through the use of RIXRATE, a text can be entered into a microcomputer and then on a sentence-by-sentence basis using RIX, the readability can be calculated.

Research conducted by Guidry and Knight (1976) indicated that when the Dale-Chall, Flesch, Fry, and Lorge formulas were used to determine readability levels of the same materials, "the Dale-Chall method seems consistently to be high in its grade-level readability and that a more valid determination can be made by subtracting − -0.891 from the final answer, . . .the Fry formula tends to yield a consistently low readability" (p. 556). When using the Fry formula, you will need to add + -0.865 as an adjustment grade-level factor. When employing the Flesch and Lorge formulas, the adjustment factors of + -0.299 and − -0.285 are suggested by Guidry and Knight. With the application of these adjustment factors, it may be possible to use these formulas with greater confidence.

Remember, however, that readability levels are only *approximations* of material difficulty; it is almost impossible to hold constant all the factors (text organization, concept difficulty, semantics, syntax, reader interest) that can affect the mastery of a given material.

The Fry Readability Graph

The Fry formula, which was first developed in 1961 and revised in 1977 is comparable in accuracy to the other readability formulas, and readability levels from grades 1 through college can be computed quickly and easily.

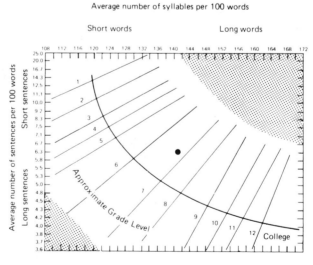

Figure 12-1. Fry Readability Graph. (From Edward Fry, "Readability Formula That Saves Time," *Journal of Reading,* 11 (April 1968), pp. 513–516, 575–577.)

It is presented here to help you determine the readability of materials that might be appropriate to students (see Figure 12-1).

HOW TO USE THE FRY GRAPH

1. Select three hundred-word passages from near the beginning, middle, and end of the book. Start at the beginning of a sentence and be sure to include proper nouns, initials, and numerals (e.g., Bill, IRA, 1984, &).
2. Count the total number of sentences in each hundred-word passage (estimating to the nearest tenth of a sentence). Average these three numbers (add together and divide by 3).
3. Count the total number of syllables in each hundred-word sample. There is a syllable for each vowel sound; for example, cat (1), blackbird (2), continental (4), 1984 (4), IRA (3), & (1). Do not be fooled by word size; for example, ready (2), stopped (1), bottle (2). It may be convenient to count every syllable over one in each word and add 100. Average the total number of syllables for the three samples.
4. Plot on the graph the average number of sentences per hundred words and the average number of syllables per hundred words. Most plot points fall near the heavy curved line. Perpendicular lines mark off approximate grade-level areas. For example, the following samples can be plotted on the Fry Graph.

Example	*Sentences Per 100 Words*	*Syllables Per 100 Words*
100-word sample, p. 5	9.1	122
100-word sample, p. 89	8.5	140
100-word sample, p. 150	7.0	129
Total	24.6	391
Divide total by 3	8.2	130
	0.865	
Average	9.065	

Plotting these averages on the graph, we find that they fall in the upper end of the fourth-grade area; hence, the book is a high fourth-grade difficulty level. If great variability is encountered either in sentence length or in the syllable count for the three selections, then you should randomly select several more passages and average them in before plotting.

The task of computing readability levels for a library full of books may be much simplified by the use of microcomputers that are often available in math and science classes or elsewhere in the school. While there are programs available commercially (Goodman and Schwab, 1980; Carlson, 1980), an alternative method suggested by Judd (1981) is to utilize the skills of advanced programming students to program in the formula most useful for the situation.

Fox Reading Research Company has computed the readability of nearly eight thousand stories found in numerous basal series. This listing, *Foxes Reference*, can be secured from the company at P.O. Box 1059, Couer D'Alene, Idaho 83814.

CAUTIONS

Although readability formulas are easy to use, they must be used with great caution. It is virtually impossible to arrive at an absolute reading level for a text based on the sampling method used by most formulas; too many other factors are not considered in these formulas. Estes and Wetmore (1983) cite the following as factors that affect readability but are not included in readability formulas: figurative and poetic languages, style of writing, density of ideas, language context, organization of ideas, abstractness, and variability of reading difficulty within text material (p. 38). It is essential to remember that a readability score is only an approximation of difficulty and to use such a score judiciously.

Other factors, outside the actual text structure, may also contribute to the "real" readability level, as opposed to the level obtained by the formula used. Chief among these factors is the experiential background and interest of the reader. This problem is illustrated in the following exercises. Please read each of the following passages and answer the questions that follow each passage.

PASSAGE I

Christmas always meant going to Grandma's house. On Christmas Eve the entire family tramped out to the woods. Dad was in charge of bringing back the tree, and the rest of us cut fir branches for house decorations. That evening Grandma would distribute the homemade ornaments. We hung up a cookie universe: suns, stars, moons, and unearthly men with raisin eyes. Mom arranged candles in silvery paper on the branches. With dignity and care, Grandpa chained the tree with yards of cranberries and popcorn. We decorated the tree the way Grandma had when she was young; we were learning tradition.

Questions

1. Who cut the Christmas tree? _____
2. What was Grandpa's job? _____
3. Who was in charge of decorating the tree? _____
4. Why did the author of this paragraph go to the woods? _____
5. What does the phrase "cookie universe" mean? _____
6. How did the author of this paragraph learn tradition? _____

PASSAGE II

One of the oldest drinks known to man is milk. Man requires liquids as well as solids to remain healthy because he is a mammal, a warm-blooded being. Prehistoric man did not consume as much liquid as modern man. He devoured fruit from the trees he inhabited. However, man had to change his habits to exist on the arid plains. No longer a fruit-eater, he soon began to hunt plains animals. This new activity required much energy; man perspired and needed to drink liquids directly. To this day man needs liquids such as milk to be able to exist.

Questions

1. What does man need to remain healthy? _____
2. Where did prehistoric man live? _____
3. What is a mammal? _____
4. Why did ancient man not have to drink liquids directly? _____
5. What made man change his eating habits? _____
6. What happened to man's body as he hunted animals? _____

Did you find one passage more difficult than the other? Did you score equally on each passage? If you found one passage more difficult, it will be interesting for you to ask yourself; "What factors within the passage created the difficulty?" Both passages, according to the readability formulas, are extremely similar. The statistics on each of the passages are

	Christmas	*Milk*
Number of words	100	100
Number of sentences	8	8
Average sentence length	12.5	12.5
Number of syllables	146	146

This chart demonstrates some of the pitfalls of relying exclusively on readability formulas to determine passage difficulty. If you could answer more questions correctly on one of the passages, it may have been because you found that passage more interesting than the other. You may have performed better on one passage than the other because of your experience; for example, you may have celebrated Christmas in the same way as the people did in the passage. On the other hand, you may have performed less well on the Christmas passage because of a lack of experience; you may not have celebrated Christmas at all, and therefore you would not have been able to read the passage from an experiential point of view.

On the surface, the two passages are similar (number of words, syllables, etc.), but if you carefully analyze the two passages, using some of the recent findings from linguistic and information processing research, you will find that the"Milk" passage is really far more difficult. It contains several instances where the reader has to *double* process; that is, the reader has to unravel the information in order to put the information into a logical sequence. To process information about the habitat of later-day man, the reader has to compare and contrast prehistoric and later-day man and the habitat of each (prehistoric man, trees; later-day man, dry plains).

An additional factor that makes the "Milk" passage more difficult than the "Christmas" passage is the requirement for the reader to sort "prehistoric man" from "man" and the habitats of each by processing inferred relationships between the concepts; for example, the reader has to infer unwritten relationships, as the following facts are not stated explicitly: (1) man moved from the trees, (2) the dry plains did not have fruit, (3) he needed to gain food and liquid supply from a source other than fruit, (4) fruit was the source of liquid, and (5) gathering fruit did not force man to exert himself.

As these examples illustrate, there is more to determining the readability level of written materials than counting syllables or sentences and performing mathematical computations. Use these formulas with caution and as tools to establish probable rather than absolute grade-level equivalents for reading material.

Diagnosing Individual Needs

Although it is important to be prepared to help your students by understanding the range of reading levels they may exhibit and to have determined readability scores for classroom materials, more important, indeed vital, to your role in teaching reading is diagnosing the reading needs of each individual. To accomplish this complex task, you must first evaluate your students to determine their strengths and needs. Through diagnosis, you will be able to plan prescriptive programs to develop individual skills. Do not be alarmed; although we are suggesting that you will need to develop the skills of individual students, we are not suggesting that you must work with each student in isolation. The classroom management techniques we discuss later in Chapter 12 will help you to understand and implement flexible grouping techniques that are necessary for prescriptive teaching.

To begin diagnosing, you need to consider the following points:

1. The strengths and needs of the students.
2. The role of diagnostic evaluation in the classroom. Remember, evaluation is a process of decision making that can be used to diagnose and plan a curriculum.
3. The knowledge brought by the students to a specific topic.
4. The skills needed to pursue the study of this topic.

In thinking about these areas, you are already evaluating the competencies of your students.

Diagnostic evaluation is not new; it has always been part of American education in one form or another. Standardized testing became part of educational evaluation at the turn of the century when Alfred Binet and Therese Simon (1916) developed standardized intelligence tests in an attempt to differentiate normal from retarded children. They eventually broadened their studies to include the measurement of intelligence of all children.

IQ vs. IF

Intelligence tests, as they are currently designed, do not measure intellectual potential (IQ). Instead, they measure a student's present level of *intellectual functioning* (IF). Intellectual functioning is a measure of both cultural experiences and information acquired through daily interactions with a variety of stimuli, in an environment ranging from people to objects. If children have been exposed to cultural experiences that are measured on a given intelligence task, they often perform well on such a measure. If the tasks are outside their range of experience, they are often considered intellectually inferior, when they may only be missing daily exposures to such tasks or interactions.

Cultural exposures, coupled with biological factors, determine the potential of mental development (intelligence). Inherent biological characteristics determine potential, while environment encourages the full or partial development of this potential. It is becoming more clear, as research continues into intelligence testing, that no one test can possibly claim to measure a person's intelligence quotient, which must include both potential and realized intellectual ability. Combinations of tests, using traditional instruments, and electronic devices such as the ERTL Index,* may eventually provide us with an accurate means of measuring an individual's total intelligence potential (Fischer, Hunt, and Randhawa, 1978).

When children are born, their intellectual potential is determined by biological structures. In certain cases, brain damage, chromosome abnormality, or other physical factors may affect potential academic or scholastic achievement. For example, research by Smith et al. (1983) indicates that specific reading disabilities within families may be genetically transmitted from one generation to the next through a particular chromosome,

---

*The ERTL Index is an electronic device that attempts to analyze neural efficiency. Neural efficiency is processed in a period of fewer than 3 minutes. A helmet equipped with electrodes that are supposed to collect brain waves is placed on the person being tested. A flashing light stimulates the brain while a computer analyzes the efficiency with which the brain processes the light flashes. An oscilloscope, on which the waves can be monitored visually, and a device to amplify the waves are also parts of the machine. For more detailed information, see William Tracy, "Goodbye IQ, Hello EI (ERTL Index)," *Phi Delta Kappan* (October 1972), 89–94; and J. Trout, G. Packwood, and Barry Wilson, "Ertl's Neural Efficiency Analyzer: Still Promising—But What?" *Phi Delta Kappan* (March 1976), 448–451.

number 15. In cases such as these, where biological considerations are a factor, the degree of fulfillment of normal potential is realized through environmental exposures and daily experiences. Thus, IQ should be defined as normal intellectual and biological potential plus present intellectual functioning. Biological functioning is innate; present intellectual functioning is developed through daily experiences.

Available intelligence tests are used in many ways, for example, to determine school placement, to determine the need for vocational guidance, to predict juvenile delinquency tendencies, or to predict college success. However, such scores must be interpreted with great caution. IQ tests cannot measure innate intellectual potential; they do, however, provide data regarding present intellectual functioning as a result of environmental exposures.

Certain social, emotional, and cultural influences (affective dimensions) may also affect one's IF. However, you, as a classroom teacher, must also be aware that the IF is influenced by one's drive, persistence, will, and sense of preservation. These psychological factors may be studied within the context of the conative domain. To better understand the IF of the student, you will need to study the *affective* and *conative* dimensions of learning as well as the child's *cognitive* skills.

In utilizing the results of intelligence tests to analyze the strengths and needs of children, you must exercise caution before labeling a child as intellectually inferior in any way. To base an educational program solely on these test results is a regrettably frequent error. Once children are labeled as dull or retarded, they are generally treated that way, and expectations for educational accomplishments diminish. When the test scores are viewed as measuring only the present level of intellectual functioning, and a program is developed to challenge a child from that point, the intellectual capacity is then tapped and the child can be encouraged to higher educational achievement levels.

Because existing tests do not measure intelligence (intellectual potential + cultural experiences) but instead measure one's present level of intellectual functioning (IF), we believe that the term *IQ testing* should be replaced by *IF testing*. Perhaps the realization and understanding of the need for this substitution will enable us to avoid erroneous, inappropriate labels. We cannot measure intellectual potential (IQ), but we do have some measures that begin to assess one's *present level of intellectual functioning* on a given task. In the next few pages, we will use the term IF to refer to what has previously been called IQ.

MA + IF

In addition to being interested in a student's IF score and his reading level scores, teachers are often anxious to determine a student's *mental age* (MA). Why? Because many tests are scored according to the age at which a majority of the population succeeds at a given task. For example, a student who succeeds on the items at the 11-year level and fails at the 12-year level has a mental age of 11. If his chronological age is less than

11, the child may be considered to be very competent in behaviors being measured by the test. If his chronological age is greater than 11, he may need instruction or exposure to the behaviors measured by the test.

Mental age refers to one's level of mental development as compared with others on a given set of standardized tasks. MA is one's IF (present intellectual functioning level) expressed in units of age.

One's MA is easily determined through use of the following formula.

$$MA = \frac{IF}{100} \times CA$$

Thus, if a child's IF is 80 and his CA (chronological age) is 8, his MA is 6.4.

$$\frac{80}{100} \times 8 = \frac{640}{100} = 100\overline{)\begin{array}{c} 6.4 \\ 640 \\ \underline{600} \\ 400 \end{array}}$$

Or a child whose CA is 10 who has an IF of 140 has an MA of 14.0

$$\frac{140}{100} \times 10 = 14.0$$

If we accept that an IF of 120 means that a student has intellectually grown at the rate of 1.2 years for each chronological year until age 15, while an IF of 80 means that the student has advanced intellectually at the rate of 0.8 for each chronological year, the commonly used formulas $(MA = IF \times CA)$ and $(IF = \frac{MA}{CA} \times 100)$ become easier to interpret.

READING EXPECTANCY LEVELS

For decades, educators have used a homogeneous system of grouping by age, assuming that the teacher's sophisticated knowledge about individualizing instruction would result in in-class grouping by actual ability level. As you attempt to implement such personalized groupings within a given grade level, remember that the actual achievement level of each student should be compared with his or her learning functioning, not his or her grade placement.

Several formulas have been developed to help you determine a student's reading expectancy level. As we look at the following examples, however, bear in mind this warning by Burns (1982):

> Reading expectancy, like other indices, can be in error and therefore cannot and should not be interpreted in isolation. . . . A reading expectancy score might be a useful component in the overall evaluation process. However, the determination of reading expectancy will not be useful, and could actually be detrimental, if the possibility of error is ignored and other factors in a child's environment are not considered (p. 453).

Bond and Tinker (1979).   Reading expectancy level (REL)=IF/100×years of reading instruction+1. This formula is interpreted as follows: Donnie, who is an 8-year-old and is in the second grade, has had 2 years of reading instruction and has an IF of 120. Donnie's REL is 3.4: (120/100×2)+1=240/100=2.4+1=3.4 (measured in grade levels).

Harris and Sipay (1978)

$$REL = \frac{2\ MA + CA}{3}$$

Can you refer to the statistics on Donnie and determine his REL using the Harris and Sipay formula? First we must determine his MA.

Remember: $MA = \dfrac{IF}{100} \times CA$

Thus: $MA = \dfrac{120}{100} \times 8 = 9.6$

Now that we have Donnie's MA we can proceed:

$$REL = \frac{2\ MA + CA}{3} = \frac{2(9.6) + 8}{3}$$

$$= \frac{19.2 + 8}{3} = \frac{27.2}{3} = 9.1 \quad \text{(reading expectancy measured in years)}$$

The REL, as well as the MA, CA, and IF, is a rough estimate of a child's ability that can be employed with great discretion in your classroom. Note that the formula of Bond and Tinker (1979) reports the reading expectancy level in *grade-level units*, whereas the Harris and Sipay formula (1978) reports the REL in *chronological age units*. The importance of these two formulas is the following:

1. It is useful for you to know the approximate level of a student's current capacity for reading so that your expectations are realities for *every* student.
2. It is useful to know both the Bond and Tinker formula and the Harris and Sipay formula because children are often in grades that do not reflect their current ages, for example, some 10-year-olds are in the third grade and some 10-year-olds are in the fifth or sixth grade.
3. It is useful to know both formulas because some schools have an ungraded system.

Norm-Referenced and Non-Norm-Referenced Tests

Both norm-referenced and non-norm-referenced tests can be useful instruments to measure a student's achievement. The basic difference between the two methods lies, as the names suggest, in what the test results are *referenced* or compared to. Norm-referenced tests assess performance of a task in relation to others who have taken the same test. They are standardized based on this information. Non-norm-referenced tests assess student performance of a task, but do not compare the results to any previously established population. Tests of this type are not standardized.

It is also possible to say that *all* tests are criterion-referenced; that is, all tests measure achievement of a particular criterion or task. Normed test results are interpreted in statistical terms including percentile rankings, stanine scores, grade levels, and IFs. Non-norm-referenced tests provide information regarding placement on a performance continuum relative to a given behavior, the extreme ends being mastery and non-mastery of the task.

Norm-referenced testing became prominent in the 1930s as only one dimension of the process of evaluation. It is useful to think of norm-referenced tests as survey instruments, designed to measure competency in a broad manner, rather than as diagnostic tools (Stanley and Hopkins, 1972). They are useful for measuring student progress when administered infrequently (i.e., each year), and nationally normed tests provide an "external basis of comparison" (Shepard, 1979, p. 29) that highlights a student's or program's relative strengths and weaknesses in the national context. State and local norms are often available, and these may provide a more useful and accurate picture of individual and program accomplishment.

Norm- and non-norm-referenced measures differ in the ways in which they are designed, as well as in the type of information conveyed through student responses (see Table 12-1). Non-norm-referenced tests can function well as diagnostic instruments due to the precise nature of the test items. Items on a non-norm-referenced achievement test must reflect competencies within a specified behavioral domain. For a non-norm-referenced instrument to be effective, this domain of behavior must be "well-defined." According to Nitko (1980),

> a domain is well-defined when it is clear to both the test developer and the test user which categories of performance (or which kinds of tests) should and should not be considered as potential test items. Well-defined domains are a necessary condition for criterion referencing since the basic idea is to generalize how well an examinee can perform in a broader class of behaviors, only a few of which happen to appear on a particular test form. (p. 465)

The scoring of the non-norm-referenced instrument should be designed to provide information about the developed skills and existing needs of a student. If behavioral objectives have been written to define the competencies to be tested within the specified domain and the test items accurately reflect these objectives, the problem of assessing the examinee's degree of demonstration is minimized. For example, the end product of a non-norm-referenced measure should provide descriptive information regarding an individual's degree of competence on a specified task. A criterion might be, "Can Beth recite her ABCs?" The criterion is clear, and the assessment is relatively simple. Here Beth is compared to an es-

TABLE 12-1

A Comparison of Norm-Referenced and Non-Norm-Referenced Tests

Test Feature	Norm-Referenced	Non-Norm-Referenced
Test design	Design is related to subject matter information and process skills.	Design is related to specific instructional behavioral objectives.
Item preparation	Test is designed to determine variances among students.	Test is designed to measure individual competency on a given task.
Item types	Many types are used (multiple choice, true-false, completion).	Many types are used (multiple choice, true-false, completion).
Item difficulty	Difficulty is moderate; test is designed to determine a middle range.	Wide variance exists, but with adequate instructional preparation, responses are generally correct.
Interpreting results	A student is compared to the accomplishments of a norm group by computing his or her subscore or total test score.	A student's performance on a specified behavioral item is determined by comparing his or her response to the correct question.
Test availability	Consult Oscar Buros's *Mental Measurement Yearbook* to ascertain information about norm-referenced tests.	The tests, which are often designed by teachers for use in the classrooms, may now also be maintained as part of the *management systems* of many basal reading programs.
Test use	Test determines a comparative score between one pupil and a normative group and determines global student achievement.	Test diagnoses student strengths and needs and evaluates an instructional program.

tablished criterion; that is, she can or cannot recite her ABCs. The test is criterion referenced, but not norm referenced.

You can use the non-norm-referenced instrument to assess individual competencies and design alternate programs based on individual needs. The norm-referenced tests can also look at the individual's competency, as he or she is related to others in the group. The question being asked is, "How do the various students rank on the ABC test?" The criterion is performance on an ABC task. Each of these measures assesses the same behaviors, but each has a different purpose. Therefore, when you are selecting or developing an instrument for use in your classroom, you need to specify your reasons for testing, and you need to specify the criterion being tested.

Until recently, the practice has been to evaluate students against some norm group, either their own or an arbitrarily chosen group. This has at least two disadvantages: (1) it makes the same students fall at the bottom in every situation, and (2) it encourages the development of curriculum unrelated to the needs of the students. Because of these and other disadvantages, the advantages of using properly designed non-norm-referenced tests are (1) comparison problems are minimized because a child is being evaluated *only* against *himself*, and (2) development may be informal and done by the classroom teacher to measure a specific behavior.

VALIDITY

The basic question to be answered is, "Does the test measure what you think it is measuring?" For example, if a college instructor announces a test and says it will measure understanding and application, and then she asks five questions related to details of a footnote on page 47, is it measuring what she thinks (or says) it is? Obviously not. We say the test has no content validity. If, as a teacher, you want to measure problem-solving ability through story problems and you proceed to give a page of fifty long-division examples, your test will have no content validity.

Content validity must be established for achievement tests. This may be accomplished by first deciding what it is you intend to measure and then deciding if your test (or the standardized test) gives a representative sample of the entire field you are interested in testing. If it does, your test has content validity.

Researchers often discuss three other kinds of validity: *predictive validity, construct validity,* and *concurrent validity.* Predictive validity determines how successful the test is at predicting success or achievement at a future time. Most informal measures in the elementary or secondary level are not concerned with this aspect of validity.

Construct validity refers to the relationship between test scores and other criteria of behavior that logically relate to the test. It examines an ability, aptitude, trait, or characteristic that is hypothesized to explain some aspect of human behavior.

Concurrent validity compares the outcome of a test at approximately the same time as the predictor test is taken. For instance, a vocational interest test may be compared with interests exhibited by members of the vocation already. Designers of elementary school measures that are formal or informal are more concerned with content validity than they are with other types of validity.

RELIABILITY

Another factor that must be determined is the stability of your test (informal or standardized). If you give a reading comprehension test on Monday and again on Friday, and the scores are not similar for each student, then the test may not be reliable. Ambiguous test items are not reliable because students are guessing at answers. For the most part, the students seldom guess twice in the same way. Long tests and very difficult tests are often unreliable because students tend to guess from fatigue; very short tests are seldom reliable because the sample of work is so limited that you may or may not have selected the items that the student knows.

A *correlation coefficient* indicates the reliability of a test. The coefficient of correlation represents the relationship between two specific behaviors of a group of students. The tendency of the students to have systematic similar or dissimilar relative positions in the two distributions is reflected through computing a correlation coefficient. A positive correlation exists between the two measures if students who are high or low in one distribution are also high or low in a second distribution. For example, if Catherine receives a high score on each of two measures and Todd receives a low score on each of the same two measures, the correlation coefficient is positive. If $r/tt = .00$ (read: the correlation equals zero), the test is completely unreliable. If $r/tt = 1.00$ (read: the correlation equals 1), the test is completely reliable. Unfortunately, tests are never completely reliable, but a correlation of .75 to .99 is usually acceptable as a measure of reliability.

If a test is both reliable and valid and you want to use it as a criterion-referenced test, you have no further concerns. However, if you want to use it as a norm-referenced test, you must investigate appropriate norming procedures.

NORMS

Norms are as important to the teacher as they are to the doctor. If you took a child to be weighed and measured, and the doctor told you that the child was greatly overweight, you would ask, "Overweight compared to whom?" If you believed the comparison to be inappropriate, you would reject the doctor's statement.

The same is true for achievement tests. The score that the child receives may be accurate, depending on the validity and the reliability of the test, but the comparisons you make may be totally inappropriate. A child can only be compared with his or her own group—that is, a 10-year-old urban child should be compared with other 10-year-old children in similar urban environments. To make the wrong comparisons is totally misleading and provides no helpful information. In fact, the information may be considered destructive if the child is labeled intellectually inferior because of his score on measures with which he has had no preparation.

A test can also be used if the appropriate norms are not supplied. For example, you may wish to use the score in the context of the child's own classroom group, use the test for a diagnostic purpose, or establish a set of norms for your own school. It really is not a difficult process. Farr (1970), a leading reading evaluator, suggested the following procedures for norming your informal reading test:

1. Administer a standardized silent reading test to a group of students (a sample size of 100 is usually best). Several teachers may cooperate on the project.
2. Develop an informal reading test based on the instructional reading materials used in the classes. Use appropriate questions (as described) and decide on criteria for establishing instructional reading levels.
3. Use the results of the standardized test to rank the students from highest to lowest. Use a composite reading score (not subscores) for this ranking.
4. Randomly select three students from each decile of the ranking. That is, select three students from the top 10, select three students from the second 10, and so on until you have selected 30 of the total 100 students.
5. Administer the informal reading test to these students.
6. From this procedure you can develop equivalency (IRI reading levels) for students scoring at various points on the standardized reading test.

Let us assume that the students who are being tested are fourth-graders. After you have completed the administration of the standardized test and selected your deciles, you should study the test manual and re-code the scores into reading grade levels. The next step is to assume that the scores are accurate for each decile, that is, that students who score at seventh-grade level are capable of performing on other tests at a seventh-grade level. Now you are ready to administer the informal reading test with test questions you have developed. The scores of each of your groups will establish norms for your informal reading test. The following chart illustrates this procedure.

| | Standardized Test | | | |
| | *Mean Raw Score* | *Mean Reading Grade Level* | *Mean Informal Reading Test Scores (highest = 10 pt)* | *Estimated Grade Level* |
Group				
A	85	7.0	9	7.0
B	50	4.0	6	4.0
C	30	1.0	3	1.0

From this chart you can see that the scores for your informal reading test are easily correlated with estimated reading levels. However, these scores should probably be used only to determine grade-level criteria. In this case, a score of 6 out of 10 will approximate a reading level score of 4.0. There are several cautions that we would like to point out if you intend to use this procedure:

1. This procedure only approximates a reading level.
2. It is assumed that the objective of your informal reading test conforms

to the objectives of the standardized reading test. Your informal reading test may have an entirely different purpose than the standardized reading test, and therefore, the score may not accurately reflect reading level ability for this particular task.

3. There is a statistical concern with this procedure. If one student in group A scores 2 out of 10 and most of the other students score 9 or 10 and if the mean is equated at 8, then a score of 8 may not accurately reflect the group's scores. Therefore, you may want to use the median score as the norm instead of the mean score.

In addition to examining reliability, validity, and norming samples when you are choosing a test, you should also consider the following:

1. *Original publication date and/or most recent test revision.* Remember that words and concepts change with each generation. Many children today have never heard of an "outhouse" or an "icebox."
2. *Type of test.* Individual or group scoring; by hand or machine.
3. *Scoring.* If test is scored by the testing company, remember to request that the student answer sheets be returned. You can plan instruction if you know the consistency of errors made by the students. An IQ score of 103 or a reading score of 6.2 tells you nothing that will aid your planning.
4. *Availability of test forms.* If you plan to retest after instruction, you will need twice as many forms.
5. *Administration time.* Be careful to measure desired behavior rather than rate.
6. *Cost.*
7. *Availability of subtests.* It is often unnecessary to administer the entire test to measure the desired behavior. (Behavior is used in the sense of desired cognitive or affective outcome or performance. Behavioral objectives will be explained in detail later in this chapter.) Sometimes one subtest is so highly correlated with all of the other subtests in a specific test that you only need to give one subtest to ascertain reading achievement information for a child. To determine if you can use one subtest as a valid predictor of overall achievement, consult the statistics provided in the manual for each standardized test.
8. *Legibility of tables, maps, and graphs.*
9. *Clarity of directions.* Lack of clarity in giving directions often measures the ability to interpret directions as well as, or instead of, the previously desired behavior. The directions should be written in vocabulary appropriate to your grade level. Would it invalidate the test if you explained the directions to your students?

Some of this information will be found in the manual. However, keep in mind that the manual is written by an author or a publisher whose major intent is to sell the tests. A less biased review of most tests can be found in the *Mental Measurement Yearbook*, edited by Buros (1968–1978).

This reference should be consulted before investing time and money in a testing program.

As a teacher you will already know a great deal about the abilities of your students. Use testing to fill in the gaps and tell you what you *don't* know. There is little point in overtesting your students. It is important that you know your reason for testing: What do I want to know about this student? How will this knowledge help me in planning better activities for him or her? After answering these questions, carefully select your instrument, using the previously stated criteria. After scoring, diagnose and plan your curriculum accordingly. No one has to pass or fail as the student is only competing with himself or herself.

Go one step farther and explain to your principal that the standardized tests being given to your class at the beginning of the year are really of little instructional value if you only have a list that supplies you with a single grade-level score for each student. Ask for a breakdown of the test by category/components, for example, vocabulary score and syllabication score.

As you attempt to analyze student assessment further, you may want to use a diagnostic test; an instrument of this type is designed to provide you with a more thorough analysis of individual skill competency. For example, a standard reading survey test will provide you with general information regarding student skill in vocabulary, comprehension, and rate, whereas a diagnostic instrument provides scores in knowledge of consonant sounds, blending, syllabication, morphemes, comprehension, study skills, and reading rate. A more thorough analysis of information is provided through the diagnostic test.

Diagnostic tests are often individually administered and require administrative and scoring skills because interpretation may be a complex task. Whichever type of test you use, if it is computer scored, remember to remind the publishing company to return the individual answer sheets so that continuing diagnosis can take place.

Standardized achievement test results, which can be used to diagnose and plan instructional needs, can be correlated with informal test results to acquire a more valid understanding of individual student skills. Correlation of standardized and informal tests, if correctly used, will provide a reliable and accurate assessment of student growth.

Informal Non-Norm-Referenced Measures

In a diagnostic-prescriptive curriculum, you need as much information as possible about each student to best serve his or her needs. In addition to standardized tests, you will find that informal assessments also provide valuable information regarding the reading competencies of your students. Informal instruments differ from standardized measures because they do not involve the formalized procedures for constructing, administering, and scoring. The quality of the informal measures used in your classroom will depend on *your competency* to design, implement, and evaluate them.

Informal measures that will be useful to you as a reading teacher are *informal reading inventories, teacher-made tests,* and the *cloze readability technique.*

IRI: INFORMAL READING INVENTORY

An effective and easily constructed diagnostic instrument, the informal reading inventory (IRI) is generally a teacher-made tool designed to assess a student's reading level. Quite often IRIs are made by selecting passages from material at the required grade level and individually administering them as a *silent* and/or *oral* reading exercise. The IRI is seldom used by content specialists because of the time (15 to 20 minutes per student) needed for individual administration. Questions on context and vocabulary help to assess the comprehension level of the student. IRIs are useful in determining a student's *independent reading level, instructional reading level,* and *frustrational level.* The independent level is believed to be the one on which the student can read successfully with little or no aid because fluency and comprehension are developed well enough to master materials at this level. The student's instructional level is the level at which he or she requires teacher assistance. At this level, the student's fluency and comprehension skills are not as well developed as when he or she reads at the independent level. The frustrational reading level signals an area of difficulty to be avoided by the student. The level of a book at the student's frustrational level is too difficult.

Through the use of an IRI, an approximation of a student's reading level can be assessed based on the number and types of errors made in oral reading. Johnson and Kress (1965) maintain that a student is reading at her independent reading level if she scores 99 to 100 percent (one error) in her oral reading word analysis skills in a hundred-word passage. If the child averages two to five errors, or 95 to 98 percent, she is considered to be reading at her instructional reading level. The child has reached her frustrational reading level when she cannot master at least 94 percent of the text.

On the silent reading test of the IRI, a student is believed to be reading at her independent reading level if she is able to answer correctly 90 to 100 percent of the questions. If 70 to 90 percent of the questions are correctly answered, the student is believed to be reading at her instructional level. Her instructional plan is now developed.

Careful planning of instructional procedures will eliminate any areas of weakness that were evidenced at this level. The frustrational reading level has been reached if the student cannot answer at least 70 percent of the posed questions.

Administering an Oral Reading IRI

1. Select a 100-word passage from the material you wish the student to read.
2. Ask the student to read the passage orally.
3. Record the following types of errors. You may record the reading and score the student afterward.

Types of Errors

Mispronunciation:	Record the incorrect response above the word missed.
Substitution:	Record the substituted word above the one missed.
Omission:	Circle the omitted word or words.
Insertion:	Caret in the extra word.
Hesitations:	Supply the needed word and write "H" if the student pauses for longer than 5 seconds.
Repetitions:	Draw a wavy line under repeated words.

Recording Miscues

While the student may make some oral reading errors, be sure not to plan extensive instruction based on these findings because the oral reading section of the IRI should help you to understand each student's word-recognition and word analysis skills. Record the errors but do not plan detailed instruction until you have assessed comprehension through silent reading.

We make this suggestion because many readers make perceptual reading errors that do not interfere with comprehension. This often happens when the student is participating in an oral reading activity.

If you wish to assess the student's ability to comprehend during an oral reading activity, you may wish to refer to the next section, "Administering a Silent Reading IRI," for guidance in designing comprehension questions.

The silent reading portion of the IRI will help to determine the student's ability to comprehend when reading silently.

Administering a Silent Reading IRI

1. Prepare questions that determine the student's ability to use various parts of the text (index, glossary, etc.):
   a. On what pages will you find information about prehistoric man?
   b. How does the author define prehistoric?
2. Prepare questions that measure both the *vocabulary* and *comprehension* of what has been read:
   a. Where did prehistoric man originate?
   b. Define the word *skeletal* used by the author in the following sentence.

3. When preparing these questions, you must be careful to provide items that assess the many operations of comprehension skills. Please refer to Chapter 7 for practice in developing a complex range of questions.
4. Direct the students to read the selection and answer the appropriate questions.
5. Students can be timed if you are interested in measuring reading rate.
6. Assess the correct responses to determine the student's reading level. This is done by counting the number of correct responses and dividing it into the total number of items. If the student is asked ten comprehension questions and he correctly responded to seven, he completed 70 percent of the questions correctly. Look at the following chart, which can help you to interpret student scores.

Informational Reading Inventory Standards

Level	Oral Reading	Comprehension
Independent	99–100%	99–100%
Instructional	95–98%	70–90%
Frustrational	Below 94%	Below 70%

We can conclude that the text from which the passages were drawn are at the reader's instructional level. Now you must provide instruction that is based on the type of errors made.

Based on the information you obtain through this assessment, you may want to devise a chart similar to that in Figure 12-2 that will help you to determine student need at a glance. If you record a student's score in each area you have assessed, you will be able to obtain a more comprehensive view of his or her reading proficiency.

Be flexible when designing this instruction because a student may differ only slightly from one of the stated standards and still be reading at one of the levels. Remember, all instruments are designed to facilitate your decision making about students' needs and competencies. The final decision is yours; therefore, we encourage you to judge wisely and flexibly, remembering that you, not an instrument, are the trained teacher.

Consider precautions when employing IRIs:

1. The type of error may be more important than the number of errors.
2. Inventory accuracy may be hampered by teacher inexperience in construction, administration, and scoring.

For more information on IRIs, refer to

Bader, L. *Bader Reading and Language Inventory*. New York: Macmillan Publishing Company, 1983. preprimer–grade 12.

Ekwall, E. *Ekwall Reading Inventory*. Boston: Allyn & Bacon, Inc., 1979. preprimer–grade 9.

Name / Reading Skills	Parts of Book	Vocabulary	Recall of Explicit Information	Main Ideas	Cause/Effect	Inference	Evaluation	Recognizing Details
Chu, Gin								
Cunningham, Mary								
Deasy, Antia								
Deleo, Sadie								
Hess, Pearl								
Hill, Gertrude								
Houlden, Trevor								
Kavanaugh, Marty								
Ramirez, Jim								
Rivera, Daryl								
Tubaugh, Harold								
Vanek, Sarah								

Figure 12-2. Assessment chart

Goodman, Y., and C. Burke. *Reading Miscue Inventory*. New York: Macmillan Publishing Company, 1972. grades 1–7.

Johnson, M. S., and R. A. Kress. *Informal Reading Inventories*. Newark, Dela.: International Reading Association, 1965. grades 1–8.

Silvaroli, N. J. *Classroom Reading Inventory*. Dubuque, Iowa: Wm. C. Brown Company, Publishers, 1976. grades 2–10.

Smith, E. H., and W. G. Bradtmueller. *Individual Reading Placement Inventory*. Chicago: Follett Publishing Company, 1970. youths and adults reading below grade 7.

Reading Miscue Inventory

The Reading Miscue Inventory (RMI) is an informal diagnostic inventory that provides an analysis of the student's reading proficiency. A psycholinguistic theory of reading is the basis for the measure, which was originally designed by K. Goodman (1969) who refers to oral reading errors as miscues. More recent versions have been designed by Y. Goodman (1972).

The focus of this inventory is on the type of response being made rather than on the number of errors. The term *miscue* refers to any oral reading response. Goodman suggests that many miscues are made by readers as they try to make "better sense" of the passage.

Example

Text reads: Wait a moment.
Reader responds: Wait a <u>minute</u>.
Text reads: Please pass some cake.
Reader responds: Please pass <u>me the</u> cake.
Text reads: One day at dinner . . .
Reader responds: One day at <u>the</u> dinner . . .
Text reads: Mildred gulped the biscuits.
Reader responds: Mildred gulped <u>down</u> the biscuits.
Text reads: May ran into the store.
Reader responds: <u>Mary</u> ran <u>in</u> the store.

ADMINISTRATION OF READING MISCUE INVENTORY

1. Select a passage above your student's independent level of reading.
2. Ask student to read the selection orally.
3. Use a recorder to tape the child's reading.
4. Have the child retell the story and answer questions about portions of the story that have been omitted from his retelling.
5. If the child has comprehended the story well enough to be able to re-tell it, he is believed to be reading successfully.
6. If the reader cannot successfully retell the story, you must code the miscues according to *graphic similarity* (look-alike words, e.g., house-horse), *sound-alike similarity* (dark-park), *dialect variation, intonation changes,* and *syntactic, semantic/meaning changes.*

We must be careful not to confuse miscues and errors since miscues may be viewed as an indicator of strength when language and meaning are not distorted; however, when this does not occur they may be viewed as reader weakness.

7. After you have coded the miscues, determine existing patterns and plan appropriate instructional strategies to alleviate student needs.

Teacher-Made Tests

Teacher-made tests are useful for understanding students' progress. The examples that follow may help you to design some of your own tests.

A simple exercise to test letter discrimination skills is shown below. The target letter is the first letter in each row. Students should draw a circle around the letter that matches it.

	Uppercase			
M	M	W	N	E
B	P	B	D	R
E	E	F	P	L
T	F	L	I	T

	Lowercase			
k	f	k	y	w
g	j	a	g	p
b	b	p	d	q
i	i	l	f	j

You can use a similar exercise to test students' abilities to discriminate the initial or final phoneme in a word. Give the students charts like the following examples (omitting the target words). As you read each word, have the students draw a circle around the letter of the initial or final sound.

Initial Phoneme

television	t	l	p	v
baseball	l	d	b	s
lost	t	s	l	f
water	v	w	m	r

Final Phoneme

cat	t	k	l	r
hard	p	d	b	r
fun	m	f	n	s
top	b	t	d	p

Cloze Reading Technique

The *cloze* procedure, which was developed by Taylor in 1953, is an informal reading comprehension technique. Assessment is made by judging the acceptability of student responses when supplying words deleted from a passage. If a student comprehends a passage, he or she will have little difficulty in filling in the blanks.

The cloze technique may be used as an instructional as well as a diagnostic technique since it provides the student with exercises in using contextual (semantic/syntactic) cues for word recognition and comprehension. If a student is presented with a passage he or she is unable to complete, you may use the passage and instruct the student in how to use the specific cues to gain meaning.

INTERPRETATION OF CLOZE TEST

1. If a student scores 58 to 100 points, the material being read is at the student's independent level. When a score of 44 to 57 occurs, the material being read is at the student's instructional level. A score below 43 indicates that the material is at the student's frustrational level.

2. Determine mean scores for each passage. When you retest, you will then be able to use only the passage that most closely approximates the mean difficulty of the text.
3. A low score indicates that the reader is unable to utilize context cues and language redundancy to read with meaning.

ADMINISTRATION

1. Select a student text with a passage of approximately 250 words.
2. Use only 250 words, even if that means stopping in the middle of a sentence.

Manuel Amado, his parents, and his sister, Rachel, were flying from Rio to Brasilia. They had arrived at the airport late. The four of them were the last people to get on the airplane.

Now Manuel sat with his nose pressed against the airplane window. There were tears in his eyes. "Why do we have to leave Rio?" he asked. "I don't want to move away."

Mr. Amado sighed. "I told you, Manuel, I am going to work for our country. To do that I have to live in our capital. My office will be there."

"You children will like Brasilia," Mrs. Amado said. "It is beautiful too, in a different way from Rio. Things there are all new and shiny. Our apartment is completely modern and so is your school."

"But I liked our old apartment in Rio," said Rachel. "It was close to the beach and we could go swimming with our friends. We don't know anyone in Brasilia."

"You will make many friends at your new school," said Mr. Amado. Mrs. Amado added, "And there is a playground and swimming pool near our apartment. Won't that be nice?"

Mr. and Mrs. Amado had been saving the big surprise for last. "Children, guess what will be waiting for us at the airport! A new car!"

"Will we drive around the country on our holiday?" Manuel asked excitedly. "Yes, we will and on weekends too, sometimes," answered his father. "There will be many wonderful things to see."

Suddenly someone called, "Manuel, Rachel, what are you doing here?" There in the aisle stood Pedro Vargas, grinning from ear to ear. "Are you moving to Brasilia too?" he asked. "We didn't see you at the airport."

"That is because we were late," said Manuel. He was so happy to see his friend. "Maybe we will go to the same school. That would be wonderful."*

---

*D. H. Madison and R. E. Sterling, *Communities*, pp. 231–233. © 1979. Reprinted by permission of D. C. Heath and Co.

3. Delete every fifth word and substitute a straight line in place of each missing word.
4. A passage should contain approximately fifty straight lines after deletions have been made.

Manuel Amado, his parents, _____ his sister, Rachel, were _____ from Rio to Brasilia. _____ had arrived at the _____ late. The four of _____ were the last people _____ get on the airplane. _____ Manuel sat with his _____ pressed against the airplane _____. There were tears in _____ eyes. "Why do we _____ to leave Rio?" he _____. "I don't want to _____ away."

Mr. Amado sighed. "_____ told you, Manuel, I _____ going to work for _____ country. To do that _____ have to live in _____ capital. My office will _____ there."

"You children will _____ Brasilia," Mrs. Amado said. "_____ is beautiful too, in _____ different way from Rio. _____ there are all new _____ shiny. Our apartment is _____ modern and so is _____ school."

"But I liked _____ old apartment in Rio," _____ Rachel. "It was close _____ the beach and we _____ go swimming with our _____. We don't know anyone _____ Brasilia."

"You will make _____ friends at your new _____," said Mr. Amado. Mrs. _____ added, "And there is _____ playground and swimming pool _____ our apartment. Won't that _____ nice?"

Mr. and Mrs. _____ had been saving the _____ surprise for last. "Children, _____ what will be waiting _____ us at the airport! _____ new car!"

"Will we _____ around the country on _____ holiday?" Manuel asked excitedly. "_____, we will and on _____ too, sometimes," answered his _____. "There will be many _____ new things to see."

_____ someone called, "Manuel, Rachel, _____ are you doing here?" _____ in the aisle stood Pedro Vargas, _____ from ear to ear. "_____ you moving to Brasilia _____?" he asked. "We didn't _____ you at the airport." "_____ is because we were _____," said Manuel. He was _____ happy to see his _____. "Maybe we will go to the same school. That _____ be wonderful." *

5. If you are unsure of standardization of text difficulty, select twelve 250-word passages that are approximately eight pages apart. This wide range of passages will ensure a representative sample of text difficulty. If you have previously selected a passage that represents difficulty, administer it.
6. Give every student all of the passages.
7. Students are asked to insert the missing words. No time limits are set.

*Ibid.

8. Responses are correct even if misspelled.
9. Each correct closure is worth 2 points.

Suggested Readings Related to Goals. We encourage you, at this time, to review the goals at the beginning of this chapter. If you feel you would like to explore one or more of these areas in greater depth, please refer to the cross-indexed bibliography at the end of the book.

13 Reading for Bilingual and ESL Students

BREAKING THE CODE

This how they come:
on plastic water wings,
on bamboo sticks,
a plywood board,
across the Mekong.
By airlift,
snatched from Thailand hills
of rice, maize, poppy,
and the gas.
Our word today is "am."
I am from Laos.
I am from Vietnam.
I am Hmong.
My students of black hair,
"unaccompanied minors"
from the camps.
Mai smiles at me
with her grandmother's face,

Ah's skeleton is borrowed
from his village elder.
Suane has a scar
soldered across his chest
above his top shirt button.
They are here,
I am here,
room 249,
sitting in a circle
calling the Dolch list.
There are no books.
We write our own.
Instead of Dick and Jane,
we read of Thor, Suane, Ah, Souvantha,
Bounlay, Kao, Shanthala.
Sometimes we do Carolyn Graham
jazz chants and laugh.

[G. Cook]

Goals

To help the student understand
1. The needs of students who are learning English
2. Linguistic differences between several languages and English
3. Different methodologies of reading instruction in both the native language and English
4. Appropriate methods of evaluating the effectiveness of materials for students who are learning English

315

In many American schools, there are students who are proficient speakers, readers, and writers of both their native language (L$_1$), which may be Spanish, Portugese, Chinese, or Italian, and English (L$_2$), which is their second language. These students are referred to as *balanced bilinguals*. There are also other students who exhibited a range of competency in speaking, writing, and reading both their native language (L$_1$) and English (L$_2$). There are many issues to consider when faced with the task of developing the language/reading/writing skills of all these students. For the sake of simplicity, we will refer to these students collectively as *bilingual* students since the goal of the curriculum in the schools where these students reside must be to develop balanced bilingual education.

Although it may seem obvious, it is important to remember that bilingual students are *not* disadvantaged. In fact, they have the privilege of understanding two languages. This language abundance sometimes will call for instruction in the native language, English only, or both.

The topic of bilingual education is extremely important for the rapidly growing bilingual population in the United States. These students need educators to answer such questions as (1) How do we educate language minority students who come to school speaking a language other than English? (2) How do we help these students grow in content area concepts while learning English and maintaining facility with their own language?

There is a need for bilingual education as evidenced by the growing numbers of limited English speaking students who continue to enter our schools. In an attempt to address this need, we will pose a series of questions that are often asked by teachers and others who work with bilingual students. The answers to these questions will be the beginning of your pursuit of knowledge on the topic of instruction for bilingual learners.

Before we investigate these questions, you may need to develop familiarity with the following terms.

1. *Bilingual education:* Teachers are trained to teach in a bilingual setting where the students are often taught in two languages in the course of the day.
2. *TESOL or TESL:* Teaching English to Speakers of Other Languages; Teaching English as a Second Language.
3. *TEFL:* Teaching English as a Foreign Language.

You will often hear the expressions ESL and EFL; these refer to the fields of English as a second language and English as a foreign language. ESL is often a component of a bilingual program, whereas EFL would never be used as a component of a bilingual program in the United States.

4. *Bilingualism* is the ability to function in a second language in addition to one's home language.
5. *Biculturalism* is the ability to behave on occasion according to selected patterns of culture other than one's own.
6. *Bilingual schooling* is the particular organizational scheme of instruction that is used to mediate curricula in the home language and in a second language.

7. *Bilingual education* is a process by which the learning experiences provided in the home and other educational and societal institutions enable a person to function in a second language in addition to the home language.
8. *Language (L_1) dominant* students can speak, read, and write in their native language (L_1) but are not yet proficient in speaking, reading, or writing their second language (L_2, English).
9. *Balanced bilingual* students are equally proficient at speaking, reading, and writing both their native language (L_1) and English, which is their second language (L_2).
10. *Bilingual/bicultural education* is a process in which a person learns and reinforces his or her own language and culture and also acquires the ability to function in a second language.

How Can the Goal of English Literacy Be Accomplished for Bilingual Students?

The bilingual approach developed out of the frustration and ineffectiveness of attempts to educate limited–English-proficient (LEP) students through English-only instruction. Eleanor Thonis, a consultant in bilingual education for the Marysville, California, schools and the author of numerous publications on bilingual literacy (1976, 1983), describes the effects of pushing students into English reading:

> The sooner we had pupils with books in hand, the more virtuous we felt and the more reading proficiency we thought we were offering our pupils. It was disappointing to us that many of our best efforts failed. A few hardy pupils did learn to read well, several survived in spite of us, and an overwhelming number of pupils gave up and left us as soon as they were old enough. (p. 10)

While many still believe that the more basic skills instruction students receive in English, the greater will be their yield in scholastic achievement, low test scores, high dropout rates, and rampant unemployment for limited–English-proficient students who have been schooled in an English-only manner provide ample evidence that the monolingual method is not an effective method of instruction.

As we consider how to obtain this goal, we may need to ask the following minor questions.

What Types of Interference Hamper the Attainment of This Goal?

CULTURAL DIFFERENCES

The needs of bilingual students are often special because of their ethnic heritage (Ching, 1976). Both teachers and students may experience some cultural interference problems when the ideas, values, or practices of one differ from another (Zintz, 1975). One such example is presented by Lado (1976, pp. 114–115) in his description of the differences being experienced by American and Spanish spectators as they observe a bullfight.

2. Comparison of Cultures.

2.1 If the native culture habits are transferred when learning a foreign culture, it is obvious that, by comparing the two culture systems, we can predict what the trouble spots will be. Obviously, this is a huge undertaking, and we will present a few examples that may facilitate cultural analysis and comparison.

2.2 *Same form, different meaning.* We will expect trouble when the same form has different classification or meaning in the two cultures.

2.2.1 A very interesting kind of trouble spot is seen when any element of the form of a complex pattern has different classification or meaning across cultures. The foreign observer gives to the entire pattern the meaning of that different classification of one element.

Example. Bullfighting has always been in my observation a source of cross-cultural misinformation. It is a particularly difficult pattern of behavior to explain convincingly to an unsophisticated United States observer. I therefore choose it as a test case.

Form. A bullfight has a very precise, complex form. A man, armed with a sword and a red cape, challenges and kills a fighting bull. The form is prescribed in great detail. There are specific vocabulary terms for seemingly minute variations. The bullfighter, the bull, the picadors, the music, the dress, etc. are part of the form.

Meaning. The bullfight has a complex of meaning in Spanish culture. It is a sport. It symbolizes the triumph of art over the brute force of a bull. It is entertainment. It is a display of bravery.

Distribution. The bullfight shows a complex distribution pattern. There is a season for bullfights on a yearly cycle, there are favored days on a weekly cycle, and there is a favored time on a daily cycle. The bullfight occurs at a specific place, the bull ring, known to the least person in the culture.

Form, meaning, and distribution to an alien observer. An American observer seated next to a Spanish or Mexican spectator will see a good deal of the form, though not all of it. He will see a man in a special dress, armed with a sword and cape, challenging and killing the bull. He will see the bull charging at the man and will notice that the man deceives the bull with his cape. He will notice the music, the color, etc.

The meaning of the spectacle is quite different to him, however. It is the slaughter of a "defenseless" animal by an armed man. It is unfair because the bull always gets killed. It is unsportsmanlike—to the bull. It is cruel to animals. The fighter is therefore cruel. The public is cruel.

The distribution constitutes no particular problem to the American observer, since he has the experience of football, baseball, and other spectacles.

Misinformation. Is there an element of misinformation here, and if so, wherein is it? I believe there is misinformation. The secondary meaning "cruel" is found in Spanish culture, but it does not attach to the bullfight.

The American observer ascribing the meaning cruel to the spectator and fighter is getting information that is not there. Why?

Since the cruelty is interpreted by the American observer as being perpetrated by the man on the bull, we can test to see if those parts of the complex form—the bull and the man—are the same in the two cultures.*

This example can serve as a reminder that cultural differences influence our perceptions and behaviors. The fact that your students may be from a culture other than yours increases the need for your sensitivity toward individual cultural differences.

TIME FOR LANGUAGE DEVELOPMENT

While socioeconomic considerations and cultural differences contribute to lack of performance in English, there is yet another factor. This is the problem LEP students have when they confront English print and are forced to deal with a symbol of a symbol—a graphic representation of speech sounds with which they are simply not familiar. These students do have many meanings based on their experiences in their own language, but they cannot attach meaning to the sounds, graphemes, and structures that are encountered in English. It is unrealistic for educators to expect students to learn to listen, to understand, to speak, to read, and to write in English while they are struggling to learn new ideas, concepts, and content through the medium of the same new language. While it is true that within two or three years most of these students are able to learn a "survival English" that has lots of context to support it, they have not yet had sufficient time to master the abstract cognitive English required for academic success.

As Thonis (1983, p. 235) suggests, the development of literacy skills takes time for *any* student in *any* language. Ordinarily, monolingual students have five years of oral language practice at home before entering the reading classroom. After a period of readiness for reading, students are offered reading instruction for the next five or six years. Usually, the students who leave the fifth or sixth grade have the necessary fluency and literacy skills to use in their junior and senior high school years. From this point on, there is little attention given to the teaching of reading as a subject. The curriculum emphasis shifts to subject matter, and students are expected to acquire content, knowledge, and skills. In terms of chronological age, students have enjoyed approximately eleven or twelve years in which to acquire the fluency and literacy skills that will serve them well the rest of their lives. Teachers recognize that skill acquisition takes appropriate instruction, guided practice, and time.

For students who spend the first five years of their lives in a Spanish environment, their oral language in Spanish may be adequate for supporting a program of reading readiness in Spanish but is most inadequate

---

*From R. Lado, *Linguistics Across Cultures*, pp. 114–115, © 1976, University of Michigan, Ann Arbor, Mich. Reprinted with permission.

for an English reading readiness program. When the next few years of schooling provide opportunities for instruction in Spanish reading and writing, these students at the end of their fifth or sixth grades should have literacy skills comparable to their English-speaking peers. During the oral English lessons and the opportunities to acquire English through the many informal contacts with English-speaking classmates, comprehension of speech should be coming right along. As students *add* the literacy skills of English, they are building *balanced* skills in both languages and are moving toward the oral *and* written control of English as well as Spanish. These valuable proficiencies take time and patience.

How Can Literacy in One Language Be Transferred to Literacy in a Second Language?

As Thonis (1983), Cummins (1981), and Krashen (1981) suggest, learning a second language should be guided by the principles of how one learns a first language. Students should learn to listen, understand, and speak English in a natural way before they learn to read and write it.

Learners often transfer the forms and meanings of their native language and culture to the second language and culture. Lado (1976) sug-

Learning a second language should be guided by the principles of how one learns a first language. Students should learn to listen, understand, and speak English in a natural way before they learn to read and write it. (Photo by Linda Lungren.)

gests that learners do this both when attempting to speak and when trying to understand the new language.

Lado (1976), Thonis (1983), and others have compared the speech and print systems of Spanish and English and have concluded that there is tremendous opportunity for transfer of language, literacy and thinking skills. Students who are already reading in Spanish bring a wealth of skills, habits, and concepts from their successful experiences with Spanish directly into English.

As teachers, we can assume that once students have facility with one language, they have stored many meanings that they can refer to both when they are receiving and when they are sending messages. In addition to this competency, the students have also added the written system of their language. They have made the associations between print and speech, and they are able to represent their speech in print. Because these students can express and receive written language, Thonis (1983) reminds us, they are literate and they only learn to read once. Literate students have experienced their language proficiency across all language processes. They can understand, speak, read, and write. Their auditory symbol system—speech—supports their visual symbol system—print.

These bilingual speakers value their ability to function well in oral and written language. This successful functioning in communication has caused them to value themselves. Success and the expectation of success will transfer into English in the same way that language elements that are shared between the two languages will transfer.

Because English and Spanish have many similarities, Lado (1976, p. 14) states,

> Some of these cognates survived in Spanish as it evolved from Latin and were borrowed into English from Latin or French. Some go back earlier to forms presumably found in Indo-European, the common ancestor of English and Spanish, which belong to what is known as the Indo-European family of languages. Whatever the cause of the similarity, these words usually constitute the lowest difficulty group—they are easy. In fact, if they are similar enough, even Spanish-speaking students who have never studied English will recognize them.

Such cognates often appear in the sciences, but students must be cautious about transferring meaning simply on the basis of word appearance. Many false cognates look the same in Spanish and English, but meaning is entirely different. In addition, Thonis (1983) reminds us, recognizing words through context is another skill that transfers readily from Spanish to English.

The thinking strategies associated with comprehension are exactly the same in any language. The cognitive skills of identifying the main idea, recalling story details, understanding cause and effect, making inferences, sequencing, making judgments, making predictions, differentiating between reality and fantasy, and identifying an author's point of view are all part of the student's intelligence once they have been developed in the first language. To effect these same skills in English, Thonis (1983) suggests, simply requires the learning of the appropriate terminology and vocabulary in English.

This is not to say that transfer from another language to English takes place automatically. Transfer requires careful planning and organization on the part of the teacher. Thonis (1983) further suggests that teachers must know how to make transfer happen by assisting students to recognize transfer possibilities and by consciously working transfer teaching into the curriculum whenever it seems appropriate and wise. Teachers are the best resource for the transferability of skills as they arrange instruction for transfer to take place and tell the students about skill transfer whenever a possibility exists. Thus we move toward the goal of dual literacy.

When Will Bilingual Students Be Ready to Learn to Read in English?

Although adult learners who already read their native language frequently learn to read English before speaking it, bilingual children need to speak English before they learn to read English. The major issue that must be addressed is not if these students should learn English but what is the most *effective* means of accomplishing the goal. The age of your students and their competence in English must determine if they are ready to learn to read English.

The following example of transition criteria was developed by Emily J. Palacio for use by the Calexico Unified School District, Calexico, California.

READING TRANSITION CRITERIA*

To determine when a student can successfully make a transition to the second language reading system will be determined by the following criteria:

Criterion 1:   Students must be reading successfully in the dominant language.

Criterion 2:   Students must have an oral command of the second language to the extent determined by the oral language proficiency instrument.

---

*Emily J. Palacio, *Reading Transition Criteria*, Calexico Unified School District Calexico, CA, 1985.

Definitions for 1 and 2

Successful Reader in the Dominant Language

Minimum of 2.5 grade level in the dominant language for grades 1 through 3. Not more than one year below grade level in the dominant language for grades 4 through 6. All testing to be done on a standardized norm-referenced test to be administered in the dominant language.

Oral Command of the Second Language

Students in the Calexico Unified School District are administered the Bilingual Syntax Measure I and II (published by Harcourt Brace Jovanovich) to determine oral language proficiency. The suggested guidelines for transition to second language reading are as follows:

> Level 4 on Bilingual Syntax Measure I for ages 4–8
> Level 4 on Bilingual Syntax Measure II for ages 9 and above

Exceptions

A variation of the foregoing criteria might include one or more of the following conditions:

1. A student new to the program who has transferred from an all English curriculum who is already successfully reading in the second language.
2. Age and grade-level factors should be a consideration. For older students having recently immigrated from Mexico who demonstrate skills at grade level or higher in the primary language, a lower oral language score could be considered.
3. Attitude might be another consideration after evidence indicates that a student or parent who is adamantly opposed to placement in primary language reading is hindering the reading process of the student.
4. When teacher judgment based on other indicators/observations merit consideration such as one or more of the following factors:
   a. Results on other language criteria such as Student Oral Language Observation Matrix
   b. Progress on the primary language reading continuum
   c. High motivational factors demonstrated by student

Bilingual students require reading instruction in four general categories:

1. *Experiential information/conceptual background.* It is difficult to read about something that is totally outside one's experience. For example, the excitement of a roller coaster ride is hard to convey to someone who has never ridden one.

2. *Auditory discrimination.* Because the phonological structures of different languages are never identical, the student from a non-English background may have trouble learning which sounds are relevant in English and which are irrelevant. For example, the initial sound of *key* and *cut* are "identical" in English but significantly different in Arabic. Similarly, the "k" sounds of *key* and *ski* are identical in English, but different in Hindi.

3. *Vocabulary.* In dealing with Hispanic students, for instance, one must beware of "false cognates," words that look or sound similar to English words but have quite different meanings. For example,

libreria	bookstore, *not* library
embarazada	pregnant, *not* embarrassed

4. *Syntax.* The most common problem areas are
   a. *Word order:* Many languages (e.g. Spanish, French) permit or prefer placement of adjectives after nouns.

La casa blanca	the white house
Les libres jaunes	the yellow books

   b. *Articles:* Many languages, particularly Oriental languages, have no articles (a, an, the). Students often have difficulties deciding when to use an article and which one is appropriate.

   c. *Verb forms:* Some languages (e.g., Russian) do not use linking verbs in the present tense as English does. Speakers of other languages may be confused about the use of "to be" in English, resulting in constructions such as

   She home.
   Today Mario work at library.

   d. *Plurals, comparatives, and possessives:* These tend to be difficult:

   We saw gooses at the zoo.
   This box is more heavy.
   Is sick the dog of Jackie?

Can I Teach All of my Bilingual Students in a Similar Manner?

Students from language groups other than English have specific problems with learning to read in English. We will present some possible sources of difficulty for the second language student as well as many insights into the contrasts between the student's language and English.

The two languages presented here have been selected as representatives of the many languages your students may speak. If you have the opportunity to work with students whose first language is not Spanish or Chinese, it is important for you to research the language of the student to understand some basic principles of its sound system and syntactic system. This is crucial to help the student learn to read.

Spanish

Spanish is the second most frequently spoken language in the United States. It is possible that you will eventually work with a Spanish-speaking student. In the next few pages, you will find information useful for teaching a Spanish-speaking student to read English.

Obviously, there is no one reading methodology for all bilingual and ESL students. A matrix similar to the following one can help you to understand some of the differences among bilingual students with regard to reading and writing ability. Five different combinations are represented:

	Student 1	Student 2	Student 3	Student 4	Student 5
Speaks	Spanish —	Spanish, English	Spanish —	Spanish, English	Spanish, English
Reads	— —	— —	Spanish —	— English	Spanish, English

You will note that students 3, 4, and 5 have no problem per se because each of them speaks and reads at least one language. Teaching student 3 to read in English or student 4 to read in Spanish depends upon several factors: age, the student's progress in English at the present time, and the need for reading in a second language. The following is an example of a prescriptive approach for teaching each of these students.

Student No. 1. Teach oral English before reading instruction in either language. Begin reading instruction in Spanish (if desired by student or parents).

Student No. 2. Begin reading instruction in one of the two languages, depending on the following factors:

    a. Student preference
    b. Local expertise
    c. Age
    d. Cultural factors
    e. Family preference

Student No. 3. Begin oral instruction in English. Begin reading instruction in English.

Student No. 4. Begin reading instruction in Spanish (if desired by student).

Student No. 5. Continue. You are doing an excellent job.

The following rules are presented to introduce you to the phonological and grammatical variations between Spanish and English:

1. Spanish-speaking students will have difficulty pronouncing the following vowels:

   /i/ sit   /a/ cat   /u/ pull

2. Spanish does not rely on voiced (sit - hit) or voiceless (buzz - bus) sounds for specific contrasting meanings.
3. The speaker of Spanish eliminates or replaces the following sounds in his or her language:

   /v/ voice   /θ/ then   /z/ zone   /j/ juice

4. Words ending in /r/ plus the consonants /d/, /l/, /p/, /s/, /t/ are pronounced by the Spanish speaker without the final consonant.
5. The Spanish language has no /s/ cluster.
6. The following grammatical differences exist between the two languages:

	English	*Spanish*
Subject Predicate	The dog sleeps.	The dogs sleeps.
Verb tense	He needed help yesterday.	He need help yesterday.
Negatives	I am not going home.	I no go home.
Omission of noun determiners	He is a dancer.	He is dancer.
Omission of pronouns	She is a doctor.	Is doctor.
Objective ordering	The green dress is beautiful.	The dress green is beautiful.
Comparisons	It is bigger.	Is more big.

The following chart lists some sounds in English that are not present in Spanish:

/p/ *point*	/z/ *pleasure*	/h/ *hear*
/t/ *take*	/v/ *vine, vote*	/y/ *yet*
/k/ *car*	/r/ *rode*	/w/ *what*
/j/ *judge*	/tt/ *cotton*	/s/ *shoe*

This information is useful for you, as a teacher of reading, because you will be able to understand the difficulty that a Spanish-speaking student may encounter when he or she is trying to read English words that contain these sounds.

Spanish-speaking students may encounter these problems when learning to speak and read English:

Possible Problems in the Pronunciation of Vowel Sounds

Sound	Example	Possible Error
1. long e	*leave, feel*	live, fill
2. short i	live, fill	*leave, feel*
3. long a	*mate, bait*	met, bet
4. short e	met, bet	*mate, bait*
5. short a	*hat, cat*	hot, cot
6. short o	*hot, cot*	*hat, cat*
7. long o	*coal, hole*	call, hall

Possible Problems in the Pronunciation of Consonants/Blends in Initial, Middle, and Final Position

Sound	Example	Possible Error
1. /θ/ and /ð/	*thin, then, path*	*sin, den, pass*
2. /š/	*shoe, show, wash*	*sue, choe, bus, or bush*
3. /č/	*chew, chop, witch*	*choe* or *jew, cash, wish*
4. /b/	*bin, beer, tab, rabbit*	*pin, pear, tap, rapid*
5. /g/	*goat, wing*	*coat, wink, duck*
6. /w/	*way, wash*	*gway, gwash* (with more proficiency, pronounced *gwash* or *watch*)
7. /y/	*yellow, yale*	*jello, jail*
8. /v/	*vote, vail*	*best, bail*

Chinese

The following is a brief overview of selected variations between English and Chinese that may be useful if you teach Chinese students.

There are many dialects of Chinese. Mandarin, which is spoken by approximately 70 percent of the Chinese people, is the national dialect in the People's Republic of China and Taiwan. Cantonese, another important dialect, is spoken by most of the Chinese families that come to the United States from Hong Kong, Kowloon, or Macao. The Cantonese dialect is the one that is discussed here.

1. The Chinese language does not have as many vowels as English; therefore, a Chinese student learning to speak English may have difficulty with these vowel sounds:

   /ay/ buy   /iy/ meat   /ey/gait

2. Chinese speakers seldom use consonants in final positions.
3. There is no direct correspondence between some English and Chinese sounds:

   rich   *shed*

4. Chinese speakers may indicate plurals through the use of numerical designations or auxiliary words:

   three dog = three dogs

5. The Chinese speaker expresses grammatical relationships by auxiliary words and word order:

   She gave me two cars.   (English)
   Yesterday she give I two cars.   (Chinese)

6. Chinese speakers use tone or pitch to distinguish word meanings whereas speakers of English combine pitch and intonation in sentence meaning.
7. The Chinese speaker may exclude subjects or predicates if the context is understandable:

   English   *Chinese*

   It is raining.   It rains.
   The car is shiny.   Car shiny.

8. English speakers invert the noun and verb forms when asking questions. The Chinese speaker does not follow this inversion but, instead, adds the empty words *ma* or *la* to the sentence:

   English   *Chinese*

   Are you happy?   You are happy ma?

9. Chinese speakers use a time word or phrase to indicate the tense of a verb:

   She go "jaw." translates "She went."

In Chinese, there are as many as one hundred spoken dialects, but only one writing system.

Tonal Language.   In Mandarin Chinese there are several tones, which can be represented in the following way:

Pluralization.   The plural concept in English is developed in the following way:

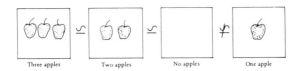

In Chinese, pluralization is similar to the following:

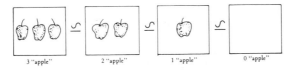

This brief presentation of language differences in Spanish and Chinese was intended only as an introduction to the multiple factors that you will need to investigate and understand when you are teaching a bilingual student to read. Although the task seems complex, it is not an impossibility. It is encouraging to note that many Americans are competent readers and speakers of two different languages. With your help, your non-English speakers will soon be reading in English.

How Can I Assess the Needs of Bilingual Students?

We will now introduce you to tests and instruments that are useful for diagnosing student difficulties and evaluating student progress. It should be pointed out immediately that most norm-referenced reading tests in English have been standardized on native English-speaking populations. The scores that bilingual students receive on these tests must be interpreted with extreme caution and sensitivity.

Where Do I Begin?

The first question you will ask when you are working in English with a second language student is, "How much English does the student know?"

In asking this question, you are beginning the process of teaching a bilingual or ESL student to read. The first issue is to assess the English proficiency. Remember that students have different proficiencies within their language ability. In most cases, it may be advantageous for you, as the teacher, to conduct a structured, but informal, nonthreatening interview to determine the student's proficiency and ease in speaking English.

Most tests that have been designed to assess language dominance have ignored the fact that students have many variations in their language abilities. Sometimes their native language is their dominant, preferred lan-

TABLE 13.1
Teacher Observation
Student Oral Language Observation Matrix*
(SOLOM)

Student's Name: _____

Language Observed: _____

	1	2
A. Comprehension	Cannot be said to understand even simple conversation.	Has great difficulty following what is said. Can comprehend only "social conversation" spoken slowly and with frequent repetitions.
B. Fluency	Speech is so halting and fragmentary as to make conversation virtually impossible.	Is usually hesitant; is often forced into silence by language limitations.
C. Vocabulary	Vocabulary limitations are so extreme as to make conversation virtually impossible.	Exhibits misuse of words; very limited vocabulary make comprehension quite difficult.
D. Pronunciation	Pronunciation problems are so severe as to make speech virtually unintelligible.	Is very hard to understand because of pronunciation problems. Must frequently repeat in order to make self understood.
E. Grammar	Errors in grammar and word order are so severe as to make speech virtually unintelligible.	Grammar and word order errors make comprehension difficult. Must often rephrase and/or restrict self to basic patterns.

*The student oral language matrix has five categories on the left, A. Comprehension, B. Fluency, C. Vocabulary, D. Pronunciation, E. Grammar, and five numbers on the top, 1 being the lowest mark to 5 being the highest.

According to your observation, indicate with an X across the square in each category that best describes the child's abilities. Those students whose (X) check marks are to the right of

Grade: _____ Signature: _____

3	4	5
Understands most of what is said at slower than normal speed with repetitions.	Understands nearly everything at normal speed, although occasional repetition may be necessary.	Understands everyday conversation and normal classroom discussions without difficulty.
Speech in everyday conversation and classroom discussion is frequently disrupted by the student's search for the correct manner of expression.	Speech in everyday conversation and classroom discussions is generally fluent, with occasional lapses while the student searches for the correct manner of expression.	Speech in everyday conversation and classroom discussions is fluent and effortless, approximating that of a native speaker.
Frequently uses the wrong words; conversation somewhat limited because of inadequate vocabulary.	Occasionally uses inappropriate terms and/or must rephrase ideas because of lexical inadequacies.	Use of vocabulary and idioms approximates that of a native speaker.
Pronunciation problems necessitate concentration on the part of the listener and occasionally lead to misunderstanding.	Always intelligible, though one is conscious of a definite accent and occasional inappropriate intonation patterns.	Pronunciation and intonation approximates that of a native speaker.
Makes frequent errors of grammar and word order that occasionally obscure meaning.	Occasionally makes grammatical and/or word order errors that do not obscure meaning.	Grammatical usage and word order approximates that of a native speaker.

the darkened line will be considered for reclassification to *FES*, if test scores and achievement data also indicate English proficiency.
SOURCE: Adapted from materials used in Evergreen School District, San Jose, and the San Jose Area Bilingual Curriculum.

guage for a particular task, but sometimes it is not. This seems eminently logical because many adults experience the same phenomenon; that is, a Spanish-speaking adult who studies advanced statistics in England may prefer to use English when he is discussing statistics. Therefore, before globally assessing a student's language dominance, we need to ask, "What is the specific task that the person is being asked to perform?" and "What is the language of the person to whom the student will speak during the instructional period?" The answers to these questions will provide you with a great deal of useful information that will enable you to begin your instructional program.

In determining language proficiency, you will want to extract information about several aspects of language so that you can build a program for each student. An example of such a test that gathers information about the reading, writing, speaking, and listening skills of the bilingual student is the Marysville Test, which is administered in English and Spanish. Other tests are also available in other languages on a variety of reading levels. Many of these tests are available through the following sources:

Bilingual Syntax Measure, 1973 (grades K–2)
Harcourt Brace Jovanovich, Inc.
Testing Department
757 Third Ave.
New York, N.Y. 10017

Dos Amigos Verbal Language Scales, 1974 (grades 1–4)
Academic Therapy Publications
1539 Fourth St.
San Rafael, Calif. 94901

James Language Dominance Test, 1974 (grades K–1)
Learning Concepts, Speech Division
2501 N. Lamar
Austin, Tex. 78705

Spanish-English Language Dominance Assessment, 1972 (grades 1–2)
Professor Bernard Spolsky
The University of New Mexico
1805 Roma N.E.
Albuquerque, N. Mex. 87106

What Are the Components of an Effective English-as-a-Second-Language Curriculum?

As suggested in a recent editorial (*San Diego Union*, June 10, 1984, p. A-12), effective bilingual programs seem to have several features in common. These programs often have a strong emphasis on language development, utilize staff members who are competent and who are sensitive to the needs of students from language minority populations and have the necessary resources to carry out effective instruction. Another key element common to successful bilingual programs is that strong skills are developed through a developmentally sequenced curriculum. Furthermore, there is a strong emphasis on developing a solid oral language base as preparation for reading in English through an English-as-a-second-language component.

You may not have any bilingual students at the present time, but it is likely that at some point you will have one or more bilingual students in your classroom. An entire English-as-a-second-language curriculum cannot, of course, be condensed into a few pages, but you may find the following scope and sequence chart helpful.

Various skills should be introduced at different stages in your program. "I" notes the time for the introduction of a skill, and "M" notes the time for its maintenance.

Skills	K	1	2	3	4	5	6–12
A. Language functions							
Vocabulary concerning							
Greetings	I	I	M	M	M	M	M
Commands	I	I	M	M	M	M	M
Following directions	I	I	I	M	M	M	M
Giving directions	I	I	I	M	M	M	M
Eating	I	I	I	M	M	M	M
Foods	I	I	I	M	M	M	M
Parts of the body	I	I	I	M	M	M	M
Clothing	I	I	I	M	M	M	M
Furniture	I	I	I	M	M	M	M
Time	I	I	I	M	M	M	M
Numbers	I	I	I	M	M	M	M
Family relations	I	I	I	M	M	M	M
Colors	I	I	I	M	M	M	M
Occupations	I	I	I	M	M	M	M
Days of the week	I	I	I	M	M	M	M
Months of the year	I	I	I	M	M	M	M
Animals	I	I	I	M	M	M	M
Holidays	I	I	I	M	M	M	M
Geographic names	I	I	I	M	M	M	M
Two-word verbs (wait for, hang up)		I	I	M	M	M	M
Directionality		I	I	M	M	M	M
Count nouns		I	I	M	M	M	M
Simple contrasts (good/bad)		I	I	M	M	M	M
Shopping expressions				I	M	M	M
Health				I	M	M	M
Government				I	M	M	M
Money				I	M	M	M
Daily living skills					I	M	M
Driving						I	M
Postal regulations							I
Traffic regulations							I
Idioms				I	I	I	I
Multiple meanings				I	I	I	I
Figurative language					I	I	I
Requesting/deference					I	I	I
Giving compliments					I	I	I

Skills	K	1	2	3	4	5	6–12
B. Grammatical Structures							
1. Verbs							
Present/progressive	I	M	M	M	M	M	M
Imperative	I	M	M	M	M	M	M
Modals				I	M	M	M
There is/are				I	M	M	M
There was/were				I	M	M	M
Simple past/							
past progressive					I	M	M
Future					I	M	M
Irregular past						I	M
Past perfect/							
present perfect							I
Passive voice							I
2. Nouns							
Plurals	I	M	M	M	M	M	M
Irregular plurals				I	M	M	M
Progressives				I	M	M	M
3. Adjectives	I	M	M	M	M	M	M
Articles	I	M	M	M	M	M	M
Demonstratives	I	M	M	M	M	M	M
Possessives	I	M	M	M	M	M	M
Descriptives	I	M	M	M	M	M	M
Comparative/superlative				I	M	M	M
4. Adverbs							
Frequency				I	M	M	M
Comparative				I	M	M	M
Descriptive				I	M	M	M
5. Pronouns							
Subject	I	I	M	M	M	M	M
Demonstrative	I	I	M	M	M	M	M
Object				I	M	M	M
Relative				I	M	M	M
6. Conjunctions	I	I	I	M	M	M	M
7. Contractions	I	I	I	M	M	M	M
C. Reading							
1. Focus on comprehension							
Main idea			I	I	I	I	I
Supporting details				I	I	I	I
Predicting outcomes				I	I	I	I
Fact/opinion				I	I	I	I
Drawing conclusions			I	I	I	I	I
Making inferences			I	I	I	I	I
Sequencing		I	I	I	I	I	I
Plot			I	I	I	I	I
Theme					I	I	I
Characterization					I	I	I
Cause/effect				I	I	I	I
2. Focus on Study Skills							
Following directions		I	I	I	I	I	I

Skills	K	1	2	3	4	5	6–12
Dictionary/glossary/ table of contents				I	I	I	I
Reference sources						I	I
Outlining						I	I
Summarizing						I	I
Note taking							I
Graphs						I	I
Maps						I	I
Charts/diagrams						I	I
D. Writing							
Handwriting	I	I	I	I	I	I	I
Spelling	I	I	I	I	I	I	I
Standardized punctuation		I	I	I	I	I	I
Correct English usages			I	I	I	I	I
Writing as process							
Prewriting			I	I	I	I	I
Composing			I	I	I	I	I
Editing			I	I	I	I	I
Sentence writing			I	I	I	I	I
Story writing				I	I	I	I
Organization and writing of essays, autobiographies					I	I	I
Writing to an audience				I	I	I	I
Writing for a purpose				I	I	I	I
Writing research reports							I

Teaching Individual Words

The question often arises, "If I begin to teach individual words, which words should I teach first?" An obvious answer is to teach the words that appear most frequently in English. The *American Heritage Word Frequency Book** can be a very useful tool in supplying information about English word frequency. For example, we know that English has a distinctive word frequency distribution. Ten percent of all the words written and printed in books, magazines, and newspapers for children and for adults are *the* and *of;* 20 percent of all the words written and read are *the, of, and, to, a,* and *in.* A computer was used to find

1. The separate word forms and their frequencies in over a million words selected from the most technical adult material in all fields
2. The relative frequency of 86,761 words in 5,088,721 running words, carefully selected from 1,045 textbooks most commonly used in grades 3 through 9

The American Heritage Word Frequency Book, pp. 565–567. Copyright © 1971 by Houghton Mifflin Company. Reprinted by permission from *The American Heritage* Word Frequency Book.

TABLE 13-2
Heritage List of Service Words

the		so		must		head		use
of	10%	these		because		above		may
and		would		does		kind		water
a		other		part		began		long
to		into		even		almost		little
in		has		place		live		very
is	20%	more		small		page		after
you		her		every		got		words
that		two		found		earth		called
it		like		still		need		just
he		him		between		far		where
for		see		name		hand		most
was		time		should		high		know
on		could		Mr.		year		get
are		no	45%	home		mother		through
as		make		big		light		trees
with		than		give		how		I'm
his		first		air		up		lady
they		been		line		out		upon
at	30%	its		set	55%	ever		family
be		who		own		paper		later
this		now		under		hard		turn
from		people		read		near		move
I		my		last		sentence		face
have		made		never		better		door
or		over		us		best		cut
by		did		left		across		done
one		back		end		during		group
had		much		along		today		true
not		before		while		others		half
but	35%	go		might		however	60%	sentences
what		good		next		sure		red
all		new	50%	sound		means		fish
were		write		below		knew		plants
when		our		saw		it's		living
we		used		something		try		wanted
there		me		thought		told		black
can		man		form		young		eat
an		too		food		miles		short
your		any		keep		sun		United States
which		day		children		ways		run
their		same		feet		thing		kinds
said		right		land		whole		book
if		look		side		hear		gave
do		think		without		example		order
will		also		boy		heard		well
each		around		once		several		such
about	40%	another		animals		change		here
them		came		life		answer		take

then	come	enough	down	why
she	work	took	only	things
many	three	sometimes	way	help
some	word	four	find	put
years	want	questions	quite	moving
different	school	blue	carry	care
away	important	meaning	goes	low
again	until	coming	distance	else
off	1	instead	although	gold
went	hot	either	added	build
old	anything	held	doing	glass
number	held	friends	sat	rock
great	state	already	pictures	tail
tell	list	warm	possible	covered
men	stood	taken	names	alone
brought	hundred	gone	heart	reached
close	shows	finally	having	bottom
nothing	tea	summer	writing	walk
though	fast	understand	real	forms
started	seemed	moon	simple	takes
idea	felt	animal	snow	check
call	kept	mind	getting	dog
lived	America	outside	rain	shown
makes	notice	power	suddenly	mean
became	can't	says	easy	English
looking	strong	problem	leaves	rest
add	voice	longer	lay	perhaps
become	probably	winter	open	certain
grow	needed	Indian	ground	six
draw	birds 65%	deep	lines	feel
yet	area	mountains	cold	fire
hands	horse	heavy	really	ready
less	Indians	carefully	table	green
John	sounds	room	remember	yes
wind	matter	sea	tree	built
places	stand	against	000	special
behind	box	top	course	ran
cannot	start	turned	front	full
letter	that's	3	known	town
among	parts	learn	American	complete
4	country	point	space	oh
A	father	city	inside	person
letters	let	play	ago	Tom
comes	night	toward	making	energy
able	following	live	Mrs.	week
both	2	using	early	explain
few	picture	himself	I'll	passed
those	being	usually	learned	lost
always	study	money	let's	spring
looked	second	seen	least	travel
show	eyes	didn't	problems	wrote
large	soon	car	followed	cities

TABLE 13-2
Heritage List of Service Words

often	times	morning	books	farm
together	story	given	tiny	circle
asked	boys	ship	hour	cried
house	since	themselves	B	whose
don't	white	begin	happened	bed
world	days	fact	foot	working
going	road	third	plant	measure
straight	grass	wild	language	North
base	plane	weather	job	teacher
mountain	pieces 70%	Mother	points	happy
caught	sides	Miss	music	changed
hair	pulled	carried	buy	products
bird	follow	pattern	window	C
per	beautiful	sky	mark	bright
wood	beginning	walked	ideas	sent
running	moved	6	heat	present
color	everyone	main	grow	plan
South	leave	someone	listen	played
class	everything	ones	ask	island
piece	game	center	changes	standing
slowly	system	named	single	there's
surface	bring	field	French	we'll
river	watch	stay	clear	opposite
numbers	shall	itself	material	barn
common	dry	worked	talking	sense
stop	hours	boat	isn't	cattle
am	written	building	thousand	million
talk	10	question	sign	anyone
quickly	stopped	wide	examples	rule
whether	within	village	guess	science
fine	floor	object	begins	helps
5	Bill	stain	forward	farmers
round	ice	placed	huge	afraid
dark	soil	Joe	needs	women
glide	human	age	closed	produce
past	trip	minute	ride	pull
ball	woman	wall	region	son
girl	eye	b	largest	meant
tried	milk	meet	answers	broken
rather	choose	record	nor	interest
length	north	copy	period	ends
looks	discovered	forest	finished	woods
speed	houses	River	blood	Henry
machine	seven	months	rich	8
information	easily	especially	team	inches
except	famous	dogs	waves	street
figure	pages	necessary	corner	George
you're	late	lower	Mary	couldn't
minutes	rocks	smaller	eat	reason

free	flowers	he's	groups	difference
fell	pay	unit	war	tells
suppose	sleep	flat	members	maybe
natural	iron	7	fly	larger
ocean	trouble	direction	yourself	history
government	store	south	decided	mouth
lives	beside	reading	seem	middle
trying	oil	fall	thus	step
horses	modern	poor	logs	thousands
the	filled	map	nearly	steps
s	fun	scientists	square	cars
baby	catch	friend	England	child
taking	size	c	moment	opened
thinking	pounds	wear	objects	shore
strange	beyond	act	fit	throughout
eggs	seeds	wings	students	compare
wish	Bob	Paul	turns	Sam
position	produced	bat	clouds	dollars
hear	fingers	arm	equal	quiet
hope	send	believe	War	ancient
song	100	major	value	Jack
	love	becomes	yard	stick
missing	materials	gray	Americans	afternoon
France	cool	died	beat	silver
heard	laughed	bones	inch	nose
playing	cause	sitting	walking	century
control	man's	wonder	sugar	saying
spread	stands	include	key	therefore
knows	feeling	interested	product	flying
evening	facts	describe	desert	level
brown	please	electric	bank	you'll
picked	meat	sold	farther	death
clean	lady	visit	won	hole
wouldn't	west	15	total	coast
section	glad	sheep	wall	directions
spent	British	I'd	wire	cross
Dan	action	waiting	rose	sharp
ring	subject	shoes	cotton	fight
higher	skin	30	moves	capital
raised	wasn't	office	spoke	Old
9	I've	amount	rope	fill
weeks	Europe	liked	rules	deal
teeth	New York	garden	four	patterns
growing	yellow	led	chance	divided
business	ships	note	homes	greatest
countries	arms	various	thick	happens
helped	party	race	sight	pass
gives	force	developed	pretty	20
exactly	test	bit	12	returned
Jim	bad	clothes	train	adding
King	temperature	uses	sets	ears
reach	pair	result	fresh	soldiers

TABLE 13-2
Heritage List of Service Words

lot	ahead	greater	faster	type
won't	wrong	fields	Washington	attention
answered	practice	New	drive	shouted
case	sand	brother	lead	gas
speak	tail	addition	break	World
shape	wait	doesn't	sit	actually
eight	difficult	states	bought	kitchen
edge	general	dead	hundreds	alike
seems	cover	weight	radio	pick
soft	areas	thin	method	scale
interesting	walls	stone	gets	basic
watched	Africa	hit	king	West
formed	showed	wife	similar	President
stories	safe	contains	return	Uncle
works	grown	row	corn	Johnny
busy	cost	contain	decide	happen 75%

Using the *Heritage* list (Table 13-2) can help you plan instruction based on this English word frequency.

How Can I Evaluate the Effectiveness of my Program for Bilingual Speakers?

In evaluating a program, it is necessary to examine the difficulty and effectiveness of materials as well as the progress of each student. On the following pages you will find information that will help you to evaluate your program and materials.

Materials

In Chapter 12 we discussed readability formulas and their uses. You may use these formulas to estimate the readability level of a text that will be used by a bilingual student, but *employ caution*. After the initial placement, reexamine the choice to see if the level is indeed appropriate.

If you are using materials written in Spanish, you may want to use a formula developed by Spaulding (1956) to determine the reading difficulty level. Spaulding created a readability instrument to be used for assessing the reading difficulty level of materials written in Spanish. He suggests the following for the selection of a sample of content.*

*The following discussion is taken from S. Spaulding, "A Spanish Readability Formula." *Modern Language Journal*, 40 (December 1956), 435. Reprinted with permission from the University of Wisconsin Press.

1. In long selections, analyze samples of 100 words every ten pages.
2. In shorter selections, analyze samples of 500 words every 1,000 words.
3. In selections of 500 words or less, analyze the entire passage.

Procedures

1. Count the number of words in the sample.
2. Count the number of sentences.
3. Divide the number of words by the number of sentences. Result is average sentence length.
4. Check the words against the accompanying Buchanan and Rodriguez Bou Word List and count the number of words not on the list.
5. Divide the number of words not on the list by the number of words in the sample. The result is the density or complexity of the vocabulary.
6. Using the table, find the number that corresponds to the density.
7. Find the number that corresponds to the average sentence length.
8. Draw a line to connect the two points of density and average sentence length.
9. The point at which the two lines intersect the central column represents the relative difficulty of the sample.

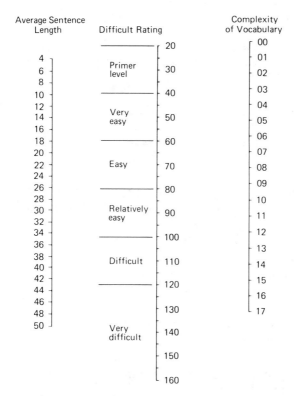

Figure 13-1. Index of Reading Difficulty

The Index of Reading Difficulty (Figure 13-1) ranges from 20 to 160 and can be divided as follows:

20–40 Primer level
40–60 Very easy   40 Grade 1
                                50 Grade 2
                                60 Grade 3
60–80 Easy   60 Grade 4
                                70 Grade 5
                                80 Grade 6
80–100 Relatively easy   Grades 6, 7, 8
100–120 Difficult   Grades 8, 9, 10
120–160 Very difficult   Grades 11, 12, and above

The following word list of Spanish words with their English equivalents (Table 13-3) has been included for two reasons: it is an essential part of the Spaulding formula, and it will provide teachers who decide to begin instruction in Spanish with the basis of their word program. Before moving on to more difficult words, teachers should be certain that their children can read the words in this list.

In planning a bilingual program, you will need to purchase a variety of materials. If you are in a position to purchase materials for use in your own classroom or in your school, you will probably want to establish criteria for their selection.

	Yes	No
1. Teacher competency		
a. Must you be a content specialist to use the materials successfully?	___	___
b. Must you be bilingual to use the materials?	___	___
c. Are the materials usable by inexperienced teachers?	___	___
d. Does the publishing company or the school system provide consultants to instruct you in the use of the materials?	___	___
2. Learners		
a. Do the materials provide for student differences in intelligence, experience, and language fluency?	___	___
b. Do the materials contain stories of equal interest to both males and females?	___	___
c. Do the materials contain high-interest, low-vocabulary selections?	___	___

TABLE 13-3
Buchanan and Rodriguez Bou Word List

asombrar—to astonish
aspecto—aspect
aspirar—to aspire
asunto—subject
atar—to tie
atención—attention
atender—to attend
atento—attentive
atrás—behind
atrevesar—to go through
atreverse—to dare
aumentar—to increase
aun, aún—even, still
aunque—although
ausencia—absence
autor—author
autoridad—authority
auxilio—help
avanzar—to advance
ave—bird
aventura—adventure
avisar—to notify
ay—alas!
ayer—yesterday
ayudar—to help
azúcar—sugar
azul—blue

bailar—to dance
bajar—to lower
bajo—low
balcón—balcony
bañar—to bathe
barba—beard
base—base
bastante—enough
bastar—to suffice
batalla—battle
batir—to shake
beber—to drink
belleza—beauty
bello—beautiful
bendecir—to bless
bendito—blessed
besar—to kiss
beso—a kiss
bestia—beast
bien (s., adv)* well
blanco—white

blando—soft
boca—mouth
boda—wedding
bondad—goodness
bonito (adj.)—pretty
bosque—forest
bravo—brave
brazo—arm
breve—brief
brillante—brillant
brillar—to shine
buen(-o)—good
burla—mockery
burlar—to ridicule
buscar—to seek

caballero—gentleman
caballo—horse
cabello—hair
caber—to go in or into
cabeza—head
cabo—cape
cada—every, each
cadena—chain
caer—to fall
café—coffee
caida—fall, tumble
caja—box
c(u)alidad—quality
calma—calmness
calor—heat
callar—to keep silent
calle—street
cama—bed
cambiar—to change
cambio—change, barter
caminar—to walk
camino—path, road
campaña—bell
campana—campaign
campo—country, field
cansar—to tire out
cantar—to sing
cantidad—quantity
canto—I sing
capa—cape
capaz—capable
capital—capital
capitán—captain

capítulo—chapter
cara—face
carácter—character
cárcel—jail
cargar—to carry
cargo—burden
caridad—charity
cariño—affection
carne—meat
carrera—career
carro—car
carta—letter
casa—house
casar—to marry
casi—almost
caso—case, event
castellano—Castillan
castigar—to castigate
castigo—punishment
causa—cause
causar—to cause
ceder—cede, to yield
celebrar—to celebrate
celebre—famous
centro—center
ceñir—to surround
cerca—near
cercano—neighboring
cerebro—brain
cerrar—to close
cesar—to cease
ciego—blind
cielo—sky
ciencia—science
cierto (-amente) certain,
  true
circunstancia—circum-
  stance
citar—to convoke
ciudad—city
civil—civil
claridad—clarity
claro—clear
clase—class
clavar—to nail
cobrar—to collect
cocer—to sew
coche—coach
coger—to catch

TABLE 13-3
Buchanan and Rodriguez Bou Word List

cólera—anger
colgar—to have
colocar—to arrange
color—color
columna—column
combatir—to combat
comedia—comedy
comenzar—to begin
comer—to eat
cometer—to commit
comida—food
como, cómo—how, as, like
compañero—companion
compañiá—company
comparar—to compare
complacer—to please
completo—complete
componer—to compose
comprar—to buy
comprender—to understand
común—common
comunicar—to communicate
con—with
concebir—to conceive
conceder—to concede
concepto—concept
conciencia—conscience
concluir—to conclude
conde—count
condenar—to condemn
condesa—countess
condición—condition
conducir—to conduce
conducta—conduct
confesar—confess
confianza—confidence
confiar—confide
conforme—in agreement
confundir—confuse
confusión—confusion
confuso—confused
conjunto—joined
conmigo—with me
conmover—affect
conocer—to know
conocimiento—knowledge
conque—condition

conquista—conquest
consagrar—to consecrate
consecuencia—consequence
conseguir—to obtain
consejo—advice
consentir—to allow
conservar—to conserve
considerar—to consider
consigo—with him
consistir—to consist
constante—constantly
constituir—to constitute
construir—to contract
consuelo—consolation
consumir—to consume
contar—to count
contemplar—contemplate
contener—to contain
contento—glad
contestar—to answer
contigo—with you
continuar—to continue
continuo—continuous
contra—against
contrario—contrary
contribuir—to contribute
convencer—to convince
convenir—to convene
conversación—conversation
convertir—to convert
convidar—to invite
copa—cup
corazón—heart
corona—crown
correr—to run
corresponder—to correspond
corriente—current
cortar—to cut
corte—court
corto—short
cosa—thing
costa—coast
costar—to cost
costumbre—custom
crear—to create
crecer—to grow

creer—to believe
criado—bred, raised
criar—to raise
criatura—child
cristal—glass
cristiano—Christian
cruel—cruel
cruz—cross
cruzar—to cross
cuadro—picture
cual, cuál—which, which one
cuando—since
cuándo—when
cuanto, cuánto—how much —as much as
cuarto (s.)—room
cubrir—to cover
cuello—neck
cuenta—account
cuento—story
cuerpo—body
cuestión—dispute
cuidado—care
cuidar—to take care of
culpa—blame
culto—cult
cumbre—top
cumplir—to fulfill
cura—cure
curiosidad—curiosity
curioso—curious
curso—course
chico—boy

dama—lady
daño—harm
dar—to give
de—(prep.) of, from
debajo—under
deber—to owe
débil—weak
decidir—decide
decir—to say
declarar—to declare
dedicar—dedicate
dedo—finger
defecto—defect
defender—to defend

defensa—defense
dejar—to leave
del—of the
delante—in front of
delicado—delicate
demás—others
demasiado—too much
demonio—demon
demonstrar—to demon-
   strate
dentro—inside
derecho (-a)—the right to
derramar—to spill
desaparecer—to disappear
descansar—to rest
desconocer—not to know
describir—to describe
descubrir—to discover
desde—since
desear—to desire
deseo—wish
desesperar—to become
   desperate
desgracia—disgrace
desgraciado—unfortunate
deshacer—to undo
desierto—desert, deserted
despedir—to emit
despertar—to awaken
despreciar—to scorn
después—after
destinar—to destine
destino—destiny
destruir—to destroy
detener—to detain
determinar—to determine
detrás—in back of
día—day
diablo—devil
diario—diary
dicha—luck
dicho (s.)—saying
dischoso—lucky
diente—tooth
diferencia—difference
diferente—different
difícil—difficult
dificultad—difficulty
difunto—dead
digno—worthy
dinero—money
dios—God

dirección—direction
directo—direct
dirigir—to direct
discreto—discrete
discurrir—to contrive
discurso—discourse
disgusto—displeasure
disponer—to dispose
disposición—disposition
distancia—distance
distinguir—to distinguish
distinto—distinct
diverso—diverse
divertir—to divert
dividir—to divide
divino—divine
doblar—to fold
doble—fold
doctor—doctor
dolor—pain
dominar—dominate
don, D.—Mr.
donde, done—wherever,
   where
dōna, Da.—Mrs.
dormir—to sleep
drama—drama
duda—doubt
dudar—to doubt
dueño—owner
dulce—candy, sweet
dulzura—sweetness
durante—during
durar—to last
duro—hard

echar—to throw
edad—age
edificio—building
educación—education
efecto—effect
ejecutar—to execute
ejemplo—example
ejercer—to execute
ejército—army
el, él—he, the
elegir—to elect
elemento—element
elevar—to elevate
ella—she
emoción—emotion
empensar—to pawn

empezar—to begin
emplear—to employ
emprender—to undertake
empresa—enterprise
en—in
enamorar—to make love to
encantador—enchanting
encanto—enchantment
encargar—to order
encender—to light
encerrar—to enclose
encima—on top
encontrar—to find
encuentro—encounter
enemigo—enemy
energia—energy
enfermedad—sickness
enfermo—sick
engañar—to fool
engaño—deception
enojo—anger
enorme—large
enseñanza—teaching
enseñar—to teach
entender—to understand
enterrar—to bury
entero—complete
entonces—then
entrada—entrance
entrar—to enter
entre—between
entregar—to turn in
entusiasmo—enthusiasm
enviar—to send
envolver—to enfold
época—era
error—error, mistake
escapar—to escape
escaso—scarce
escena—scene
escalvo—slave
escoger—to select
esconder—to hide
escribir—to write
escritor—writer
escuchar—to listen
escuela—school
ese, ése—that, that one
esfuerzo—spirit, vigor
eso—that
espacio—space
espada—spear

TABLE 13-3
Buchanan and Rodriguez Bou Word List

espalda—back, shoulders
español—Spanish
esparcir—to scatter
especial—special
especie—kind
espejo—mirror
esperanza—hope
esperar—to wait
espeso—thick
espíritu—spirit
esposo—husband
establecer—to establish
estado—state
estar—to be
estatua—statue
este, éste—this, this one
estilo—style
estimar—to estimate
estrecho—narrow
estrella—star
estudiar—to study
estudio—studio
eterno—eternal
evitar—to avoid
exacto—exact
examinar—to examine
excelente—excellent
exclamar—to exclaim
exigir—demand
existencia—existence
existir—to exist
experiencia—experience
experimentar—to experi-
    ment
explicar—to explain
exponer—to expose
expresar—to express
expresión—expression
extender—to extend
extensión—extension
extranjero—foreigner
extrañar—to banish
extrano—strange
extraordinario—extraordi-
    nary
extremo—extreme

fácil—easy
facultad—faculty

falda—skirt
falso—false
falta—lack
fama—fame
familia—family
famoso—famous
fantasía—fantasy
favor—a favor
favorecer—to favor
fe—faith
felicidad—happiness
feliz—happy
fenómeno—phenomenon
feo—ugly
fiar—to bail
fiel—faithful
fiesta—party
figura—figure
figurar—to figure
fijar—to make firm
fijo—firm
fin—end
final—final
fingir—to fake
fino—fine
firme—firm
físico—physical
flor—flower
fondo—fund
forma—form
formar—to form
formidable—formidable
fortuna—fortune
francés—French
franco—Frank
frase—phrase
frecuente—frequently
frente—front
fresco—fresh
frío—cold
fruto—fruit
fuego—fire
fuente—fountain
fuera—outside
fuerte—strong
fuerza—strength
función—function
fundar—to raise
futuro—future

galán—courtier
gana—desire
ganar—to win
gastar—to spend
gato—cat
general—general
género—class, kind
generoso—generous
genio—genius
gente—people
gesto—gesture
gitano—gypsy
gloria—glory
glorioso—glorious
gobernar—to govern
gobierno—government
golpe—stroke, hit
gota—drop
gozar—to enjoy
gracia—grace
gracioso—funny
grado—grade
gran(-de)—grand, big
grandeza—grandeur
grave—ponderous
griego—Greek
gritar—to scream
grito—shriek
grupo—group
guapo—handsome
guardar—to keep
guerra—war
guiar—to drive
gustar—to like
gusto—taste

haber—to have
habitación—residence
habitar—to dwell
hablar—to talk
hacer—to do
hacia—toward
hacienda—estate
hallar—to find
hambre—hunger
harto—satiated
hasta—until
he aquí—here is
hecho (s.)—made or done

helar—to freeze
herida—wound
herir—to wound
hermano—brother
hermoso—handsome
hermosura—beauty
hervir—to boil
hierro—iron
hijo—son
hilo—thread
historia—history
hogar—home
hoja—leaf
hombre—man
hombro—shoulder
hondo—deep
honor—honor
honra—reverence
honrar—to honor
hora—hour
horrible—horrible
horror—horror
hoy—today
huerta—irrigated land
hueso—bone
huevo—egg
huir—to escape
humanidad—humanity
humano—human
humo—smoke
hundir—to submerge

idea—idea
ideal—ideal
idioma—language
iglesia—church
ignorar—ignore
igual—equal
iluminar—illuminate
ilusión—illusion
ilustre—illustration
imagen—image
imaginación—imagination
imaginar—to imagine
imitar—to imitate
impedir—to hinder
imperio—empire
imponer—to impose
importancia—importance
importante—important
importar—to matter
imposible—impossible

impresión—impression
impreso—printed matter
imprimir—to print
impulse—impulse
inclinar—incline
indicar—indicate
indiferente—indifferent
individuo—individual
industria—industry
infeliz—unhappy
infierno—hell
infinito—infinite
influencia—influence
ingenio—inventive
inglés—English
inmediato—immediate
inmenso—immense
inocente—innocent
inquieto—restless
inspirar—to inspire
instante—instant
instrumento—instrument
inteligencia—intelligence
intención—intention
intentar—to intend
interés—interest
interesante—interesting
interesar—to interest
interior—interior
interrumpir—to interrupt
íntimo—intimate
introducir—to introduce
inútil—useless
invierno—winter
ir (-se)—go, to go
ira—wrath
isla—island
izquierdo—left

jamás—never
jardín—garden
jefe—chief
joven—young
juego—game
juez—judge
jugar—to play
juicio—judgment
juntar—to join, connect
junto—together
jurar—promise
justicia—justice
justo—just

juventud—youth
juzgar—to judge

la—(fem.) the
labio—lip
labor—work
labrador—farmer
lado—side
ladrón—thief
lágrima—tear
lanza—lance
lanzar—to throw
largo—long
lástima—pity
lavar—to wash
lazo—bow
lector—reader
lecho—bed, couch
leer—to read
legua—league
lejano—distant
lejos—far
lengua—tongue
lento—slow
letra—letter
levantar—to lift
leve—of little weight
ley—law
libertad—liberty
librar—to set free
libre—free
libro—book
ligero—fast
limitar—to limit
limite—limit
limpio—clean
lindo—pretty
línea—line
líquido—liquid
lo—(art., neut.,) the
loco—crazy
locura—insanity
lograr—to gain
lucha—struggle
luchar—to struggle
luego—later on
lugar—place
luna—moon
luz—light
llama—call
llamar—to call
llano—even

TABLE 13-3
Buchanan and Rodriguez Bou Word List

llanto—flood of tears	mérito—merit	nada—nothing
llave—key	mes—month	nadie—no one
llegar—to arrive	mesa—table	natural—natural
llenar—to fill	meter—to put in	naturaleza—nature
lleno—full	mezcla—mixture	necesario—necessary
llevar—to take	*mi, mí	necesidad—necessity
llorar—to cry	miedo—fear	necesitar—to need
	mientras—while	necio—stupid
madre—mother	militar—military	negar—to deny
maestro—teacher	ministro—minister	negocio—business
magnifico—magnificent	minuto—minute	negro—black
majestad—majesty	mio—mine	ni—neither, nor
mal (-o)—adj., bad, bad-	mirada—glance	ninguno—none
ness s. o adv.	mirar (v.) to look	niño—boy
mandar—to command	misa—mass	no—no
manera—manner	miserable—miserable	noble—noble
manifestar—manifest	miseria—misery	noche—night
mano—hand	mismo—same	nombrar—to name
mantener—maintain	misterio—mystery	nombre—name
mañana—tomorrow	misterioso—mysterious	norte—north
máquina—machine	mitad—half	nota—grade, mark
mar—sea	moderno—modern	notable—notable
maravilla—wonder	modesto—modest	notar—to note
marcar—to mark	modo—mode	noticia—news
marchar—to march	molestar—molest	novio—bridegroom
marido—husband	momento—moment	nube—cloud
mas, más—more; (conj.)	montaña—mountain	nuevo—new
but	montar—mount	número—number
masa—dough	monte—mountain	numeroso—numerous
matar—to kill	moral—moral	nunca—never
materia—matter	morir—to die	
material—material	mortal—mortal	obedecer—obey
matrimonio—matrimony	mostrar—to show	objeto—object
mayor—greatest	motivo—motive	obligación—obligation
†me	mover—move	obligar—obligate
médico—doctor	movimiento—movement	obra—work
medida—measure	mozo—young man	obscuridad—obscurity
medio—half	muchacho—boy	obscuro—obscure
medir—to measure	mucho—much	observación—observation
mejor—better	mudar—move	observer—observe
mejorar—to improve	muerte—death	obtener—obtain
memoria—memory	mundo—world	ocasión—occasion
menester—need, want	murmurar—murmur	ocultar—conceal
menos—less	música—music	oculto—hidden
mentir—to lie	muy—very	ocupación—occupation
mentira—a lie		ocupar—occupy
menudo—small	nacer—to be born	ocurrir—occur
merced—mercy	nación—nation	odio—hatred
merecer—to deserve	nacional—national	ofender—to offend

oficial—official
oficio—occupation
ofrecer—offer
oído—ear
oír—to hear
ojo—eye
olor—odor
olvidar—to forget
opinión—opinion
oponer—to oppose
oración—prayer
orden—order
ordenar—to order
ordinario—ordinary
oreja—ear
orgullo—pride
orígen—origin
orilla—shore
oro—gold
otro—other

paciencia—patience
padecer—to suffer
padre—father
pagar—to pay
página—page
país—country
pájaro—bird
palabra—word
palacio—palace
pan—bread
papel—paper
par—pair
para—for
parar—to stop
parecer (v.)—to seem
pared—wall
parte—part
particular—particular
partida—departure
partido—party
partir—to depart
pasado—past
pasar—to pass
pasear—to take a walk
paseo—stroll
pasión—passion
paso—pace, step
patria—native country
paz—peace
pecado—sin
pecho—chest

pedazo—piece
pedir—to ask
pegar—to stick
peligro—danger
peligroso—dangerous
pelo—hair
pena—penalty, pain
penetrar—penetrate
pensamiento—thought
pensar—to think
peor—worse
pequeño—small
perder—to lose
perdón—pardon
perdonar—to forgive
perfecto—perfect
periódico—newspaper
permanecer—to stay
permitir—to permit
pero—but
perro—dog
perseguir—to follow
persona—person
personaje—character
personal—personal
pertenecer—to pertain
pesar (v. o s.)—to weigh,
  or cause regret
peseta—coin
peso—weight, dollar
picar—to prick, pierce
pico—beak
pie—foot
piedad—piety
peidra—rock
piel—skin
pieza—piece
pintar—to paint
pisar—to step on
placer—pleasure
planta—plant
plata—silver
plato—dish
plaza—market
pluma—pen
población—population
pobre—poor
poco—scanty
poder (v. o s.) to be able,
  power
poderoso—powerful
poeta—poet

política—politics
político—political
polvo—dust
poner—to put
poquito—a little bit
por—(prep.) by, for
porque—because
por qué—why
porvenir—time to come
poseer—to possess
posesión—possession
posible—possible
posición—position
precio—price
precioso—precious
preciso—precise
preferir—prefer
pregunta—question
preguntar—to ask
premio—prize
prenda—piece of jewelry
prender—to turn on
preparar—to prepare
presencia—presence
presentar—to present
presente—present
presidente—president
prestar—lend
pretender—to pretend
primero—first
primo—cousin
principal—principal
príncipe—prince
principio—principle, be-
  ginning
prisa—in a hurry
privar—to deprive
probar—to try
proceder—proceed
procurar—ask for
producir—produce
profundo—profound
prometer—promise
pronto—soon
pronunciar—pronounce
propiedad—property
propio—own
propener—propose
proporción—proportion
proporcionar—to propor-
  tion
propósito—purpose

TABLE 13-3
Buchanan and Rodriguez Bou Word List

proseguir—to pursue
protestar—to protest
provincia—province
próximo—next
prueba—proof
publicar—to publish
público—public
pueblo—town
puerta—door
puerto—port
pues—(conj.) because
punta—point
punto—dot, period
puro—pure

que, qué—that—what?
quedar (-se)—to stay
queja—complaint
quejarse—to complain
quemar—to burn
querer—to love
querido—loved one
quien, quién—who, who?
quienquiera—whoever
quitar—to take away
quizá, quiza(s)—maybe,
  perhaps

rama—branch
rápido—fast
raro—strange
rato—a while
rayo—ray
raza—race
razón—reason
real—real
realidad—reality
realizar—realize
recibir—receive
recién—recent
reciente—recently
reclamar—reclaim
recoger—pick up
reconocer—to know
recordar—remember
recorrer—to go over
recuerdo—remembrance
reducir—reduce
referir—refer

regalar—give away
región—region
regla—rule
reina—queen
reinar—to rule
reino—kingdom
reir—to laugh
relación—relation
relativo—relative
religión—religion
religioso—religious
remedio—remedy
remoto—remote
rendir—subdue
reñir—quarrel
reparar—to repair
repartir—to divide
repetir—to repeat
replicar—to reply
reposar—to rest
reposo—repose
representar—to represent
república—republic
resistir—to resist
resolución—resolution
resolver—resolve
*respe(c)tar
†respe(c)to
respirar—to breathe
responder—to respond
respuesta—answer
resto—rest
resultado—result
resultar—to result
retirar—to retire
retrato—picture
reunión—meeting
reunir—to meet
revolver—to resolve
rey—king
rico—rich
ridículo—ridiculous
riesgo—risk
rigor—rigor
rincón—corner
río—river
riqueza—richness
risa—laughter
robar—to steal

rodar—to move
rodear—to surround
rodilla—knee
rogar—to plead
rojo—red
romper—to break
ropa—clothes
rosa—rose
rostro—face
rubio—blond
rueda—wheel
ruido—noise
ruina—ruins
rumor—rumor

saber (v.)—to know
sabio—wise
sacar—to take out
sacerdote—priest
sacrificio—sacrifice
sacudir—to shake
sagrado—sacred
sal—salt
sala—living room
salida—exit
salir—to go out
saltar—to leap
salud—health
saludar—to greet
salvar—to save
sangre—blood
sano—healthy
santo—saint
satisfacer—satisfy
satisfecho—satisfied
se—to know
seco—dry
secreto—secret
seguida—continued, suc-
  cessive
seguir—to follow
según—according to
segundo—second
seguridad—security

triunfo—triumph
tropezar—stumble
**tu, tu
turbar—confuse

ultimo—last	velar—to watch	viento—wind
††un, uno (-a)	vencer—to conquer	vino—wine
único—only one	vender—sell	violencia—violence
unión—union	venganza—revenge	violento—violent
unir—to unite	venir—to come	virgen—virgin
usar—to use	venta—sale	virtud—virtue
uso—use	ventana—window	visión—vision
usted—you	ventura—fortune	visita—visit
útil—useful	ver—see	visitar—to visit
	verano—summer	vista—view
vacío—empty	veras—reality	visto—obvious, clear
vago—lazy	verbo—verb	viudo—widower
valer—to protect	verdad—truth	vivir—to live
valiente—valiant	verdadero—truthful	vivo—alive
valor—value	verde—green	volar—to fly
valle—valley	vergüenza—sham	voluntad—voluntary
vanidad—vanity	verso—verse	volver—to return
vano—vain	vestido—dress	voto—vote
vapor—vapor	vestir—to dress	voz—voice
variar—vary	vez—turn, time	vuelta—turn
vario—various	viaje—trip	
varón—boy	vicio—vice	
vaso—glass	víctima—victim	y—and
vecino—neighbor	vida—life	ya—already, right away
vela—candle	viejo—old	yo—I

†me = first person, personal pronoun; dative, accusative, and reflexive of Yo.

*mi, mí: mi = singular possessive pronoun, my; mí = personal pronoun, oblique case of pronoun Yo, used after preposition.

*Respectar = to concern, regard; respetar = to respect, revere.
†Respecto = relation, proportion; respeto = respect.
**Tu = personal pronoun, second person, m. or f., thou; tu = possessive pronoun, m. or f. (pl. tus), thy.
††Un, una = indefinite article, a, an.

3. Program sequence
   a. Does the developmental sequence of the program closely parallel the natural development of language learning?   ____ ____

   b. Does the program build on the natural language strengths of the student?   ____ ____

   c. Does the program make provisions for the development of all of the language arts?   ____ ____

   e. Do the materials provide for individualizing instruction?   ____ ____

   f. Are the materials free from cultural stereotyping?   ____ ____

g. Can the materials be integrated within an existing
program? ⎯⎯ ⎯⎯

4. Program packaging
   a. Do the materials contain charts, filmstrips, flashcards, and other supplementary materials? ⎯⎯ ⎯⎯

   b. Are the supplementary aids easily used by students? ⎯⎯ ⎯⎯

   c. Are materials provided for reinforcement, review,
   and evaluation? ⎯⎯ ⎯⎯

   d. Are the costs consistent with available program
   funds? ⎯⎯ ⎯⎯

   e. Are program time constraints consistent with time
   allowances for classroom implementation? ⎯⎯ ⎯⎯

Student Progress

Most educators agree that literacy is measurable, but they do not always
agree upon the most appropriate instruments for measuring student progress. We cannot "protect" our students or ourselves from accountability.
The argument about standardized tests is not whether to use them, but
which ones should be used. "Which instruments adequately assess the
abilities of bilingual students at their present age of development in English?" If a student, age 5 or 15, is just beginning English instruction, let
us be absolutely certain that our tests take into consideration this level of
limited exposure to English. By way of example, let us present the following fictional test item.

Instructions

Read this brief passage and answer the two questions that follow:

   "There he is up around the bend;

   "Come on down over here," Ian said.

   "We will box him in and ambush him like Butch Cassidy used to do
with the Sundance Kid."

Answer the following:

1. To whom is Ian talking?
2. What is Ian's suggested plan of action?

There are very few polysyllabic words in the passage; most of the words
are monosyllabic. The only word to be counted as a difficult word, using

the Dale-Chall readability formula, would be ambush. Almost any young native English speaker would be able to comprehend this passage, but it would be extremely difficult for someone just learning English for the following reasons:

Syntax: The syntax is complex; *used to* is a sophisticated structure.

Idioms: This brief selection uses two idioms that the bilingual student may not be able to understand: "*up around* the bend" and "*Come* on down *over* here."

Cultural/Experiential Background: The student needs to have some knowledge of Butch Cassidy to fully appreciate the passage.

There are many items in this short passage that would be impossible for a bilingual student to interpret. A second example may further illustrate the point:

Had he gone to the dentist on time, his mother wouldn't have yelled at him.

Again, a young native English speaker probably would be able to interpret this utterance, but a bilingual student, recently exposed to English, would have an extremely difficult time comprehending this complex English syntactic pattern.

We urge extreme caution when using any standardized test to measure the reading growth of bilingual students. We urge you to analyze the test thoroughly and to interpret it in light of the student's present level of functioning in English. If test items are based on complex syntactic structures, English idioms, and English lexical items demanding a specific cultural experience, make a note of the items and interpret your student's scores according to your knowledge of his or her level of English proficiency.

Summary

For the rapidly growing limited–English-speaking population, bilingual education is a critical issue since many of these students are not in bilingual programs but, instead, are "submerged" in English. They can seldom attach meaning to the sounds, graphemes, and structures they encounter in English. After only a few years, they are usually able to communicate in English at a "survival" level, but they do not become proficient in the abstract, cognitive English necessary for academic success. As a result, limited–English-speaking students in English-only programs tend to score low on English achievement tests, lag several years behind grade level, and have twice the retention rate and double the dropout rate of Anglo students. This has always been a problem for immigrants to the United States. It unfortunately takes too many years (three generations) before a new group experiences school success.

Some educators believe the LEP students should learn to listen, understand, and speak English before learning how to read it. They advocate that students be given an opportunity to develop thinking skills by learning to read first in the native language and then later transferring these skills to English.

There is ample evidence to indicate that high-quality bilingual programs can help to develop English academic proficiency for language minority students who come to school speaking languages other than English. An emphasis on language development, competent and sensitive staff members, ample resources, strong skill development in their native language, a solid oral base in English, and instructional strategies that maximize the transfer potential between languages are essential for success.

Suggested Reading Related to Goals.   We encourage you at this time to review the goals at the beginning of this chapter. If you feel you would like to explore one or more of these areas in greater depth, please refer to the cross-indexed bibliography at the end of the book.

14 Teaching Reading to Special Students

Reading teachers must expand their traditional knowledge base about the physical, intellectual, and emotional difficulties involved in order to effectively teach all students.

[J. Gillet and C. Temple]

Goals

To help the student understand
1. The history and significance of Public Law (P.L.) 94–142 and mainstreaming
2. Classroom considerations and teaching techniques for several types of handicapped students
3. The nature of learning disabilities

Overview

With the implementation of P.L. 94–142, the Education for All Handicapped Children Act, all classroom teachers must have some understanding of special education, the teaching of special students. In addition to the ever-present disparity of reading levels within one classroom, you now must also integrate or mainstream into your instructional framework students with severe visual and/or auditory difficulties, mentally retarded or emotionally disturbed students, and those with learning disabilities. The task certainly appears awesome, but with the proper use of personnel, facilities, and funds, plus an understanding of the handicaps afflicting these

355

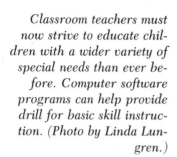

Classroom teachers must now strive to educate children with a wider variety of special needs than ever before. Computer software programs can help provide drill for basic skill instruction. (Photo by Linda Lungren.)

special students, teaching strategies can be devised to meet this challenge. This chapter provides a brief overview of how and why America is mainstreaming and what the law itself provides and gives information about the handicaps delineated in P.L. 94–142; it also gives you specific techniques and educational considerations that apply to each group. Particular attention is paid to the learning disabled student because this handicap offers special challenges to the reading teacher, P.L. 94–142, and mainstreaming.

Historical Background

Dating back to ancient times, handicapped persons have a long history of social ostracism. It was not until the midnineteenth century that changes began to occur. Residential schools to house the blind, deaf, and mentally retarded were established largely through the efforts of such educators and social activists as Horace Mann, Samuel Gridley Howe, Dorothea Dix, and the Reverend Thomas Gallaudet (Cruickshank and Johnson, 1975). Although housing, care, and education for the handicapped was at last being provided, these residential institutions still kept the handicapped out of the mainstream of society, placating humanitarian instincts yet adhering to an "out-of-sight, out-of-mind" philosophy. This attitude began to change during and after World Wars I and II when so many men who had been "normal" returned from the fighting with physical or mental disabilities. At about the same time, the moving force in changing public opinion that finally resulted in P.L. 94–142 emerged. This force was the parents of handicapped children.

Legal Actions

Dating from 1940, when a group of concerned parents timidly began to organize what became the New York State Cerebral Palsy Association, to 1975 when Congress passed P.L. 94–142, the American public has done an "about face" in its attitudes about the treatment of handicapped individuals. Civil rights, human rights, and the quality of life have all been major social and political issues in the last four decades, and many court cases reflected this public concern over the plight of the handicapped. The first major ruling that had an effect on education for handicapped students was *Brown* v. *Board of Education* (1954). This was essentially a racial integration decision that found that separate facilities are inherently unequal. Equal education for all was the theme when the Supreme Court stated

> Today, education is perhaps the most important function of state and local governments. . . . It is required in the performance of our most basic public responsibilities. . . . It is the very foundation of good citizenship. Today it is the principal instrument in awakening the child to cultural values, in preparing him for later professional training, and in helping him to adjust normally to his environment. In these days, it is doubtful that any child may reasonably be expected to succeed in life if he is denied the opportunity of an education. Such an opportunity, where the state has undertaken to provide it, is a right which must be made available to all on equal terms. (*Brown* v. *Board of Education*, 1954)

Other landmark decisions were the class action suit, *Pennsylvania Association for Retarded Children* v. *Commonwealth of Pennsylvania* in 1971 and, in 1972, *Mills* v. *Board of Education of the District of Columbia*. In the former case, the court decided in favor of the plantiffs representing the mentally retarded population of Pennsylvania, who had been excluded from the public education system. In the latter case, the plaintiffs included children who had been excluded from public school because they were mentally, physically, emotionally, or otherwise handicapped. Again, the court found in favor of the plaintiffs and disallowed the defendant's contention that it was lack of funds that resulted in the exclusion. The court ruled that exceptional children should not be made to bear more of the financial consequences than the normal children. Both these cases, and most especially the *Mills* case, are considered to be major precedent setters in the cause for equal education for all.

P.L. 94–142

Combining state and federal decisions for the education of the handicapped is Public Law 94–142, the Education for All Handicapped Children Act, passed by Congress in 1975 as an amendment to P.L. 93–380, the Education of the Handicapped Amendments of 1974. P.L. 94–142 became enforceable in 1977. This law has had an enormous impact on the classroom teacher who is essentially responsible for the success of this valiant effort finally to provide "free appropriate public education" for all children. The law covers every aspect of the issue, from searching out those individuals who are not receiving any education at all to funding requirements and the role of the U.S. Commissioner of Education; it has been written about and explained in detail by many authors (Corrigan, 1978; Council for Exceptional Children, 1977; Turnbull and Schulz, 1979). As the focus of this chapter is on the classroom consequences of P.L. 94–142, only the main points that affect you as a teacher are outlined here.

The main thrust of the law is to provide a "free appropriate public school education" to all handicapped individuals between the ages of 3 and 21 years. The key word for teachers is "appropriate" because it is in seeking to provide the most suitable instruction that P.L. 94–142 delineates four essential guidelines for what occurs in the classroom as well as outside it. These guidelines are

1. Handicapped students will be protected against discrimination in the evaluation process by ensuring that the testing materials utilized for placement will be free from racial and cultural bias and, when possible, will be administered in the child's native language. Tests will have established validity, be administered by trained personnel, and will test specific areas of educational need rather than strictly IQ. Students with sensory or physical handicaps will be tested in a manner consistent with their handicap. Further protection comes from the guarantee that no single test will be used as the sole evaluation instrument but that other factors, including socialization, physical, and emotional development, will be considered by a team of specialists before placement is made. Placement will always be made in a regular classroom unless the total evaluation process contraindicates such a step.
2. Handicapped students will be placed in "the least restrictive environment commensurate with their needs." In most cases, this means the regular classroom, but for many exceptional students, combinations of special classes and instructors along with instruction in the classroom will best meet their needs. In severe cases, special schools or institutions will be necessary.
3. An individualized educational program (IEP) for each child is required. It includes a written statement of the child's present educational level, annual goals, instructional objectives, and any special education or related services provided for the child. The plan must be developed jointly by parents, educators, and, when appropriate, the child in question; it will be reviewed at least annually.
4. Procedural safeguards have been written into this law to protect the rights of all concerned. Parents have access to all the student's records and have the right to obtain an outside evaluation if desired. They are to be given prior notice for approval of any change in the placement of their child, and they have the right to challenge anything done by the teacher or the school, including the right to court action. The par-

ents and the schools have the right to appeal any decision made regarding the placement of a handicapped student. During any hearing, the child in question will be allowed to remain in school or be admitted to school until the final decision has been reached.

It is obvious why P.L. 94–142 has been called "the most important piece of educational legislation in this country's history" (Corrigan, 1978). The classroom teacher's job has become more demanding and, at the same time, potentially more rewarding.

Who Are Handicapped Students?

The definition of handicapped students includes the mentally retarded, hard of hearing, deaf, speech impaired, visually handicapped, seriously emotionally disturbed, orthopedically impaired or other health impaired, or those with specific learning disabilities.

Each of these handicaps will be discussed in a separate section of this chapter, with the exception of the seriously emotionally disturbed, who would not be placed in a regular classroom. Students with mild emotional problems may well be in your classroom, but for the most part, managing these students is quite similar to managing any other student, as their problems are simply exaggerations of emotions that everyone has. Guidelines must be established as to what constitutes unacceptable behavior, and consistency in enforcing these rules is critical. It has been said that children with emotional difficulties, mental retardation, and learning disabilities have many of the same behavioral and cognitive problems (Hallahan and Kauffman, 1977); for this reason, teaching suggestions listed for the mentally retarded and learning disabled may be useful for instructing an emotionally handicapped student. (For further reading and references on emotionally handicapped students, see Hallahan and Kauffman, 1978, Chap. 4; Berkowitz and Rothman, 1960; Hewett, 1968.)

The Mentally Retarded

DEFINITION

The definition adopted by the American Association on Mental Deficiency (AAMD), the most accepted in the field, reads: "Mental retardation refers to significantly subaverage general intellectual functioning existing concurrently with deficits in adaptive behavior, and manifested during the developmental period" (Grossman, 1973). The emphasis on a relationship between intelligence, as measured by a standardized intelligence test, and socially adaptive behavior pinpoints the modern concept of mental retardation. In the past, too much importance was given to a test score, so much so that many children who functioned quite normally, efficiently, and happily outside of school became labeled as retarded to their teachers and school administrators. As will be stressed throughout this chapter and elsewhere in this text, relying solely on an IQ score (or on any single test score) is misleading as to the student's overall ability and potential and may actually limit his or her academic career.

The commonly accepted categories of mental retardation are those provided by the AAMD. While based on intelligence scores, they are also descriptive of functional traits. The general breakdown is IQ score 70–55, "mild"; 55–40, "moderate"; 40–25, "severe"; and 25–0 "profound." The terms EMR (educable mentally retarded) and TMR (trainable mentally retarded) are educational labels that attempt to define the instructional needs of retarded children whose IQs fall within the ranges of 75–50 and 50–25, respectively. Remember that these scores cannot be used as hard and fast break-off points for inclusion or exclusion in educational programs; the *whole* individual must be evaluated. As with other students, ongoing assessment must be made for mentally retarded students because, contrary to some ideas about mental retardation, gains in IQ scores are possible, especially for the mildly retarded, with the proper education (Kirk, 1958; Klaus and Gray, 1968).

CLASSROOM CONSIDERATIONS

It is most unlikely that a severely retarded student would be placed in a regular school environment as his or her specialized needs generally are best met in residential institutions or in the home. Even a moderately retarded student usually requires a special education situation for academic subjects; he or she may be integrated into the regular school program only for such activities as physical education, music, and art. All but the most mildly retarded student would likely spend part of the day with a specialist and part of the day in the regular classroom, so it is important to coordinate your teaching efforts with those of the specialist.

Remember that mildly retarded students may be functioning at a mental age from two to four years below their chronological age and should not be expected to perform the same academic exercises as other students. In the early grades, they may require readiness training long after the other children have moved on to reading. The secondary grades should emphasize adult survival skills, vocational training, and successful social interactions that will prepare them to take part in the community once their school days are over. Generally, the more severe the retardation disability is, the more the concentration should be on social functioning skills as opposed to academics. Although much of the program will be individualized, group activities in which the handicapped student is actively included are important. Being a member of a team and being a partner are essential to developing peer relationships.

INSTRUCTIONAL METHODS

The most successful technique, especially in the severe and profound categories, has been Skinner's behavior modification or operant conditioning (see Robinson and Robinson, 1976). While the mildly retarded may not need a strictly classical approach to behavior modification, a well-structured program that is very task oriented seems appropriate. Lessons should be broken down into small tasks that can be successfully completed in a short period of time. As with the learning disabled, the emphasis here is on structure and success. Acceptable behavior should be quickly reinforced. New information should build directly on what has just been learned. The suggestions for teaching the learning disabled student are equally appropriate for the mildly retarded student in the regular classroom; you may refer to that section of this chapter for other instructional methods.

TEACHING TECHNIQUES

In addition to those suggestions given for learning disabled students, the following ideas may be useful for teaching the mentally retarded student.

1. Use the game of "Concentration" (pairs of cards placed face down in random order) to improve visual memory skills. Begin very simply with four to six cards and progress as skill improves.
2. To aid in comprehension skills, highlight main ideas of a story in one color and supporting details in another. Have the student read the color-coded copy first, then present a plain copy, and ask him or her to use the colored pencils to mark main idea and details. Students can compare the two copies for immediate feedback.
3. Using a tape recorder, have the student record material to be learned (vocabularly, spelling words, sequence of a story, facts of a history lesson), listen to the tape, repeat it into the tape using no notes, and then check the answer. Verbal repetition is effective in teaching the mentally retarded.
4. Drill and repetition may be useful in learning new concepts. Use similar exercises from different series of skills books to reemphasize an idea (such as parts of speech, sentence construction, vocabulary, etc.). Have the student "wallpaper" a cubicle with repeated spelling words written in colorful ink. Change the "wallpaper" when the words are learned.
5. Charts showing student successes (such as books read, words spelled correctly, acceptable behavior, participation in class, etc.) are a positive reinforcement to behavioral and academic goals. Notes in the form of "awards" or "medals" allow the student to take home commendations from the teacher.

The Hearing Impaired

DEFINITION

Individuals with hearing impairments are generally classified as either deaf or hard of hearing. Definition of this classification has stirred considerable debate; there are two basic systems for classifying the hearing impaired. The first is strictly physiological, based on auditory performance as measured by an audiologist. The most accepted definition, by Davis (1970), uses decibels (dB), a measurement for the intensity or loudness of sounds, as the criterion for placement. A hearing loss up to 25 dB is considered normal; for 25 dB to 93 dB is classified as hard of hearing; and any further loss beyond 93 dB is categorized as deaf. The second method of classification is a more practical one for educational purposes; it is based on the individual's *functional* ability to hear and speak. The preferred definition in this instance was formulated by the Conference of Executives of American Schools for the Deaf:

> A **deaf** *person is one whose hearing disability precludes successful processing of linguistic information through audition, with or without a hearing aid.*
> A **hard-of-hearing** *person is one who, generally with the use of a hearing aid, has residual hearing sufficient to enable successful processing of linguistic information through audition.* (Report of the Ad Hoc Committee to Define Deaf and Hard of Hearing, 1975, p. 509)

CLASSROOM CONSIDERATIONS

Perhaps the most devasting aspect of a hearing impairment is its effect on communication abilities, including language acquisition, speech production, and reading skills. The lack of adequate auditory feedback both from oneself and from others, coupled with the inability to hear an adult model speak the language, contribute greatly to a difficulty with language acquisition. Since reading is essentially the translation of a printed code into the sounds that make up language, a hearing impairment that has resulted in reduced language skills usually interferes with learning to read. Five basic factors that influence language acquisition and, consequently, reading skills should be considered when working with hearing-impaired children (Birch, 1975):

1. The *nature of the hearing loss* relates to what frequencies (tones) and level of intensity are affected.
2. The *degree* of the impairment refers to how much residual hearing there is.
3. The *age of onset*, or when the hearing loss occurred, is extremely important. The later the age of onset, the more chance the person has of acquiring language in a normal way.
4. *Intelligence level* may be a significant educational factor in that children with higher IQs may be better equipped to compensate for their handicap. [The intellectual ability of the hearing impaired is a controversial issue, with some professionals arguing that without language there can be no cognitive processing (Vygotsky, 1962) and others maintaining that this is not the case (Furth, 1961, 1971).]
5. The *quality of stimulation*, the amount and kind of daily exposure to language, may determine how thoroughly language is acquired.

Perhaps the most important consideration for hearing-impaired students is that they are all individuals and cannot be expected to perform in the same way just because they share a common difficulty. With this in mind, here are some general suggestions for making mainstreaming easier for the hearing impaired:

1. *Seating arrangement.* A seat near the front of the room that offers a good view of the teacher as well as the other students is essential for the hearing impaired, whether they rely on their residual hearing or on speech reading. However, depending on the degree of their hearing loss or their ability to compensate for it, some students may prefer to sit in other parts of the room. Allow the student to experiment with his or her seating arrangement, within reason, always providing the seat near the front if necessary.

2. *Talking to the student or addressing the class.* Try to refrain from moving about; keep your hands, pencil, paper, and so on away from your mouth to provide as clear a sound and image as possible. Write on the board first and then talk about it rather than speak with your back to the class. Enunciate clearly and speak at a moderate pace, but don't exaggerate speech. Students trained in speech reading have been taught to read normal speech. When repeating instructions or ideas, rephrase what has been said rather than repeat it verbatim. If the student didn't understand it the first time, new words may help give context clues to the idea. Shouting does not help with the hearing impaired; if they are using a hearing aid, the amplification distorts the voice or blasts them in the ear. Try to stand where the light is good and not in a shadow or where the student will be facing a glare while looking at you.

3. *Attending and comprehending skills.* Be sure that hearing-impaired students are not just looking attentive but are actually understanding what is going on in class. Verify that they understand instructions and assignments and that they are following class discussion as much as possible. Don't, however, expect them to attend all the time, as it is extremely hard work and very tiring. It is best to schedule breaks for them when they may work alone. Encourage asking questions if they don't understand what was said and giving you feedback on how they are adjusting to the class.

4. *Integration into the Classroom.* Natural classroom opportunities (e.g., a unit on the senses, science lesson, discussion pertaining to broadcasting, sound waves) can foster an understanding of the nature of a hearing impairment so that other students will be more at ease with a handicapped classmate's disability. An understanding of why a deaf or hard-of-hearing student may sound unusual or hard to comprehend when he or she speaks may help the other students try harder to listen and be friendly. Above all, set reasonable goals for the hearing impaired; it is better to err on the side of high expectations.

As many hearing-impaired children use some form of amplification (e.g., hearing aid), it is important for you to understand how they work and be able to make minor essential adjustments such as changing a battery or cord. Consult the school specialist for instruction and keep a supply of the necessary items available in the classroom.

INSTRUCTIONAL METHODS

It is highly unlikely that any classroom teacher would be faced with the very specialized task of teaching reading to a hearing-impaired student who has no communication skills at all. Before being placed in a regular classroom, on either a full- or part-time basis, the student will have been taught to communicate by using one or more of the following approaches:

1. *Oral approach.* This method stresses the use of residual hearing, incorporating amplification when appropriate and speech reading, looking at the mouth and face to gain understanding of the words and tone of speech. This method also encourages the hearing-impaired student to learn to verbalize and develop oral language.
2. *Manual approach.* The knowledge of finger spelling (or the manual alphabet) and sign language are essential to this method so that the deaf and hard of hearing have the means for total expression, rather than the (they feel) often inadequate results achieved when the deaf attempt to produce speech.
3. *Total communication approach.* This method allows the student to use a combination of both methods to achieve the most efficient communication skills available.

Unless an interpreter is provided, chances are only those students functioning with oral skills will be mainstreamed into the regular classroom. Instructional methods that are appropriate for teaching hearing students to read may be useful for the hearing impaired if they are not based on an auditory system. Visual methods that present new words and concepts in as concrete a manner as possible are most beneficial.

Hearing-impaired students need a variety of life experiences, along with the language to describe both the experience and how they feel about it. Field trips, neighborhood walks, guest speakers, and so on should all be discussed before, during, and after the event to prepare the hearing-impaired student for what is to happen. Continuing work on syntax and grammar is important, and the *language experience* approach is an excellent means for working with the student's existing vocabulary while describing these new experiences.

TEACHING TECHNIQUES

Here are some suggestions for teaching the hearing-impaired student in the regular classroom.

1. Present new vocabulary words by writing them down, pronouncing them, and using them in sentences. New words may also be written down for the student to take home to study with outside help.
2. Provide "previews" of the topics to come by listing the main points and new words so that the student may prepare in advance and be more familiar with the material when the class discusses it.
3. Create a "buddy" or "note taker" system to aid the handicapped student with details missed during class. Note takers are especially useful

because it is very difficult to watch the speaker intently and write at the same time. Note takers themselves benefit by taking more complete notes.
4. A unit on hearing aids, finger spelling, American Sign Language, and speech reading, with demonstrations by the school specialist, will be of interest to the whole class while providing the hearing-impaired student a chance to demonstrate special skills.
5. Photographs and illustrations from magazines provide excellent stimuli for vocabulary development. Scrapbooks and photograph albums compiled by the student (using pictures he or she has taken) with written captions are excellent ways in which to improve language skills. Make this an ongoing journal of day-to-day experiences. Some journal entries could be expanded into essays in which the students practice more refined writing skills by making rough, intermediate, and final drafts.

The Speech Impaired

DEFINITION

Speech is the action of vocally reproducing the sounds, in proper sequence, of a language; a speech impairment, then, is a condition that interferes with this sound-producing process. A speech impairment differs from a language disorder, which is the inability to use or comprehend the actual semantic and grammatical code system by which ideas are communicated. Since language disorders are generally characteristic of other handicaps (deafness, mental retardation, learning disabilities, etc.), they are discussed in the sections relating to the associated condition.

Whether or not speech is in fact impaired or just deviant is highly subjective. Strong regional dialects may make speech incomprehensible to an outsider, yet be totally understandable to residents of the area. However, two definitions of speech disorders provided guidelines to determining when and if an impairment exists.

> Speech is defective when it is ungrammatical, unintelligible, culturally or personally unsatisfactory, or abusive of the speech mechanism. (Perkins, 1971, p. 4)

> Speech is defective when it deviates so far from the speech of other people that it calls attention to itself, interferes with communication, or causes the possessor to be maladjusted. (Van Riper, 1984, p. 34)

A speech impairment can have many causes (e.g., a cleft palate, cleft lip, or cerebral palsy), but it generally falls into (or overlaps) three categories: articulation disorders, voice disorders, or fluency disorders.

Articulation Disorders. These generally consist of errors of sound production involving *omissions* (e.g., ru for run; ift for lift), *substitutions* (e.g., bery for very), *additions* (e.g., puraple for purple), and *distortions* (e.g., consistently mispronouncing /r/) (Perkins, 1971). Misarticulation is common in young children, but by the age of 7 or 8, these mistakes should disappear naturally unless a speech problem exists.

Voice Disorders. Although it is very difficult to quantify voice qualities, problems generally fall into these areas:

pitch: high or low, depending on age and sex of the individual

intensity: loudness or volume

quality: how the voice "sounds": sweet, rough, mellow. Problem qualities are hoarseness, breathiness, and nasality. These may indicate the need for medical treatment.

flexibility: the ability to modulate pitch and intensity to put expression in the voice. Monotone and sing-song voices indicate a problem with flexibility.

Fluency Disorders. When the flow of speech is interrupted to such a degree that it becomes unintelligible or unpleasant to listen to, the speaker is suffering from a fluency disorder, commonly known as *stuttering.* The interruptions consist of repetitions and prolongations of sounds, hesitations and interjections (uh, uh . . .).

There is no conclusive evidence as to what causes stuttering, although many theories have been advanced, ranging from underlying emotional conflicts to organic dysfunctions (for discussion of these theories, see Van Riper, 1984; Bloodstein, 1969; Ainsworth, 1970). While the problem of stuttering is a familiar disorder, the actual number of stutterers is very small—1 percent of the population (Hull et al., 1969), and it seems to disappear as mysteriously as it comes on (Van Riper, 1973).

CLASSROOM CONSIDERATIONS

Speech impairments can cause social and emotional trauma if afflicted persons are not made to feel accepted. Academic problems may result if the student does not participate in class discussions or ask questions about concepts that are not understood or becomes so uncommunicative that language ability itself begins to degenerate. The primary role of the classroom teacher is to put the student at ease in the group and make speaking experiences pleasant and nonthreatening.

The speech impairment must be acknowledged by both the student and the teacher so that, together with the student's parents and speech clinician, a plan can be developed to help the student fit into the classroom. Acceptance by other students is important; as with any other handicap, knowledge of a condition will facilitate understanding better than ignorance. Once the handicap has been acknowledged, it is best to concentrate on *what* is being said rather than on *how* it is being said. Patience and attentiveness and acceptance will encourage a speech-impaired student to speak up in class.

INSTRUCTIONAL METHODS

Speech pathologists generally believe that disorders of voice and misarticulation are learned behaviors, not inherent qualities (Schiefelbusch and Lloyd, 1974; Sloane and MacAulay, 1968). Consequently, it becomes the clinician's job to use learning techniques to teach the appropriate new speech skills. Many of these teaching strategies are highly structured, programmed learning systems that incorporate behavior modification techniques as well as generally relying on modeling (i.e., imitation) and positive reinforcement.

The clinical process has three steps: (1) the actual teaching of the new skill, (2) transferring the use of the skill to general usage, as opposed to only responding to the teaching stimuli, and finally (3) making a habit of using the skill so that it becomes the new way of speaking long after the clinical sessions have ended. The classroom teacher is an especially important part of this clinical process because the student must be encouraged and reminded to use appropriate speech when participating in classroom discussions. As imitation is an important aspect of learning to speak clearly, the teacher must be considered as the ultimate model and be conscious of speaking well and clearly. It might also help to seat the student near others who speak especially well or place the speech-impaired student in a small discussion group with especially articulate peers. The tape recorder is an excellent tool for use with these students as it can be used for both modeling and monitoring of speech. As with all handicapped students who require the services of a specialist, keep an open channel of communication with the clinician so that the student has consistency of educational philosophy and reinforcement.

TEACHING TECHNIQUES

Making speech and language occasions pleasant may be the most important part of your job when working with mainstreamed speech-impaired students. Fortunately, that objective is equally important for all students in the class so most of these activities can be readily used for everyone.

1. Stimulate discussion by having students create and present a reader's theater production. Rehearsals should stress good articulation and expressive use of voice.
2. Allow students to use a camera for taking slides on a subject of their choice; then have them arrange and present a slide show with either live narration or tape-recorded narrative.
3. Make a game out of using descriptive language by blindfolding a student, handing him an object, and having him describe its qualities. Individual or team points could be scored based on the number of adjectives used or qualities mentioned, as well as if the student guesses what the item is. As an individual venture, a "touch" box can be constructed in which various items are placed; the student is asked to describe into the tape recorder how each item feels.

4. A file of pictures and photographs that serve as a stimulus to creating stories about events or emotions can be useful not only for written assignments (which could be read orally) but for spontaneous or prepared oral stories that can be taped or read to the class.

5. A group story can be formulated using one of the pictures by having one student begin a story with a statement and then having each student contribute another statement to the story based on the preceding one. Stories become quite outrageous and language experience can be enhanced further by doing this in small groups so students can have more than one chance to participate in a given story.

The Visually Impaired

DEFINITION

The category of the visually impaired includes individuals who are referred to as *partially sighted*, which indicates a visual acuity of 20/70 after correction, and *blind*, indicating a visual acuity of 20/200 after correction. As with most definitions regarding individuals, these terms are almost useless as educational criteria for assessing student abilities and needs. The scores that form the basis for this definition are from the Snellen Chart, which measures only distance reading ability. Since reading instruction is done at a close range and since individuals use their residual vision with differing degrees of competency, the numbers 20/70 or 20/200 say very little (Gearheart and Weishahn, 1976). Other classification and measurement scales of visual ability have been proposed that essentially stress that teachers should not base any instruction strictly on test scores but on observation of the student's functional abilities (Genensky, 1970; Barraga, 1970; Harley, Spollen, and Long, 1973).

CLASSROOM CONSIDERATIONS

Since reading is largely a visual process, it is obvious that visually-impaired students may encounter many difficulties including concept development, left to right orientation, and clarity of the word image itself (Degler and Risko, 1979). They may be behind their peers in reading level due to a slower reading rate or inappropriate instructional methods (Turnbull and Schulz, 1979), but visually handicapped students, whether partially sighted or blind, are easily accommodated into the regular classroom with minimal adaptations.

Putting a student at ease in the school environment is essential to successful instruction. Two key words when working with visually handicapped youngsters are "orientation," which refers to a person's spatial placement in relation to objects in the environment, and "mobility," which refers to the ability to move about in the environment. Mobility and orientation instruction are special skills, and most students will receive this training from a specialist before entering the regular classroom. The classroom teacher must, however, assist in orienting the student to the classroom and school environment. Suggestion for accomplishing this are

1. Spend time with the student in the classroom before the school year begins or, if this is not possible, make time available before or after school. Make sure that the student is comfortable with the surroundings and knows how to find the appropriate desk, books, and materials. Similarly, acquaint the student with the layout of the entire school, including the cafeteria, library, and restrooms. When appropriate, ask other students to perform this orientation to help the student become acquainted with some of his or her classmates.
2. Discuss and practice the fire drill procedure and route.
3. Arrange for extra traveling time for the visually-impaired student either before or after the other students.
4. Encourage these students to ask for help when they need it and instruct sighted students to assist when called upon. Special training provided by a mobility instructor in how to guide a blind or partially sighted person might be both useful and interesting for the other students.
5. Provide ample work space for extra equipment such as Braille books, magnifying devices, typewriter, and tape recorder.
6. Be sure to call the student by name and encourage classmates to identify themselves until the student learns their voices.
7. Include the visually handicapped student in as many of the regular class activities as possible, as all the students will profit from this interaction.

INSTRUCTIONAL METHODS

Any method of teaching reading can be used with the visually handicapped student as long as you use a *multisensory* approach and present concepts in as *concrete* a manner as possible. Blind children and those with extremely low vision rely heavily on auditory and tactile input to process information. Classroom activities and field trips should be explained or narrated to provide a vivid picture of what is going on. New concepts must be explained in nonvisual, concrete terms. Whenever possible, tactile experiences should be provided to illustrate elements or characteristics of the concept being discussed. For example, instead of saying that a mouse is a small, furry animal, say that a mouse can be held in the palm of your hand and provide a piece of fur for the student to stroke. Better still, of course, would be to present a real mouse. Models can be useful for concept development as long as they are not overused to the point of presenting a distorted or limited idea of reality (Ward and McCormick, 1981).

Most of the techniques listed here are useful for students who have low vision or who are blind; however, special consideration must be made for differences in these groups.

Low Vision. Students with low vision should be seated to avoid glare and may wish to use a portable lamp. Proper illumination, be it bright or dim, and print that is very clear are perhaps more important than is the size of the print (Sykes, 1972). Large-type books are available for students who require them. If a student with low vision has trouble keeping lines of print separate, encourage the use of a marker or the sweep of the hand to keep the eyes on line.

Blindness. Braille is the main tool for use in teaching reading to the blind. Although Braille instruction is usually done by specialists, a slight knowledge of Braille is very useful for the classroom teacher. In addition to the readiness required for regular reading (Chapter 4), reading readiness for learning Braille requires a refined sense of touch. Sorting tasks—moving from large, clearly defined items to small, subtle items—are quite useful for developing this skill.

TEACHING TECHNIQUES

1. Include prereading activities such as discussion of new vocabulary words and concepts, using the concrete multisensory approach outlined earlier in this section. For low-vision students, large clear pictures are useful for explaining ideas, as well as promoting creative language experience stories. To illustrate such concepts as "velvety" or "corrugated," for example, cards can be covered with any number of substances to provide the desired tactile response. Sound effects and the actual objects themselves are also useful for presenting new ideas to visually-impaired students.
2. To develop listening skills for the visually impaired, the teacher can use tape-recorded material, sighted readers, and everyday classroom activity. Tape recorders are essential and may be used to record sentences or passages from stories and have the student repeat them into the tape and play back for correction. On tape, record a series of sounds using bells, drums, and so on. This can be used as a game by several students, awarding points for the longest correct series recalled.
3. Reader's Theater is very beneficial to visually handicapped students because it gives them a chance to participate in oral, expressive reading with their classmates. Although their reading rate may be slower than that of other students, with practice an accomplished production can be performed.
4. Plan activities especially for the visually-impaired students and include the regular class in the activity. For example, a nature walk with emphasis on smells, shapes, and textures and asking the students to verbalize how things smell and feel is an excellent way to build up oral language fluency. It also creates an appreciation for the fact that there is more to objects than their appearance.

The Orthopedically and Other Health Impaired

DEFINITION

This category covers a wide range of disabilities, from cerebral palsy to diabetes to missing limbs. The common link among these persons is that the primary difficulty is the result of a nonsensory physical handicap. There are few common learning problems associated with this group, as many physical impairments have no real effect on cognitive ability or learning potential, while others such as cerebral palsy and spina bifida may have significant neurological complications that contribute to severe communication problems. Perhaps the most common characteristic of this group is the psychological aspect of coping with a very obvious disfiguring or life-threatening disability. In this context, as with all handicapping conditions, the individual's ability to adapt to a given condition or disease has a dramatic impact on the functional severity of the disability, regardless of the medical prognosis.

There are two basic categories of physical disabilities: *orthopedic* and *neurological impairments*, including cerebral palsy, muscular dystrophy, spina bifida, epilepsy, multiple sclerosis, congenital malformations, and impairments due to accident; and other *health impairments*, including cardiac conditions, diabetes, cancer, tuberculosis, sickle cell anemia, cystic fibrosis, hemophilia, and other chronic or terminal diseases. (For a general description of these disorders, see Hallahan and Kauffman, 1978, Chap. 8; Meyer, 1978, Chap. 8.)

CLASSROOM CONSIDERATIONS

Federal law (P.L. 93–112, Section 502) now requires architectural access and adequate toilet facilities for wheelchairs; therefore, your major environmental concern should be for proper placement of the physically handicapped student in the classroom. Where the student sits should depend on any accompanying sensory handicaps and accessibility (e.g, maneuvering space) to various parts of the classroom (the student's desk, free reading center, individual study carrels, media center, games) so that the disabled student is as free to participate in the same learning options as the other students with as little special help as possible.

After the student is physically at ease in the class environment, your main concern must be to help the student attain a positive self-concept, which, for the physically impaired, involves, to a large extent, fostering independence and an acceptance of the handicapping condition (Bigge and O'Donnel, 1977). Family attitude is obviously highly significant in the psychological health of a handicapped student, but the teacher is influential in helping the other students to relate to the disabled student, thus easing the crucial task of establishing peer relationships. Confer with the family and appropriate professionals involved with the student to understand how he or she feels about the condition and how much is understood about it. Encouraging honest answers to questions regarding a physical handicap will help classmates to shift their curiosity from that aspect of the student to the individual as a person.

Some practical concerns regarding work load for a physically handicapped individual include absenteeism, fatigue, and motor problems associated with writing. Here are some suggestions for dealing with these problems:

Absenteeism.   When practical and appropriate, send work home with classmates who live nearby, allowing the student contact with his or her peers and providing tutoring which benefits both parties. If the absence is prolonged or hospitalization is required, special tutors may be engaged to help the student keep up with the class work. Encourage the student to keep a journal during the confined time and periodically have the class write letters or visit the student when possible.

Fatigue.   Students with health or mobility problems tire easily, and the class work should be varied or flexible enough to include rest periods in which the student can read, draw, or nap as indicated. Do not expect a handicapped student to keep up with the pace of the rest of the class, but always include the student, providing the choice to rest if he or she is tired.

Writing Problems.   Alternatives to handwritten assignments may include the use of a typewriter or computer (sometimes it is necessary to use a head wand, when hand coordination is not sufficient to type with the fingers) or a tape recorder for oral responses.

INSTRUCTIONAL METHODS AND TEACHING TECHNIQUES

The learning problems of the physically impaired may range from those of the mentally retarded to the gifted; therefore, it is impossible to offer specific techniques unique to this class of handicap. Suggestions offered in the other sections of this chapter as well as those in other chapters of this text can help you to plan appropriate instruction. Emphasis should always be first on self-help, survival, and social skills, with more academic pursuits based on these initial skills. As with all special students, never underestimate them! A challenge should always be presented, keeping a close watch on frustration levels.

Learning Disabilities

DEFINITION

In 1963, Samuel Kirk coined the term "learning disabilities," which has since been used to describe a series of problems that affect an individual's ability to learn. The most important aspect of a definition of learning disabilities is that it is not one single condition and consequently cannot be treated in one single way. In 1968, the National Advisory Committee on Handicapped Children presented this definition of learning disabilities to Congress for use in funding programs designed for these students:

> Children with special learning disabilities exhibit a disorder in one or more of the basic psychological processes involved in understanding or in using spoken or written language. These may be manifested in disorders of listening, thinking, talking, reading, writing, spelling, or arithmetic. They include conditions which have been referred to as perceptual handicaps, brain injury, minimal brain dysfunction, dyslexia, developmental aphasia, etc. They do not include learning problems which are due primarily to visual, hearing, or motor handicaps, to mental retardation, emotional disturbance, or to environmental disadvantage.

This definition may provide the traditional and legal delineation of learning disabilities, but it does not bring the educator much closer to determining what exactly constitutes a learning disability and what to do about it. Any definition of learning disabilities provokes great controversy, but there is professional agreement about two of the most common components of these definitions:

1. A learning disabled student does not achieve up to his or her academic potential. This potential is usually measured by comparing scores on a standardized intelligence test with those on a standardized achievement test; however, other methods using a formula for ratio discrepancy (Mykelbust, 1968) may provide a more accurate picture of expected versus actual achievement.
2. A learning disabled student has a wide range of achievement that spreads across the academic spectrum. The student may be strong in reading but weak in spelling or math, or have excellent oral communication skills but be unable to write a coherent sentence.

There is debate over three of the other most common aspects of learning disabilities definitions: presence of brain injury, lack of environmental disadvantage, and lack of mental retardation or emotional handicaps (Hallahan and Kauffman, 1978).

The field of learning disabilities has some of its roots in work done by Werner and Strauss with brain-damaged mentally retarded children in the 1930s. Because many underachieving students were found to have some of the same behavioral characteristics as the brain-injured mentally retarded children, the assumption was made that the children were not learning because their brains were in some way damaged. Although much of this early work has been refuted due to its nonstatistical and introspective nature, the possibility that neurological disturbances are the cause of learning disorders has been central to research in the field (Cruickshank, 1975). It is now assumed that learning disabled youngsters are not necessarily brain injured unless neurological testing so indicates. As more sophisticated neurological examinations are increasingly more possible, perhaps the true nature of the relationship between brain dysfunction or damage and learning disabilities will be revealed.

The objections to definitions that state that the environment has nothing to do with learning disabilities arise from an increasing awareness that environment strongly affects the realization of potential in nearly every aspect of development—intelligence, artistic achievement, emotional maturity, and so on. Gearheart and Weishahn (1976) suggest that the exclusion of culturally disadvantaged or different children from classification as learning disabled was to prevent "wholesale placement of black, Mexican–American, Puerto Rican–American, and the very poor of all races in special, segregated, or semisegregated programs" (p. 8). If culturally disadvantaged students exhibit the characteristic behavior pattern of the learning disabled as they are likely to do (Cravioto and DeLicardil, 1975; Hallahan and Cruickshank, 1973), then they too deserve whatever special help is available.

A similar argument can be made for the exclusion of the mentally retarded or emotionally disturbed student. If these students are not achieving up to their expected potential, they too can be considered as learning disabled. Many professionals (Cruickshank and Johnson, 1975; Hallahan and Kauffman, 1976) feel that the phenomenon of learning disabilities cuts across every IQ level.

There is no universally acceptable definition of learning disabilities. Somewhere between the Advising Committee's statement quoted earlier in this text and the terse contention that "a learning disabled child is simply not achieving up to his potential" (Hallahan and Kauffman, 1978) exists a student who for some reason has trouble learning; it is your job as a teacher to teach that student.

CAUSES

Because the term "learning disability" encompasses a vast array of disorders, it seems obvious that the condition cannot have one single cause. More accurately, a learning disability is the result of a complex integration of biophysical, emotional, environmental, intellectual, and perceptual difficulties that create various problems of varying degrees. The two most common areas discussed as causes of learning disabilities are biological and organic disorders and environmental factors.

Biological and Organic Disorders. The traditional culprit in learning disability cases—neurological impairment—may be the result of an unusual prenatal or birth experience (Pasamanick and Knoblock, 1960). Any maternal illness, medication, or the use of alcohol or tobacco during pregnancy are now all commonly believed to affect the fetus. Fetal malnutrition due to lack of proper nutrition during pregnancy is another prenatal cause of neurological distress (Birch, 1971). Prolonged labor, lack of oxygen to the child, breech birth, or forceps delivery are also cited as unusual birth experiences. The theory of mixed dominance (for example, preferred use of the right hand and left foot as opposed to a complete preference for one side of the body) claimed that this condition was a sign of a neurological problem that was responsible for learning disabilities (Orton, 1937). The theory has been disproved (Belmont and Birch, 1965), but research into the complexities of the relationships between hemispheric dominance and learning continues.

Other theories that have enjoyed media success but that have not been supported by research are those of a biochemical nature. Feingold (1975) believes that artificial food colors and flavorings cause hyperactivity, one of the main characteristics of learning disabled children, and Cott (1972) attributed a disorder that prevents the body from synthesizing vitamins as a cause of learning disabilities.

Environmental Factors. Although it is true that children from a disadvantaged environment tend to have learning problems, it is unclear whether these problems stem from emotional-psychological factors or from biophysical factors. Hunger or conflict in the home may prevent a student from concentrating on school work, which presents a learning problem. However, malnutrition or lack of proper medical care can result in neurological disorders that cause learning problems (Hallahan and Cruickshank, 1973).

Another environmental factor may be lack of proper teaching (Bateman, 1973). This phrase—teaching disability—has been used to mean that the problem lies more in inefficient instructional methods in the early years than in the ability or disability of a student to learn.

CHARACTERISTICS

For organizational reasons, we have divided characteristics into categories, but remember that children will not fall nicely into line behind a banner marked "Language difficulties" or "Perceptual-motor disorders." Not all learning disabled students will display all these characteristics; conversely, some students with no learning problem may exhibit certain problems listed here. This delineation seeks to provide a guideline for understanding the complexities of a learning disability and also to aid in diagnosing a learning disability when one is suspected.

Lack of Appropriate Impulse Control. Research dating from the early work of Werner and Strauss (1941) through more recent research (Tarver and Hallahan, 1976; Sabatino and Ysseldyke, 1972) has recognized that the learning disabled tend to exhibit disorders of attention, hyperactivity, and impulsivity. Rappaport (1964) used the term "inadequate impulse control or regulation" to describe these activities, and Cruickshank (1975) summed up all these behaviors as "the inability of the child to refrain from reaction to extraneous external or internal stimuli" (p. 260). The student has difficulty sorting out which elements in the environment require attention and which do not. The result might be disorders of attention that include a short attention span, perseveration (the repetition of an idea in speech or writing), and distractibility, wherein the student is unable to focus attention on the task at hand due to external or internal distractions. Hyperactivity is perhaps one of the best known characteristics of the learning disabled and shows itself in the youngster who is constantly in motion, whose motor activity is too high for his or her age group. Impulsivity is the inability to control spontaneous inclinations to act or speak regardless of the circumstances and may cause problems both in social behavior and problem-solving ability (Heins et al., 1976).

Perceptual Disorders. Perception can be defined as the process of becoming aware of the nature of something through the senses. In reading, good visual perception is important to comprehension of the printed symbols that comprise the written code of language. Similarly, auditory perception influences reading ability because the visual symbol of the word must then be related to the sound it represents. Research indicates that poor visual and auditory perception are common traits of learning disabled individuals (Leton, 1962; Devol and Hastings, 1967; Skubic and Anderson, 1970); consequently, many authorities have advocated strong programs of visual and auditory perception training to improve reading skills. While this training is certainly indicated for some individuals, it does not offer *the* solution to reading problems and should be coupled with other techniques that deal with other aspects of the reading difficulties.

Perceptual-motor problems, or the inability to move the body in accordance with what the mind directs, are also characteristic of the learning disabled. These difficulties can be of a gross (large muscle coordination) or fine (small muscle coordination) nature and may influence everything from the ability to play in motor games to the ability to write legibly. Again, many professionals (most notably Kephart, 1971) advocate programs of perceptual-motor training to improve this coordination, but these methods alone will not necessarily improve the learning skills of the individual. They are a *part* of a total program and will serve the student best in a social way by making him or her more accepted by the peer group.

Language Problems. The learning disabled may have language problems described as difficulties with "receptive language" and "expressive language" (Hallahan and Kauffman, 1978) or "input" and "output" (Johnson and Myklebust, 1967). Receptive or input problems result from a lack of comprehension of spoken language, which may impede, for example, following directions and understanding class discussions. Expressive or output disabilities result in the inability to express thoughts using oral language. Complications of the notion of input and output may produce students who can understand what is spoken but cannot speak the ideas themselves, or those who may be able to say what they mean but not write it down. A student with this aspect of a learning disability may be mistaken for one who does not pay attention or is shy about speaking up in class.

Memory and Cognitive Difficulties.   Any learning process requires the ability to remember information long enough to assess it or relate it to other information. The time required to perform this operation may be short term (the time it takes to associate the visual symbol to its corresponding sound) or long term (storing vocabulary and syntax rules); dysfunctions of either memory type can create learning problems. Research supports the notion that learning disabled children experience memory deficiencies (Vande Voort and Senf, 1973; Wiig and Roach, 1975), but it offers no conclusions as to why. Some theories suggest a lack of efficient skill in organizing the material to be remembered (Parker, Freston and Drew, 1975) and that verbal information causes particular memory problems (Farnham-Diggory and Gregg, 1975; Velluntino et al., 1975).

Cognitive difficulties may manifest themselves in impulsive problem-solving strategies (Keogh and Donlon, 1972) and conceptual disorders (Walters and Doan, 1962). In a classic study by Werner and Strauss (1941), replicated in 1951 by Dolphin and Cruickshank, learning disabled youngsters, given a task of sorting objects into groups based on similar aspects, were consistently distracted by nonessential details of the objects, which resulted in bizarre groupings, displaying troubled thought processes (e.g., a wire was grouped with a fire engine because it was long and thin like a hose). Although some of this behavior appears creative and imaginative (e.g., a whistle and sunglasses go together because police officers may wear them when directing traffic), the problem is that the student loses sight of the main task.

Emotional Instability.   Frequent mood changes in the learning disabled may be associated with a low self-concept. The failure syndrome so often found in underachieving students operates here with the learning disabled. Lack of success in learning tasks causes students to lose confidence, motivation, and self-esteem; this in turn produces more failure in terms of teacher and parental disapproval. Rappaport (1964) also discusses a *low frustration tolerance* and *flight from challenge,* which may result in a physical or verbal attack on someone if the individual does not achieve immediate success with the task. Overcompensation for insecurities may result in the student reverting to something he or she is successful at, which might be totally irrelevant to the task at hand (e.g., singing Gilbert and Sullivan songs or reciting baseball statistics). Control or manipulation of others, power struggles, and negativism are other defense mechanisms that may show up in the behavior of the learning disabled student trying to cope with a difficult situation.

Classroom Considerations

Learning disabilities are very complex. A wide variety of teaching strategies must be employed to meet the needs of these students in the regular classroom. Ranging from the hyperactive child who creates general chaos to the quiet student who cannot seem to follow directions, learning disabled students ideally should have individualized programs to meet their specific educational requirements and, at the same time, allow them to participate with the rest of the class whenever possible to encourage correct socialization. The approaches and suggestions described in the following sections may be adapted for use either individually or in a class situation.

1. Never *assume* that these students have understood directions even if the instructions are perfectly clear to everyone else.
2. Try to make class exercises short and success oriented. Team games are especially useful when there is no direct individual pressure on the members (e.g., Blackboard Scrabble) and if the student can cope with the excitement.
3. Alternative teaching and response methods (e.g., a typewriter, computer, or tape recorder) may be useful with some learning disabled students for completing assignments.
4. Structure the time into small segments with varying activities—quiet independent work, work with a tutor or aide, classroom work, physical work (filing, board games, etc.).

Remember that you are a crucial person in the life of a learning disabled student and that your relationship with the student must be as close and as understanding as possible. Rappaport (1966) calls for a "relationship structure," which he defines as the "ability of the adult (parent or teacher or therapist or otherwise) to understand the child sufficiently well at any given moment, through his verbal and nonverbal communications, to relate in a way which aids the child's development of impulse control and other ego functions" (p. 26). This, of course, is the dream relationship between every pupil and teacher; however, it is even more important to students who have met with so little academic and social success that they are caught up in a failure syndrome.

INSTRUCTIONAL METHODS

Since learning disabilities are a composite of many difficulties that are unique to each individual, no one method of teaching will satisfactorily meet the needs of any student. Many theories or methods for teaching learning disabled students exist, and it is necessary to compose a comprehensive instructional framework (CIF) for each student. This consists of selecting those methods (or aspects of them) that will best remediate the deficiencies exhibited by a particular individual. Once the theoretical methods of instruction are chosen, an individualized educational program, pinpointing specific goals, techniques, and exercises, can be developed. By first establishing an educational outline based on the major instructional approaches to learning disabilities, the actual teaching techniques and the rest of the classroom program will easily and naturally build up around this theoretical framework.

Hallahan and Kauffman (1978) present five convenient categories of teaching approaches, which represent the consensus of professionals, for learning disabled students.

Process Training. This theory claims that it is possible to know what "underlying processes" are used in learning and that, if there is difficulty in learning, then the specific psychological process is the target for reha- bilitation or remediation. The malfunctioning process most commonly cited is perceptual-motor integration, which has led to many programs stress- ing perceptual-motor training. Frostig and Horne (1964), Getman, Kane, and McKee (1968), and Kephart (1971) are among the more popular pro- ponents of this method of instruction; generally, they stress the acquisi- tion of motor skills, moving on to matching visual skills to them. Research has indicated that process training achieves very little real academic gain for the disabled learner (Hallahan and Cruickshank, 1973); however, as part of a comprehensive instructional framework, the use of visual-motor training in particular may serve to elevate a student's level of coordina- tion. This improves self-esteem, which may contribute positively in atti- tude toward academic success.

Multisensory Approaches. Fernald's VAKT (visual, auditory, kines- thetic, and tactile) method of instruction serves as the standard upon which most other multisensory methods are based (Fernald, 1943). By using all the sensory mechanisms available rather than focusing on just visual and/ or auditory, it is felt that students have a better chance of learning be- cause individuals differ in how they process sensory information.

Stimulus Reduction. Designed for use with hyperactive and distractible students, characteristics among the most common found in the learning disabled, techniques to reduce environmental and instructional stimuli may be beneficial to all learning disabled students. This method, advocated originally by Strauss and Warner and applied experimentally by Cruick- shank (1961), basically seeks to reduce any source of distraction for the student, be it in the form of environmental factors (ornate bulletin boards, books on a shelf, other children, noise, etc.) or an instructional program in which the student is called upon to make choices. Stimuli reduction is accomplished in the latter instance by providing a totally teacher-structured program, which eliminates the frustration of choice until the student can be sufficiently educated to handle some decision making. Environmental control consists of providing a quiet, relatively stimulus-free work space where attention can be focused on the learning task (e.g., undecorated walls in a corner of the room or a cubicle). Cruickshank found that al- though academic skills did not automatically improve, attending skills did; since attention and concentration are essential to learning, this approach may contribute significantly to the CIF of certain learning disabled stu- dents.

Cognitive Training. Modeling and self-instructional training are two re- lated methods that attempt to teach learning disabled students with impulsive problem-solving strategies how to slow down and reflect on the task before responding. Both methods utilize an adult or peer model to demonstrate the appropriate behavior and then provide positive reinforcement either directly or indirectly for any successes achieved. Self-instruction further provides a verbal stimulus to modeling by developing in the student the ability to "talk to himself" while performing the task, thus using verbal control. Meichenbaum (1975), a major advocate of the system, provides the following format for self-instructional training:

1. An adult model performed a task while talking to himself out loud (cognitive modeling);
2. The student performed the same task under the direction of the model's instruction (overt self-guidance);
3. The student whispered the instructions to himself as he went through the task (faded, overt self-guidance);
4. The student performed the task while guiding his performance via private speech (covert self-instruction). (pp. 16, 17)

Modeling can be very effective in changing student behavior; it can be easily accomplished by seating the child near peers who normally exhibit the desired behavior. An individualized program can also be instituted if necessary.

Behavior Modification. Reinforcing appropriate behavior and ignoring inappropriate behavior—behavior modification—has been used successfully with learning disabled children suffering from hyperactivity and distractibility (Hallahan and Kauffman, 1975); it has also been shown to improve math scores and linguistic skills (Smith and Lovitt, 1975; Lovitt and Smith, 1972). The "engineered classroom," devised by Frank Hewett (1967, 1968), has been successful in improving attention skills by offering tokens or marks for tasks successfully completed or for acceptable behavior. Prizes are then available that students "buy" with their tokens or checkmarks.

TEACHING TECHNIQUES

Any method of reading instruction with which the teacher is competent and comfortable can be used to teach learning disabled students to read. Certain modifications of the material are necessary for certain types of problems, and suggested techniques for adapting existing academic material are presented here.

1. Exaggerate the item being taught, which causes the student to focus all of his or her attention on the task. For example;

   When teaching new vocabulary words in context, highlight the new word with larger print or color.
   When teaching minimal pairs, highlight the distinguishing letter as above.

2. Break up stories, lessons, worksheets, and other assignments into small parts that culminate in success-oriented tasks. For example;

   Determine how much the student can read before frustration sets in and divide the stories into sections that can be handled successfully. Ask questions after each section to reinforce the skill being taught, aid in recall, and spark interest in continuing.

   The use of a typewriter, tape recorder, computer, or other audio-visual tools provides useful diversions between reading tasks; assignments can be related to what was just done or preview what is coming up.

3. If a restricted environment is indicated for certain activities, create "offices" from carrels, partitions, or appliance crates that are free from distracting stimuli. Students may be assigned "office hours" when the space is for their own private use. Behavior modification principles can be applied to "buy" more or less office time (depending on which is considered more desirable by student and teacher).

4. IEPs for learning disabled students require a great deal of monitoring to be certain that the correct instructional level is being used and that the instructions are understood. Utilize peer tutors when possible to help in the lessons, thus making use of the modeling technique at the same time. Sharing "office" space with a responsible, well-organized student may foster better skills, even if the students work side by side in isolation.

High Technology and the Special Child

During our discussions of instructional methods and classroom techniques, we have purposely omitted reference to recent advances in technology. In no way should it be inferred that these advances are unimportant. Most of them, however, are in their formative stages of development and experimentation so it is difficult to determine the scope and degree of instructional benefit each will offer to the special child.

For the classroom teacher, the use of computers and related technologies will require the development of some new instructional strategies and the adaptation of some existing strategies:

> The importance of developing new instructional strategies which fully use and teach about technology is more than a desirable program enhancement. Current and future technologies hold the potential to be normalization agents for the exceptional person both in school and in the community. Properly developed, they can overcome physical barriers, facilitate communication, compensate for biological deficiencies and serve as daily living prosthetic devices. (Cain, 1984, p. 239)

New technologies offer great promise for meeting many needs of special students. We encourage teachers to keep abreast of technological advances through professional journals, inservice training, and/or college/university course offerings.

Suggested Readings Related to Goals.   We encourage you at this time to review the goals at the beginning of this chapter. If you feel you would like to explore one or more of these areas in greater depth, please refer to the cross-indexed bibliography at the end of the book.

15 Developing and Managing Your Reading Program

Assessment is virtually meaningless if instructional programming does not follow.

[A. Archer]

Goals

To help the student understand
1. The factors contributing to effective classroom management
2. How to develop and implement thematic teaching
3. Successful grouping techniques
4. Behavioral objective as an essential instructional tool
5. The capabilities of different media and their usefulness as classroom aids
6. The importance of continuous evaluation

In this chapter, like all others in this text, we provide you with a variety of instructional strategies, methods, and materials necessary to implement a successful reading program. We continue to advocate an individualized approach to reading as the optimal one for meeting the needs of *all* of your students. The present chapter will help you to organize your reading program smoothly by incorporating the principles of systems management into the knowledge you have acquired about the individual needs of your students. Continuous evaluation by you as the teacher and by the students as the principal users of your system is crucial to the success of any management system.

You might assume that when an institutionalized program is not meeting the individual needs of students or teachers, a more efficient change in the system would be welcome. However, some people are resistant to change and are reluctant to throw out what they know, even when familiarity has bred contempt. O'Donnell and Moore (1980) found seven categories of "stumbling blocks" to organizational change in education: (1) administration, (2) parents, (3) community, (4) resources, (5) assessment and evaluation, (6) willingness to change, and (7) the problem of working with large numbers of students. They suggest that "the most persuasive and obvious stumbling block was the self-fulfilling prophecy: 'But our school just doesn't have the staff or resources to do it; therefore, I can't do it' " (p. 187).

These stumbling blocks can be overcome, and an innovative, efficient management system designed to meet the needs of those involved in a classroom reading program can be implemented. The classroom teacher will need to establish an interactional base for this system that includes parents, students, teachers, administrators, school boards, and community leaders, all working together with mutual, well-correlated goals.

The Foundation: A Working System

"School is much more interesting this year," eleven-year-old Erin was overheard telling her brother Jay. "We don't just read the same old readers; we also read interesting and exciting books and magazines. This year I like reading as much as science!"

The enthusiasm exuded in student comments like this one indicates involvement in a reading program that is not only instructionally invigorating but also well managed. As a teacher, how you manage the classroom will contribute greatly to the success of your reading program.

Think about the type of learning environment you would want to establish. It should include provisions for

1. Giving *all* students specific information regarding their competencies
2. Encouraging student participation in the planning of program goals
3. Having all students participate in evaluating their own progress
4. Encouraging students to make decisions about participation in alternate learning activities designed to accomplish the specified goals

Such an environment requires you, as the teacher, to be a classroom manager; you will need to determine

1. Reading program goals
2. Student competencies
3. Procedures for individual or group progress
4. Techniques and materials needed to implement appropriate procedures

5. Continuous evaluation of the goals, student competencies, processes, and techniques

Equipped with a working philosophy of education, it is then important to determine specific means for helping students to accomplish their goals. Too often, classroom teachers intend to implement a very personalized model of education but are unable to do so because they lack the skills needed to manage one. The use of management systems in educational planning is expanding, following the lead of business management, which, since the 1950s and 1960s has made increasing use of advanced technology in this area. Through such a system, the teacher is able to compare student growth with stated objectives and reschedule or recycle student programs according to exhibited competencies. Many textbook companies have been developing basal reading series that provide the teacher with a management system model; for example, Ginn Reading Program (1983), Houghton Mifflin Reading program (1981), and Holt Basic Reading (1980). For a complete review of these and other basal reading series components, see Aukerman (1981).

In exploring the processes of defining and developing a classroom management system, several key questions must be addressed. Where is the classroom located? What is the socioeconomic stratification? What is the school building like? How involved are the parents? What are the students like? and What existing curricular and societal structures predetermine classroom interactions?

Such questions can be formulated by examining the schemata of an educational management system given in Figure 15-1.

Existing Structures and Individuals

Consideration must be directed toward the existing structures that directly affect the happenings within your classroom. Although some of these structures may be governed by you (philosophy and psychology), others (societal influence, budget allocations) may be outside your range of authority, and still other areas (curricular requirements, time schedules) may have been established before your arrival, but can be changed.

You must be familiar with all the structures in your environment and the extent of your decision-making power regarding each. You may gain initial insights into this area through social and professional interactions with colleagues and administrators. A review of existing school policies, as well as curriculum guides, will offer you some insights into the parametric structure of the existing curriculum. As you begin to collect information about existing structures, remember to ask the following questions:

1. How is the day divided?
2. Is the time schedule predetermined? By whom?
3. Is your classroom self-contained?

EDUCATIONAL MANAGEMENT SYSTEM

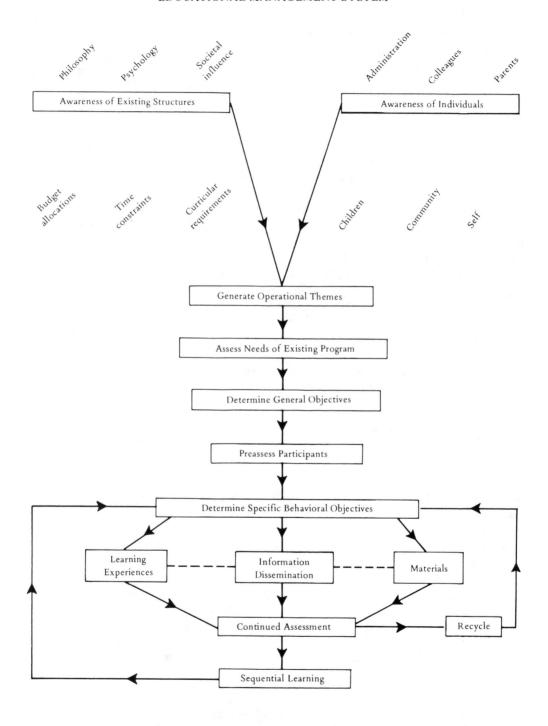

Figure 15-1. Educational management system

4. What special teachers (music, art) or special services (gym, theater) are provided?
5. Is there an organized curriculum committee? If so, how can you join?
6. What funds are available to you?
7. How are text materials adopted?

These questions are extremely important. Always attempt to compare the answers you receive with your philosophy of teaching. Is there compatibility? If not, is there room for negotiation and change? In what areas and to what extent can you compromise without violating your own educational beliefs?

One reason for becoming a teacher is enjoyment of working with others to help students learn. Consequently, it is important to consider your own feelings about education and how you relate to others.

Ask yourself questions such as these: Who am I? Who am I working for? Answers to such questions may be found through your interactions with the administration, colleagues, parents, community, students, and yourself.

ADMINISTRATION

1. What appears to be the major objectives of the administration?
2. How are these objectives related to education?
3. How is their apparent philosophy similar to or different from mine?
4. What are the line-staff relationships (line of command) with this administration?
5. *What* decisions are made by *whom?*

COLLEAGUES

1. Who are my colleagues?
2. Do major educational beliefs appear to be shared by the majority of this faculty?
3. What are the faculty's initial impressions of me?
4. What will be my role as a member of this educational community?
5. What decision-making responsibilities are mine?

PARENTS

1. Who are the parents of my students?
2. What are their values with regard to the educational training of their children?
3. Are they heavily involved with the decision-making processes of this school?
4. How do they view the existing faculty and administration?

COMMUNITY

1. Is the surrounding community well represented (economically, socially) by the family makeup of the students within my classroom?
2. What segment of the community controls school board decision making?
3. What are the apparent and less apparent feelings of the school board with regard to the administration, faculty, and education?

STUDENTS

1. Who are my students?
2. What have been their life exposures thus far?
3. What may be their projected life goals?
4. Are their life exposures similar or dissimilar to mine?
5. What will be their projected view of me?

SELF

1. What will be my function in this educational community?
2. Do I harbor any prejudices or fears with regard to the people within the community?
3. Are there any barriers that may interfere with my functioning effectively?
4. If so, how is it possible to alter these barriers?

As a veteran or as a beginning teacher, you continually need to pursue answers to these questions. You will probably find that your students are similar to students in most middle grades: multiethnic and culturally diverse, with various dialects, levels of cognitive development, levels of sensory and perceptual readiness, degrees of physical health, degrees of social and emotional development, various interests and attitudes about learning, and a great variety of oral and silent reading skills.

In attempting to meet the needs of your individual students, it is wise to look closely at the existing program structures at your school. You might begin by

1. Reviewing the specific sequence of reading skills covered in the school basal reading program. The levels of student reading ability within a middle grade might range from about second grade to tenth grade. It is a good idea to design a scope and sequence checklist of reading skills, ranging from phonic and structural analysis to study skills and evaluative and interpretive reading skills.
2. Surveying school libraries and book closets to determine the range of available reading materials.
3. Informally discussing with the principal and fellow teachers their philosophies about reading instruction.
4. Surveying community attitudes toward reading instruction.

Operational Themes

After acquiring a general understanding of the existing structures and individuals within your educational community, as well as their decision-making effects on the management of your classroom, you can begin planning your classroom curriculum. Think about general student interests and needs to determine the topics you might share with your students. You will probably want to share decision-making situations with your students, but never lose sight of the fact that your experiences are broader and more far-reaching than those of your students. It will also probably be the case that many of the themes will be those provided through the management system of the basal program you are using.

At this point, let us brainstorm to determine the general themes you may plan to share with your students.

Life Cycles (biological, emotional, social)
Making Choices (family, school, friends, careers)
Exploring Your Environment (geographically, culturally, emotionally)
Life in the American Past (family, environment, economic structures)
Building a Nation (the Constitution, interstate and international relations)

As you add to this list of themes, keep in mind that several themes may be operating simultaneously because some of your students will not have the same interests or the same reading levels. Your intent in any theme will be to convey the basic skills of communication as well as the skills and areas of information that will foster the development of independent learners.

> Students need to learn far more than the basic skills. Children who have just started school may still be in the labor force in the year 2030. For them, nothing could be more wildly impractical than an education designed to prepare them for specific vocations or professions or to facilitate their adjustment to the world as it is. To be practical, an education should prepare a man for work that doesn't yet exist and whose nature cannot even be imagined. This can be done only by teaching people how to learn, by giving them the kind of intellectual discipline that will enable them to apply man's accumulated wisdom to new problems as they arise, the kind of wisdom that will enable them to recognize new problems as they arise. (Silberman, 1970, pp. 83–84)

It may be helpful to select themes that facilitate the incorporation of science, math, and social studies lessons. Think of your themes as topics that may be expanded to become an integrated curriculum unit.

Many schools today have competency-based educational curriculum and testing programs that, on the surface, seem to discourage thematic teaching. Teachers find themselves expected to teach discrete reading, writing, and/or problem-solving skills that will enable students to pass school competency tests. While it is important to remember that students must possess basic skills in these areas, the development of strong communication and study skills takes place only when the instruction is interesting, practical, and useful. Students will understand, synthesize, and enhance these skills most effectively if they can practically apply them in daily life.

Thematic teaching is challenging in that it calls upon the teacher to integrate content area learning, language arts, and study skills into a manageable, practical, interesting learning endeavor. Difficult as it may be, we contend that such an orientation to instruction is the essence of good teaching.

Needs of the Existing Program

Once you have selected some general themes, which you have altered after assessing student interest, you will want to assess the needs of the existing program. In making this program assessment, you should ask the following questions:

1. What previous themes have been explored at this grade level?
2. Do these themes apply to the objectives of the system?
3. Am I infringing on material that my colleagues may cover?
4. What resources are available to me?

After thinking about the existing curriculum, you will want to develop general program objectives.

General Objectives

Based on information derived from the program assessment, general objectives can be formulated. Following this, you can develop instruction for these objectives that is thematic in nature. For example;

Theme	*General Objectives*
Life cycles	1. Define a life cycle.
	2. Develop an understanding of the life cycle of plants.
	3. Develop an understanding of the biological life cycle of animals.
	4. Promote an awareness of emotional and psychological cycles in humans.
	5. Establish an appreciation for each stage of life from birth to death.
	6. Develop a personal awareness of one's own physical and emotional place in the cycle.
	7. Evaluate personal and societal feelings about life and death.

Exploring Your Environment
1. Develop an awareness of self.
2. Identify significant others.
3. Identify geographic boundaries.
4. Identify cultural boundaries.
5. Compare strengths and weaknesses of boundary limitations.
6. Evaluate social change you can effect.

As you plan these general thematic objectives, you will become more aware of the interrelatedness of the content areas and of the basic skills each student will need to study this topic successfully. For example, within the thematic study of "exploring your environment," the student encounters geography, history, sociology, and mathematics as well as reading, writing, and speaking. Through the integration of these areas, the learner explores standard, basic content skills while he or she explores areas of practical self-interest.

Because students have varying degrees of readiness for a new learning experience, it is important to assess entry-level competencies when you are planning to individualize instruction.

Student Assessment

In a study on teacher decisions regarding reading instruction, Borko, Shavelson, and Stern (1981) asked the question, "Do teachers use all of the available information about students to form reading groups?" (p. 452). The short answer to their question is "no"; teachers tend to base these decisions largely on information about reading ability rather than on any other aspect of the student or situation. While grouping strictly by reading ability has been popular in the past, it is now felt that other information such as students' interest, attitudes, and emotional needs should be considered.

To determine individual needs, the teacher must begin the process of diagnosing student competencies. Through *formal* measures, such as standardized reading tests, and *informal* measures, such as observation scales, teacher-made checklists, interest inventories, and textbook placement exams, you can assess each student's

1. Sensory and perceptual developmental needs
2. Emotional and social needs
3. Knowledge of oral reading, noting each student's difficulties with sight words and knowledge of vowel situations, consonant elements, and structural and contextual clues
4. Silent reading comprehension skills, focusing each student's attention to inferential and evaluative comprehension skills
5. Interests

According to this initial diagnosis, groups were designed based on student interests and needs. Correlation of student needs and interests is possible by first determining the reading needs of each student and then accommodating student interests through alternate activities.

FORMING GROUPS

After instructional levels have been determined through informal and standardized testing, students can be grouped according to their skill development needs, achievement, interests, purposes for reading, and attitudes toward reading. Grouping allows for individualization of instruction and provides for economy of teacher effort and increased student participation. It is more efficient for a teacher to instruct a group of students with similar needs, interests, and purposes than it is to work with a total classroom of separate individuals. Materials can be matched to the learner more effectively than would be possible if instruction were geared to a whole class. Grouping is beneficial to the learner because the instruction is matched with interests, needs, purposes, and skills. Table 15-1 shows an example of grouping patterns.

Although there are five groups with various reading levels within this classroom, there must not necessarily be at least five groups. First, there may be individuals who already possess the reading behaviors that have been set as the terminal outcome of instruction prior to the initiation of instruction. The teacher has two options for proceeding with the instructional program for these students: allow them to advance to a new and different program or let them proceed with the original program independently with minimal teacher guidance.

Second, other individuals may emerge who are unable to handle the materials required in the instructional program because they lack the skills that are necessary for dealing with the content. They would be totally incapable of benefiting from the instructional program as it is now planned. These students would be considered to be functioning on the frustrational level. To make instruction meaningful for them, the program would have to be revised to begin with the skills that the students already possess and build the skills that are needed to master the original program.

Finally, another group of students may emerge, those who can handle the materials and the instructional program but who still require teacher guidance and instruction. These students can be considered to be functioning at the instructional level, and they may proceed with the program as it was originally devised. There can be as many groups as necessary to meet the needs of the learners, but teacher energies must be taken into consideration. It may be that, in a given class, there are no students at the frustrational level when working within a certain theme; however, at the same time, students may be at various points within the instructional level. You may form two, three, four, or five groups within the instructional level, each with different skills, interests, and purposes.

Grouping is intended to increase participation for students; therefore,

TABLE 15-1
Example of Grouping Patterns

Reading Level	Number of Students	Needs	Grouping Plans
2^8	1	(Non-native speaker) Has difficulty with syntax, vocabulary; needs cultural exposure.	Group A: Introduce language experience activities, games and drills using basic word lists, high-interest/low-vocabulary reading materials.
3^4	1	Have limited sight vocabularies; need practice with word analysis strategies.	
3^5	1		
4^2	2	Need motivating; difficulty with cause and effect, comparison, and contrast.	Group B: Develop organizational skills and critical thinking skills; utilize newspapers, skits, humor, and satire.
4^7	3	Have difficulty with patterns of organization; needs practice with inferential skills.	
5^1	4	Need review and practice with literal and critical comprehension skills; also study skills, particularly outlining and establishing purpose for reading.	Group C: Discuss and analyze magazine articles and stories; research articles for oral report on Skylab.
5^8	2		
6^1	5	Students read at grade level.	Group D: Reinforce basic reading skills; extend mastery of study skills.
6^3	3		
7^2	1	Students read independently above grade level.	Group E: Develop study skills and aid students in transferring and applying them to content area situations; write, critique, and perform play or story.
7^6	1		
8^1	1	Students read independently well above grade level.	
8^5	1		

instructional materials are not necessarily uniform for all groups. For instance, the practice of grouping elementary school readers into "red," "blue," and "yellow" birds has often been the extent of grouping. Having groups use the same materials, purposes, and teaching methods, but at differing rates, is highly questionable because purpose, teaching methods, and materials should be modified, changed, and geared to meet the needs of the learners in a specific group in accordance with the various themes being pursued.

Remember that grouping must be based on students' thematic interests whenever possible and that groups will have to change accordingly. Groups can also be modified according to specific instructional objectives. As a student progresses through the program and fulfills the objectives, the group for which that program has been formed may become unnecessary for all the learners because each student does not necessarily progress at the same speed. If the objective has been met or if it is determined to be unrealistic, the group may be dissolved. New objectives may then be formed for different purposes and different instructional objectives. The same individuals may or may not be part of both groups. Also, students who progress faster than others may profit from working independently. For grouping to be effective, specific instructional objectives need to be defined and constant evaluation of student progress is necessary to maintain the validity of the group. Although grouping allows a teacher to make pedagogical decisions based on the group rather than on each individual in the class, never forget that the groups are comprised of individuals who do not remain static.

Because students' skills change constantly, there is a need for continual evaluation, regrouping, elimination of some groups, and formation of new groups. Groups should be viewed as temporary and changing, recognizing that not all students need to be included in groups all the time. This is especially true of students who are functioning at the independent levels.

Assessment instruments used for grouping are much the same as those that are used in determining reading levels: standardized tests, informal tests, textbook tests, and teacher observations. The standardized reading tests can be used to provide evaluations of reading levels to determine groups if the skills measured by the test are the same as those included in the instructional program and are tested in the same manner as the skills to be taught. Informal tests also provide reliable indications of reading levels for the creation of groups because they are constructed from the actual materials used in the programs and contain questions related specifically to instructional goals. The validity of the informal test for groups and for determining reading levels is often dependent on the competence of the teacher who devises it. Finally, teacher observations and textbook tests are especially useful in grouping. Such measures can provide a readily available means of assessing student progress toward attaining the program objectives.

In summary, successful grouping practices are contingent on the definition of what is to be taught and how it is to be taught and the anticipated terminal behavior. It is also dependent on continuous assessments of student behavior, on flexibility of established groups, and on changing the instructional program to meet the needs of the students. In general, the following steps should be followed in using tests for grouping:

1. Identify the objectives of the instructional program and the teaching methodology.

2. Preassess student reading behavior by using a standardized test (if it matches the objectives and definitions established for the instructional program), an informal test, a teacher checklist, and/or any combination of the three.
3. Form groups according to preassessment (for example, reading levels, thematic interests, purposes for reading, content of instruction, and student attitudes).
4. Evaluate student progress continuously by using informal tests, teacher checklists, or standardized tests (that match the instructional objectives), with the intent of moving students to independent activities if possible or regrouping on the basis of new instructional goals when the original ones have been met. Eliminate groups when they are no longer necessary.

Once group composition and needs have been determined, specific behavioral objectives should be developed for each learner or for each learning group.

Behavioral Objectives

A behavioral objective states an instructional goal in terms of measurable student performance. If objectives are well-formulated, they will enable the teacher to move smoothly into the actual development and use of instructional materials. A behavioral objective has three basic components: (1) the operational *conditions* to be present when the behavior occurs, (2) the terminal *behavior* the student should be able to exhibit upon completing instruction, and (3) the level of *performance* needed to determine mastery.

Operational conditions are the circumstances or restraints under which the behavior is to be performed. If, for example, it is necessary for the student to be in a particular environment or to have specific tools/resources when performing the behavior, such conditions must be stated.

Acceptable

1. Given a short article containing numerous grammatical errors . . .
2. Given a list of ten prefixes . . .
3. Given six pictures showing poor water conservation practices . . .

Unacceptable

1. Given a lesson on grammar . . .
2. After instruction on prefixes . . .
3. After reading a brochure on water conservation methods . . .

(Note that, although the unacceptable condition statements relate closely to the acceptable conditions, they do not specify the precise resources/tools the student will have available to him or her when actually performing the desired behavior.)

An acceptable statement of terminal *behavior* describes the student's behavior with such specificity that it cannot be misinterpreted. It answers the question, "What will the student be doing to demonstrate that the goal has been met?" Let's look at the following examples:

Acceptable

1. The student will be able to write . . .
2. The student will be able to identify . . . (verbally, visually)
3. The student will be able to read . . .

Unacceptable

1. The student knows . . .
2. The student will enjoy . . .
3. The student will acquire an appreciation of . . .

An acceptable statement of *performance* level describes how well the student must perform to meet the objective. It must be *specific*, as these examples show:

Acceptable

1. . . . at least six of the following professions.
2. . . . with at least 75 percent accuracy.
3. . . . with no more than three errors.

Unacceptable

1. . . . showing marked improvement over previous scores.
2. . . . with greater accuracy than before the lesson.
3. . . . better than last week.

While some researchers (Hambleton et al., 1978) feel there is a trend toward using "domain specifications" (Popham, 1975) or "amplified objectives" (Millman, 1974), it is still essential for a teacher to understand and use behavioral objectives accurately. A review of the literature (Lapp, 1972b) suggests that the acceptance or rejection of behavioral objectives as a relevant component to a thematic reading program has largely been based on speculation rather than research.

Unfortunately, the training of prospective teachers, which includes instruction in writing behavioral objectives, often is not accompanied by training in the utilization of such objectives. The teacher is never sure of the value of behavioral objectives in thematic curricular planning and evaluation. According to Gilpin (1962), an adequately prepared teacher can develop instructional objectives more effectively if the following questions and procedures are followed:

1. What is it that we must teach?
2. How will we know when we have taught it?
3. What materials and procedures will work best to teach what we want to teach? (p. viii)

Sometimes a general objective is conceived first and is then designed into a behavioral objective. For example, a classroom objective may be to introduce students to the theme of space-age careers. The following is a behavioral objective derived from such a broad objective:

Given a question about space-age career options, the student will be able to name at least three such careers and describe two ways in which the careers benefit society.

Why should you use behavioral objectives? There are many reasons; behavioral objectives will help you to determine

1. If the accomplishment of the stated objective is really of any value to the total development of the student
2. If the student has accomplished the objective:
   a. If there are related objectives within the theme that are to be designed and utilized at this time
   b. Methods of instruction and performance level needed for implementation of related objectives
3. If the student has not accomplished the objective:
   a. Whether the objective can be accomplished by this student at this time
   b. Whether the performance level of the objective was too difficult
   c. What new methods of instruction are needed to better enable the student to accomplish the objective

Information Dissemination

METHODS AND MATERIALS

Following the establishment of groups, needs, and objectives, the teacher will determine methods of instruction for each group. For example, although you may reinforce reading and language arts skills whenever you teach content specific subjects, you may choose to allot 1 hour each morning for reinforcing the basic processes and skills of reading. Obviously, you will not be able to meet with each group for the entire period, so it is wise to develop methods of instruction that could be operationalized without your immediate physical presence. You still manage the entire program, but you need not always be directly involved with the instructional input of each activity.

In developing these activities, you will refer to the specific behavioral objectives you established to enable you to determine the nature of the learning experience as well as the method and materials that would be used to convey the information. Information can be conveyed in a variety of ways, some of which are (1) the teacher, (2) the text, and (3) other instructional media. Some examples of instructional media are

1. Reference books	6. Films
2. Trade books	7. Records
3. Magazines	8. Tape recordings
4. Maps	9. Video recorders
5. Models	10. Computer software

All these materials can be considered as classroom aids. Each medium has particular capabilities that make it an effective instructional tool. Understanding these capabilities will allow the teacher to create meaningful instruction that does not require your direct physical presence.

CLASSROOM AIDS

Audio Aids.   Audio equipment includes record players, radios, language laboratories, telelectures, and tape recorders. The portability and relatively low cost of such equipment increase their classroom utility. The tape recorder can be used to highlight developmental language creativity by designing a sound collage that involves collecting environmental or commonplace sounds on tape, camouflaging these sounds through speed modification and tape loops, and then organizing and combining the sounds to form new combinations of sounds.

The sound collage can be used in a variety of ways: as a composition of its own, in a study of sound classification, or as a stimulus for creative writing.

The language laboratory is used primarily to offer students instruction in foreign languages. Students listen to a recording and then verbally model the sounds they have heard. The teacher is able to monitor this experience through a mechanical device that enables him or her to listen to the conversation. The idea of the language laboratory has been incorporated within many reading programs because of its ability to provide specialized individualized attention for students in developing language and listening skills. It is also valuable for students whose native language is not English.

The telelecture enables groups of students to listen to prearranged conversations with renowned speakers. For example, a class studying the undersea world might greatly desire to speak personally with Jacques Cousteau.

Audio devices can be used in isolation or in conjunction with visual aids to create the setting necessary to experience totally pictorial representations. For example, music by Palestrina would enhance one's learning about the Renaissance. Audio devices not only offer the means to reach large groups, but they also provide an opportunity for individual student tutoring. Your role as the teacher becomes less burdensome because you are freed from repeating lessons.

Visual Aids.   Visual aids primarily include chalkboards, bulletin boards, opaque projectors, filmstrip and overhead projectors, teaching machines,

Using audio and visual aids enhances the classroom teacher's ability to provide individualized instruction. The teacher can utilize available curriculum materials that are based on sequential development. (Photo by Linda Lungren.)

textbooks, and video recorders. Of all the visual aids, the textbook is the one most frequently used. In many classes, the textbook is the major information source, and teachers are viewed as extensions of textbooks. Alternatively, the teacher may serve as the central factor synthesizing information from many textbook sources. The chalkboard is closely identified with this process because it has been used in learning situations for decades as a tool by which information can be transmitted.

Another long-time classroom material used to transmit information has been the display or bulletin board. Two-dimensional demonstrations are often found on felt, bulletin, or display boards. Through these sources, information can quickly be conveyed or reinforced.

The filmstrip projector is certainly the most commonly found projector in American schools. Filmstrips, made from 35mm film, can be used by individuals or groups of students. This instructional device also frees the teacher for working with individuals who are having difficulty with particular concepts.

The slide projector can be used to impart visual information as well as to spark creativity. By combining tapes and groups of slides that are prepared commercially or by the teacher or the students themselves, an audiovisual production can be made. With the accessibility of inexpensive cameras and slide development, the slide show can serve as a means of personal expression for student work.

Optical reflection is the principle on which the opaque projector operates. A darkened classroom is required for use because light is reflected off the projected material. This projector is widely used by students who wish to view photographs, drawings, documents, or other such materials. The opaque projector, like many other visual and audio aids, is a means of transmitting information without the total aid of the classroom teacher.

The overhead projector is also found in many school environments. It is used to transmit information to both large and small groups and it presents tables, graphs, and lists with considerable clarity.

Teaching machines that convey information on just about every subject are found in many classrooms. Although automated features may be characteristic of some teaching machines, this is not standard. Teaching machines differ primarily in their presentation of information and questioning.

Many educators look askance at programmed material and teaching machines because of their early use as review, drill, and testing. Although today's programs still serve these objectives, they are also being designed to individualize programs for independent study.

Using audio and visual aids enhances the classroom teacher's ability to provide individualized instruction. The teacher can utilize available curriculum materials that are based on sequential development. Students can be matched to materials according to their strongest learning modality. Finally, use of these classroom aids may provide the teacher with more planning time.

Multisensory Aids.   Media that involve more than one sense in the learning experience are commonly referred to as multisensory aids. Motion pictures, television, video recorders, sand tables, sandpaper cutouts, indented objects, and felt or velvet boards are the most common multisensory aids found in educational settings.

The use of motion pictures primarily involves the senses of hearing and sight, as well as the extension of emotional and other human experiences. Simplicity of operation and a vast range of personal involvement have been two prime factors in encouraging motion picture adoption as a teacher aid. Students can explore their own world and those of others through film.

Television is a medium that has advantages similar to those of film. While offering students the possibility of exploring the lives of others, television also capitalizes on the present, providing students with an opportunity for involvement in events as they happen.

In recent years, most schools have acquired *video recorders*. Video recordings combine the advantages of film and television; in addition, the greatest advantage may be that particular video recordings can be shown when it is most beneficial for the students rather than relying on TV schedules or schedules for borrowing films. They can also be used to record in-class or in-school productions, much to the students' delight.

Computer Aids.   The use of computers in today's society and also in the classroom is underemphasized even by the word "revolution." Today's young students will one day not remember a time without computers, much as the students of the 1950s don't remember times without television. As O'Donnell (1982) says, "Computers are not a fad, they are not too expensive, and they won't go away" (p. 490). Even so, some teachers seem reluctant to use this type of classroom aid.

In a recent survey (Lungren, Lapp, and Flood, 1983), language arts teachers were asked if they were reticent to enroll in computer courses. Of the 150 (K–12) teachers polled, 87 percent stated that they were reticent because they found that the literature addressed them as though they were computer programmers rather than computer users. As computer users, they felt they needed help in understanding the computer as an *educational tool* that could be used to facilitate individualized and small-group instruction. Recent advances in both computer hardware and software are reducing the need for teachers to have a strong knowledge of computer programming. Higher-quality commercial software programs and increasingly user-friendly educational authoring languages are begin-

Effective instructional use of microcomputers in the classroom will become a reality only when teachers understand how to integrate computer-assisted instruction into the curriculum. (Photo by Linda Lungren.)

ning to make the microcomputer a more practical and nonthreatening instructional and management tool.

But the effective instructional use of microcomputers in the classroom will become a reality only when teachers understand how to integrate computer-assisted instruction (CAI) into the curriculum. Through preservice/inservice instruction, teachers need to be taught how to use the computer as an instructional tool. Investigate the offerings of your local school district, nearby districts, or institutions of higher learning. If you do not find the instruction you are seeking, suggest the topic for upcoming seminars. Teachers at all grade levels in all content areas would welcome the opportunity to learn how the computer can be used as an educational tool.

Computer-assisted instruction is too vast a subject to be condensed in a short space, but the following information will give you a brief overview with references you can explore further.

Computer-related Glossary.   The following terms will be useful to you in exploring computer-assisted instruction.

Courseware: Computer programs written especially for educational purposes.
Disk: Can be either "floppy" or "hard." A disk is used to store computer programs. A "floppy" disk is small and inexpensive and made of flexible material. A "hard" disk contains more information and accesses that information faster than does a "floppy" disk.
Disk Drive: The "record player" of the computer. The disk drive transfers information from the disk to the memory of the computer.
Memory: The amount of characters of information that can be stored by the computer. ROM—permanent memory of computer; RAM—temporary memory of the computer.
Microcomputer: Small, self-contained desktop computers such as the Apple, IBM, Kaypro, Commodore, TRS-80, Atari, and PET.
Modem: Device for communicating to a computer via a telephone line. Electronic bulletin boards are accessed via a modem.
Program: A set of instructions or commands composed of letters, symbols, or words for directing computers to perform desired operations.
Software: Programs (set of instructions) that govern the operation of a computer. (Hardware is the computer itself.)
Teachers' utility: A utility program that assists the teacher in producing customized materials used in teaching, such as crossword puzzles, multiple choice tests, parent reports, and gradebooks.
Word processing program: Software that turns the computer into a "typewriter." It allows correcting, editing, rearranging, and storing information before printing.

Computer Journals for Educators.   The following journals will provide helpful resources for using the computer in education.

Classroom Computer Learning
Pitman Learning, Inc.
19 Davis Drive
Belmont, Calif. 94002

Computer-Using Educators (CUE)—organization and journal
P.O. Box 18547
San Jose, Calif. 95158

Computers, Reading, and Language Arts (CRLA)
P.O. Box 13247
Oakland, Calif. 94661–0247

Electronic Learning and Teaching and Computers
Scholastic, Inc.
730 Broadway
New York, N.Y. 10033

Infoworld, The Newsweekly for Microcomputer Users
375 Cochituate Road
Framingham, Mass. 01701

Personal Computing
P.O. Box 2941
Boulder, Colo. 80321

Plus numerous specialized computer magazines for specific computer systems.

Computer Uses in the Classroom.   Computers can be used in two important ways when planning and implementing a reading program. First, CAI can be used to bolster the teacher's ability to teach both basic and more abstract communication skills. Second, the teacher can use CMI (computer-managed instruction) to facilitate classroom management tasks.

Computer-Assisted Instruction.   There are a variety of commercially produced software programs for reading and language arts. These programs run the gamut from drill and practice in spelling and vocabulary to speed reading. Programs in the area of composition and more advanced writing skills development (computer-based invention) are also emerging. These programs combine selected CAI programs with word processing programs. Schwartz (1984) advocates the use of computerized word processing with the observation:

> Word processing can change the way students write and their attitudes toward writing. In fact, the protean malleability of text with word processing is ideally suited for tutoring students in writing improvement. Writing is not like arithmetic with discrete, masterable component units. It is more like producing a symphony, with different parts cooperating to produce an overall effect. The players need to get through the piece, even if it isn't very good the first time. (pp. 239–240)

Bean (1983) also found that computerized word processing had positive effects on students' editing and revision of written work.

When selecting CAI for your classroom, it is important to consider several factors. First, what are the particular instructional needs of your students? Are there glaring gaps or weaknesses in the curriculum that CAI might help to alleviate? What seem to be the major instructional needs of students who are having great difficulty acquiring basic skills? What instruction might be beneficial for accelerated students? Can selected CAI programs address these individual needs?

Once you have decided upon the desired content, it is then important to evaluate individual software programs for their instructional quality. Brown, Lewis, and Harcleroad (1983) suggest that teachers ask the following questions when evaluating instructional software:

1. Will the program run on your brand or model of microcomputer?
2. Does the program run well? Is it free of errors in language and content? Are instructions clear and concise? Can the students control the pace of instruction (when appropriate)?
3. Does the program take advantage of the computer capability to be an interactive learning tool? Is feedback truly instructional? (pp. 552–553).

Many authors have exhibited a concern with software evaluation, and numerous evaluation forms have been developed. Several computer magazines now devote a section to software product reviews so more and more information is now available to the prospective consumer. However, one must approach these reviews critically.

Consider the source of the review and the background of the reviewer. Is the review unnecessarily focused on technical quality with an exclusion of content validity? Is the review unnecessarily biased toward creativity, with content being considered secondarily?

It would be in your best interest as the classroom manager to select an evaluation system that works for you and to use the evaluation regularly and consistently. Cumbersome forms will not be filled out, so use one that is concise, readily available, and informative. We have chosen to include the Lungren Quick Software Review to illustrate an evaluation that presents pertinent information in a concise manner (see Figure 15-2).

A review such as this will provide useful information to you as well as to other teachers at your school.

Computer-Managed Instruction.   The micrcomputer can also be used as a powerful management tool. Record-keeping software can assist the teacher in monitoring and evaluating individual student progress. With this information, the teacher can guide students through a sequence of custom-made instructional activities. Such programs also provide the teacher with an easily accessible printed profile of each student, which can aid in the accountability process.

Other types of CMI include programs in text readability levels, test administration, cloze tests, and assessment. These programs can help the

LUNGREN QUICK SOFTWARE REVIEW

Program name: _____ Publisher address: _____

_____

Price: _____ No. of disks: _____ Backup Disks? _____
Computer brand/model: _____

Peripherals:

_____ paddles/joystick   _____ voice digitizer   _____ color monitor

_____ disk drive(s)   _____ cassette   _____ printer

_____ other

Type of work:

_____ Independent   _____ Team   _____ Teacher Directed

Ease or difficulty of use (i.e., documentation: code words, etc.) _____

_____

Instructional system–drill/practice tutorial _____

simulation game word processing _____

teacher utility etc.: _____

Management system/record keeping:

_____ on disk/long term   _____ short term/on screen   _____ provided in manual/paper

_____ aid/hindrance

Grade level:

Concept _____   Actual format _____

Objectives (skills): _____

_____

General reaction: _____

_____

Anticipated student reaction to program: _____

_____

Subject area:

How can this be used in *my* classroom? _____

_____

Where does it fit into *my* curricular design? _____

_____

Can I modify this program to suit my needs? (words lists, etc.)

_____ yes   _____ no

Would I purchase this software (why/why not)? _____

_____

Figure 15-2. Lungren Quick Software Review

teacher to evaluate a variety of instructional materials to determine their appropriateness for students.

The computer can be used in many ways to enhance the teacher's over-all instructional effectiveness. If you still are unsure about the pros and cons of computers, you may wish to examine content area books focusing on specific applications of the micrcomputer in the classroom.

Selected Computer Education References

Grady, M., and J. Gawronski (eds.). *Computers in Curriculum and Instruction.* Alexandria, Virginia: Association for Supervision and Curriculum Development, 1983.

Hofmeister, Alan. *Micromputer Applications in the Classroom.* New York: Holt, Rinehart and Winston, 1984.

Lathrop, Ann, and B. Goodson. *Courseware in the Classroom.* Reading, Mass.: Addison-Wesley Publishing Company, 1983.

Mason, G., J. Blancard, and D. Daniel. *Computer Applications in Reading.* Newark, Dela.: International Reading Association, 1983.

NEA Educational Computer Service. *The Yellow Book of Computer Products for Education.* Bethesda, Md.: NEA Educational Computer Service, 4720 Montgomery Lane, 20814, 1984 (annual revisions).

Standifor, A., K. Jaycey, and A. Auten. *Computers in the English Classroom: A Primer for Teachers.* Urbana, Ill.: National Council for Teachers of English, 1982.

Willis, J., D. Johnson, and P. Dixon. *Computers, Teaching, and Learning: A Guide to Using Computers in Schools.* Beaverton, Ore.: Dilithium Press, 1984.

LEARNING PRESCRIPTIONS

The instructional media just discussed can help you to personalize your learning environment. Providing each student with an individualized prescriptive learning packet will encourage his or her active participation in the learning process. Each packet contains the daily learning assignments as well as grouping arrangements for each student. Assignments and grouping arrangements are determined through formal and informal assessment techniques. Such a system will allow the classroom teacher to meet the various needs of all students yet maintain a manageable program. Classroom arrangement facilitates the addressing of individual needs and accommodates short-term grouping situations. The size and composition of the groups fluctuates in response to the rate of individual skill development. A well-designed reading class is presented in Figure 15-3.

1. Three students who were members of group C and two students from group D were reading directions, discussing plans, and building a scale model rocket. These students were working in the building production area.

2. Three students from group D were in the committee meeting area dis-

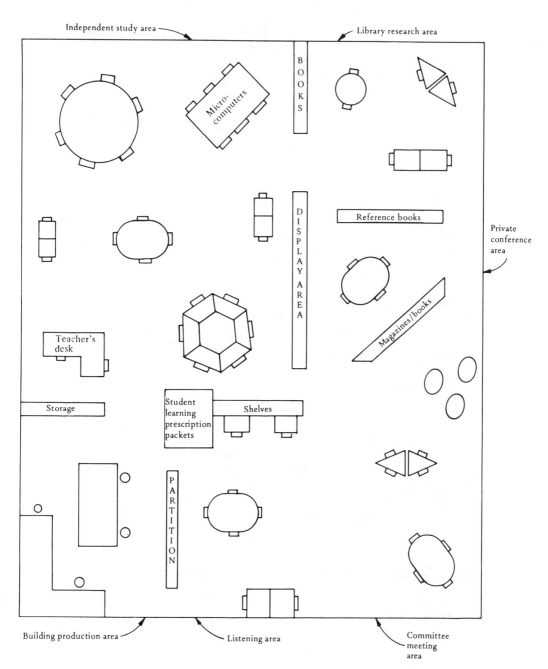

Figure 15-3. Well-designed classroom

cussing their answers to a set of study questions that involved their ability to sequence information as well as predict and hypothesize future similar events. Four students from group E were also working in the committee meeting area, discussing changes and revisions in a play script.

3. Three students from group D were working independently on their assignments. These students were dispersed throughout the independent study area as well as the library, because their learning prescriptions required use of the card catalog and reference books.

4. Two students from group B and two students from group C were sitting together in the independent study area reading a newspaper story and developing a time line. This activity aided the students in understanding sequential development, which is essential for total comprehension.

5. One student also from group C and one from group B were in the listening area listening to a newscast. All these students were interested in media and social-political events. Their assignment was to listen for cause-effect social happenings presented by the newscasters. After the newscast, these students were asked to survey the morning newspaper to determine if they had accurately interpreted the newscast.

6. Two other students from group B were in the independent study area working on a computer-assisted instructional program that supplements their basal reader.

7. One student from group A was in the listening area equipped with a headphone set. He was listening to and reading a primer. This activity reinforced basic sight-word reading skills.

8. Two other children from group A were with the teacher in the private conference tutorial area discussing a basal story they had just finished reading.

How can so many students be involved in such a variety of instructional activities simultaneously? The key is a system of management through learning prescriptive contracts. This approach enables students to take responsibility for their work tasks. A prescriptive contract is simply a note to each student that specifies (1) daily goals, (2) assignments and time schedule, and (3) grouping arrangements. Each student's prescriptions are kept in a manila folder for easy reference. The following is an example of a prescriptive contract for a student named Erin:

Good morning, Erin!

Please work on the following:

9:00–10:30 A.M.
1. End-of-Unit Test, p. 31, in *Signs of the Times*.
2. After the test, you may do any *two* of the following:
   a. Continue editing and revising your short story (due Friday).
   b. Browse through the science books in the library to get an idea of what you might do for your science project.
   c. Work on one of the study skills worksheets (level F) in the independent study area.

We'll check your test together later, and then I'll give you reading assignments for Tuesday and Wednesday.

10:30–10:45 A.M.   Clean-up and break.

10:45–11:30 A.M.
   Math—Please complete the math assignment from last Friday. If you have trouble with the ratio problems, ask Jim, Tokiko, or Carla for help. Also, finish lesson 6 in your math book. Continue to work on this task on Tuesday and Wednesday.

11:30 A.M.–12:15 P.M.
   Science (Monday–Wednesday)—Work with your group on the science experiment we discussed last Thursday. Refer to contract sheet no. 23 for specific instructions.

12:15–1:15 P.M. Lunch.

1:15–2:00 P.M.
   Social Studies—Meet in the independent study area. Complete your project. I'll assign new groups on Tuesday.

2:00–2:15 P.M.   Clean-up and break.

2:15–2:30 P.M.
   On Monday please meet me in the private conference area. We'll talk about your work. On Tuesday and Wednesday you may use this time to finish a task of your choice, or you may choose a new area of interest. You might like to read the new *Discover* magazine.

2:30–3:00 P.M.
   Complete the unfinished tasks or engage in
   1. Reading your library book
   2. Rehearsing your oral presentation
   3. Reading a magazine
   4. Completing a bonus mystery packet (level F)

Erin, if you have anything you want to share with me, please write it on the attached sheet. Have a good day and I'll see you tomorrow.

Although each student's tasks are clearly stated in the prescriptive learning packet, the teacher must continually mingle with groups of students, as well as individuals, to determine if any immediate issues need to take precedence over the prescriptive task. Each student has many individual encounters with the teacher during any given day.

Although initially time consuming, the use of individual learning prescriptions allows the teacher to monitor and evaluate individual student progress quite effectively. Continuous evaluation is an essential part of a good reading program because succeeding assignments are based on the competencies and needs of each student as he or she completes his or her tasks.

From observation and teacher report, we have found that it takes a teacher approximately 10 to 12 minutes to review a student's completed prescription. Given a class of twenty-six students, if a teacher develops each prescription for three-day periods and reviews seven to nine prescriptions daily, the total daily time spent on this process is approximately 2 hours. This 1- to 2-hour process requires no more time than the daily grading of individual workbooks and worksheets in a more traditional nonindividualized classroom.

When developing, evaluating, and replanning a student's prescriptive program, it is useful to ask the following questions.

1. Is the student successfully completing the learning task?
2. How can I continue to motivate this learner?
3. Does the student work better at long or short assignments?
4. How can I best reinforce each student's learning successes?
5. What types of materials are most meaningful and interesting to this student?
6. How can I encourage the student to take more responsibility for his or her learning?
7. What learning techniques encourage the effective development of memory skills?
8. How can I best help this learner to transfer what has been learned in one subject area to other areas?
9. How can I best encourage the student to synthesize and generalize the information being learned?
10. How can I best encourage the student to make evaluative decisions about the validity of the information being learned?

By answering these questions, the teacher is able continually to evaluate what has been mastered and to plan the next step for each student. You may also want to pursue these questions if you are interested in implementing program strategies.

Assessment, Recycling, and Sequential Learning

It is important to remember that you will be constantly evaluating each student's progress against your general and behavioral objectives. This assessment will help you to determine the effectiveness of your instructional program, and it will be a "red flag" to you if a particular student is either having undue difficulty or needs to have his or her learning prescription reevaluated.

Students who are successfully meeting objectives will be given new challenges as your various groups change, both in content and in the student composition. Well-managed sequential learning activities are at the core of a successful instructional program.

With the help of an educational management system, you can survey, plan, implement, reimplement, or sequence an integrated theme. Continuous evaluation is the prime ingredient for success in a program of this type. A system of management enables you, as a teacher, to state clearly desired terminal behaviors, evaluate instructional effectiveness, and determine sequential learning.

Mastery of instruction may be affected by the amount of instructional time utilized for topical presentation, background readiness of your students, manner or method of presentation, complexity of material, and student interest. As suggested in earlier chapters, instruction needs to be carefully sequenced to encourage the students to formulate the concept, interpret the information, and apply the learned principles and facts. The works of Piaget (1959), Gagné (1965), Bloom (1967), and Taba (1967) offer many insights into the educational procedures that should be used when you are sequencing instruction.

As you review the information in this chapter, consider the following facts:

1. Sequencing instruction through the aid of a management system enables you to avoid a hit-or-miss, ineffectual type of teaching.
2. Sequencing instruction through the use of a management system enables students to proceed according to their developing competencies.
3. Sequencing instruction through the aid of a management system enables you to manage complex skills better by presenting them in smaller, subordinate parts.
4. Sequencing instruction through the aid of a management system enables you to develop a clearer understanding of how students learn.

Remember that a program of this type is certainly not a "new idea." You will be able to succeed in your attempts if you always remain cognizant of the following facts:

1. Students are not "on their own" in learning. The degree of decision-making responsibility shared by the student must be commensurate with his or her experience and ability. It is the teacher's responsibility to plan the program and thus guide each student's independence and initiative in learning situations. The learner will, however, have a new role in the individualized program. A student will no longer be found resting contentedly in a program where all of the decisions are made for him or her. You will provide each with options, and from these options the student will choose what, where, when, and how to pursue the learning task. Students in your classroom will no longer know the frustrations of being tagged a "slow learner." Through individualized learning prescriptions, students will no longer pursue learning in a lockstep fashion.
2. The degree of program individualization must depend on the task to be accomplished, the readiness exposures of the student for the given task, and your abilities to manage multiple methods for accomplishing a given task. You may be more successful in your attempts to individualize your program if you start with only one content area. Once you

are successful with initial attempts, you may want to expand the program. You are the program manager. Be careful not to design a program that you are unable to manage.

3. Use the materials you currently have to individualize your program. Do not use a lack of materials as an excuse for not individualizing your curriculum. Your incentive is the prime factor in the success of these initial attempts.

4. The major portion of your time will be spent in planning instructional procedures that may be independently executed by your students. This will be difficult for you in the beginning because you have previously spent as much time implementing as planning. Your planning of learning prescriptions will be based on what the student has previously accomplished. You may want to develop anecdotal file cards or checklists to enable you to assess the competencies as they are acquired by each individual student.

5. Students will be involved with both the implementing and correcting responsibilities of their learning. Because each learning prescription will be designed with the learner as the central focus, students will feel that their efforts have been worthwhile.

6. As a teacher you are responsible for the individual development of each student. Your professional expertise must be conveyed in a variety of ways if each student is to grow intellectually and emotionally from the encounter. You cannot teach students only today's body of literal facts and expect them to be critical decision makers tomorrow. Your curriculum must encourage this growth by being custom tailored to each learner.

This program will become a reality only if you believe that there is no one best way to learn. If this is your belief, select a small portion of your curriculum and begin the process of designing a manageable individualized program. Whatever your choice, good luck in your endeavors.

Suggested Readings Related to Goals.   We encourage you at this time to review the goals at the beginning of this chapter. If you feel you would like to explore one or more of these areas in greater depth, please refer to the cross-indexed bibliography at the end of the book.

Bibliography

The boldface numbers that come after each reference refer to the goals that are itemized at the beginning of every chapter. A few references do not have these goal numbers.

Chapter 1

Baumann, J. V. "Implications for Reading Instruction from the Research on Teacher and School Effectiveness." *Journal of Reading*, 28, 2 (November, 1984), 109–117.   **2**

Birthoff, A. E. "Is Teaching Still Possible? Writing, Meaning, and Higher Order Reasoning." *College English*, 46, 8 (December, 1984), 743–755.   **2**

Cannella, G. S. "Beginning Reading: Cognitive Developmental Research." *Journal of Instructional Psychology*, 7 (Fall 1980), 139.   **1**

Cleland, C. J. "Piagetian Implications for Reading Models." *Reading World*, 20 (October 1980), 10–15.   **1**

Cohen, A., and G. G. Glass. "Lateral Dominance and Reading Ability." *The Reading Teacher*, 21 (November 1968), 343–348.   **1**

Dennard, K. "Commentary: A Black Educator Speaks About 'Black English.'" *The Reading Teacher*, 35 (November 1981), 133.   **2**

DeStefano, J. S. *Language, the Learner, and the School.* New York: John Wiley & Sons, Inc., 1978.   **1**

Dewey, J. *Experience and Education.* New York: Macmillan Publishing Company, 1938.   **1**

Drucker, P. "The New Philosophy Comes to Life." *Harper's Magazine* (August 1957), 37–40.   **1**

DuBois, D., and G. Stice. "Comprehension Instruction: Let's Call It for Repair." *Reading World*, 20 (March 1981), 173–84.   **3**

Dunn, R., and M. Garbo. "The Reading Game: How to Improve the Odds for Every Youngster." *Learning*, 8 (August–September 1979), 34–36+.   **3**

Feeley, J. T. "Teaching Non-English Speaking First-Graders to Read." *Elementary English*, 47 (February 1970), 199–208.   **2**

Flood, J., and D. Lapp. "In Search of the 'Perfect Question': Questioning Strategies for Developing Story Comprehension in Young Children." *Principal*, 56 (October 1980), 220–23.   **2**

Florio-Ruane, S., and J. Dohanick. "Research-Currents: Communicating Findings by Teacher/Researcher Deliberation." *Language Arts,* 61, 7 (November, 1984), 724–730.   2

Freire, P. "Reading the World and Reading the Word: An Interview." *Language Arts,* 62, 1 (January, 1985), 15–21.   3

Glatthorn, A. A. *A Guide for Developing an English Curriculum for the Eighties.* Urbana, Ill.: National Council of Teachers of English, 1980.   3

Goldbecker, S. S. *Reading: Instructional Approaches.* Washington, D.C.: National Education Association, 1975.   4

Gordon, W. J. J. *Synectics: The Development of Creative Capacity.* New York: Harper & Row, Publishers, 1961.   4

Guthrie, J. T. *Comprehension and Teaching: Research Reviews.* Newark, Dela.: International Reading Association, 1981.   4

Harris, L. A., and C. B. Smith, eds. *Individualizing Reading Instruction: A Reader.* New York: Holt, Rinehart and Winston, 1977.   3

Harris, T. L., and R. E. Hodges. *A Dictionary of Reading.* Newark, Dela.: International Reading Association, 1981.   3

Hoover, N. L. "Teachers' Self-Reports of Critical Decisions in Teaching Reading." *The Reading Teacher,* 38, 4 (January 1985), 440–445.   1

Hunt, R. L. "Why Teachers Fail." *The Clearing House,* 12 (April 1938), 176.   3

Jersild, A. T. *When Teachers Face Themselves.* New York: Bureau of Publications, Teachers College Press, Columbia University, 1955.   3

Johnson, T., ed. *Complete Poems of Emily Dickinson.* Boston: Little, Brown and Company, n.d.   3

King, E. M. "The Influence of Teaching on Reading Achievement." In *Reading for All,* ed. R. Karlin. Proceedings of the Fourth IRA World Congress on Reading, pp. 110–115.   3

Klein, M. L. "Key Generalizations About Language and Children." *Educational Leadership,* 38 (March 1981), 446.   3

LaBerge, D., and S. J. Samuels. "Toward a Theory of Automatic Information Processing in Reading." In *Theoretical Models and Processes of Reading,* ed. H. Singer and R. Ruddell, pp. 548–579. Newark, Dela.: International Reading Association, 1976.   3

Lapp, D. "Beyond the Redbirds, Bluebirds, and Yellowbirds." *Reporting on Reading,* 5 (March 1979), 1–9.   1

———. "Individualizing Reading Instruction Made Easy for Teacher." *Early Years* 34 (February 1977), 34–37.   1

Lenneberg, E. H. "On Explaining Language." In *Language and Reading—An Interdisciplinary Approach,* ed. D. V. Gunderson. Washington, D.C.: Center for Applied Linguistics, 1970.   1

Lohnes, P. R., and M. M. Gray. "Intelligence and the Cooperative Reading Studies." *Reading Research Quarterly,* 3 (Spring 1972), 3–25.   1

Malmquist, E. "Perspectives of Reading Research." In *Reading for All,* ed. R. Karlin. Proceedings on the Fourth IRA World Congress on Reading, pp. 142–155. Newark, Dela.: International Reading Association, 1973.   1

Menyuk, P. "Language Development and Reading." In *Understanding Reading Comprehension,* ed. J. Flood. Newark, Dela.: International Reading Association, 1984.   1

Mitchell, K. A. "Patterns of Teacher-Student Responses to Oral Reading Errors as Related to Teachers' Theoretical Frameworks." *Research in the Teaching of English,* 14 (October 1980), 259.   1

Neuman, S. B. "Effect of Teaching Auditory Perceptual Skills on Reading

Achievement in First Grade." *The Reading Teacher*, 34 (January 1981), 422–426.   1

Noyce, R. M. "Try the Enrichment Triad in Reading Class." *Journal of Reading*, 24 (January 1981), 326–330.   4

Philadelphia Teachers' Learning Cooperative. "On Becoming Teacher Experts: Buying Time." *Language Arts*, 61, 7 (November 1984), 731–736.   1

Piaget, J. *Plays, Dreams, and Imitation in Childhood*. New York: W. W. Norton & Company, Inc., 1962.   4

Preston, E. F. "Those We Flunked." *The Clearing House*, 12 (April 1938), 176.   4

Robinson, D. *Preparation for Teaching: Making It Relevant*. Washington, D.C.: National Education Association, 1982.   1

Rousseau, J. J. *Emile, Julie, and Other Writings*. New York: Barron's Educational Series, Inc., 1964.   2

Santa, C. M., and B. L. Hayes. *Children's Prose Comprehension: Research and Practice*. Newark, Dela.: International Reading Association, 1981.   2

Silbiger, F., and D. Woolf. "Perceptual Difficulties Associated with Reading Disability." *College Reading Association Proceedings*, 6 (Fall 1965), 98–102.   2

Singer, H. "A Century of Landmarks in Reading and Learning from Text at the High School Level: Research, Theories, and Instructional Strategies." *Journal of Reading*, 26 (January 1983), 332–341.   4

Skinner, B. F. *Beyond Freedom and Dignity*. New York: Alfred A. Knopf, Inc., 1972.   2

Smith, D. "The Future of Teacher Evaluation: Needed Research and Practices." A Draft of a paper presented for the Future of Teachers Education Conference, Texas A&M University, College of Education, College Station, Tex., May 1982.   2

Spache, G. D. "Psychological and Cultural Factors in Learning to Read." In *Reading for All*, ed. R. Karlin. Proceedings of the Fourth IRA World Congress on Reading, pp. 671–679. Newark, Dela.: International Reading Association, 1973.   2

Spivak, G. C. "Reading the World: Literacy Studies in the 80's." *College English*, 43 (November 1981), 671–679.   2

Stewig, J. W. "Planning Environments to Promote Language Growth." In *Discovering Language with Children*, ed. G. S. Pinnell. Urbana, Ill.: National Council of Teachers of English, 1980, 52–55.   4

Susi, G. L. "The Teacher/Writer: Model, Learner, Human Being." *Language Arts*, 61, 7 (November 1984), 712–716.   3

Tinker, M., and C. M. McCullough. *Teaching Elementary Reading*, 4th ed. Englewood Cliffs, N.J.: Prentice-Hall, Inc., 1975.   4

Tremans-Ziremba, M., J. Michayluk, and L. Taylor. "Examination of Some Predictors of Reading Achievement in Grade 4 Children." *Reading Improvement*, 17 (Winter 1980), 264.   4

Wanat, S. F. "Language Acquisitions: Basic Issues." *The Reading Teacher*, 25 (November 1971), 142–47.   4

White, N. J. "I've Taught Them All." *The Clearing House*, 12 (November 1937), 151, 192.   4

Wolf, T. "Reading Reconsidered." In *Thought and Language/Language and Reading*, ed. M. Wolf, M. McQuillan, and E. Radwin, pp. 109–127. Cambridge, Mass.: President and Fellows of Harvard College, 1980.   1

Chapter 2

Almy M. "The Importance of Children's Experience to Success in Beginning Reading." In *Research in the Three R's*, ed. J. Hunnicutt and W. Iverson, 48–52. New York: Harper & Row, Publishers, 1958.   **1–4**

Alyeshmerni, M., and P. Tauber. *Working with Aspects of Language*. New York: Harcourt Brace Jovanovich, Inc., 1975.   **2**

Anderson, P., and D. Lapp. *Language Skills in Elementary Education*. New York: Macmillan Publishing Company, 1979.   **1–4**

Babbs, P., and A. Moe. "Metacognition: A Key for Independent Learning from Text." *Reading Teacher*, 36 (January 1983), 422–426.   **1**

Beck, I. L. *A Longitudinal Study of the Reading Achievement Effects of Formal Reading Instruction in the Kindergarten: A Summative and Formative Evaluation*. Unpublished doctoral dissertation, University of Pittsburgh, 1973.   **2**

Berko-Gleason, J. "The Child's Learning of English Morphology." *Word*, 14 (1958), 150–177.   **2**

Brown, R., and C. Fraser. "The Acquisition of Syntax." In *Verbal Behavior and Learning*, ed. C. N. Cofer and B. Musgrave, 158–197. New York: McGraw-Hill Book Company, 1963.   **2**

Bullock, Sir A. *A Language for Life*. Report for the British Government, 1975.   **1**

Chapparo, J. "A New Look at Language Experience." In *A Successful Foundation for Reading in a Second Language Conference*, San Diego, Calif., February 1975.   **2**

Chomsky, C. S. *The Acquisition of Syntax in Children from 5 to 10*. Cambridge, Mass.: M.I.T. Press, 1969.   **2**

Chomsky, N. *Syntactic Structures*. Gravenhage: Mouton, 1962.

———. *Aspects of the Theory of Syntax*. Cambridge, Mass.: M.I.T. Press, 1965.   **2**

———. *Language and Mind*. New York, Harcourt Brace Jovanovich, 1972.   **2**

Clark, H. H. "Semantics and Comprehension." In *Current Trends in Linguistics*, Vol. 12, *Linguistics and Adjacent Art Sciences*, ed. T. A. Sebeok. The Hague: Mouton, 1976.   **2**

Dasch, A. "Aligning Basal Reader Instruction with Cognitive Stage Theory." *Reading Teacher*, 36 (January 1983), 428–434.   **1**

DeFord, D., and J. Harste. "Child Language Research and Curriculum." *Language Arts*, 6 (September 1982), 590–600.   **2**

Durkin, D. *Children Who Read Early: Two Longitudinal Studies*. New York: Bureau of Publications, Teachers College Press, Columbia University, 1966.   **3**

———. "Listen to Your Children." *Instructor*, 8 (February 1972), 87–88.   **1**

———. *Teaching Young Children to Read*, 3rd ed. Boston: Allyn & Bacon, Inc., 1980.   **1–4**

———. *Teaching Them to Read*, 4th ed. Boston: Allyn & Bacon, Inc., 1983.   **1–4**

Flood, J. "Parental Styles in Reading Episodes with Young Children." *The Reading Teacher*, 30 (May 1977), 864–867.   **3**

Flood, J., and P. Salus. *Language and the Language Arts*. Englewood Cliffs, N.J.: Prentice-Hall, Inc., 1984.   **2**

Fox, B. "'Freshness and the Growth of Autonomy in Children's Poetry." *Language Arts*, 62, 1 (January, 1985), 22–33.   **2**

Hess, R. D., and V. C. Shipman. "Early Experience and the Socialization of Cognitive Modes in Children." *Child Development*, 36 (1965), 869–886.   1

Indrisano, R., and J. Gurry. "In Search of Structure, Reading and Televison." In *Promoting Reading Comprehension*, ed. J. Flood. Newark, Dela.: International Reading Association, 1984.   4

Jakobson, R. *Kindersprache, Aphasie, und Allegmeine Lautgesetze*. Uppsals: Almquist and Wiksell, 1941. English translation, *Child Language, Aphasia and Phonological Universals*. The Hague: Mouton, 1968.   2

Jones, J. P. *Intersensory Transfer, Perceptual Shifting, Modal Preference, and Reading*. Newark, Dela.: International Reading Association, 1972.   3

Kagan, J. *Change and Continuity in Infancy*. New York: John Wiley & Sons, Inc., 1971.   3

Lambert, D., M. Bramwell, and G. Lawter (eds.). *The Brain: A User's Manual*. New York: Perigee Books, 1982.   1

Leifer, G. "Children's Theater Workshop." Cambridge, Mass.: Harvard Educational Workshop, 1974.   4

Lenneberg, E. H. *Biological Foundations of Language*. New York: John Wiley & Sons, Inc., 1967.   2

MacKinnon, P. *How Do Children Learn to Read?* Montreal: The Copp Clark Co., 1959.   **1–4**

McCarthy, D. "Language Development in Children." In *Manual of Child Psychology*, 2nd ed., ed. L. Carmichael, pp. 492–639. New York: John Wiley & Sons, Inc., 1954.   1

Menyuk, P. "Language Development and Reading," In *Understanding Reading Comprehension*, ed. J. Flood, 101–121. Newark, Dela.: International Reading Association, 1984.   2

National Council of Teachers of English. "Essentials of English." *College English*, 45 (February 1983), 184–189.   2

Piaget, J. *The Origins of Intelligence in Children*. New York: W. W. Norton & Company, Inc., 1963.   1

Ploghoft, M., and W. Sheldon. "Television Viewing Skills." In *Teaching Reading Through the Arts*, ed. J. Cowen, 11–33. Newark, Dela.: International Reading Association, 1983.   4

Poincaré, H. *Science and Hypothesis*. New York: Dover Publications, Inc., 1952.

Probst, R. "Film, Television, and Reality." *English Journal*, 72 (January 1983), 86–89.   1

Roser, N. L. "Electric Company Critique: Can Great Be Good Enough?" *The Reading Teacher*, 17 (April 1972), 680–684.   4

Rumelhart, D., and D. Norman. "Analogical Processes in Learning," in *Cognitive Skills and Their Acquisition*, ed. J. R. Anderson, 335–360. Hillsdale, N.J.: Lawrence Erlbaum Associates, 1981.   **1–4**

Slobin, D. I. *Psycholinguistics*. Glenview, Ill.: Scott, Foresman and Company, 1979.   2

Spache, G. D., and E. B. Spache. *Reading in the Elementary School*, 4th ed. Boston: Allyn & Bacon, Inc., 1977.   **1–4**

Steinberg, H. "Reading and TV Viewing—Complementary Activities." *Journal of Reading*, 26 (March 1983), 510–514.   4

Sternberg, R. J. "Component Processes in Analogical Reasoning." *Psychological Review*, 84, 4 (1977), 353–378.   **1–4**

Sternberg. R. J. (ed.). *Handbook of Human Intelligence*. New York: Cambridge University Press, 1982.   1

Swift, M. "Training Poverty Mothers in Communication Skills." *The Reading Teacher*, 23 (January 1970), 360–367.   3

Templin, M. *Certain Language Skills in Children*. Minneapolis: University of Minnesota Press, 1957.   4

Vernon, M. D. "The Perceptual Process in Reading." *The Reading Teacher*, 13 (October 1959), 2–8.   1

Vygotsky, L. S. *Thought and Language*. Cambridge, Mass.: M.I.T. Press, 1962.   2

Chapter 3

Anderson, P. S., and D. Lapp. *Language Skills in Elementary Education*. New York: Macmillan Publishing Company, 1979.   1

Bellugi, U., and R. Brown, eds. *The Acquisition of Language*. Monographs of the Society for Research in Child Development, No. 29, 1964.   1

Berry, K. S. "Talking to Learn Subject Matter/Learning Subject Matter Talk." *Language Arts*, 62,1 (January, 1985), 34–42.   3

Brandenburg, R. "The Language of a Three-Year-Old Child." *Pedagogical Review*, 21 (March 1915), 89.   3

Burrows, A. T., et al. *They All Wanted to Write*. New York: Holt, Rinehart and Winston, 1964, p. 88.   4

Carroll, J. B. "Language Development." In *Child Language*, ed. A. Bar-Adon and F. L. Weiner, pp. 200–211. Englewood Cliffs, N.J.: Prentice-Hall, Inc., 1971.   3

Cazden, C. "Environments for Language Learning." *Language Arts*, 60 (January 1983), 121–122.   1

Collins, C. "The Power of Expressive Writing in Reading Comprehension." *Language Arts*, 62,1 (January, 1985), 48–54.   4

Combs, W. E. "Further Effects of Sentence Combining Practice on Writing Ability." *Research in the Teaching of English* (Fall 1976), 147.   4

Davis, F. "In Defense of Grammar." *English Education*, 16,3 (October, 1984), 151–164.   3

Devine, T. G. "Listening: What Do We Know After Fifty Years of Research and Theorizing?" *Journal of Reading*, 21 (January 1978), 296–304.   2

Dunn, S., and E. Gaffney. "Poems." *College English*, 46,8 (December, 1984), 795–796).   1

Feldman, A. K. "The Effect of Reinforcement of Listening Skills of the Culturally Deprived." Master's thesis, The Ohio State University, Columbus, 1967.   2

Flood, J., and D. Lapp. *Language/Reading Instruction for the Young Child*. New York: Macmillan Publishing Company, 1981.   1

Flood, J., and P. H. Salus. *Language and the Language Arts*. Englewood Cliffs, N.J.: Prentice-Hall, Inc., 1984.   1

Foley, D. *Teaching Writing in the Elementary Curriculum*. Indianapolis: Indianapolis Public Schools/Lilly Endowment, Inc., 1981.   4

Friedman, P. G. *Listening Processes: Attention, Understanding, Evaluation. What Research Says to the Teacher*. Washington, D.C.: National Education Association, 1978.   2

Fulwiler, T. "Writing and Learning, Grade Three." *Language Arts*, 62,1 (January, 1985), 55–59.

Gere, A. R. "Teaching Writing Teachers." *College English*, 47,1 (January, 1985), 58–65.   4

Glatthorn, A. A. *A Guide for Developing an English Curriculum for the Eighties.* Urbana, Ill.: National Council of Teachers of English, 1980.   1

Hayes, J. R., and L. Flower. "The Process of Writing." In *Cognitive Processes in Writing*, ed. L. Gregg and E. Steinberg, 3–30. Potomac, Md.: Lawrence Erlbaum Associates, 1980.   4

Joos, M. *The Fine Clocks.* New York: Harcourt Brace Jovanovich, 1967.

Indrisano, R. "Reading and Writing Revisited." *Ginn Occasional Papers*, No. 18. Lexington, Mass.: Ginn and Company, 1984.   1

Kantor, K. J. "Appreciating Children's Writing." *Language Arts*, 56 (October 1979), 742–746.   4

Kendall, J. "Fireproof Your School with Writing." *English Journal*, 74,1 (January, 1985), 59–61.

Langer, J. A. "Reading, Thinking, Writing . . . and Teaching." *Language Arts*, 59 (April 1982), 336–341.   4

Lapp, D., and J. Flood. "The Impact of Writing Instruction on Teachers' Attitudes and Practices." Yearbook National Reading Conference, ed. J. Niles, 1985 (in press).

Loban, W. *The Language of Elementary School Children.* Urbana, Ill.: National Council of Teachers of English, 1976.   1

Lundsteen, S. W. *Listening: Its Impact on Reading and the Other Language Arts*, NCTE/ERIC Clearinghouse on Reading and Communication Skills. Urbana, Ill.: National Council of Teachers of English, 1979.   2

McAfee, D. C. "Effect of Sentence-Combining Instruction on the Reading and Writing Achievement of Fifth-Grade Children in a Suburban School District." Unpublished Ph.D. dissertation, Texas Woman's University, Denton, Tex., 1980.   4

Meier, T., and C. Cazden. "Research Update: A Focus on Oral Language and Writing from a Multicultural Perspective." *Language Arts*, 59 (May 1982), 504–512.   3, 4

Mellon, J. C. *Transformational Sentence-Combining: A Method for Enhancing the Development of Syntactic Fluency in English Composition.* Urbana, Ill.: National Council of Teachers of English, 1969.   4

Menyuk, P. "Language Development and Reading." In *Understanding Reading Comprehension*, ed. J. Flood, 101–121. Newark, Dela.: International Reading Association, 1984.   1

Mollick, L. B., and K. S. Etra. "Poor Learning Ability . . . or Poor Hearing?" *Teacher*, 98 (March 1981), 42–43.   2

Murray, D. M. *A Writer Teaches Writing: A Practical Method of Teaching Composition.* Boston: Houghton Mifflin Company, 1968.   4

National Council of Teachers of English. "Essentials of English." *College English*, 45 (February 1983), 184–189.   1

O'Hare, F. *Sentence Combining: Improving Student Writing Without Formal Grammar Instruction.* Urbana, Ill.: National Council of Teachers of English, 1973.   4

Olson, D. "Perspectives: Children's Language and Language Teaching." *Language Arts*, 60 (February 1983), 226–233.   1

Pearson, P. D., and L. Fielding. "Research Update: Listening Comprehension." *Language Arts*, 59 (September 1982), 617–629.   2

Petrosky, A., and J. Brozick. "A Model for Teaching Writing Based upon Current Knowledge of the Composing Process." *English Journal* (January 1979), 96–101.   4

Russell, D. H., and E. J. Russell. "Listening Aids Through the Grades." New

York: Bureau of Publications, Teachers College Press, Columbia University, 1959.   **2**

Sager, C. "Improving the Quality of Written Composition Through Pupil Use of Rating Scale." Unpublished Ed.D. dissertation, Boston University School of Education, Boston, Mass., 1972.   **4**

Sealey, L., N. Sealey, and M. Millmore. *Children's Writing (An Approach for the Primary Grades)*. Newark, Dela.: International Reading Association, 1979.   **4**

Shane, H. G., and M. Walden, eds. *Classroom-Relevant Research in the Language Arts*. Washington, D.C.: Association for Supervision and Curriculum Development, 1978.   **1**

Smith, E. B., et al. *Language and Thinking in the Language Arts in the Elementary School*. New York: Holt, Rinehart and Winston, 1970.   **1**

Stammer, J. D. "MAPPing Out a Plan for Better Listening." *Teacher*, 98 (March 1981), 37–38.   **2**

Tierney, R., and P. D. Pearson. "Toward a Composing Model of Reading." In *Composing and Comprehending*, ed. J. Jensen, pp. 33–47. Urbana, Ill.: NCTE and ERIC, 1984.   **4**

Wilkinson, A. *The Foundations of Language*. London: Oxford University Press, 1971.   **3**

Wilt, M. "A Study of Teacher Awareness of Listening as a Factor in Elementary Education." *Journal of Educational Research*, 43 (April 1950), 626–636.   **2**

Chapter 4

Almenoff, P. "A Comparison of Kindergarten Predictors for Forecasting Second Grade Reading Achievement." Unpublished doctoral dissertation, Hofstra University, Hempstead, N.Y., 1979.   **2**

Arthur, G. "A Quantitative Study of the Results of Grouping First Grade Children According to Mental Age." *Journal of Educational Research*, 12 (October 1925), 173–185.   **1**

Ausubel, D. P. "Viewpoints from Related Disciplines + Human Growth and Development." *Teachers College Record*, 60 (February 1959), 245–254.   **1–4**

Barrett, T. C. "Visual Discrimination Tasks as Predictors of First Grade Reading Achievement." *The Reading Teacher*, 18 (January 1965), 276–282.   **2**

Bellugi, U., and R. Brown (eds.). *The Acquisition of Language*. Chicago: University of Chicago Press, 1971.

Bond, G. L., and R. Dykstra. "The Cooperative Research Program in First Grade Reading Instruction." *Reading Research Quarterly*, 2 (Summer 1967), 5–142.   **2, 3**

Brubaker, V., and E. Keiser. "Reading to Your Child: A Pilot Program." *Journal of Reading*, 25 (April 1982), 693–694.   **3**

Bruno-Golden, B., and B. Cutler. "The Development of Perception, Memory, and Counting Skills: At Home or School." *Exceptional Parent*, 9 (April 1979), 58–59.   **2, 3**

Bryan, B. "Relative Importance of Intelligence and Visual Perception in Predicting Reading Achievement." *California Journal of Educational Research*, 15 (February 1964), 2–6.   **2**

Caldwell, B. M. "The Usefulness of the Critical Period Hypothesis in the Study of Filiative Behavior." In *Contemporary Issues in Developmental Psychology*, eds. N. D. Endler, L. R. Boulter, and H. Osser, pp. 213–223. New York: Holt, Rinehart and Winston, 1968.   **2**

Calfee, R., R. Chapman, and R. Venezky. "How a Child Needs to Think to Learn to Read." In *Cognition in Learning and Memory,* ed. L. Gregg, pp. 139–182. New York: John Wiley & Sons, Inc., 1972.   **2, 3**

Calfee, R., and K. Hoover. "Policy and Practice in Early Education Research." Paper presented at the California Council for Educational Research, November 1973, Los Angeles, Calif.   **1–4**

Carswell, M. D. "Attainment of Selected Concepts Related to Reading by Kindergarten and First Grade Children." Unpublished doctoral dissertation, University of Georgia, Athens, Ga., 1978.   **2–4**

Chisholm, D., and J. Knafle. "Letter-Name Knowledge as a Prerequisite to Learning to Read." Paper presented at the American Education Research Association Convention, April 1975, Washington, D.C.   **2**

Croft, D. R. *An Activities Handbook for Teachers of Young Children,* 2nd ed. Boston: Houghton Mifflin Company, 1975.   **2–4**

DeHirsch, K., J. J. Jansky, and W. S. Langford. *Predicting Reading Failure.* New York: Harper & Row, Publishers, 1966.   **1–4**

Durkin, D. *Children Who Read Early: Two Longitudinal Studies.* New York: Bureau of Publications, Teachers College Press, Columbia University, 1966.   **2, 3**

———. "A Language Arts Program for Pre-First Grade Children: Two-Year Achievement Report." *Reading Research Quarterly,* 5 (Summer 1970), 534–565.   **2, 3**

———. *Teaching Young Children to Read,* 3rd ed. Boston: Allyn & Bacon, Inc., 1983.   **1–4**

———. *Teaching Them to Read,* 4th ed. Boston: Allyn & Bacon, Inc., 1983.   **1–4**

Durrell, D. D. "First Grade Reading Success Story: A Summary." *Journal of Education,* 140 (February 1958), 2–6.   **2, 3**

Dyson, A. H. "N Spell my grandmama: Fostering Early Thinking about Print." *The Reading Teacher,* 38, 3 (December, 1984), 262–271.   **2**

Ellis, D. W., and F. W. Preston. "Enhancing Beginning Reading Using Wordless Picture Books in a Cross-Age Tutoring Program." *The Reading Teacher,* 37, 8 (April 1984), 692–698.   **3**

Farr, R., and N. Roser. *Teaching a Child to Read.* New York: Harcourt Brace Jovanovich, Inc., 1979.   **1–4**

Flood, J., and D. Lapp. *Language/Reading Instruction for the Young Child.* New York: Macmillan Publishing Company, 1981.   **1**

———, D. Lapp, and S. Flood. "Types of Writings Found in the Early Levels of Basal Reading Programs: Preprimers Through Second Grade Readers." Orton Society Bulletin, 34 (1984), 241–255.

Fromkin, V., and R. Rodman. *An Introduction to Language.* New York: Holt, Rinehart and Winston, 1974.   **1–4**

Ganschow, L., D. B. Weber, and S. K. Suelter. "To Remediate Reading-Like Behavior, Teach a Beginner to Self-monitor." *The Reading Teacher,* 37, 8 (April 1984), 718–721.   **3**

Gates, A. I. "The Necessary Mental Age for Beginning Reading." Elementary School Journal, 37 (March 1937), 497–508.   **1, 2**

———. "The Role of Personality Maladjustment in Reading Disability." In *Children with Reading Problems,* ed. G. Matchez, pp. 80–86. New York: Basic Books, Inc., Publishers, 1968.   **1, 2**

———, and G. L. Bond. "Reading Readiness: A Study of Factors Determining Success and Failure in Beginning Reading." *Teachers College Record,* 37 (May 1936), 679–685.   **1–4**

Gavel, S. R. "June Reading Achievements of First-Grade Children." *Journal of Education*, 140 (February 1958), 37–43.   **2, 3**

Gentile, L., and J. Hart. "Kindergarten Play: The Foundation of Reading." *The Reading Teacher*, 36 (January 1983), 436–439.   **3**

Gesell, A, *The First Five Years of Life*. New York: Harper & Row, Publishers, 1940.   **1, 2**

———, and F. Ilg. *The Child from Five to Ten*. New York: Harper & Row, Publishers, 1946.   **1, 2**

Gibson, E. J., J. J. Gibson, A. D. Pick, and H. A. Osser. "A Developmental Study of the Discrimination of Letter-Like Forms." *Journal of Comparative and Physiological Psychology*, 55 (December 1962), 897–906.   **2, 3**

Goetz, E. M. "Early Reading: A Developmental Approach." *Young Children*, 34 (1979), 4–11.   **1**

Goins, J. T. "Visual Perception Abilities and Early Reading Progress." *Supplementary Educational Monograph*, 87 (1958), 116–128.   **2–4**

Goodall, M. "Can Four Year Olds 'Read' Words in the Environment?" *The Reading Teacher*, 37, 6 (February 1984), 478–483.   **2**

Goodfield, B. A., and C. E. Snow. "Reading Books with Children: The Mechanics of Parental Influence on Children's Reading Achievement." In *Promoting Reading Comprehension*, ed. J. Flood, pp. 204–215. Newark, Dela.: International Reading Association, 1984.   **2**

Haley-James, S. "When Are Children Ready to Write?" *Language Arts*, 59 (May 1982), 458–463.   **2, 3**

Hallgren, B. "Specific Dyslexia: A Clinical and Genetic Study." *Acta Psychiatrica et Neurologia*, 65 (1950), 1–237.   **2**

Heald-Taylor, B. G. "Scribble in First Grade Writing." *The Reading Teacher*, 38, 1 (October 1984), 4–9.   **3**

Hiebert, E. H. "Developmental Patterns and Interrelationships of Preschool Children's Print Awareness." *Reading Research Quarterly*, 16, 2 (1981), 238–259.   **2, 3**

———. "Knowing About Reading Before Reading: Preschool Children's Concepts of Reading." *Reading Psychology*, 3–4 (July–December 1983), 253–260.   **2, 3**

Hillerich, R. *Reading Fundamentals for Preschool and Primary Children*. Columbus, Ohio: Charles E. Merrill Publishing Company, 1977.   **2–4**

Holmes, M. C. "Investigation of Reading Readiness of First Grade Entrants." *Childhood Education*, 3 (January 1927), 215–221.   **1, 2**

Huey, E. B. *The Psychology and Pedagogy of Reading*. New York: Macmillan Publishing Company, 1908.   **1, 2**

Ingram, T. S. "The Nature of Dyslexia." In *Early Experience and Visual Information Processing in Perceptual and Reading Disorders*, eds. F. A. Young and D. B. Lindsley, pp. 405–444. Washington, D.C.: National Academy of Sciences, 1970.   **2**

Jansky, J., and K. DeHirsch. *Preventing Reading Failure*. New York: Harper & Row, Publishers, 1972.   **2, 3**

Kak, A. K. "Schemata: Its Role in the Early Reading Process of Children." *Reading World*, 19 (March 1980), 295–301.   **2**

Lincoln, A. *Speeches and Letters*. In *The Oxford Dictionary of Quotations*, 2nd ed. London: Oxford University Press, 1966, p. 314.

Lohnes, P. R., and M. M. Gray. "Intelligence and the Cooperative Reading Studies." *Reading Research Quarterly*, 3 (Spring 1972), 53–61.   **2, 3**

MacGinitie, W. N. "Evaluating Readiness for Learning to Read: A Critical Review and Evaluation of Research." *Reading Research Quarterly*, 4 (Spring 1969), 396–410.   **1–4**

Mallon, B., and Berglund, R. "The Language Experience Approach to Reading." *The Reading Teacher*, 37, 9 (May 1984), 867–873.   **3**

Manning, M. M., and G. L. Manning. "Early Readers and Nonreaders From Low Socioeconomic Environments: What Their Parents Report." *The Reading Teacher*, 38, 1 (October, 1984), 32–35.   **2**

Menyuk, P. "Syntactic Structures in the Language of Children." *Journal of Child Development*, 34 (1963), 407–422.   **2**

———. *The Acquisition and Development of Language*. Englewood Cliffs, N.J.: Prentice-Hall, Inc., 1971.   **2**

———. "Language Development and Reading." In *Understanding Reading Comprehension*, ed. J. Flood, pp. 101–121. Newark, Dela: International Reading Association, 1984.   **3**

Monroe, M. "Reading Aptitude Tests for the Prediction of Success and Failure in Beginning Reading." *Education*, 56 (September 1935), 7–14.   **1, 2, 4**

Morphett, M., and C. Washburne. "When Should Children Begin to Read?" *Elementary School Journal*, 31 (March 1931), 496–503.   **1**

Muehl, S., and S. Kremenack. "Ability to Match Information Within and Between Auditory and Visual Sense Modalities and Subsequent Reading Achievement." *Journal of Educational Psychology*, 57 (August 1966), 230–239.   **2, 3**

Nessel, D. D. "Storytelling in the Reading Program." *The Reading Teacher*, 38, 4 (January 1985), 378–381.   **3**

Olson, A. V. "Growth in Word Perception Abilities as It Relates to Success in Beginning Reading." *Journal of Education*, 140 (February 1958), 25–36.   **2**

Owens, F., P. Adams, and T. Forrest. "Learning Disabilities in Children: Sibling Studies." *Bulletin of the Orton Society*, 18 (1968), 33–62.   **2**

Piaget, J. *Plays, Dreams, and Imitation in Childhood*. New York: W. W. Norton & Company, Inc., 1962.

———. *The Origins of Intelligence in Children*. New York: W. W. Norton & Company, Inc., 1963.   **1, 2**

Reed, M. M. *An Investigation of Practices in First Grade Admission and Promotion*. New York: Bureau of Publications, Teachers College Press, Columbia University, 1927.   **1, 2**

Richek, M. A. "Readiness Skills That Predict Initial Word Learning Using Two Different Methods of Instruction." *Reading Research Quarterly*, 13 (1977–78), 200–221.   **2–4**

Russell, D. *Manual for Teaching the Reading Readiness Program*. Lexington, Mass.: Ginn and Company, 1967.   **3, 4**

Samuels, S. J. "The Effect of Letter-Name Knowledge on Learning to Read." *American Educational Research Journal*, 9 (Winter 1972), 65–74.   **2**

Satz, P., and G. K. van Nostrand. "Developmental Dyslexia: An Evaluation of a Theory." In *The Disabled Learner: Early Detection and Intervention*, eds. P. Satz and J. J. Ross. Netherlands: University of Rotterdam Press, 1973.   **2, 3**

Silberberg, N., et al. "The Effects of Kindergarten Instruction in Alphabet and Numbers on First Grade Reading," Final Report. Minneapolis: Kenny Rehabilitation Institute, 1968.   **2, 3**

Silvaroli, N. J. "Factors in Predicting Children's Success in First Grade Reading." In *Reading and Inquiry*, Vol. 10, ed. J. A. Figurel, pp. 296–298. Newark, Dela.: International Reading Association, 1965.   **2, 3**

Silver, L. B. "Familial Patterns in Children with Neurologically Based Learning Disabilities." *Journal of Learning Disabilities*, 4 (August–September 1971), 349–358.　**2, 4**

Sitting, L. H. "Involving Parents and Children in Reading for Fun." *The Reading Teacher*, 36 (November 1982), 166–168.　**2**

Spache, G. D., and E. B. Spache, *Reading in the Elementary School*, 4th ed. Boston: Allyn & Bacon, Inc., 1977.　**2, 3**

Teale, W. H. "Positive Environments for Learning to Read: What Studies of Early Readers Tell Us." *Language Arts*, 55 (November–December 1978), pp. 922, 932.　**2, 3**

Vukelich, C. "Parent's Role in the Reading Process: A Review of Practical Suggestions and Ways to Communicate with Parents." *The Reading Teacher*, 37, 6 (February 1984), 472–477.　**3**

Weiner, M., and S. Feldman. "Validation Studies of a Reading Prognosis Test for Children of Lower and Middle Socio-Economic Status." *Educational and Psychological Measurement*, 23 (Winter 1963), 807–814.　**2, 4**

Wilson, F. T., and C. W. Fleming. "Grade Trends in Reading Progress in Kindergarten and Primary Grades." *Journal of Educational Psychology*, 31 (January 1940), 1–13.　**1, 2**

Zirkelbach, T. "A Personal View of Early Reading." *The Reading Teacher*, 37, 6 (February 1984), 468–471.　**3**

Chapter 5

Bromley, K. D. "Teaching Idioms." *The Reading Teacher*, 38, 3 (December 1984), 272–276.

Burmeister, L. "Vowel Pairs." *The Reading Teacher*, 21 (February 1968), 447–498.　**3, 4**

Coleman, E. *Collecting a Data Base for an Educational Technology*, Parts I and III. El Paso: University of Texas, 1967.　**3, 4**

Dolch, E. "A Basic Sight Vocabulary." *Elementary School Journal*, 36 (February 1936), 456–460.　**1**

Durkin, D. *Teaching Them to Read*. Boston, Mass.: Allyn and Bacon, 1974.

Fairbanks, G. *Experimental Phonics: Selected Articles*. Urbana: University of Illinois Press, 1966.

Fries, C. *Linguistics and Reading*. New York: Holt, Rinehart and Winston, 1963.　**2, 3**

Fulwiler, G., and P. Groff. "The Effectiveness of Intensive Phonics." *Reading Horizons*, 21 (Fall 1980), 50–54.　**3, 4**

Garner, W. I. "Reading Is a Problem-solving Process." *The Reading Teacher*, 38, 1 (October 1984), 36–41.　**3**

Gibson, E., and H. Levin. *The Psychology of Reading*. Cambridge, Mass.: M.I.T. Press, 1975.　**3**

Groff, P. *The Syllable: Its Nature and Pedagogical Usefulness*. Portland, Ore.: Northwest Regional Educational Laboratory, 1971.　**3, 4**

———. "Teaching Reading by Syllables." *The Reading Teacher*, 34 (March 1981), 659–664.　**3, 4**

———. "A Test of the Utility of Phonics Rules." *Reading Psychology*, 3–4 (July–December 1983), 217–226.　**3**

———. "Resolving the Letter Name Controversy." *The Reading Teacher*, 37, 1 (January 1984), 384–390.　**1**

Hoover, K. "The Effect of Sequence of Training in Kindergarten Children." Unpublished Ph.D. dissertation, Stanford University, Stanford, Calif., 1975.   **4**

Jenkins, J., R. Bausel, and L. Jenkins. "Comparison of Letter Name and Letter Sound Training as Transfer Variables." *American Educational Research Journal,* 9 (February 1972), 75–86.   **2, 3, 4**

Kibby, M. W. "The Effects of Certain Instructional Conditions and Response Modes on Initial Word Learning." *Reading Research Quarterly,* 15, 1 (1979), 145–171.   **3, 4**

Marchbanks, B., and H. Levin. "Cues by Which Children Recognize Words." *Journal of Educational Psychology,* 56 (September 1965), 57–61.   **1–4**

Moon, L., and C. Scorpio. "When Word Recognition Is OK—Almost." *The Reading Teacher,* 37, 9 (May 1984), 825–827.   **4**

Murphy, H., and D. Durrell. *Speech to Print Phonics.* New York: Harcourt Brace Jovanovich, Inc., 1972.   **1–4**

Shimron, J., and D. Navon. "The Dependence on Graphemes and on Their Translation to Phonemes in Reading: A Developmental Perspective." *Reading Research Quarterly,* 17, 2 (1982), 210–228.   **1–4**

Shwedel, A. "Must We Use Phonology to Read? What Chinese Can Tell Us." *Journal of Reading,* 26 (May 1983), 707–713.   **2–4**

Silberberg, N., M. Silberberg, and I. Iverson. "The Effects of Kindergarten Instruction in Alphabet and Numbers on First Grade Reading." *Journal of Learning Disabilities,* 5 (March 1972), 254–261.   **3–4**

Thorndike, E. *The Teaching of English Suffixes.* New York: Bureau of Publications, Teachers College Press, Columbia University, 1932.   **3, 4**

Tovey, D. R. "Children's Grasp of Phonics Terms vs. Sound-Symbol Relationships." *The Reading Teacher,* 33 (January 1980), 431–437.   **3, 4**

Webster, N. *The American Spelling Book,* 1831. Reprint, New York: Bureau of Publications, Teachers College Press, Columbia University, 1961, p. 19.   **1, 2**

Chapter 6

Anderson R. C., and P. Freebody. *Vocabulary Knowledge and Reading.* Center for the Study of Reading, University of Illinois, Reading Educational Report No. 11, 1979.   **4**

Ashton-Warner, S. *Teacher.* New York: Bantam Books, Inc., 1963.   **1–3**

Barrett, M. T., and M. F. Graves. "A Vocabulary Program for Junior High School Remedial Readers." *Journal of Reading,* 25, 2 (November 1981), 146–151.   **4**

Bean, T. W., N. B. Inabinetti, and R. Ryan. "The Effect of a Categorization Strategy on Secondary Students' Retention of Literacy Vocabulary." *Reading Psychology,* 3–4 (July–December 1983), 247–253.   **4**

Beech, J. R., and L. M. Harding. "Phonemic Processing and the Poor Reader from a Developmental Log Viewpoint." *Reading Research Quarterly,* 29, 3 (Spring 1984), 357–366.   **1–4**

Bengston, J. K., and L. L. Smith. "A Comparison of Procedures for Training Efficient Word Processing." *Reading Psychology,* 3–4 (July–December 1983), 227–236.   **4**

Berlo, D. *The Process of Communication.* New York: Holt, Rinehart and Winston, 1960, p. 175.

Biemiller, A. "Changes in the Use of Graphic and Contextual Information as Functions of Passage Difficulty and Reading Achievement Level." *Journal of Reading Behavior,* 11 (Winter 1979), 307–318.   **3**

Brown, B. "Enrich Your Reading Program with Personal Words." *The Reading Teacher,* 35 (October 1981), 40–43.   1

Calfee, R. C. "The Book: Components of Reading Instruction." Unpublished paper, Stanford University, Stanford, Calif., 1981   4

Carnine, L., D. Carnine, and R. Gersten. "Analysis of Oral Reading Errors Made by Economically Disadvantaged Students Taught with a Synthetic-Phonics Approach." *Reading Research Quarterly,* 29, 3 (Spring 1984), 343–356.   2

Curtis, M. E. "Development of Components of Reading Skill." *Journal of Educational Psychology,* 72 (1980), 656–669.   4

Coleman, E. *Collecting a Data Base for an Educational Technology,* Parts I and III. El Paso: University of Texas, 1967.   1–3

Dale, E. "A Comparison of Two Word Lists." *Educational Research Bulletin* (December 1931), 484–489.   1

Dolch, E. "A Basic Sight Vocabulary." *Elementary School Journal,* 36 (February 1936), 456–460.   1

Draper, A. G., and G. H. Moeller. "We Think with Words (Therefore to Improve Thinking, Teach Vocabulary)." *Phi Delta Kappan,* 52, 8 (April 1971), 428–484.   4

Durrell, D. D. *Improving Reading Instruction.* New York: Harcourt Brace Jovanovich, Inc., 1966,   1–3

Frager, A. M. "An 'Intelligence' Approach to Vocabulary Instruction." *Journal of Reading,* 28, 2 (November, 1984), 160–165.   4

Fries, C. C. *Linguistics and Reading.* New York: Holt, Rinehart and Winston, 1963.   1–3

Gleason, J. B. "Language Development in Early Childhood." In *Oral Language and Reading,* ed. J. Walden. Urbana, Ill.: National Council of Teachers of English, 1969.   1–3

Graves, M. F. "Selecting Vocabulary to Teach in the Intermediate and Secondary Grades." In *Promoting Reading Comprehension,* ed. J. Flood, pp. 245–260. Newark, Dela.: International Reading Association, 1984.   4

————, and S. D. Bender. "Preteaching Vocabulary to Secondary Students: A Classroom Experiment." *Minnesota English Journal,* 10, 5 (1980), 27–34.   4

Guszak, F. *Diagnostic Reading Instruction in the Elementary School.* New York: Harper & Row, Publishers, 1972.   1–3

Haber, L., et al. "Word Length and Word Shape as Sources of Information in Reading." *Reading Research Quarterly,* 18, 2 (1983), 165–189.   1

Haber, R. N., and L. R. Haber. "The Shape of a Word Can Specify Its Meaning." *Reading Research Quarterly,* 16, 3 (1981), 334–345.   1

————, and R. Schindler. "Errors in Proofreading: Evidence of Syntactic Control of Letter Processing?" *Journal of Experimental Psychology: Human Perception and Performance,* 7 (1981), 573–579.   1

Harris, A., and M. Jacobsen. *Basic Elementary Reading Vocabularies.* New York: Macmillan Publishing Company, 1972.

Jenkins, J. R., D. Pany, and J. Schreck. *Vocabulary and Reading Comprehension: Instructional Effects.* Center for the Study of Reading, University of Illinois, Technical Report No. 100, 1978. (ED 160 999)   4

Juel, C. "Comparison of Word Identification Strategies with Varying Context, Word Type, and Reader Skill." *Reading Research Quarterly,* 15, 3 (1980), 358–376.   1

————. "The Development and Use of Mediated Word Identification." *Reading Research Quarterly,* 19, 3 (1983), 306–327.   3

Kucera, H., and W. Francis. *Computational Analysis of Present-Day American English*. Providence, R.I.: Brown University Press, 1967.   **1–3**

Marchbanks, B., and H. Levin. "Cues by Which Children Recognize Words." *Journal of Educational Psychology*, 56 (September 1965), 57–61.   **3**

McHugh, J. "Words Most Useful in Reading." Compiled at California State University, Hayward, Calif., 1969.   **1**

Murphy, H., and D. Durrell. *Letters in Words*. Wellesley, Mass.: Curriculum Associates, Inc., 1970.   **1**

Nagy, W. E., and R. C. Anderson. "How Many Words Are There in Printed School English?" *Reading Research Quarterly*, 19, 3 (Spring 1984), 304–330.   **4**

Rayner, K. "Developmental Changes in Word Recognition Strategies." *Journal of Educational Psychology*, 68 (June 1976), 323–329.   **1**

———. "Eye Movements in Reading and Information Processing." *Psychological Bulletin*, 85 (May 1978), 618–660.   **1**

Ruddell, R. *Reading-Language Instruction*. Englewood Cliffs, N.J.: Prentice-Hall, Inc., 1974.   **1–3**

Shuy, R. "Some Relationships of Linguistics to the Reading Process." In *Teachers' Edition of How It Is Nowadays*, by T. Clymer and R. Ruddell, Reading 360 Series. Lexington, Mass.: Ginn and Company, 1973.   **1, 2**

Spache, G. D., and E. Spache. *Reading in the Elementary School*, 4th ed. Boston: Allyn & Bacon, Inc., 1977.   **1–3**

Stotsky, S. L. *Toward More Systematic Development of Children's Reading Vocabulary in Developmental Reading Programs for the Middle to Upper Elementary Grades*. Unpublished doctoral dissertation, Harvard University, Cambridge, Mass., 1976.   **4**

Thorndike, E. *The Teaching of English Suffixes*. New York: Bureau of Publications, Teachers College Press, Columbia University, 1932.   **2**

Veatch, J., et al. *Key Words to Reading: The Language Experience Approach Begins*, 2nd ed. Columbus, Ohio: Charles E. Merrill Publishing Company, 1979.   **1**

Chapter 7

Anderson, R. C., R. J. Spiro, and W. E. Montague, eds. *Schooling and the Acquisition of Knowledge*. Hillsdale, N.J.: Lawrence Erlbaum Associates, 1977.   **1**

Armbruster, B. B., and T. H. Anderson. *The Effect of Mapping on the Free Recall of Expository Text*, ERIC ED 182 735. Washington, D.C.: National Institute of Education (DHEW), February 1980.   **2, 4**

Bartlett, B. *Top-Level Structure as on Organizational Strategy for Recall of Classroom Text*. Unpublished doctoral dissertation, Arizona State University, Temple, Ariz., 1978.   **3**

Bartlett, J. R. *Remembering: A Study in Experimental and Social Psychology*. Cambridge: Cambridge University Press, 1932.   **1**

Blachowicz, C. "Showing Teachers How to Develop Students' Predictive Reading." *The Reading Teacher*, 36 (March 1983), 680–684.   **4**

Blecha, M. K., P. C. Gega, and M. Green. *Exploring Science*. River Forest, Ill.: Laidlaw Publishers, 1980, pp. 40–42.

Bloom, B. S., ed. *Taxonomy of Educational Objectives. Handbook I: Cognitive Domain*. New York: David McKay Co., Inc., 1956.   **1–4**

Calfee, R. "Acquisition and Development of Schema." Paper delivered at the National Reading Conference, San Diego, Calif., December 1980.

Carr, K. "The Importance of Inference Skills in the Primary Grades." *The Reading Teacher*, 36 (February 1983), 518–522.   **2, 4**

Chapman, J. "Comprehending and the Teacher of Reading." In *Promoting Reading Comprehension*, ed. J. Flood, pp. 261–272. Newark, Dela.: International Reading Association, 1984.   **4**

Crossen, H. "Effect of the Attitudes of the Reader upon Critical Reading Ability." *Journal of Educational Research*, 42 (December 1948), 289–298.   **4**

Cunningham, R. "Developing Question-Asking Skills." In *Developing Teacher Competencies*, ed. J. Weigand. Englewood Cliffs, N.J.: Prentice-Hall, Inc., 1971.   **4**

Dehn, N. "An AI Perspective on Reading Comprehension." In *Understanding Reading Comprehension*, ed. J. Flood, pp. 82–100. Newark, Dela.: International Reading Association, 1984.   **1, 2**

Eller, Wm., K. Hester, and R. Farr. *Blue-Tailed Horse*. River Forest, Illinois: Laidlaw Brothers Publisher, 1984, p. 27.   **4**

Elliott, S. N. "Effect of Prose Organization on Recall: An Investigation of Memory and Metacognition." Unpublished doctoral dissertation, Arizona State University, Tucson, Ariz., 1978. Cited by B. Meyer, "Organizational Aspects of Text: Effects on Reading Comprehension and Applications for the Classroom." In *Promoting Reading Comprehension*, ed. J. Flood, pp. 113–138. Newark, Dela.: International Reading Association, 1984.   **3**

Fisher, D. F., and C. W. Peters, eds. *Comprehension and the Competent Reader*. New York: Praeger Publishers, Inc., 1981.   **1–3**

Flood, J. "The Effects of First Sentences on Reader Expectations in Prose Passages." *Reading World*, 17 (May 1978), 306–315.   **2, 3**

———. (ed.) *Promoting Reading Comprehension*. Newark, Dela.: International Reading Association, 1984. (a)   **1–4**

———. (ed.) *Understanding Reading Comprehension*. Newark, Dela.: International Reading Association, 1984. (b)   **1–4**

———, and D. Lapp. *Language/Reading Instruction for the Young Child*. New York: Macmillan Publishing Company, 1981, pp. 356, 361.   **1–4**

———, and D. Lapp. *Comprehension Plus, Levels A–F*. Englewood Cliffs, N.J.: Prentice-Hall, Inc., 1983.   **4**

———, and D. Lapp. "Inference: A Scoring System for Operations Performed by Readers in Text Recall." Paper presented at National Reading Conference, St. Petersburg, Fla., December 1977.   **2**

———, and D. Lapp. "In Search of the 'Perfect Question': Questioning Strategies for Developing Story Comprehension in Young Children." *Principal*, 56 (October 1980), 20–23.   **4**

———, and D. Lapp. "Prose Analysis and the Effects of Staging on Prose Comprehension." Paper presented at the Second Annual Reading Association of Ireland Conference, Dublin, Ireland, 1977.   **3**

Frederiksen, C. H. "Inference and Structure of Children's Discourse." Paper for the Symposium on the Development of Processing Skills, Society for Research in Child Development Meeting, New Orleans, 1977.   **3, 4**

Gibson, E., and H. Levin. *The Psychology of Reading*. Cambridge, Mass.: M.I.T. Press, 1975.   **1**

Gough, P. B. "One Second of Reading." In *Language by Eye and Ear*, ed. J. F. Kavanaugh and I. G. Mattingly, 331–358. Cambridge, Mass.: M.I.T. Press, 1972.   **1**

Groff, P. J. "Children's Attitudes Toward Reading and Their Critical Reading Abilities in Four Content Type Materials." *Journal of Educational Research*, 55 (1962), 313–317. **3**

Guthrie, J. "Research Reviews: Story Comprehension." *The Reading Teacher*, 30, 5 (1977), 575–577. **2**

———, ed. *Comprehension and Teaching: Research Reviews*. Newark, Dela.: International Reading Association, 1981. **1**

Halliday, M., and R. Hasan. *Cohesion in English*. London: Longman Press, 1976. **3**

Hansen, J. "An Inferential Comprehension Strategy for Use with Primary Grade Children." *The Reading Teacher*, 34 (March 1981), 665–669. **4**

Housel, T. J., and S. J. Acker. *Schema Theory: Can It Connect Communication Discourse?* ERIC Document ED 177 614. Washington, D.C.: U.S. Educational Resources Information Center, May 1979. **2**

Huey, E. B. *The Psychology and Pedagogy of Reading*. New York: Macmillan Publishing Company, 1908. **1, 4**

Johnson, C. J., II. "A Study and Analysis of the Relationships at the Intermediate Grade Levels Between Attitude as Reflected in Certain Thematic Content and Recalled Comprehension." Unpublished doctoral dissertation, University of California, Berkeley, Calif., 1967. **1**

King, R. M., D. K. Bracken, and M. A. Sloan. *Communities and Social Needs*. River Forest, Ill.: Laidlaw Publishers, 1977.

LaBerge, D., and S. J. Samuels. "Toward a Theory of Automatic Information Processing in Reading." *Cognitive Psychology*, 6 (1974), 293–323. **1**

Lapp, D., and J. Flood. *CLUES for Better Reading*. Wellesley, Mass.: Curriculum Associates, Inc., 1982. Kits for grades 1–8. **4**

———, and J. Flood. "Promoting Reader Comprehension Instruction Which Ensures Continuous Reader Growth." In *Promoting Reading Comprehension*, ed. J. Flood, pp. 273–288. Newark, Dela.: International Reading Association, 1984. **4**

———, J. Flood, and G. Gleckman. "Classroom Practices Can Make Use of What Researchers Learn." *The Reading Teacher*, 35 (March 1982), 578–585. **4**

Lueers, N. "The Short Circuit Model of Reading: A Synthesis of Reading Theories." *Reading Psychology*, 4 (January–March 1983), 79–94. **1**

Mandler, J. M., and N. S. Johnson. "Remembrance of Things Parsed: Story Structure and Recall." *Cognitive Psychology*, 9 (January 1977), 111–151. **3**

Marshall, N. "Using Story Grammar to Assess Reading Comprehension." *The Reading Teacher*, 36 (March 1983), 616–620. **2**

Marshall, N., and M. D. Glock. "Comprehension of Connected Discourse: A Study into the Relationships Between the Structure of Text and Information Recalled." *Reading Research Quarterly*, 14, 1 (1978–79), 10–56. **3**

McConaughy, S. "Developmental Changes in Story Comprehension and Levels of Questioning." *Language Arts*, 59 (September 1982), 580–589+. **2, 4**

McKillop, A. S. *The Relationship Between the Reader's Attitude and Certain Types of Reading Responses*. New York: Bureau of Publications, Teachers College Press, Columbia University, 1952. **4**

Menyuk, P. "Syntactic Competence and Reading." In *Language Learning and Reading Disabilities: A New Decade*, ed. J. Stark and S. Wurzel. New York: Proceedings of Queens College CUNY Conference, 1981. **3**

———. "Language Development and Reading." In *Understanding Reading Comprehension*, ed. J. Flood. Newark, Dela.: International Reading Association, 1984.

430

———, and J. Flood. "Linguistic Competence, Reading, Writing Problems and Remediation." *Orton Society Bulletin*, 31 (1981), 13–28.   **3, 4**

Merritt, J. E. "Developing Competence in Reading Comprehension." In *Reading Instruction: An International Forum*. Proceedings of the First World Congress on Reading. Newark, Dela.: International Reading Association, 1967, pp. 91–98.   **4**

Meyer, B. J. *The Organization of Prose and Its Effects on Memory*. Amsterdam: North-Holland Publishing Company, 1975.   **3**

———. "Organizational Aspects of Text Effects on Reading Comprehension and Applications for the Classroom." In *Promoting Reading Comprehension*, ed. J. Flood, pp. 113–138. Newark, Dela.: International Reading Association, 1984.   **3**

———, and A. G. Rice. *The Amount, Type, and Organization of Information Recalled from Prose by Young, Middle, and Old Adult Readers*, ERIC ED 191 003. Paper presented at the annual meeting of the American Psychological Association, Montreal, Canada, September 1980, p. 6.   **3**

Micklos, J. "A Look at Reading Achievement in the United States: The Latest Data." *Journal of Reading*, 25 (May 1982), 760–762.   **4**

Mikulecky, L. "Preparing Students for Workplace Literacy Demands." *Journal of Reading*, 28, 3 (December 1984), 253–257.   **4**

National Assessment of Educational Progress. *Reading in America: A Perspective on Two Assessments*. Denver, Colo.: NAEP, 1981.   **4**

Niles, O. *School Programs: The Necessary Conditions in Reading: Process and Program*. Urbana, Ill.: National Council of Teachers of English, 1970.   **3**

Pearson, P. D., and D. Johnson. *Teaching Reading Comprehension*. New York: Holt, Rinehart and Winston, 1978.   **1, 4**

Reder, L. M. "The Role of Elaborations in the Comprehension and Retention of Prose: A Critical Review." *Review of Educational Research*, 50 (Spring 1980), 5–53.   **2**

Reutzel, D. R. "Story Maps Improve Comprehension." *The Reading Teacher*, 38, 4 (January 1985), 400–405.   **4**

Rumelhart, D. "Toward an Interactive Model of Reading," Technical Report No. 56. Center for Human Information Processing, University of California, San Diego, 1976.   **1**

———. "Understanding Understanding." In *Understanding Reading Comprehension*, ed. J. Flood, pp. 1–20. Newark, Dela.: International Reading Association, 1984.   **1, 2**

———, and A. Ortony. "The Representation of Knowledge in Memory." In *Schooling and the Acquisition of Knowledge*, ed. R. C. Anderson, R. J. Spiro, and W. E. Montague, pp. 99–135. Hillsdale, N.J.: Lawrence Erlbaum Associates, 1977.   **1**

Schank, R. C., and R. P. Abelson. *Scripts, Plans, Goals, and Understanding: An Inquiry into Human Knowledge Structures*. Hillsdale, N.J.: Lawrence Erlbaum Associates, 1977.   **2, 3**

Sendak, M. *Where the Wild Things Are*. New York: Harper & Row, Publishers, 1969.

Senta, C., and B. Hayes. *Children's Prose Comprehension*. Newark, Dela.: International Reading Association, 1981,   **3. 4**

Sinatra, R. C., J. Stahl-Gemake, and D. N. Berg. "Improving Reading Comprehension of Disabled Readers Through Semantic Mapping." *The Reading Teacher*, 38, 1 (October, 1984), 22–31.   **4**

Smith, F. *Understanding Reading*, 2nd ed. New York: Holt, Rinehart and Winston, 1978.   **1**

Smith, N. B. *Reading Instruction for Today's Children.* Englewood Cliffs, N.J.: Prentice-Hall, Inc., 1963.   **1**

Smith, S. P. "Comprehension and Comprehension Monitoring By Experienced Readers." *Journal of Reading*, 28, 4 (January 1985), 292–300.   **4**

Stein, N. "How Children Understand Stories: A Developmental Analysis." In *Current Topics in Early Childhood Education*, ed. L. Katz, Vol. 2. Hillsdale, N.J.: Ablex, Inc., 1979.   **2**

————, and C. Glenn. "The Role of Structural Variation in Children's Recall of Simple Stories." Paper presented at the Society for Research in Child Development, New Orleans, La., 1977.   **2**

Summers, P. "Story Grammars." Handout for Course RL 780, Reading and Language Department, Boston University, Boston, Mass., April 1980.   **2**

Taylor, B. M. "Children's Memory for Expository Text After Reading." *Reading Research Quarterly*, 15, 2 (1980), 399–41.   **2, 3**

Thorndike, P. N. "Cognitive Structures in Comprehension and Memory of Narrative Discourse." *Cognitive Psychology*, 9, 1 (January 1977), 77–110.   **1, 4**

Tierney, R., and J. Mosenthal. Discourse Comprehension and Production: Analyzing Text Structures and Cohesion, ERIC ED 179 945. Champaign-Urbana, Ill.: Center for the Study of Reading, (January 1980), p. 31.   **3**

Trabasso, T. "Mental Operations in Language Comprehension." *Language Comprehension and the Acquisition of Knowledge.* Washington, D.C.: V. H. Winston, 1972.   **2**

————. "On the Making of Inferences During Reading and Their Assessment." In *Comprehension and Teaching: Research Reviews*, ed. J. Guthrie. Newark, Dela.: International Reading Association, 1981.

Vacca, R. "An Investigation of a Functional Reading Strategy in Seventh Grade Social Studies." Unpublished doctoral dissertation, Syracuse University, Syracuse, N.Y., 1973.   **3**

Wilson, C. "Teaching Reading Comprehension by Connecting the Known to the Unknown." *The Reading Teacher*, 36 (January 1983), 382–390.   **2, 4**

Winograd, T., and P. Johnston. "Comprehension Monitoring and the Error Detection Paradigm," Technical Report No. 153. Center for the Study of Reading, University of Illinois, Champaign-Urbana, Ill., January 1980.   **1, 4**

Wixson, K. "Postreading Question-Answer Interactions and Children's Learning from Text." *Journal of Educational Psychology*, 75 (June 1983), 413–423.   **4**

————. "Level of Importance of Postquestions and Children's Learning from Text." *American Educational Research Journal* 21, 2 (Summer 1984), 419–434.   **4**

Woodworth, R. S. *Experimental Psychology.* New York: Holt, 1938.   **1**

Chapter 8

Adams, A., D. Carnine, and R. Gersten. "Instructional Strategies for Studying Content Area Texts in the Intermediate Grades." *Reading Research Quarterly*, 18, 1 (1982), 27–55.   **1, 2**

Andre, M., and T. Andersen. "The Development and Evaluation for a Self-questioning Study Technique." *Reading Research Quarterly*, 14, 4 (1978–79), 605–623.   **1, 2**

Brady, M., and H. Brady. *Idea and Action in American History.* Englewood Cliffs, N.J.: Prentice-Hall, Inc., 1977.

Brown, A., J. Campione, and J. Day. "Learning to Learn: On Training Students to Learn from Texts." *Educational Researcher*, 10 (February 1981), 14–21.   **2**

Bruner, J., et al. *Studies in Cognitive Growth*. New York: John Wiley & Sons, Inc., 1967.   1

Chambers, D., and H. Lowry. *The Language Arts*. Dubuque, Iowa: Wm. C. Brown Company, Publishers, 1975, p. 75.   1, 2

Courtney, L. "Recent Developments in Reading in the Content Areas." *Conference on Reading*, 27 (1965), 134–144.   1, 2

Estes, T. "Reading in the Social Studies: A Review of Research Since 1950." In *Reading in the Content Areas*, ed. James L. Laffey, pp. 177–187. Newark, Dela.: International Reading Association, 1972.   1

Fay, L., T. Horn, and C. McCullough. *Improving Reading in the Elementary Social Studies*, Bulletin No. 33. Washington, D.C.: National Council for the Social Studies, 1961.   1

Flavell, J. H. "Metacognitive Aspects of Problem Solving." In *The Nature of Intelligence*, ed. L. B. Resnick, p. 232. Hillsdale, N.J.: Lawrence Erlbaum Associates, 1976.   1

Friedland, J., and R. Kessler. "A Top (to Bottom) Drawer Way to Teach Outlining." *Teacher*, 98 (September 1980), 110–111.   2

Garner, R., and R. Reis. "Monitoring and Resolving Comprehension Obstacles: An Investigation of Spontaneous Text Lookbacks Among Upper-Grade Good and Poor Comprehenders." *Reading Research Quarterly*, 16, 4 (1981), 569–582.   1, 2

Hartley, W., and W. Vincent. *American Civics*, 4th ed. New York: Harcourt Brace Jovanovich, Inc., 1983.

Hawkins, M. *Graphing: A Stimulating Way to Process Data*. How to Do It Series, Series 2, no. 10. Washington, D.C.: National Council for the Social Studies, 1980, p. 1.   2

Hoffman, J. "Developing Flexibility Through Reflex Action." *The Reading Teacher*, 33 (December 1979), 323–329.   2

Kiewra, K. "Acquiring Effective Notetaking Skills: An Alternative to Professional Notetaking." *Journal of Reading*, 27, 4 (January 1984), 299–301.   2

Lamberg, W., and C. Lamb. *Reading Instruction in the Content Areas*. Chicago Ill.: Rand-McNally & Company, 1980.   1, 2

The Reader's Guide to Periodical Literature. New York: The H. W. Wilson Company, June 10, 1983.

Reeves, R. *The Teaching of Reading in Our Schools*. New York: Macmillan Publishing Company, 1966.   1

Rickards, J. "Notetaking, Underlining, Inserted Questions, and Organizers in Text: Research Implications." *Educational Technology*, 20 (June 1980), 5–11.   2

Rogers, D. "Assessing Study Skills." *Journal of Reading*, 27, 4 (January 1984), 346–355.   1, 2

Russell, D. *Children Learn to Read*. Lexington, Mass.: Ginn and Company, 1961, p. 457.   1, 2

Schilling, F. C. "Teaching Study Skills in the Intermediate Grades—We Can Do More." *Journal of Reading*, 27, 7 (April 1984), 620–623.   1

Shepherd, D. *Comprehensive High School Reading Methods*, 2nd ed. Columbus, Ohio: Charles E. Merrill Publishing Company, 1978.   1, 2

Singer, H., and D. Donlan. "Active Comprehension: Problem Solving Schema with Question Generation for Comprehension of Complex Short Stories." *Reading Research Quarterly*, 17, 2 (1982), 166–186.   2

Taylor, K. "Can College Students Summarize?" *Journal of Reading*, 26 (March 1983), 524–528.   2

Tierney, R. "Learning from Text." In *Secondary School Reading: What Research Reveals for Classroom Practice*, ed. A. Berger and H. A. Robinson. Urbana,

Ill.: ERIC Clearinghouse on Reading and Communication Skills and the National Conference on Research in English, 1982, p. 109.   1

Tonjes, M., and M. Zintz. *Teaching Reading/Thinking/Study Skills in Content Classrooms*. Dubuque, Iowa: Wm. C. Brown Company, Publishers, 1981.   **1, 2**

Truman, D. "The Effects of Pictorial Aids on Inferentially Produced Interference in Younger and Older Children's Sentence Learning," Unpublished Ph.D. dissertation, The University of Wisconsin-Madison, 1981.   1

Tuten, R., et al. *Weight Training Everyone*. Winston-Salem, N.C.: Hunter Textbooks, Inc., 1983.

Vacca. R. *Content Area Reading*. Boston: Little, Brown and Company, 1981.   1, 2

Witt, M. "Developing Reading Skills and Critical Thinking." *Social Education*, 25 (May 1961), 239–241.   1

Chapter 9

Asimov, I., and R. G. Gallant. *Ginn Science Program: Intermediate Level C*. Lexington, Mass.: Ginn and Company, 1973.

Austin, M. C. "Improving Comprehension of Mathematics." In *Reading in the Secondary Schools*, ed. M. J. Weiss, pp. 391–396. Indianapolis, Ind.: The Odyssey Press, 1961.   **3**

Barnard, K., and C. Lavatelli. *Science: Measuring Things*. New York: Macmillan Publishing Company, 1970.

————, et al. *Science: A Search for Evidence*. New York: Macmillan Publishing Company, 1966.

Bisque, R., H. Pratt, and J. Thompson. *Earth Science: Patterns in Our Environment*. Englewood Cliffs, N.J.: Prentice-Hall, Inc., 1975.

Chambers, D. W., and H. W. Lowry. *The Language Arts*. Dubuque, Iowa: Wm. C. Brown Company, Publishers, 1975, pp. 75.   1

Clymer, T. *Ginn 360, 720*. Lexington, Mass.: Ginn and Company, 1970, pp. 42–76.

Corle, C. G. "Reading in Mathematics: A Review of Recent Research." In *Reading in the Content Areas*, ed. J. L. Laffey, pp. 75–94. Newark, Dela.: International Reading Association, 1972.   **3**

Courtney, L. "Recent Developments in Reading in the Content Areas." *Conference on Reading* (University of Chicago) 27 (1965), 134–144.   **1–5**

Cunningham, J., and H. Ballew. "Solving Word Problem Solving." *The Reading Teacher*, 36, 4 (April 1983), 836–839.   1

Davis, F. B. "Research in Comprehension in Reading." *Reading Research Quarterly*, 3 (Summer 1968), 499–545.   1

Dole, J., and V. Johnson. "Beyond the Textbook: Science Literature for Young People." *Journal of Reading*, 24 (April 1981), 579–582.   **4**

Dupuis, M., and S. Snyder. "Develop Concepts Through Vocabulary: A Strategy for Reading Specialists to Use with Content Teachers." *Journal of Reading*, 26 (January 1983), 297–305.   **1–5**

Estes, T. H. "Reading in the Social Studies: A Review of Research Since 1950." In *Reading in the Content Areas*, ed. J. L. Laffey, p. 177–187. Newark, Dela.: International Reading Association, 1972.   **2**

Fay, L., T. Horn, and C. McCullough. *Improving Reading in the Elementary Social Studies*, Bulletin No. 33. Washington, D.C.: National Council for the Social Studies, 1961.   **2**

Flood, J., D. Lapp, and S. Flood. "Types of Writing Found in the Early Level of Basal Reading Programs: Preprimer Through Second Grade Readers." Maryland: *Annals of Dyslexia*, 34 (1984) 241–255.   1

Forbes, J., T. Thoburn, and R. Bechtel. *Macmillan Mathematics*, Books 7 and 8. New York: Macmillan Publishing Company, 1982.

Frager, A. M., and L. C. Thompson. "Reading Instruction and Music Education: Getting in Tune." *Journal of Reading*, 27, 3 (December 1983), 202–206.   5

Gallant, R. *National Geographic Picture Atlas of Our Universe*. Washington, D.C.: National Geographic Society, 1980.

Gross, H. D., et al. *Exploring World Regions: Western Hemisphere*. Chicago: Follett Publishing Company, 1975.

Hartley, W., and W. Vincent. *American Civics*, 4th ed. New York: Harcourt Brace Jovanovich, Inc., 1983.

Herber, H. *Teaching Reading in Content Areas*, 2nd ed. Englewood Cliffs, N.J.: Prentice-Hall, Inc., 1978.   1–5

Jarolimek, J. *Social Studies in the Elementary School*, 6th ed. New York: Macmillan Publishing Company, 1982.   2

Jenkinson, M. "Ways of Teaching." In *The Teaching of Reading*, ed. R. Staiger. Paris: UNESCO, 1973.   1

Karlin, R. *Teaching Elementary Reading*. New York: Harcourt Brace Jovanovich, Inc., 1971, p. 218.   1–5

Kenworthy, L. S. *Eleven Nations*. Lexington, Mass.: Ginn and Company, 1972, p. 177.

Lamberg, W., and C. Lamb. *Reading Instruction in the Content Areas*. Chicago: Rand McNally & Company, 1980.   2–5

Lapp, D., and L. Lungren. "Musical Creativity: Exclusively an Elementary School Concept?" *American Music Teacher*, 24 (June–July 1975), 21–22.   5

———, A. Lahnston, R. Rezba, and A. Duelfer. "Is It Possible to Teach Reading Through the Content Areas?" *New England Reading Association Journal*, 13, 3 (1978), 20–25.   1

———, and J. Flood. "Promoting Reading Comprehension: Instruction Which Ensures Continuous Growth." In *Promoting Reading Comprehension*, ed. J. Flood, pp. 273–288. Newark, Dela.: International Reading Association, 1984.   1–5

Linder, B., E. Selzer, and B. Berk. *A World History*. Chicago: Science Research Associates, Inc., 1979.

Mallison, G. G. "Reading in the Sciences: A Review of the Research." In *Reading in the Content Areas*, ed. J. L. Laffey, pp. 127–182. Newark, Dela.: International Reading Association, 1972.   4

Marksheffel, N. D. *Better Reading in the Secondary School*. New York: The Ronald Press Company, 1966, p. 174.   1

Marsh, M., et al. *The Spectrum of Music with Related Arts*. New York: Macmillan Publishing Company, 1980.

McGuire, G. "How Arts Instruction Affects Reading and Language: Theory and Practice." *The Reading Teacher*, 37, 9 (May 1984), 835–839.   5

Miccinati, J. L., J. B. Sanford, and G. Hapner. "Teaching Reading Through the Arts: An Annotated Bibliography." *The Reading Teacher*, 36, 4 (January 1983), 412–417.   5

Moore, D., and J. Readence. "Approaches to Content Area Reading Instruction." *Journal of Reading*, 26 (February 1983), 397–402.   1–5

National Society for the Study of Education. *Reading in the Elementary School*, Forty-eighth Yearbook. Chicago: University of Chicago Press, 1962.   1

Patberg, J., P. Dewitz, and M. J. Henning. "The Impact of Content Area Reading Instruction on Secondary Teachers." *Journal of Reading*, 27, 6 (March 1984), 500–507.   **1–5**

Reeves, R. *The Teaching of Reading in Our Schools*. New York: Macmillan Publishing Company, 1966.   **1**

Roe, B., B. Stoodt, and P. Burns, *Reading Instruction in the Secondary School*, rev. ed. Chicago: Rand-McNally & Company, 1978.   **1–5**

Russell, D. *Children Learn to Read*. Lexington, Mass.: Ginn and Company, 1961, p. 457.

Schon, I. "Introducing Pre-Columbian and Hispanic Art and Artists to Young People Through Recent Books." *Journal of Reading*, 27, 3 (December 1983), 248–251.   **5**

Shannon, A. J. "Monitoring Reading Instruction in the Content Areas." *Journal of Reading*, 28, 2 (November, 1984), 128–135.

Shepherd, D. *Comprehensive High School Reading Methods*, 2nd ed. Columbus, Ohio: Charles E. Merrill Publishing Company, 1978.   **1–5**

Smardo, F. A. "Using Children's Literature as a Prelude or Finale to Music Experiences with Young Children." *The Reading Teacher*, 37, 8 (April 1984), 700–705.   **5**

Stone, A., and L. Sherman. *Spaceship Earth: Life Science*. Boston: Houghton Mifflin Company, 1975.

Thompson, L. C., and A. M. Frager. "Teaching Critical Thinking: Guidelines for Teacher-Designed Content Area Lessons." *Journal of Reading*, 28, 2 (November, 1984), 122–127.

Tierney, R., and D. Lapp (eds.). *National Assessment of Educational Progress*. Newark, Dela.: International Reading Association, 1979.   **1**

Tirro, R. "Reading Techniques in the Teaching of Music." In *Fusing Reading Skills and Content*, ed. H. A. Robinson and E. L. Thomas, pp. 103–107. Newark, Dela.: International Reading Association, 1968.

Tonjes, M., and M. Zintz. *Teaching Reading/Thinking/Study Skills in Content Classrooms*. Dubuque, Iowa: Wm. C. Brown Company, Publishers, 1981.   **1–5**

Wade, S. E. "A Synthesis of Research for Improving Reading in Social Studies." *Review of Educational Research*, 53, 4 (Winter 1983), 461–498.

Wallbank, T., A. Schrier, D. Maier-Weaver, and P. Gutierrez. *History and Life: The World and Its People*. Glenview, Ill.: Scott, Foresman and Company, 1980.

Wallen, N. E., and R. M. W. Travers. "Analysis and Investigation of Teaching Methods." In *Handbook of Research on Teaching*. Skokie, Ill.: Rand McNally & Company, American Educational Research Association, 1963, p. 453.   **1**

Chapter 10

Allen, R. *Report of the Reading Study Project*, Monograph No. 1. San Diego, Calif.: Department of Education, San Diego County, 1961.   **2**

———. *Language Experiences in Communication*. Boston: Houghton Mifflin Company, 1976.   **2**

Barrett, T. "Predicting Reading Achievement Through Readiness Tests." In *Reading and Inquiry, Proceedings of the International Reading Association*, ed. J. Figurel, pp. 26–28. Newark, Dela.: International Reading Association, 1965.   **2**

Black, I. *The Bank Street Readers.* New York: Macmillan Publishing Company, 1966.   **2**

Bloomfield, L., and C. Barnhart. *Let's Read: A Linguistic Approach.* Detroit: Wayne State University Press, 1961.   **2**

Bruner, J. *The Process of Education.* Cambridge, Mass.: Harvard University Press, 1960.

Buchanan, C., and Sullivan Associates. *Programmed Reading.* St. Louis, Mo.: McGraw-Hill Book Company, Webster Division, 1966.   **2**

Burmeister, L. "Content of a Phonics Program." In *Reading Methods and Teacher Improvement,* ed. N. Smith, pp. 27–33. Newark, Dela.: International Reading Association, 1971.   **2**

Carillo, L., and D. Bissett. *The Chandler Language Experience Readers.* San Francisco: Chandler Publishing Company, 1968.   **2**

Cheek, M., and E. Cheek. *Diagnostic-Prescriptive Reading Instruction.* Dubuque, Iowa: Wm. C. Brown Company, Publishers, 1980.   **2**

Clymer, T. "The Utility of Phonic Generalizations in the Primary Grades." *The Reading Teacher,* 16, 3 (1963), 252–258.   **2**

Clymer, T., et al. *Ginn Reading Program.* Lexington, Mass.: Xerox Corp., 1983.   **2**

Dale, E., and J. Chall. "A Formula for Predicting Readability." *Educational Research Bulletin,* 27 (January 1948), 11–20.   **2**

Dewey, J. *Democracy and Education.* New York: Macmillan Publishing Company, 1916.   **1**

Durkin, D. *Teaching Young Children to Read,* 3rd ed. Boston: Allyn & Bacon, Inc., 1980.   **2**

————. *Teaching Them to Read,* 4th ed. Boston : Allyn & Bacon, Inc., 1983.   **2**

Durrell, D. "Success in First Grade Reading." *Boston University Journal of Education,* 140 (February 1958), 2–47.   **2**

Eller, W., et al. *Laidlaw Reading Program.* River Forest, Ill.: Laidlaw Publishers, 1983.   **2**

Farr, R., and N. Roser. *Teaching a Child to Read.* New York: Harcourt Brace Jovanovich, Inc., 1979.   **2**

Fisher, J. "Dialect, Bilingualism and Reading." In *Reading for All,* ed. R. Karlin. Proceedings of World Congress of IRA, Buenos Aires, Argentina, 1974.   **2**

Flesch, R. *Marks of Readable Style: A Study of Adult Education.* New York: Bureau of Publications, Teachers College Press, Columbia University, 1943.   **1**

Flood, J., and D. Lapp. "The Reading/Language Arts Curriculum in Secondary Schools: What Has Been and What Might Be." *English Education,* 1985.   **3**

————, and D. Lapp. "An Investigation of Types of Writing Included in Basal Reading Programs and Standardized Reading Tests." *English Education,* 1985.   **2**

————, D. Lapp, and S. Flood. "Types of Writing Included in Basal Readers from Preprimers to Second Grade Readers," *Annuals of Dyslexia,* 34 (1985), 241–256.

Fries, C. *Linguistics and Reading.* New York: Holt, Rinehart and Winston, 1962.   **2**

————. *Reading in the Elementary School.* Boston: Allyn & Bacon, Inc., 1964.   **2**

————, et al. *Merrill Linguistic Readers.* Columbus, Ohio. Charles E. Merrill Publishing Company, 1966.   **2**

Fry, E. "Programmed Instruction and Automation in Beginning Reading." In *El-*

ementary Reading Instruction, ed. A. Beery et al., pp. 400–413. Boston: Allyn & Bacon, Inc., 1969.   2

Gattegno, C. *Words in Color.* Chicago: Learning Materials, Inc., 1980.   2

Good, C. "Doctoral Studies Completed or Underway." *Phi Delta Kappa,* 1923–1953.   1

Goodman, K. "Dialect Barriers to Reading Comprehension." *Elementary English,* 42 (December 1965), 852–860.   2

———, ed. *The Psycholinguistic Nature of the Reading Process.* Detroit: Wayne State University Press, 1968.   2

———. "Effective Teachers of Reading Know Language and Children." *Elementary English,* 51 (September 1974), 828–32   2

Goodman, Y. "Using Children's Reading Miscues for New Teaching Strategies." *The Reading Teacher,* 23 (February 1970), 455–459.   2

Gray, L., and D. Reese. *Teaching Children to Read,* 3rd ed. New York: The Ronald Press Company, 1963.   2

Gray, W. "Summary of Investigations Relating to Reading." *Elementary School Journal,* 1925–1932.   1

———, and B. Leary. *What Makes a Book Readable.* Chicago: University of Chicago Press, 1935.   1

Guthrie, J. "Research: Meaning of 'Reading.' " *Journal of Reading,* 26 (May 1983), 750–751.   3

Hafner, L., and H. Jolly. *Patterns of Teaching Reading in the Elementary School.* New York: Macmillan Publishing Company, 1972.   2

Hall, M. *Reading as a Language Experience.* Columbus, Ohio: Charles E. Merrill Publishing Company, 1975.   2

Harris, A. *How to Increase Reading Ability,* 7th ed. New York: David McKay Co., Inc., 1980.   2

Harris, A., and M. Jacobson. *Basic Elementary Reading Vocabularies.* The First R Series. New York: Macmillan Publishing Company, 1972.   2

Harris, L., and C. Smith, eds. *Individualized Reading Instruction: A Reader,* 3rd ed. New York: Holt, Rinehart and Winston, 1980.   2

Harris, T., et al. *The Economy Company Readers.* Boston: The Economy Company, 1972.   2

Jalongo, M. R., and K. Bromley. "Developing Linguistic Competence Through Song Picture Books." *The Reading Teacher,* 37, 9 (May, 1984), 840–845.

Jenkins, M., ed. "Here's to Success in Reading Self-Selection Helps." *Childhood Education,* 32 (November 1955), 124–131.   2

Lapp, D., et al. *Teaching and Learning: Philosophical, Psychological, Curricular Applications.* New York: Macmillan Publishing Company, 1975.   3

Lorge, I. "Predicting Readability." *Teachers College Record,* 45 (March 1944), 404–419.   1

Matthes, C. *How Children Are Taught to Read,* 2nd ed. Lincoln, Neb.: Professional Educators Publications, 1977.   2

Mazurkiewicz, A., and H. Tanzer. *Early to Read Program, Revised Phases 1, 2, 3.* ITA. New York: Macmillan Publishing Company, 1965–66.   2

McKim, M., and H. Caskey. *Guiding Growth in Reading,* 2nd ed. New York: Macmillan Publishing Company, 1963.   2

Pitman, Sir J., A. Mazurkiewicz, and H. Tanzer. *The Handbook on Writing and Spelling in i/t/a.* New York: i/t/a Publications, 1964.   2

Reimer, B. "Recipes for Language Experience Stories." *The Reading Teacher,* 36 (January 1983), 396–401.   2

Robinson, H., ed. "Reading: Seventy-five Years of Progress." Supplementary

Educational Monographs, No. 96. Chicago: University of Chicago Press, 1966.   **1**

————, ed. *Reading & Writing Instruction in the United States: Historical Trends.* Urbana, Ill.: ERIC Clearinghouse on Reading and Communication Skills; and Newark, Dela.: International Reading Association, 1977.   **1**

Roser, N. L. "Teaching and Testing Reading Comprehension: An Historical Perspective on Instructional Research and Practices." In *Promoting Reading Comprehension,* ed. J. Flood, pp. 48–60. Newark, Dela.: International Reading Association, 1984.   **1**

Rumelhart, D. Toward an Interactive Model of Reading. Center for Human Information Processing, Technical Report No. 56. La Jolla: University of California, San Diego, 1976.   **2**

Samuels, S. J. "The Effect of Letter-Name Knowledge on Learning to Read." *American Educational Research Journal,* 9 (Winter 1972), 65–74.   **2**

Sartain, H. "The Place of Individualized Reading in a Well-Planned Program." In *Readings on Reading Instruction,* ed. A. Harris and E. Sipay, 2nd ed., pp. 193–199. New York: David McKay Co., Inc., 1972.   **2**

Schmidt, W., J. Coul, J. Byers, and M. Buchman. "Content of Basal Reading Selections: Implications for Comprehension Instruction." In *Comprehension Instruction,* eds. G. Duffy, L. Roehler, and J. Mason. New York: Longman, Inc., 1984.   **2**

Schulwitz, B., ed. *Teachers, Tangibles, Techniques: Comprehension of Content in Reading.* Newark, Dela.: International Reading Association, 1975.

Serwer, B. "Linguistic Support for a Method of Teaching Beginning Reading to Black Children." *Reading Research Quarterly* (Summer 1969), 449–467.   **2**

Shuy, R. "Some Considerations for Developing Beginning Reading Materials for Ghetto Children." *Journal of Reading Behavior,* 1 (Spring 1969), 33–44.   **2**

Silvaroli, N. "Factors in Predicting Children's Success in First Grade Reading." In *Reading and Inquiry, Proceedings of the International Reading Association,* pp. 296–298. Newark, Dela.: International Reading Association, 1965.   **2**

Smith, C. *The Macmillan R.* New York: Macmillan Publishing Company, 1975.

————, and R. Wardhaugh. *Macmillan Reading, Series R.* New York: Macmillan Publishing Company, 1980.

————, et al. *Teaching Reading in Secondary School Content Subjects: A Book-Thinking Process.* New York: Holt, Rinehart and Winston, 1978.

Smith, F. *Understanding Reading,* 2nd ed. New York: Holt, Rinehart and Winston, 1978.   **2**

Smith, J. *Creative Teaching of Reading in the Elementary School,* 2nd ed. Boston: Allyn & Bacon, Inc., 1973.   **2**

Smith, N. *American Reading Instruction.* Newark, Dela.: International Reading Association, 1965.   **1**

Spache, G. "Psychological and Cultural Factors in Learning to Read." In *Reading for All, Proceedings of the Fourth IRA World Congress on Reading,* ed. R. Karlin, pp. 43–50. Newark, Dela.: International Reading Association, 1973.   **2**

————, and E. Spache. *Reading in the Elementary School,* 4th ed. Boston: Allyn & Bacon, Inc., 1977.   **2**

Stauffer, R. *Directing the Reading-Thinking Process.* New York: Harper & Row, Publishers, 1975.   **2**

————. *The Language-Experience Approach to the Teaching of Reading.* New York: Harper & Row, Publishers, 1970.   **2**

Strickland, R. "The Language of Elementary School Children: Its Relationship to the Language of Reading Textbooks and the Quality of Reading in Selected Children." *Bulletin of the School of Education* (Indiana University), 38 (1962), p. 4. **2**

Tinker, M., and C. McCullough. *Teaching Elementary School*, 3rd ed. New York: Appleton-Century-Crofts, 1968. **2**

Veatch, J., et al. *Key Words to Reading: The Language Experience Approach Begins*, 2nd ed. Columbus, Ohio: Charles E. Merrill Publishing Company, 1979. **2**

Chapter 11

Alexander, J., and R. Filler. *Attitudes and Reading*. Newark, Dela.: International Reading Association, 1976. **1**

Allport, G. "Attitudes." In *A Handbook of Social Psychology*, ed. C. Murchison, p. 798. Worcester, Mass.: Clark University Press, 1935. **1**

Buerger, T. A. "A Follow-Up of Remedial Reading Instruction." *The Reading Teacher*, 21 (November, 1968), 329–334.

Chaparro, J., P. Conlon-Ross, and R. Ross. *Economy Company's Reader's Theater Program*. Oklahoma City, Okla.: Economy Company, Publishers, 1981.

Christensen, J., chairperson. *Your Reading: A Booklist for Junior High and Middle School Students*. Urbana, Ill.: National Council of Teachers of English, 1983.

Ciccone, D. "Reading Attitudes and Interests of Sixth Grade Pupils." Unpublished M.A. thesis, Kean College of New Jersey, Union, N.J., 1981.

Combs, M. "Developing Concepts About Print With Patterned Sentence Stories." *The Reading Teacher*, 38, 2 (November, 1984), 178–181.

Dawson, M. "Developing Interest in Books." In *The Quest for Competency in Teaching Reading*, ed. H. Klein, pp. 36–41. Newark, Dela.: International Reading Association, 1972. **2**

Dobbs, L. W. "The Behavior of Attitudes." *Psychological Review*, 54 (1947), 135–156. **1**

Epstein, I. *Measuring Attitudes Toward Reading*, ERIC/TM Report 73. Princeton, N.J.: ERIC Clearinghouse on Tests, Measurements, and Evaluations, 1980. **1**

Estes, T. H. "Assessing Attitudes Toward Reading." *Journal of Reading*, 25 (1971), 135–138. **1**

Fishbein, M. "Attitude and the Prediction of Behavior." In *Readings in Attitude Theory and Measurement*, ed. M. Fishbein. New York: John Wiley & Sons, Inc., 1967. **1**

Gardner, R. C. A. "The Relationship of Self-esteem and Variable Associated with Reading for Fourth Grade Prima Indian Children." Unpublished doctoral dissertation, University of Arizona, Tucson, Ariz., 1972. **1**

Gordon, I. J. *Studying the Child in School*. New York: John Wiley & Sons, 1966.

Groff, P. J. "Children's Attitudes Toward Reading and Their Critical-Type Materials." *Journal of Educational Research*, 55 (April 1962), 313–314. 1

Heathington, B. S. "The Development of Scales to Measure Attitudes Toward Reading." Unpublished doctoral dissertation, University of Tennessee, Knoxville, Tenn., 1975. **1**

———. "What to Do About Reading Motivation in the Middle School." *Journal of Reading*, 22 (May 1979), 709–713. **2**

———, and J. E. Alexander. "Do Classroom Teachers Emphasize Attitudes

Toward Reading?" *The Reading Teacher*, 37, 6 (February 1984), pp. 484–490,   1

Logan, J. "ERIC/RCS Report: Developing Children's Appreciation of Literature." *Language Arts*, 60 (April 1983), 518–521.   2, 4

McDougall, W. *Body and Mind*. New York: Macmillan Publishing Company, 1921.   1

Manning, D. T., and B. Manning. "Bibliotherapy for Children of Alcoholics." *Journal of Reading*, 27, 8 (May 1984), 720–725.   1–4

Mathewson, G. "The Function of Attitude in the Reading Process." In *Theoretical Models and Processes of Reading*, 2nd ed., ed. H. Singer and R. Ruddell, pp. 665–676. Newark, Dela.: International Reading Association, 1976.   1

Miller, N., and J. Dollard. *Social Learning and Imitation*. New Haven, Conn.: Yale University Press, 1941.   1, 3

Neale, D. C., N. Gill, and W. Tismer. "Relationship Between Attitudes Toward School Subjects and School Achievement." *Journal of Educational Research*, 63 (1970), 232–237.   1

Neumann, S. B. "Television: Its Effects on Reading and School Achievement." *The Reading Teacher*, 33 (April 1980), 801–805.   1

———, and P. Prowda. "Television Viewing and Reading Achievement." *Journal of Reading*, 25 (April 1982), 666–671.   1

Nichols, J. N. "Using Prediction to Increase Content Area Interest and Understanding." *Journal of Reading*, 27, 3 (December 1983), 225–228.   1

O'Connor, W. F. "The Reading Apperception Test: An Exploration of Attitudes Toward Reading." Unpublished doctoral dissertation, Oklahoma State University, Norman, Okla., 1968.   1

Peifer, J. E. "The Development of an Attitude Scale to Measure Students' Attitudes Toward Reading in the Secondary Schools." Unpublished doctoral dissertation, Pennsylvania State University, University Park, Pa., 1962.   1

Puryear, C. "An Investigation of the Relationship Between Attitudes Toward Reading and Reading Achievement." Unpublished doctoral dissertation, University of South Carolina, Columbia, So. Car., 1975.   1

Quandt, I. *Self-concept and Reading*. Newark, Dela.: International Reading Association, 1972.   1

Ransbury, M. "Critical Factors in the Development of Attitudes Toward Reading as Defined by Individual Perceptions of Students, Their Teachers and Parents." Unpublished doctoral dissertation, Indiana University School of Education, Bloomington, Ind., 1971.   1

———. "An Assessment of Reading Attitudes." *Journal of Reading*, 17 (October 1973), 25–28.

Ratliff, G. "Reader's Theatre: The 'Theatrical' Approach to Teaching Literature." Montclair State College, Montclair, N.J., 1980.   4

Rosenblatt, L. "The Reading Transactions: What for?" In *Developing Literacy: Young Children's Use of Language*, ed. R. Parker and F. Davis, pp. 118–135. Newark, Dela.: International Reading Association, 1983.   1

Roswell, C. G. "Changes in Attitude Toward Reading and Its Relationship to Certain Variables Among Children with Reading Difficulties." Unpublished doctoral dissertation, George Peabody College for Teachers, Nashville, Tenn., 1967.   1

Schrank, F. A., and D. W. Engels. "Bibliotherapy as a Counseling Adjunct: Research Findings." *The Personnel and Guidance Journal*, 60 (November 1981), 143–147.   1–4

Schwartz, E. E. "Bibliotherapy." *New Jersey Education Association Review*, 55 (November 1981), 34–35.   **1–4**

Smith, J. A. *The Nature of Creative Teaching*. Boston: Allyn & Bacon, Inc., 1975.   **1, 3**

Somers, A., and J. Worthington. *Response Guides for Teaching Children's Books*. Urbana, Ill.: National Council of Teachers of English, 1979, p. 6.   **4**

Spiegel, D. L. *Reading for Pleasure: Guidelines*. Newark, Dela.: International Reading Association, 1981.   **4**

Stephens, J. *The Crock of Gold: Irish Fairy Tales*. New York: Macmillan Publishing Company, 1960.   **4**

Telfer, R. J., and R. S. Kann. "Reading Achievement, Free Reading, Watching TV, and Listening to Music." *Journal of Reading*, 27, 6 (March 1984), 536–539.   **1**

Thurstone, L. L. "Attitudes Can Be Measured." *The American Journal of Sociology*, 33 (1928), 529–554.   **1**

Tillman, C. E. "Bibliotherapy for Adolescents: An Annotated Research Review." *Journal of Reading*, 27, 8 (May 1984) 713–719.   **1–4**

Tullock-Rhody, R., and J. Alexander. "A Scale for Assessing Attitudes Toward Reading in Secondary Schools." *Journal of Reading*, 23 (April 1980), 609–614.   **1**

Turner, T., and J. Alexander. "Promising Practices for Improving Reading Attitudes." Paper presented at the Annual Meeting of the Southeastern Regional Conference of the International Reading Association, Nashville, Tenn., February, 1980.   **1**

White, C. S. "ERIC/RCS: Learning Style and Reading Instruction." *The Reading Teacher*, 36 (April 1983), 843–845.   **3**

Wilson, R., and M. Hall. *Reading and the Elementary School Child*. New York: Van Nostrand Reinhold Company, 1972.   **1–3**

Witty, P., and Associates. "Studies of Children's Interests—A Brief Summary." In *Readings on Reading Instruction*, ed. A. J. Harris, pp. 330–337. New York: David McKay Co., Inc., 1963.   **1–3**

Woodbury, J. "Choral Reading and Reader's Theatre: Oral Interpretation of Literature in the Classroom." In *Developing Active Readers: Ideas for Parents, Teachers and Librarians*, ed. D. Monson, pp. 65–72. Newark, Dela.: International Reading Association, 1979.   **1–3**

Chapter 12

Anderson, J. "Lix and Rix: Variations on a Little-Known Readability Index." *Journal of Reading*, 26 (March 1983), 490–496.   **1**

Aukerman, R. C. "Assessing the Readability of Textbooks." In *Reading in the Secondary School Classroom*, pp. 19–45. New York: McGraw-Hill Book Company, 1972.   **2**

———. *The Basal Reader Approach to Reading*. New York: John Wiley & Sons, Inc., 1981.   **1**

Bader, L. *Bader Reading and Language Inventory*. New York: Macmillan Publishing Company, 1983.   **2**

Binet, A., and T. Simon. *The Development of Intelligence in Children*. Baltimore: The Williams and Wilkins Company, 1916.   **2**

Bond, G. L., and M. A. Tinker. *Reading Difficulties: Their Diagnosis and Correction*, 4th ed. Englewood Cliffs, N.J.: Prentice-Hall, Inc., 1979.   **1**

Bormuth, J. "The Cloze Readability Procedure." *Elementary English,* 45 (April 1968), 426–436.   **2**

Bormuth, J. R., ed. *Readability in 1968.* Champaign, Ill.: National Council of Teachers of English, 1968.   **2**

Burns, E. "Linear Regression and Simplified Reading Expectancy Formulas." *Reading Research Quarterly,* 17, 3 (1982), 446–453.   **2**

Buros, O. K., ed. *Mental Measurement Yearbooks.* Highland Park, N.J.: Gryphon Press, 1968–1978.   **2**

Carlson, R. "Reading Level Difficulty." *Creative Computing,* 4 (April 1980), 60–61.   **2**

Collier, R. "The Word Processor and Revision Strategies." *College Composition and Communication,* 34 (May 1983), 149–155.   **4**

Combs, A. W. *The Professional Education of Teachers.* Boston: Allyn & Bacon, Inc., 1965.   **1**

Dale, E., and J. Chall. "A Formula for Predicting Readability." *Educational Research Bulletin,* 27 (1948), 11–20,   **2**

Demaine, J. "IQism as Ideology and the Political Economy of Education." *Educational Studies,* 3 (October 1979), 199–215.   **1**

Duffy, G. "Fighting off the Alligators: What Research in Real Classrooms Has to Say About Reading Instruction." *Journal of Reading Behavior,* 14, 4 (1982), 357–373.   **4**

Estes, T., and E. Wetmore. "Assessing the Comprehensibility of Text." *Reading Psychology,* 4 (January–March 1983), 37–51.   **1**

Farr, R. *Reading: What Can Be Measured?* Newark, Dela.: International Reading Association, 1969.   **2**

———, ed. *Measurement and Evaluation of Reading.* New York: Harcourt, Brace & World, Inc., 1970.   **2**

———. Unpublished Class Notes. Indiana University, Bloomington, IN, 1970.

Fischer, D. G., D. Hunt, and B. Randhawa. "Empirical Validity of Ertle's Brain-Wave Analyzer (BWAO2)." *Educational & Psychological Measurement,* 4 (Winter 1978), 1017–1030.   **1**

Flesch, R. F. *Marks of Readable Style: A Study of Adult Education.* New York: Bureau of Publications, Teachers College Press, Columbia University, 1943.   **1**

Fry, E. "Readability Formula That Saves Time." *Journal of Reading,* 11 (April 1968), 513–516.   **2**

———. "Fry's Readability Graph: Clarification, Validity, and Extension to Level 17." *Journal of Reading,* 21 (December 1977), pp. 242–252.   **2**

Gagne, R. M. *The Conditions of Learning.* New York: Holt, Rinehart and Winston, 1965.   **4**

Goodlad, J. I. *School, Curriculum, and the Individual.* Waltham, Mass.: Blaisdell Publishing Company, 1966.   **1**

Goodman, D., and S. Schwab. "Computerized Testing for Readability." *Creative Computing,* 4 (April 1980), 46–51.   **2**

Goodman, K. S. "Analysis of Oral Reading Miscues: Applied Psycholinguistics." *Reading Research Quarterly,* 5 (Fall 1969), 9–30.   **2**

Goodman, K. S. "Miscue Analysis: Theory and Reality in Reading." In *New Horizons in Reading,* ed. J. E. Merritt, pp. 15–26. Newark, Dela.: International Reading Association, 1976.   **2**

Goodman, Y. M. "Reading Diagnosis—Qualitative or Quantitative?" *The Reading Teacher,* 26 (October 1972), 32–37.   **1**

————, and C. L. Burke. *Reading Miscue Inventory: Procedure for Diagnosis and Evaluation.* New York: Macmillan Publishing Company, 1972.   1

Gray, W. S., and B. E. Leary. *What Makes a Book Readable?* Chicago: University of Chicago Press, 1935.   2

Guidry, L. J., and F. D. Knight. "Comparative Readability: Four Formulas and Newbery Books." *Journal of Reading,* 19 (April 1976), 552–556.   2

Hambleton, R. K., H. Swaminathan, J. Algino, and D. B. Coulson. "Criterion-Referenced Testing and Measurement: A Review of Technical Issues and Developments." *Review of Educational Research,* 48 (Winter 1978), 1–47.   2

Hammond, R. L. *Evaluation at the Local Level.* Miller Committee for the National Study of ESEA Title III, U.S. Office of Education, Washington, D.C., 1967, EDRS.   2

Harris, A. J. "Some New Developments on Readability." In *New Horizons in Reading,* ed. J. E. Merritt, pp. 106–118. Newark, Dela.: International Reading Association, 1976.   2

————, and E. R. Sipay. *How to Increase Reading Ability,* 7th ed. New York: Longman, Inc., 1980.   1

Johnson, M. S., and R. A. Kress. *Informal Reading Inventories.* Newark, Dela.: International Reading Association, 1965.   2

Judd, D. H. "Avoid Readability Formula Drudgery: Use Your School's Microcomputer." *The Reading Teacher,* 1 (October, 1981), 7–8.   1

Kretschmer, J. L. "Computerizing and Comparing the Rix Readability Index." *Journal of Reading,* 27, 4 (January 1984), 490–499.   1

Legneza, A., and D. Elijah. "The Cloze Procedure: Some New Applications." *Journal of Educational Research,* 6 (July–August 1979), 351–355.   2

Lorge, I. "Predicting Readability." *Teachers College Record,* 45 (March 1944), 404–419.   2

Millman, J. "Criterion-Referenced Measurement." In *Evaluation in Education: Current Applications,* ed. W. J. Popham. Berkeley, Calif.: McCutchen Publishing Company, 1974, 309–398.   2

Nitko, A. J. "Distinguishing the Many Varieties of Criterion-Referenced Tests." *Review of Educational Research,* 3 (Fall 1980), 461–485.   2

Rivera, C. "Massachusetts Bilingual Legislation: Impact on the Boston Educational System." Unpublished paper, Boston University, School of Education, Boston, Mass., 1976.   1

Roney, R. C. "Background Experience Is the Foundation of Success in Learning To Read." *The Reading Teacher,* 38, 2 (November, 1984), 196–199.   2

Russo, N. A. "The Effects of Student Characteristics, Educational Beliefs, and Instructional Task on Teachers' Preinstructional Decisions in Reading and Math." Unpublished doctoral dissertation, University of California, Los Angeles, Calif., 1978.   3

Shepard, L. "Norm-Referenced vs. Criterion-Referenced Tests." *Educational Horizons,* 1 (Fall 1979), 26–32.   2

Smith, S., W. Kimberling, B. Pennington, and H. Lubs. "Specific Reading Disability: Identification of an Inherited Form Through Linkage Analysis." *Science,* 219 (March 1983), 1345–1347.   2

Spache, G. "A New Readability Formula for Primary Grade Reading Materials." *Elementary School Journal,* 53 (March 1953), 410–413.   2

Stanley, J. C., and K. D. Hopkins. *Educational and Psychological Measurement and Evaluation.* Englewood Cliffs, N.J.: Prentice-Hall, Inc., 1972.   1

Vernon, P. E. "Intelligence Testing and the Nature/Nurture Debate, 1928–1978: What Next?" *British Journal of Educational Psychology*, 49 (February 1979), 1–14.   **2**

Weiss, B. J., et al. *Holt Basic Reading*. New York: Holt, Rinehart and Winston, 1980.   **3**

Zjawin, D. "Mother Goose Was My Paraprofessional." *Instructor*, 90 (November 1980), 60–62.   **3**

Chapter 13

Associated Press. "U.S. Hispanic Population Soars to 15.9 Million." *The San Diego Union*, April 16, 1984.   **2, 3**

Ching, D. *Reading and the Bilingual Child*. Newark, Dela.: International Reading Association, 1976.   **1**

Cook, G. "Breaking the Code." *Journal of Reading*, 25 (May 1982), p. 730.

Cummins, J. "The Role of Primary Language Development in Promoting Educational Success for Language Minority Students." In *Schooling and Language Minority Students: A Theoretical Framework*. Los Angeles: Evaluation, Dissemination and Assessment Center, California State University, 1981.   **1–4**

Gillet, J. W., and J. R. Gentry. "Bridges Between Nonstandard and Standard English with Extensions of Dictated Stories." *The Reading Teacher*, 36, 4 (January 1983), pp. 360–365.   **4**

Gondelman, J. "Bilingual Education an Emotional Issue." *San Diego Union*, June 10, 1982, pp. A1, A12.   **1, 3**

———. "Does Bilingual Education Work?" *San Diego Union*, June 11, 1984, pp. A1, A6. (a).

———. "Proposed Changes in the Law." *San Diego Union*, June 12, 1984, p. A1. (b)

Hirsch, S. "Informal Diagnostic Instruments of English Language Skills." In *Proceedings of the Boston University Bilingual Reading Laboratory*, ed. J. Flood, pp. 84–96. Boston: Boston University of Education, 1976.   **4**

Krashen, S. D. "Bilingual Education and Second Language Acquisition Theory." In *Schooling and Language Minority Students: A Theoretical Framework*. Los Angeles: Evaluation, Dissemination and Assessment Center, California State University, 1981   **2**

Lado, R. *Linguistics Across Cultures*. University of Michigan, Ann Arbor, MI, 1976.   **4**

Mace-Matluck, B. J. *Literacy Instruction in Bilingual Settings: A Synthesis of Current Research*, ERIC Document ED 222 079. National Center for Bilingual Research, Los Alamitos, CA, 1983.   **4**

Long, R. "Soviet Children's Books: Expanding Children's View of the Soviet Union." *Journal of Reading*, 27, 5 (February 1984), 418–423.   **2**

Moores, D. *Educating the Deaf: Psychology, Principles and Practices*. Boston: Houghton Mifflin Company, 1978.   **2**

National Education Association. *The Invisible Minority*. Washington, D.C.: NEA, 1966.   **1**

Past, K., and A. Past. "A Bilingual Kindergarten Immersed in Print." *The Reading Teacher*, 50 (May 1980), 907–913.   **1, 3**

Ruddell, R. *Reading-Language Instruction*. Englewood Cliffs, N.J.: Prentice-Hall, Inc., 1974.   **1**

Spaulding, S. "A Spanish Readability Formula." *Modern Language Journal,* 40 (December 1956), 435.   **2,3**

Steffensen, M., C. Joag-Dev, and R. Anderson. "A Cross-cultural Perspective on Reading Comprehension." *Reading Research Quarterly,* 5 (1979), 10–29.   **1,4**

Steinberg, L., P. L Blinde, and K. S. Chan. "Dropping Out Among Language Minority Youth." *Review of Educational Research,* 54, 1 (Spring 1984), pp. 113–132.   **1**

Thonis, E. *Teaching Reading to Non-English Speakers.* New York: Macmillan Publishing Company, 1970.   **3, 2**

———. *Teaching Reading to Non-English Speakers.* New York: Collier-Macmillan, 1976. (a)   **2**

———. *Teaching Reading to Spanish Speaking Children.* Newark, Dela.: International Reading Association, 1976. (b)   **2,3**

———. *The English-Spanish Connection.* N.J.: Santillana Publishing Company, 1983.   **2**

Unfinished Education: Outcome for Minorities in Five Southwestern States. Washington, D.C.: U.S. Government Printing Office, 1972.

Vorhaus, R. "Strategies for Reading in a Second Language." *Journal of Reading,* 27, 5 (February 1984), 412–417.   **3**

Zintz, M. *The Reading Process.* Dubuque, Iowa: W. C. Brown Company, Publishers, 1975.   **1**

Chapter 14

Ainsworth, S. "Report and Commentary." In *Conditioning in Stuttering Therapy: Application and Limitations,* Vol. 7. Memphis, Tenn.: Speech Foundation of America, 1970.   **2**

Arnold, D. G., and B. Swaby. "Neurolinguistic Applications for the Remediation of Reading Problems." *The Reading Teacher,* 37, 9 (June 1984), 831–834.   **2**

Barraga, N., ed. *Visual Efficiency Scale.* Louisville, Ky.: American Printing House for the Blind, 1970.   **2**

Bateman, B. "Educational Implications—Minimal Brain Dysfunction." In *Annals of the New York Academy of Sciences,* ed. F. F. de La Cruz, B. H. Fox, and R. H. Roberts, Vol. 205 (1973), 245–250.   **2**

Bates, G. W. "Developing Reading Strategies for the Gifted: A Research-Based Approach." *Journal of Reading,* 27, 7 (April, 1984), 590–593.   **2**

Belmont, L., and H. Birch. "Lateral Dominance, Lateral Awareness, and Reading Disability." *Child Development,* 34 (1965), 57–71.   **2**

Berkowitz, P. H., and E. P. Rothman. *The Disturbed Child.* New York: New York University Press, 1960.   **2**

Bigge, J. L., and P. A. O'Donnell. *Teaching Individuals with Physical and Multiple Disabilities.* Columbus, Ohio: Charles E. Merrill Publishing Company, 1977.   **2**

Birch, H. G. "Functional Effects of Fetal Malnutrition." *Hospital Practice,* 4 (1971), 134–148.   **2**

Birch, J. W. *Hearing Impaired Children in the Mainstream.* Minneapolis: Leadership Training Institute/Special Education, University of Minnesota, 1975.   **2**

Bloodstein, O. *A Handbook on Stuttering.* Chicago: National Easter Seal Society for Crippled Children and Adults, 1969.   **2**

Borkowski, J. G., and P. B. Wanschura. "Mediational Processes in the Re-tarded." In *International Review of Research in Mental Retardation,* ed. N. R. Ellis, Vol. 7. New York: Academic Press, Inc., 1974.   2

Bransford, J. D., N. J. Vye, and B. S. Stein. "A Comparison of Successful and Less Successful Learners: Can We Enhance Comprehension and Mastery Skills?" In *Promoting Reading Comprehension,* ed. J. Flood, pp. 216–231. Newark, Dela.: International Reading Association, 1984.   2

Brown, A. L. "The Role of Strategic Behavior in Retardate Memory." In *International Review of Research in Mental Retardation,* ed. N. R. Ellis, Vol. 7. New York: Academic Press, Inc., 1974.   2

Brown v. *Board of Education,* 347 U.S. 483, 493 (1954).   1

Cain, E. J., Jr. "The Challenge of Technology: Educating the Exceptional Child for the World of Tomorrow." *Teaching Exceptional Children,* 16, 4 (1984) 238–241.

Carr, K. S. "What Gifted Readers Need from Reading Instruction." *The Reading Teacher,* 38, 2 (November, 1984), 144–147.   3

Conference of Executives of American Schools for the Deaf. *Report of the Ad Hoc Committee to Define Deaf and Hard of Hearing,* 1975.   2

Corrigan, D. C. "Political and Moral Contexts That Produced P.L. 94–142." *Journal of Education,* 29 (1978), 11.   1

Cott, A. "Megavitamins: The Orthomolecular Approach to Behavioral Disorders and Learning Disabilities." *Academic Therapy,* 7 (1972), 245–258.   2, 3

Council of Exceptional Children. *The Education for All Handicapped Act—P.L. 94–142.* Washington, D.C.: U.S. Office of Education, 1977.   1

Cravioto, J., and E. DeLicardi. "Environmental and Nutritional Deprivation in Children with Learning Disabilities." In *Perceptual and Learning Disabilities in Children: Research and Theory,* ed. W. M. Cruickshank and D. P. Hallahan, Vol. 2. Syracuse, N.Y.: Syracuse University Press, 1975.   3

Cruickshank, W. M. "The Education of Children with Specific Learning Disa-bilities." In *Education of Exceptional Children and Youth,* ed. W. M. Cruickshank and G. O. Johnson. Englewood Cliffs, N.J.: Prentice-Hall, Inc., 1975.   3

———, and G. O. Johnson, eds. *Education of Exceptional Children and Youth,* 3rd ed. Englewood Cliffs, N.J.: Prentice-Hall, Inc., 1975.   2

———, F. A. Bentzen, F. H. Ratzeburg, and M. T. Tannhauser. *A Teaching Method for Brain Injured and Hyperactive Children.* Syracuse, N.Y.: Syr-acuse University Press, 1961.   2

Davis, H. "Abnormal Hearing and Deafness." In *Hearing and Deafness,* 3rd ed., ed. H. Davis and S. R. Silverman. New York: Holt, Rinehart and Winston, 1970.   2

Degler, L. S., and V. J. Risko. "Teaching Reading to Mainstreamed Sensory Im-paired Children." *The Reading Teacher,* 32 (May 1979), 921–925.   2

Devol, S. H., and M. L. Hastings. "Effects of Sex, Age, Reading Ability, SES, and Display Position on Measures of Spatial Relationships of Children." *Per-ceptual and Motor Skills,* 24 (1967), 375–387.   2

Dolphin, J. E., and W. M. Cruickshank. "Pathology of Concept Formation in Children with Cerebral Palsy." *American Journal of Mental Deficiency,* 56 (1951), 386–392.   2

Ellis, N. R. "The Stimulus Trace and Behavioral Inadequacy." In *Handbook of Mental Deficiency,* ed. N. R. Ellis, pp. 134–158. New York: McGraw-Hill Book Company, 1963.   2

———. "Memory Processes in Retardates and Normals." In *International Re-*

view of Research in Mental Retardation, ed. N. R. Ellis, Vol. 4, pp. 1–32. New York: Academic Press, Inc., 1970.   2

Farnham-Diggory, S., and L. Gregg. "Short-Term Memory Function in Young Readers." *Journal of Experimental Child Psychology*, 19 (1975), 279–298.   2

Feingold, B. F. *Why Your Child Is Hyperactive*. New York: Random House, Inc., 1975.   3

Fernald, G. M. *Remedial Techniques in Basic School Subjects*. New York: McGraw-Hill Book Company, 1943.   3

Frostig, M., and D. Horne. *The Frostig Program for the Development of Visual Perception: Teacher's Guide*. Chicago: Follett Publishing Company, 1964.   2

Furth, H. G. "Influence of Language on the Development of Concept Formation in Deaf Children." *Journal of Abnormal Social Psychology*, 63 (1961), 386–389.   2

———. "Linguistic Deficiency and Thinking: Research with Deaf Subjects 1964–1969." *Psychology Bulletin*, 76 (1971), 58–72.   2

Gearheart, B. R., and M. W. Weishahn. *The Handicapped Child in the Regular Classroom*. St. Louis, Mo.: The C. V. Mosby Company, 1976.   2

Genensky, S. M. *A Functional Classification System of the Visually Impaired to Replace the Legal Definition of Blindness*. Santa Monica, Calif.: The Rand Corporation, 1970.   2

Geoffrion, L. D., and R. D. Bergeron. *Initial Reading Through Computer Animation*, ERIC Document No. ED 138929. Durham: University of New Hampshire, 1977.   2

Getman, G. N., E. R. Kane, and G. W. McKee. *Developing Learning Readiness Programs*. New York: McGraw-Hill Book Company, 1968.   2

Gillet, J., and C. Temple. *Understanding Reading Problems: Assessment and Instruction*. Boston: Little, Brown and Company, 1982, p. 291.   2

Goldberg, E. P. *Social Technology for Special Children: Computers as Prostheses to Serve Communication and Autonomy in the Education of Handicapped Children*. Baltimore, Md.: University Park Press, 1979.   2

Grossman, H. J., ed. *Manual on Terminology and Classification in Mental Retardation*, 1973 rev. Washington, D.C.: American Association on Mental Deficiency, 1973.   2

Hallahan, D. P., and W. M. Cruickshank. *Psycho-education Foundations of Learning Disabilities*. Englewood Cliffs, N.J.: Prentice-Hall, Inc., 1973.   3

———, and J. M. Kauffman. "Research on the Education of Distractible and Hyperactive Children." In *Perceptual and Learning Disabilities in Children*, Vol. 2, *Research and Theory*, ed. W. M. Cruickshank and D. P. Hallahan. Syracuse, N.Y.: Syracuse University Press, 1975.   3

———, and J. M. Kauffman. *Introduction to Learning Disabilities: A Psychobehavioral Approach*. Englewood Cliffs, N.J.: Prentice-Hall, Inc., 1976.   3

———, and J. M. Kauffman. "Categories, Labels, Behavioral Characteristics: ED, LD, and EMR Reconsidered." *Journal of Special Education*, 11 (1977), 139–149.   2, 3

———, and J. M. Kauffman. *Exceptional Children: Introduction to Special Education*. Englewood Cliffs, N.J.: Prentice-Hall Inc., 1978.   2

Harley, R., J. Spollen, and S. Long. "A Study of Reliability and Validity of the Visual Efficiency Scale with Preschool Children." *Education of the Visually Handicapped*, 5 (May 1973), 38–42.   2

Heins, E. D., D. P. Hallahan, S. G. Traver, and J. M. Kauffman. "Relationship Between Cognitive Tempo and Selective Attention in Learning

Disabled Children." *Perceptual and Motor Skills*, 42 (1976), 233–234.   3

Hewett, F. M. "Educational Engineering with Emotionally Disturbed Children." *Exceptional Children*, 33 (1967), 459–467.   2

———. *The Emotionally Disturbed Child in the Classroom*. Boston: Allyn & Bacon, Inc., 1968.   2

Hull, F. M., P. W. Miekle, R. J. Timmons, and J. A. Willeford. *National Speech and Hearing Survey Report*, Project No. 50978. Washington, D.C.: U.S. Office of Education, Bureau of Education for the Handicapped, 1969.   2

Johnson, D. J., and H. R. Myklebust. *Learning Disabilities: Educational Principles and Practices*. New York: Grune & Stratton, 1967.   3

Keogh, B. K., and G. M. Donlon. "Field Dependence, Impulsivity and Learning Disabilities." *Journal of Learning Disabilities*, 5 (1972), 331–336.   3

Kephart, N. C. *The Slow Learner in the Classroom*, 2nd ed. Columbus, Ohio: Charles E. Merrill Publishing Company, 1971.   2

Kirk, S. A. *Early Education of the Mentally Retarded: An Experimental Study*. Urbana: University of Illinois Press, 1958.   2

Kirk, S. "Behavioral Diagnosis and Remediation of Learning Disabilities." In *Conference on Exploration into the Problems of the Perceptually Handicapped Child*, pp. 1–7. Evanston, Ill.: Fund for Perceptually Handicapped Children, 1963.   2

Klaus, R. A., and S. W. Gray, *The Early Training Project for Disadvantaged Children: A Report After Five Years*. Monograph of the Society for Research in Child Development 33, Ser. No. 120, 1968.   2

Lanquetot, R. "Autistic Children and Reading." *The Reading Teacher*, 38, 2 (November, 1984), 182–187.   3

Leton, D. A. "Visual-Motor Capacities and Ocular Efficiency in Reading." *Perceptual and Motor Skills*, 15 (1962), 406–432.   2

Lewis, R., and D. H. Doorlag. *Teaching Special Students in the Mainstream*. Columbus, Ohio: Charles E. Merrill Publishing Company, 1983.   2

Lovitt, T. C., and J. O. Smith. "Effects of Instructions on an Individual's Verbal Behavior." *Exceptional Children*, 38, 3 (1972), 685–693.   2

Lowenbraun, S., J. Affleck, and A. Archer. *Teaching the Mildly Handicapped in the Regular Class*, 2nd ed. Columbus, Ohio: Charles E. Merrill Publishing Company, 1981.   2

Meichenbaum, D. H. "Cognitive Factors as Determinants of Learning Disabilities: A Cognitive-Functional Approach." Paper presented at the NATO Conference on *The Neuropsychology of Learning Disorders: Theoretical Approaches*, Korsor, Denmark, June 1975.   3

Mercer, C. D., and M. E. Snell. *Learning Theory Research in Mental Retardation: Implications for Teaching*. Columbus, Ohio: Charles E. Merrill Publishing Company, 1977.   2

Meyer, E. L. *Exceptional Children and Youth: An Introduction*. Denver, Colo.: Love Publishing Company, 1978.   2

Mills v. Board of Education of District of Columbia, 348 F. Supp. 866, 880 (D. D.C. 1972).   1

Moller, B. "An Instructional Model for Gifted Advanced Readers." *Journal of Reading*, 27, 4 (1984), 324–327.   2

Myklebust, H. R. "Learning Disabilities: Definition and Overview." In *Progress in Learning Disabilities*, ed. H. R. Myklebust, Vol. 1, pp. 1–15. New York: Grune & Stratton, 1968.   3

National Advisory Committee on Handicapped Children. Conference sponsored by Bureau of Education of the Handicapped. Washington, D.C.: U.S. Office of Education, September 28, 1968.   2

Nelson-Herber, J., and H. Herber. "A Positive Approach to Assessment and Correction of Reading Difficulties in Middle and Secondary Schools." In *Promoting Reading Comprehension*, ed. J. Flood, pp. 232–244. Newark, Dela.: International Reading Association, 1984.

Orton, S. T. *Reading, Writing and Speech Problems in Children*. New York: W. W. Norton & Company, Inc., 1937.   2

Parker, T. B., C. W. Freston, and C. J. Drew. "Comparison of Verbal Performance of Normal and Learning Disabled Children as a Function on Input Organization." *Journal of Learning Disabilities*, 8 (1975), 386–393.   3

Pasamanick, B., and P. Knoblock. "Brain Damage and Reproductive Casualty." *American Journal of Orthopsychiatry*, 30 (1960), 298–305.   2

Pennsylvania Association for Retarded Children (PARC) v. *Commonwealth of Pennsylvania*, 34 F. Supp. 279 (E.D. Pa. 1972) Consent Agreement.   1

Perkins, W. H. *Speech Pathology: An Applied Behavioral Science*. St. Louis, Mo.: The C. V. Mosby Company, 1971.   2

Rappaport, S. R., ed. *Childhood Aphasia and Brain Damage: A Definition*. Narbeth, Pa.: Livingstone Publishing Company, 1964.   2

———. *Proceedings of the 1965 Pathway School Institute*. Narbeth, Pa.: Livingstone Publishing Company, 1966.   2

Report to the Ad Hoc Committee to Define Deaf and Hard of Hearing. *American Annals of the Deaf*, 120 (1975), 509–512.   2

Robinson, N. M., and H. B. Robinson. *The Mentally Retarded Child: A Psychological Approach*, 2nd ed. New York: McGraw-Hill Book Company, 1976.   2

Rubenstein, R., and A. Rollins. *Demonstration of Use of Computer-Assisted Instruction with Handicapped Children*. Cambridge, Mass.: Bolt, Beranek, and Newman, Inc., 1978.   2

Sabatino, D. A., and J. E. Ysseldyke. "Effects of Extraneous Background on Visual-Perceptual Performance of Readers and Non-readers." *Perceptual and Motor Skills*, 35 (March 1972), 323–328.   2

Schiefelbusch, R. L., and L. L. Lloyd, eds. *Language Perspectives—Acquisition, Retardation and Intervention*. Baltimore, Md.: University Park Press, 1974.   2

Sheehan, J. "Projective Studies of Stuttering." *Journal of Speech and Hearing Disorders*, 23 (1958), 18–25.   2

Skubic, V., and M. Anderson. "The Interrelationship of Perceptual-Motor Achievement, Academic Achievement, and Intelligence of Fourth-Grade Children." *Journal of Learning Disabilities*, 3 (1970), 413–420.   2

Sloane, H. N., and B. D. MacAulay, eds. *Operant Procedures in Remedial Speech and Language Training*. Boston: Houghton Mifflin Company, 1968.   2

Smith, D. D., and T. C. Lovitt. "The Use of Modeling Techniques to Influence the Acquisition of Computational Arithmetic Skills in Learning Disabled Children." In *Behavior Analysis and Education*, ed. E. Ramp and G. Semb, pp. 86–94. Englewood Cliffs, N.J.: Prentice-Hall, Inc., 1975.   3

Sykes, K. C. "Print Reading for Visually Handicapped Children." *Education of the Visually Handicapped*, 8 (1972), 117–126.   2

Tarver, S. G., and D. P. Hallahan. "Children with Learning Disabilities: An Overview." In *Teaching Children with Learning Disabilities: Personal Perspectives*, ed. J. M. Kauffman and D. P. Hallahan. Columbus, Ohio: Charles E. Merrill Publishing Company, 1976.   3

Turnbull, A. P., and J. B. Schulz. *Mainstreaming Handicapped Students: A Guide for the Classroom Teacher.* Boston: Allyn & Bacon, Inc., 1979. **2**

Vande Voort, L., and G. Senf. "Audiovisual Integration in Retarded Readers." *Journal of Learning Disabilities,* 6 (1973), 170–179. **2**

Van Riper, C. *Speech Correction: Principles and Methods,* 5th ed. Englewood Cliffs, N.J.: Prentice-Hall, Inc., 1972. **2**

————. *The Treatment of Stuttering.* Englewood Cliffs, N.J.: Prentice-Hall, Inc., 1973. **2**

Vellutino, F. R., J. A. Steger, L. Desetto, and F. Phillips. "Immediate and Delayed Recognition of Visual Stimuli in Poor and Normal Readers." *Journal of Experimental Child Psychology,* 19 (1975), 223–232. **2**

Vygotsky, L. S. *Thought and Language.* New York: John Wiley & Sons, Inc., 1962. **2**

Walters, R. H., and H. Doan. "Perceptual and Cognitive Functioning of Disabled Readers." *Journal of Consulting Psychology,* (1962), 355–361. **3**

Ward, M., and S. McCormick. "Reading Instruction for Blind and Low Vision Children in the Regular Classroom." *The Reading Teacher,* 34 (January 1981), 434–444. **2**

Weisberg, R. K. "How Consistent Is the Clinical Diagnosis of Reading Specialists?" *The Reading Teacher,* 38, 2 (November, 1984), 205–212. **3**

Werner, H., and A. A. Strauss. "Pathology of Figure-Background Relation in the Child." *Journal of Abnormal and Social Psychology,* 36 (1941), 236–248. **2**

Wiig, E. H., and M. A. Roach. "Immediate Recall of Semantically Varied 'Sentences' by Learning Disabled Adolescents." *Perceptual and Motor Skills,* 40 (1975), 119–125. **3**

Zeaman, D., and B. J. House. "The Role of Attention in Retardate Discrimination Learning." In *Handbook of Mental Deficiency,* ed. N. R. Ellis, 159–223. New York: McGraw-Hill Book Company, 1963. **2**

Chapter 15

Alkin, M. C. *The Use of Behavioral Objectives in Education: Relevant or Irrelevant.* Los Angeles: University of California, Los Angeles, Center for the Study of Evaluation, May 9, 1968, 27 pp. (ED035067). **4**

Ammons, M. "The Definition, Function, and Use of Educational Objectives." *The Elementary School Journal,* 62 (May 1962), 432–436. **4**

Archer, A. "Initial Assessment: Determining What to Teach." In *Teaching the Mildly Handicapped in the Regular Classroom,* 2d ed., eds. J. Affleck, S. Lowenbraun, and A. Archer, p. 61. Columbus, Ohio: Charles E. Merrill Publishing Company, 1980. **1**

Aukerman, Robert C. *The Basal Reader Approach to Reading.* New York: John Wiley & Sons, Inc., 1981.

Barrett, T. C. "Taxonomy of Cognitive and Affective Dimensions of Reading Comprehension." Unpublished paper. International Reading Association Conference. Newark, Dela., 1961. **3**

Bean, J. "Computerized Word-Processing as an Aid to Revision." *College Composition and Communication,* 34 (May 1983), 146–148. **5**

Bloom, B. S., ed. *Taxonomy of Educational Objectives. Handbook I: Cognitive Domain.* New York: David McKay Co., Inc., 1967. **4**

Borko, H., R. J. Shavelson, and P. Stern. "Teachers' Decisions in the Planning of Reading Instruction." *Reading Research Quarterly,* 16, 3 (1981), 449–466.

Brown, J., R. Lewis, and F. Harcleroad. *AV Instruction,* 6th ed. New York; McGraw-Hill Book Company, 1983.   **5**

Burnett, R. W. "The Classroom Teacher as a Diagnostician." In *Reading Diagnosis and Evaluation,* ed. D. L. DeBoar. Vol. XIII, Part 4, p. 4. Proceedings of the Thirteenth Annual Convention. Newark, Dela.: International Reading Association, 1970.   **1**

Burr, C. "Writing Behavioral Objectives: A Self-instruction Module." *Queensland Science Teacher,* 6 (February, 1980), 24–57.   **4**

Clymer, T. *Ginn Reading Program.* Lexington, Mass.: Ginn and Xerox, 1983.

Durr, W. K. *The Houghton Mifflin Reading Program.* Boston: Houghton Mifflin Company, 1981   **3**

Fay, L. C. *Rand McNally Reading Program: Young America Basic Series.* Lombard, Ill.: The Riverside Publishing Company, 1981.   **3**

Gagné, R. M. *The Conditions of Learning.* New York: Holt, Rinehart and Winston, 1965.   **2**

Gilpin, J. G. "Foreword." In *Preparing Instructional Objectives,* ed. R. F. Mager. Palo Alto, Calif.: Fearon Publishers, 1962.   **4**

Gronlund, N. E. *Measurement and Evaluation in Teaching,* 5th ed. New York: Macmillan Publishing Company, 1985.   **1**

Hambleton, R. H., K. Swaminathan, J. Algino, and D. B. Coulson. "Criterion-Referenced Testing and Measurement:" *A Review of Technical Issues and Developments,* 48, 1 (Winter, 1978), 1–47.   **1**

Holt Reading Program, New York, 1980.

Houghton Mifflin Reading Program. Boston, Mass., 1981.

Jarolimek, J., and B. Davis. *Lands of Promise.* New York: Macmillan Publishing Company, 1974.

Johnson, R. K. "JH/MS Idea Factory: Designs for Middle School Interdisciplinary Studies." *English Journal,* 69 (February 1980), 59–62.   **2**

Judd, D. H. "Avoid Readability Formula Drudgery; Use Your School's Microcomputer." *The Reading Teacher,* 1 (October 1981), 7–8.   **5**

Lapp, D. "Behavioral Objectives Writing Skills Test." *Journal of Education,* 154 (February 1972), 13–24. (This test may be secured from Educational Testing Services, Princeton, N.J.) (a)   **4**

———. *The Use of Behavioral Objectives in Education.* Newark, Dela.: International Reading Association, 1972. (b)   **4**

———. "Can Elementary Teachers Write Behavioral Objectives?" *Journal of Education* 155, 3 (February 1973). 13–19   **4**

———. "Individualized Reading Instruction Made Easy for Teachers." *Early Years,* 7 (February 1977), 63–67+.   **4**

Lungren, L., D. Lapp, and J. Flood. "An Investigation of Teachers' Apprehensions of Computers." Unpublished manuscript, San Diego State University, San Diego, Calif., 1983.   **5**

Millman, J. "Criterion-Referenced Measurements." In *Evaluation in Education: Current Applications,* ed. S. J. Pophorn, pp. 309–398. Berkeley, Calif.: McCutchan Publishing Company, 1974.   **4**

O'Donnell, H. "Computer Literacy. Part I: An Overview." *The Reading Teacher,* 35 (January 1982), 490–494.   **4**

O'Donnell, M. P., and B. Moore. "Eliminating Common Stumbling Blocks to Organizational Change." In *Making Reading Possible Through Effective Classroom Management,* ed. D. Lapp, pp. 186–215. Newark, Dela.: International Reading Association, 1980.   **1**

Piaget, J. *The Language and Thought of the Child,* 3rd ed. New York: The Humanities Press, Inc., 1959.

Rodrigues, R. J., and D. W. Rodrigues. "Computer-Based Intervention: Its Place and Potential." *College Composition and Communication,* 35, 1 (February 1984), 78–87.   **5**

Schwartz, H. "Teaching Writing with Computer Aids." *College English,* 46 (November 3, 1984), pp. 239–247.   **5**

————, and L. Bridwell. "A Selected Bibliography on Computers in Composition." *College Composition and Communication,* 35 (1984), pp. 71–77   **5**

Silberman, C. *Crises in the Classroom.* New York: Random House, 1970.

Stewart, J., and I. MacDonald, "Resources." *Screen Education,* 35 (Summer 1980), 91–105.   **5**

Taba, H. *Teacher's Handbook for Elementary Social Studies.* Palo Alto, Calif.: Addison-Wesley Publishing Co., 1967, 91–117.

Wallen, C. J., and L. L. Wallen. *Effective Classroom Management.* Boston: Allyn & Bacon, Inc., 1978.   **1**

Wedman, J. "Reading Software: What's Out There." *Language Arts,* 60 (April 1983), 516–517.   **5**

Zaharias, J. A. "Microcomputers in the Language Arts Classroom: Promises and Pitfalls." *Language Arts,* 60, 8 (November/December 1983), 990–998.   **5**

Name Index

Subject Index

Stimulus reduction, for teaching the learning disabled, 379
Story grammars, 126–129
Story schemata, 123
Stress point rules, 88–89
Structural analysis, 106–110
  inflectional endings, 108–109
  morphology, 106–108
Student Oral Language Observation Matrix, 330–331
Study skills. *See* Reading study skills
Stuttering, 366
Substitutions, as articulation disorder, 365
Suffixes, 106–108
Summarizing, 169–170, 175–176
Summary, as contextual clue, 110
Syllabication, 87–88
Syllogistic reasoning, in propaganda, 157–158
Synonyms
  as contextual clue, 110
  in definitions, 112
Syntax, 23, 24–25
  for bilingual students, 324
Synthesis, perception and, 22
Synthesizing, 175–176

Table of contents, 183–184
Tape recorders, 398
Taxonomic pattern, of text organization, 133
Taxonomy of reading objectives, Bloom's 134–136
Teacher
  creative thinking encouraged by, 21
  reading attitude fostered by, 259–260
  role of, 6–8
Teacher-made tests, 310–311
Teaching machines, 398–402
TEFL, 316
Telegraphic speech, 25
Telelecture, 398
Television
  as classroom aids, 400
  educational aspects of, 31–32
  effect of, 31–32
Term, 18
TESL, 316
TESOL, 316
Testimonial approach, as propaganda technique, 160
Tests
  for bilingual students, 329–332
  criterion-referenced, 299–301
  evaluating, 301–302
    norms for, 298–301
    reliability, 301–302
    validity, 301
  in grouping, 391–392
  informal, 305–311
    cloze readability technique, 311–314
    for groups, 391–392
    informal reading inventory, 306–309
    norming, 302–304
    oral reading test, 307
    silent reading test, 307–310
    teacher-made tests, 310–311
  intelligence, 295–296
  norm-referenced, 298–301
  standardized, 72, 299, 301, 304, 305
    diagnostic tests, 299–300, 302, 305
    for groups, 391–392
    of intelligence, 295–296
    oral reading tests, 306–307
    reading survey tests, 301
    See also Reading readiness; specific tests
Text
  cohesion, 134

organization, 131–134
readability formula for, 288–292
selection, 278–279
Textual analysis, 125–134
  expository, 130–134
  narrative, 126–129
Thematic teaching, 389–391
Time-order pattern, of text organization, 130, 132
Tokens, learning disabled and, 380
Top-down process view, 117, 119, 121, 122
Total communication approach, for hearing-impaired, 364
Trainable mentally retarded (TMR), 360
Transfer, as propaganda technique, 161

VAKT, 379
Validity, of a test, 301
Vane Kindergarten Test, 54
Verbs, 106, 108–109
Vision
  assessing, 69–72
  difficulties in, 69–70, 368–370
Visual aids, 398–400
Visual discrimination 54–55
  reading readiness assessed with, 54–55
Visual memory, 121
  for mentally retarded, 361
Visual perception, 21–22, 54–55, 78–79
  in learning disabled, 376
Visually impaired, 368–370
Vocabulary, 105–106
  of a basal reading program, 237, 239–240
  for bilingual students, 322, 324
  for hearing-impaired, 364
  language-experience method and, 246–247
  for learning disabled, 377
  mathematical, 208, 209–210
  for music, 223
  parents' assistance in expanding child's, 271–272
  reading readiness assessed with, 54
  of science, 215–218
  of social studies, 200–202
  See also Sight-word analysis; Word recognition skills
Voice disorder, 365–366
Voiced consonants, 91
Voiceless consonants, 91
Vowel correspondences, 84–85
Vowels, 91–95
  digraphs, 94
  diphthongs, 94
  early introduction of, 96
  long, 92–93
  schwa, 93, 188
  sequencing based on decibel rating, 96
  short, 92–93
  in teaching program, 96–98
  y, as vowel, 94

Whole-word method. *See* Sight-word analysis
Word discrimination, 81, 85
Word families, 97
Word meaning. *See* Definition; Semantics
Word outline, 174
Word problems, in mathematics, 209–210
Word recognition skill. *See* Contextual analysis; Sight-word analysis; Structural analysis; Vocabulary
Words-in-Color, 241–242
Writing skills, 42–49
  language experience approach and, 244–246
  theory, 44–45

Y, as vowel, 94